THE CAMBRIDGE COMPANION TO
THE GOSPELS

The four gospels are a central part of the Christian canon of scripture. This volume treats the gospels not just as historical sources, but also as crucial testimony to the life of God made known in Jesus Christ. This approach helps to overcome the sometimes damaging split between critical gospel study and questions of theology, ethics and the life of faith. The essays are by acknowledged experts in a range of theological disciplines. The first section considers what are appropriate ways of reading the gospels given the kinds of texts they are. The second, central section covers the contents of the gospels. The third section looks at the impact of the gospels in church and society across history and up to the present day.

STEPHEN C. BARTON is Reader in New Testament in the Department of Theology and Religion, University of Durham, England, and a non-stipendiary minister at St John's Church, Neville's Cross. His books include *The Spirituality of the Gospels* (1992), *Discipleship and Family Ties in Mark and Matthew* (1994), *Invitation to the Bible* (1997), and *Life Together: Family, Sexuality and Community in the New Testament and Today* (2001).

CAMBRIDGE COMPANIONS TO RELIGION
A series of companions to major topics and key figures in theology and
religious studies. Each volume contains specially commissioned chapters
by international scholars which provide an accessible and stimulating
introduction to the subject for new readers and non-specialists.

Other titles in the series

THE CAMBRIDGE COMPANION TO CHRISTIAN DOCTRINE
edited by Colin Gunton (1997)
ISBN 0 521 47118 4 hardback   ISBN 0 521 47695 x paperback

THE CAMBRIDGE COMPANION TO BIBLICAL INTERPRETATION
edited by John Barton (1998)
ISBN 0 521 48144 9 hardback   ISBN 0 521 48593 2 paperback

THE CAMBRIDGE COMPANION TO DIETRICH BONHOEFFER
edited by John de Gruchy (1999)
ISBN 0 521 58258 x hardback   ISBN 0 521 58781 6 paperback

THE CAMBRIDGE COMPANION TO LIBERATION THEOLOGY
edited by Christopher Rowland (1999)
ISBN 0 521 46144 8 hardback   ISBN 0 521 46707 1 paperback

THE CAMBRIDGE COMPANION TO KARL BARTH
edited by John Webster (2000)
ISBN 0 521 58476 0 hardback   ISBN 0 521 58560 0 paperback

THE CAMBRIDGE COMPANION TO CHRISTIAN ETHICS
edited by Robin Gill (2001)
ISBN 0 521 77070 x hardback   ISBN 0 521 77918 9 paperback

THE CAMBRIDGE COMPANION TO JESUS
edited by Markus Bockmuehl (2001)
ISBN 0 521 79261 4 hardback   ISBN 0 521 79678 4 paperback

THE CAMBRIDGE COMPANION TO FEMINIST THEOLOGY
edited by Susan Frank Parsons (2002)
ISBN 0 521 66327 x hardback   ISBN 0 521 66380 6 paperback

THE CAMBRIDGE COMPANION TO MARTIN LUTHER
edited by Donald K. McKim (2003)
ISBN 0 521 81648 3 hardback   ISBN 0 521 01673 8 paperback

THE CAMBRIDGE COMPANION TO ST. PAUL
edited by James D. G. Dunn (2003)
ISBN 0 521 78155 8 hardback   ISBN 0 521 78694 0 paperback

THE CAMBRIDGE COMPANION TO POSTMODERN THEOLOGY
edited by Kevin J. Vanhoozer (2003)
ISBN 0 521 79062 x hardback   ISBN 0 521 79395 5 paperback

THE CAMBRIDGE COMPANION TO JOHN CALVIN
edited by Donald K. Mckim (2004)
ISBN 0 521 81647 5 hardback   ISBN 0 521 01672 x paperback

THE CAMBRIDGE COMPANION TO HANS URS VON BALTHASAR
edited by Edward T. Oakes, S.J. and David Moss (2004)
ISBN 0 521 81467 7 hardback   ISBN 0 521 89147 7 paperback
THE CAMBRIDGE COMPANION TO REFORMATION THEOLOGY
edited by David Bagchi and David C. Steinmetz (2004)
ISBN 0 521 77224 9 hardback   ISBN 0 521 77662 7 paperback
THE CAMBRIDGE COMPANION TO AMERICAN JUDAISM
edited by Dana Evan Kaplan (2005)
ISBN 0 521 82204 1 hardback   ISBN 0 521 52951 4 paperback
THE CAMBRIDGE COMPANION TO KARL RAHNER
edited by Declan Marmion and Mary E. Hines (2005)
ISBN 0 521 83288 8 hardback   ISBN 0 521 54045 3 paperback
THE CAMBRIDGE COMPANION TO FRIEDRICH SCHLEIERMACHER
edited by Jacqueline Mariña (2005)
ISBN 0 521 81448 0 hardback   ISBN 0 521 89137 x paperback
THE CAMBRIDGE COMPANION TO THE QUR'AN
edited by Jane Dammen McAuliffe (2006)
ISBN 0 521 83160 1 hardback   ISBN 0 521 53934 x paperback

Forthcoming
THE CAMBRIDGE COMPANION TO ISLAMIC THEOLOGY
edited by Tim Winter
THE CAMBRIDGE COMPANION TO EVANGELICAL THEOLOGY
edited by Timothy Larsen and Daniel J. Treier
THE CAMBRIDGE COMPANION TO THE TALMUD AND RABBINIC LITERATURE
edited by Charlotte E. Fonrobert and Martin S. Jaffee

THE CAMBRIDGE COMPANION TO
THE GOSPELS

Edited by Stephen C. Barton
University of Durham

CAMBRIDGE
UNIVERSITY PRESS

CAMBRIDGE UNIVERSITY PRESS
Cambridge, New York, Melbourne, Madrid, Cape Town,
Singapore, São Paulo, Delhi, Mexico City

Cambridge University Press
The Edinburgh Building, Cambridge CB2 8RU, UK

Published in the United States of America by Cambridge University Press, New York

www.cambridge.org
Information on this title: www.cambridge.org/9780521002615

© Cambridge University Press 2006

First published 2006
4th printing 2012

A catalogue record for this publication is available from the British Library

ISBN 978-0-521-80766-1 Hardback
ISBN 978-0-521-00261-5 Paperback

Contents

Notes on contributors

Loveday Alexander is Professor of Biblical Studies in the University of Sheffield, England, and Canon Theologian of Chester Cathedral. She is editor of *Images of Empire* (1991), and author of *The Preface to Luke's Gospel* (1993) and *Acts in its Ancient Literary Context: A Classicist Looks at the Acts of the Apostles* (2005). Currently, she is completing two commentaries on the book of Acts, one for *Black's New Testament Commentaries*, and the other for *The People's Bible*.

Scott Bader-Saye is Associate Professor in the Department of Theology and Religious Studies, University of Scranton, USA. He is author of *Church and Israel after Christendom: The Politics of Election* (1999), and has published in journals such as *Studies in Christian Ethics, Modern Theology, Pro Ecclesia*, and *Cross Currents*. He is currently working on a book entitled *Following Jesus in a Culture of Fear*.

Stephen C. Barton is Reader in New Testament in the Department of Theology and Religion, University of Durham, England, and a non-stipendiary minister at St John's Church, Neville's Cross. His books include *The Spirituality of the Gospels* (1992), *Discipleship and Family Ties in Mark and Matthew* (1994), *Invitation to the Bible* (1997), and *Life Together: Family, Sexuality and Community in the New Testament and Today* (2001).

Stephen E. Fowl is Professor of Theology at Loyola College in Maryland, USA. His books include *The Story of Christ in the Ethics of Paul* (1990), *Reading in Communion* (with L. Gregory Jones, 1991), *The Theological Interpretation of Scripture: Classic and Contemporary Readings* (as editor, 1997), *Engaging Scripture: A Model for Theological Interpretation* (1998), and *A Commentary on Philippians* (2005).

Joel B. Green is Vice-President for Academic Affairs and Professor of New Testament Interpretation at Asbury Theological Seminary, USA. His books include *The Gospel of* Luke (1997), *Between Two Horizons: Spanning Biblical Studies and Systematic Theology* (as co-editor, with Max Turner, 2000), *Introducing the New Testament* (as co-author with Paul J. Achtemeier and Marianne Meye Thompson, 2001), and *Narrative Reading, Narrative Preaching* (as co-editor with Michael Pasquarello III, 2003). He is currently working on commentaries on 1 Peter and the Acts of the Apostles.

Richard B. Hays is the George Washington Ivey Professor of New Testament in The Divinity School, Duke University, Durham, North Carolina, USA. His books include *Echoes of Scripture in the Letters of Paul* (1989), *The Moral Vision of the New Testament* (1996), *First Corinthians* (1997), *The Faith of Jesus Christ* (2nd edn, 2002), *The Art of Reading Scripture* (as co-editor with Ellen Davis, 2003), and *The Conversion of the Imagination* (2005).

David Matzko McCarthy is an Associate Professor at Mount Saint Mary's University in Emmitsburg, Maryland, USA. He has written on the significance of the saints for moral theology in the journals *Modern Theology, Communio* and *Pro Ecclesia*. His books include *Sex and Love in the Home: A Theology of the Household* (2001) and *The Good Life: Genuine Christianity for the Middle Class* (2004).

Gordon Mursell is Bishop of Stafford, having served previously as Dean of Birmingham Cathedral. He has ministered in parishes in Liverpool, London and Stafford, and was also Chaplain and Tutor in Spirituality at Salisbury and Wells Theological College, Salisbury. His publications include *Out of the Deep: Prayer as Protest* (1989), *English Spirituality* (2 vols., 2001) and *Praying in Exile* (2005).

Sandra B. Schneiders IHM. is Professor of New Testament Studies and Spirituality at the Jesuit School of Theology and the Graduate Theological Union in Berkeley, California, USA. Her books include *Women and the Word: The Gender of God in the New Testament and the Spirituality of Women* (1986), *Beyond Patching: Faith and Feminism in the Catholic Church* (1991), *The Revelatory Text: Interpreting the New Testament as Sacred Scripture* (1999), and *Written That You May Believe: Encountering Jesus in the Fourth Gospel* (2003).

John T. Squires is Senior Lecturer in Biblical Studies at the United Theological College, North Parramatta, and Senior Academic Associate in the School of Theology, Charles Sturt University, Australia. His books include *The Plan of God in Luke-Acts* (1993), *At Table with Luke* (2000), and the commentary on the Acts of the Apostles in *The Eerdmans Commentary on the Bible* (2003).

Marianne Meye Thompson is Professor of New Testament Interpretation at Fuller Theological Seminary, Pasadena, California. Her recent books include *The Promise of the Father: Jesus and God in the New Testament* (2000), *The God of the Gospel of John* (2001), *Introducing the New Testament* (as co-author with Paul J. Achtemeier and Joel B. Green, 2001), and *A Commentary on Colossians and Philemon* (2005).

Francis Watson is Professor of New Testament Exegesis in the University of Aberdeen, having previously taught at King's College London. He has written extensively on the relation between biblical interpretation and systematic theology, including *Text, Church and World: Biblical Interpretation in Theological Perspective* (1994), and *Text and Truth: Redefining Biblical Theology* (1997). His most recent book is *Paul and the Hermeneutics of Faith* (2004).

Frances Young is Edward Cadbury Professor of Theology in the University of Birmingham and a Methodist minister. Her books include *From Nicaea to*

Chalcedon (1983), *The Art of Performance* (1990), *The Making of the Creeds* (1991), *The Theology of the Pastoral Epistles* (1994), *Biblical Exegesis and the Formation of Early Christian Culture* (1997) and *The Cambridge History of Early Christian Literature* (as co-editor with Lewis Ayres and Andrew Louth, 2004).

Abbreviations

ANRW	*Aufstieg und Niedergang der römischen Welt*
BETL	Bibliotheca ephemeridum theologicarum lovaniensium
BIS	Biblical Interpretation Series
ET	English translation
HTR	*Harvard Theological Review*
JBL	*Journal of Biblical Literature*
JSNT	*Journal for the Study of the New Testament*
JSNTS	Supplement to *Journal for the Study of the New Testament*
JSOT	*Journal for the Study of the Old Testament*
MT	Masoretic Text
NRSV	New Revised Standard Version of the Bible
NTS	*New Testament Studies*
SJT	*Scottish Journal of Theology*
SNTSMS	Studiorum Novi Testamenti Societas Monograph Series
WUNT	Wissenschaftliche Untersuchungen zum Neuen Testament

Introduction

STEPHEN C. BARTON

There can be no doubt that the four gospels of the Christian Bible are of fundamental significance for Christian life and thought. The gospel stories about Jesus' birth, life, death and resurrection, about his teaching, miracle-working and care for the poor, are read and recounted in churches throughout the world every Sunday. They shape Christian worship and sacramental practice, inspire Christian art, architecture and aesthetics, and inform Christian morality at both the individual and social levels. It could even be said that Christian life in all its aspects is an ongoing 'performance' of the gospels.[1] And, of course, to the extent that the Christian community is a part of the wider human community, the performance of the gospels contributes to the shaping of the moral, spiritual and aesthetic traditions of people worldwide whether Christian or not. It is fitting, therefore, that the *Cambridge Companion* series should include a *Companion to the Gospels*.

Of course, there are many fine introductions to the gospels, the New Testament, and the Bible as a whole, already available.[2] Most of these are written with a view to explaining the meaning and significance of the texts by means of the best tools of historical understanding currently available. They address, for example, questions about authorship and dating, about the historical context of the work, its author and audience, about the formation and transmission of the text in its various versions, and, more recently, questions about the history of the reception of the text.

Other introductions, equally valuable, have a stronger literary and aesthetic interest. Whereas the former approach the gospels more as *sources* of historical information and reconstruction, the latter approach them more from a 'readerly' point of view as *texts* to be appreciated, not only for what they communicate, but also for the way they communicate. For this kind of approach, the tools of literary criticism, in all their variety, come into their own.

What is sometimes lacking, however, is an adequate appreciation of the gospels as texts which form part of a *canon believed by Christians to be revelatory* – the canon of Christian scripture which helps to sustain the faith, life and worship of the church. It is the absence of an adequate appreciation of this kind that helps to explain the often damaging split that takes place between approaches to the gospels in academic institutions such as universities (approaches which might be characterized as 'standing *over* the text') and approaches to the gospels in the churches and in the lives of individual Christians (which might be characterized as 'standing *under* the text').

The essays in this volume have been written against this backdrop. They exemplify the best in current historical understandings of the gospels, in full recognition that the gospels are texts from the past and have, therefore, to be interpreted historically. They also exemplify the best in literary appreciation of the gospels, in recognition of the fact that the gospels are rhetorically powerful texts skilfully composed with a view to instruction and persuasion. They seek to show at the same time, however, that the gospels can be read in historically and aesthetically responsible ways that seek nevertheless to do greater justice to their theological and christological subject-matter and to their fundamental role as Christian scripture.[3]

There are three main parts. Part I is entitled 'Approaching the gospels', and deals with hermeneutical and methodological questions. In the opening essay, 'What is a gospel?', Loveday Alexander addresses the question of the genre of the gospels. She shows how much is to be gained by an awareness of a wide range of historical analogies to the gospels at various stages in their development, especially in the transition from oral tradition to written gospel. Among the analogies she explores are: oral traditional literature like the folk-tale, with its distinctive episodic character; historical reminiscence of an essentially anecdotal kind shaped and passed down in oral and written form in various ancient school settings; and the 'lives' (*bioi*) of famous men (including martyrologies) written by Greek, Roman and Jewish authors, the latter drawing strongly on narrative precedents in Hebrew scripture. But Alexander concludes that such analogies are just that, for in certain respects the gospels are *sui generis* – not least in their self-representation as 'good news', written versions of early Christian witness in teaching and preaching to the life-giving message about Jesus.

The second essay focuses on the very distinctive phenomenon of the fourfold gospel of the Christian canon. Francis Watson here points out that the concept of a fourfold gospel was unknown both to the earliest, first-century Christians and to the evangelists themselves; rather, it was a development of the second half of the second century whereby church leaders sought to stabilize oral and written testimony about Jesus and to discriminate between competing claims to represent the truth about him. Thus, the fourfold gospel canon is the result of a choice between competing options. It meant a rejection of a number of possibilities: first, the primacy of (potentially uncontrollable) oral traditions about Jesus in favour of the written gospel; second, the privileging of one gospel over others, especially a gospel (like the *Gospel of Thomas*) claiming special authority as the revelation of an esoteric Jesus; third, the offer of a 'purified' gospel in which, as with Marcion, Jesus is stripped of both his material setting in Judaism and his scriptural setting in the line of the patriarchs and prophets; fourth, the offer of supplementary gospels which seek to fill in the gaps about Jesus by expanding the tradition with material of an apocryphal kind; and fifth, a harmonization of the gospels with the contradictions ironed out (as in Tatian's *Diatessaron*) and the fourfold gospel reduced to one. The decision in favour of a fourfold gospel is a decision in favour of a plurality within limits: the limits sustaining the coherence of the apostolic testimony to Jesus, and the plurality allowing the richness and complexity of the truth about Jesus to be displayed.

A wise interpretation of the canonical gospels draws upon an understanding of the genre of the gospels and a recognition of their fourfold plurality. Richard Hays's essay on 'the canonical matrix of the gospels' shows that another dimension of the interpretative task is important also: close attention to the profound ways in which the gospel stories of Jesus are indebted to and shaped by the scriptures. Focusing on the Gospel of Mark in particular, but with illustrations from Matthew, Luke and John also, Hays shows that the scriptures constitute what he calls the gospels' 'generative milieu'. The question here is not the old-style question common in certain kinds of Christian apologetic about 'Jesus' use of the Old Testament'; it is, rather, a question about the literary phenomenon of intertextuality – how the gospels tell their respective stories of Jesus as part of the larger scriptural story of God's self-revelation in creation and redemption, played out especially in the story of Israel, and, conversely, how the story of Jesus allows the scriptural story to be read in new and previously unforeseen ways.

It is one thing to interpret the gospels and the Jesus of the gospels by attending to their scriptural matrix; but is it not important to try to 'get behind' the gospels to find out about who Jesus *really* was? As Stephen Fowl explains in his essay, this latter concern became the dominant scholarly question in the modern period. Based upon the presupposition that the 'real' Jesus is not the Jesus of scriptural revelation and that this real Jesus can be discovered only by the independent, 'value-free' exercise of human reason, tools of criticism of both literary and historical kinds were applied to the gospels in order to allow the real Jesus – now referred to as 'the historical Jesus' – to surface. But, argues Fowl, so-called value-laden theology and value-free history cannot be disentangled so easily, and the gospels themselves resist dichotomies of this kind; and he demonstrates this by looking critically at two recent, and significantly different, accounts of the historical Jesus: by John Dominic Crossan and by N. T. Wright. For Fowl, however, following Luke Timothy Johnson, what is important in reading the gospels is, not bringing the world (in the form of historical criticism) to the gospels, but bringing the gospels (in the form of scriptural witness to God's love revealed in Christ) to the world. In making this suggestion, Fowl is arguing for a move beyond modernity and its preoccupation with (historical-critical) method to ways of reading more characteristic of classic Christianity in the pre-modern period, ways of reading to which, interestingly enough, the ethos of postmodernity is, in some respects, more hospitable.

Ways of reading are also the concern of the final essay in Part I, on 'The gospels and the reader', by Sandra Schneiders. Here, important questions of theological and philosophical hermeneutics – relevant not just to interpreting the gospels but also to biblical interpretation as a whole – are addressed. Where the previous essays focus primarily on the text as the object of interpretation, Schneiders focuses on the reader as *the subject who interprets the text* in the process of reading. First, she surveys what she terms 'pragmatic' approaches to the text, where the situation and concerns of the reader (as subject) constitute the starting-point and the text is read for its potential to change that situation for the better. As examples, she discusses liberationist and feminist hermeneutics, along with readings which have a strong ethical commitment, as well as 'spiritual readings' which promote personal transformation. Then she offers an account of hermeneutics as a global philosophical theory of interpretation, and therefore a grounding for particular ways of reading. This she does with special reference to Paul Ricoeur and Hans-Georg Gadamer, two of the most important hermeneutical theorists of the twentieth century. Finally, she turns to questions about the text, the reader, and reading which arise from a reader-oriented approach to interpretation. Sensitive to approaches which are totalizing and potentially abusive when worked out in practice, Schneiders advocates an approach to validity in interpretation which is hospitable to a plurality of possibilities – possibilities that commend themselves in relation both to inherited tradition critically received and to their transformative potential in the world.

Attention to hermeneutical and methodological considerations in approaching the gospels gives way in Part II of the *Companion* to the subject-matter of the gospels themselves. The intention of this part is to give a taste of the contents of each of the gospels, taken in canonical order, in a way that makes clear their distinctive and overlapping testimonies to the truth about Jesus. Where appropriate, attention is drawn also to significant break-throughs in their interpretation.

The editor's contribution comes at this point with an account of the Gospel of Matthew. Drawing on the fruit of a generation of scholarly study, this essay seeks to display the dynamic way in which Matthew, in his care-fully constructed story of Jesus, brings together traditions old and new in such a way as to present Jesus as Son of God and Israel's Messiah, the hope of salvation for Israel and the nations. Matthew's christology, soteriology and eschatology have not taken shape in a vacuum, however. In all like-lihood, his story of Jesus reflects tensions between church and synagogue in the period after Easter – more specifically, the period after the destruction of Jerusalem in the war of 66–70. Thus, Matthew's gospel speaks from the past to the present and addresses in its own way the profound and com-plex question of the relation between emergent Christianity and formative Judaism. And, as an essentially open-ended text, Matthew speaks beyond itself to other situations of communities in conflict. Into such situations it speaks words of reassurance – in the 'I am with you always' of the risen Christ.

In ways which reinforce what Loveday Alexander says about the gospels as 'biography' and what Richard Hays says about intertextuality, Joel Green shows how important, in recent interpretation of the Gospel of Mark, has been the attention given to its quality as narrative. What is particularly remarkable is the subtle way in which the story of Jesus – focusing above all as it does on his passion – is set within a larger story about God, a story conveyed in considerable measure by means of intertextual links with Isaiah and other texts of scripture. These post-exilic texts speak of God's act of salvation of Israel in the event of the exodus, an act of salvation which offers a basis for hope for Israel in exile. They allow Mark to announce as 'good news' that the coming of Messiah Jesus is the beginning of a new act of liberation by God and inaugurates a new exodus. At the heart of the 'good news', however, is a disturbing paradox: the power of God at work in Jesus his 'Son' does not exempt Jesus from misunderstanding, opposition and suffering. Indeed, accepting the way of the cross is the mark of Jesus' obedience to the will of God. That is the way that leads to resurrection – not only for Jesus, but also for his followers.

What of the Gospel of Luke? According to John Squires, Luke employs the techniques of history-writing familiar at the time to give his fellow believers a comprehensive account of Jesus and the beginnings of the Christian movement as the basis for a well-grounded faith and for sacrificial witness in the ongoing circumstances of daily life. Luke sets the story of Jesus in continuity both with the scriptures and the story of Israel in the past, as their eschatological fulfilment, and with the story of the apostles and Christian mission which follows, and which Luke, alone of the four evangelists, narrates in a second volume. In writing thus, Luke displays his underlying conviction that the plan of God for the salvation of humankind and the whole of creation – a plan in which Israel, Jesus and the apostolic church play leading roles – is coming to fruition. Particularly expressive of this conviction is his account of the way Jesus as Messiah, Lord and Saviour manifests the kingdom of God in his teaching, healing and table fellowship, and welcomes the poor and the marginalized into the company of God's people. Implicit in the carrying over of these themes into Luke's story of the Spirit-inspired apostles in Acts is a summons to the church to carry on Christ's work as God's agent of salvation in all the world.

The revelation of the salvation of the world through Christ is at the heart of the message of the Gospel of John also. But as Marianne Meye Thompson shows, by comparison with the synoptic gospels, John's account is distinctive. Thus, for example, it is characteristic of John that themes and images with counterparts in the synoptics are explored and elaborated in much greater breadth and depth; witness the great revelatory 'I AM' sayings, for instance. Alternatively, some themes and images central to the synoptics are relegated to the margins apparently to be replaced by others: thus, 'kingdom of God' in the synoptics gives way to 'eternal life' in John. At stake throughout is the truth or otherwise of the claim that Jesus is the embodiment of God's presence in the world, the Son from the Father, who uniquely reveals the way to the Father and imparts life and light. Explanations for John's distinctiveness are suggested: John offers a theologically creative reworking of synoptic tradition; he draws on tradition independent of synoptic tradition; he is seeking to communicate the meaning and significance of Jesus to a wider audience and so uses imagery that has a universal appeal; the christological intensity of John results from conflict between synagogue and church over the truth of Jesus' claim to messiahship; and so on. Whatever the explanation – and it is likely that a range of factors played a part – the Gospel of John makes an irreducible contribution to the Christian understanding of who Jesus is.

Part III of the *Companion*, on the 'afterlife' of the gospels, offers four essays on what might be called 'gospel effects' in church and society down the ages. The essays are particular case-studies in how the gospels have been received and appropriated in times past and present – how as scripture (or scripture in the making) they have been heard as speaking beyond their own time and place.

First in this group is Frances Young's study of the impact the gospels had on the development of doctrine in the early church. The story is not a straightforward one. It begins with the contested status of the fourfold gospel in the first two centuries (which Francis Watson explores in more detail, in chapter 2), raising the question whether, for the early period, emerging doctrine determined which gospels were acceptable, or whether acceptable doctrine was derived from the gospels regarded as most reliable. More important than the written gospels, at this stage, was the gospel in the form of confessional summaries, of the kind found in Rom 1.1–4. Even when the four gospels had been accepted as canonical, what shaped doctrine most was the overarching sense – epitomized in the 'rule of faith' and summed up in the creeds – of what scripture *as a whole* was about. Thus, in the very significant christological debates of the fourth and fifth centuries, where exegesis played a major part, the focus of the exegesis was not exclusively on the gospels, but on scripture as a whole interpreted in light of the creeds. In other words, the gospels were read *doctrinally*; and in a concluding section, Young suggests that doctrinal reading and liturgical reading – that is, readings informed by an understanding of the overarching story of God in Christ received and celebrated in worship – remain fundamental if engagement with the fourfold gospel is to make accessible the reality of the incarnation.

Interpretation of the gospels is reflected not only in *thought* – the development of doctrine, for example. It is seen also in *action*: not least, in the lives of the saints and martyrs of the church. This is the subject of David Matzko McCarthy's essay on 'The gospels embodied'. Drawing in the first instance upon the life story of Ignatius of Loyola, author of the seminal *Spiritual Exercises*, McCarthy shows how the meaning of a gospel text can be both discerned and displayed in very profound ways by men and women who respond to scripture as making a direct, existential call on their lives. There are four gospel-text case-studies. The meaning of the renunciation for which Jesus calls in Matt 19.21 is explored through the lives of Antony of Egypt, Francis of Assisi, his near-contemporary Clare of Assisi, and Charles de Foucauld. The nature of true kinship spoken of in Matt 12.50 (also 10.37) is elaborated by attention to Augustine in the Late Roman period, Catherine

of Siena from the fourteenth century, and Franz Jägerstätter, in his opposition to Nazism in the early 1940s. The understanding of what it means
to engage in the practice of works of mercy of the kind spoken of in Matt
25.40 is displayed through the life stories of Martin of Tours and Dorothy
Day. Finally, the meaning of forgiveness and reconciliation as exemplified
in Christ's prayer from the cross for the forgiveness of his enemies, in Lk
23.34, is explored in the martyrdom stories of Stephen and Polycarp in the
early period and of Maximilian Kolb and Martin Luther King Jr in the modern period. Taken together, the lives of saints and martyrs are a kind of
extension of the scriptural canon. The canon of scripture produces a canon
of saints.

That the gospels are more than historical sources or literary artefacts
is seen, not only in their embodiment in the lives of saints and martyrs,
but also in their formative role in the practices of Christian prayer and worship. This is the issue explored in Gordon Mursell's wide-ranging essay. He
points out that for the entire pre-modern period, exposure to the gospels for
the great majority of Christians took place when the gospels were read in
the context of worship. Reminiscent of David McCarthy's essay, his chapter
also points to the profound influence, especially in early and medieval spirituality, of reading the gospels for the guidance they gave for the *imitatio
Christi* ('imitation of Christ'), even – drawing on the imagery of the Gospel
of John – for mystical union with Christ. Particular strategies for engaging
with the subject-matter of the gospels developed over time and in various
places. One was the practice of *lectio divina* ('spiritual reading'); another
was the discipline of the rosary with its concentration on various 'mysteries' in the life of Christ and his mother Mary; another, increasingly popular
with the invention of printing and the availability of Bibles in the vernacular,
was individual meditation; yet another, and of huge significance throughout
Christian history, has been engagement with the gospels through music and
the singing of hymns. In all this, Mursell shows that the field of influence
was not just one-way – from the gospels to prayer and worship. Rather,
practices of prayer, worship and Christian life ('spirituality') allowed the
gospels themselves to be seen and interpreted in new and often fruitful
ways.

The final essay, by Scott Bader-Saye, brings the question of the 'afterlife'
of the gospels into the public realm – the realm of morality and politics.
According to Bader-Saye, the gospels are misunderstood if they are confined
to the service of privatized religion and personal ethics. Rather, set within
a narrative horizon of creation, covenant, redemption and resurrection, the
gospels are a summons to a moral life shaped in community by practices

of *dispossession* after the pattern of Christ, with a view to participation in a world being made new. Against this backdrop, Bader-Saye offers a selective history of moral and political interpretations of Jesus' ethic of dispossession, taking Augustine, Immanuel Kant, Reinhold Niebuhr and John Paul II as examples. Augustine represents the attempt – normal in the pre-modern period but falling into disrepute in modernity – to 'read' the world in terms of the eschatological reality of heaven and the City of God. With Kant, by contrast, the life of Jesus offers, not the *standard* of the good, but *examples* of the good, now judged in accordance with the light of universal reason. Like Kant, Niebuhr understood Jesus as pointing to a moral ideal but, unlike Kant, he concluded that attainment of the ideal was impossible in the real world of human history. All that is possible is to live 'in the shadow' of the ideal of love and self-dispossession that Jesus taught. With John Paul II, however, we witness (in the encyclical *Veritatis Splendor*) a recovery of a reading of the gospels as themselves reality-defining and reality-shaping. Here, freedom is not the autonomy of Kantian modernity: rather, shaped by the gospel story of Christ, true freedom takes the form of self-giving in love. It is this alternative way of seeing the world and defining 'the real' that makes reconciliation and new community possible.

Taken as a whole, the essays demonstrate the vitality of current scholarly engagement with the gospels. Even more, they show the vitality of the gospels themselves as texts of Christian scripture. When read for their witness to Christ, and 'performed' in daily life in church and society, the gospels, like Christ himself, are for many a fount and wellspring of life.

Notes

1. For an elaboration of the metaphor of performance, see Nicholas Lash, 'Performing the Scriptures', in his collection of essays, *Theology on the Way to Emmaus* (London: SCM Press, 1986), 37–46; also Stephen C. Barton, 'New Testament Interpretation as Performance', in his *Life Together: Family, Sexuality and Community in the New Testament and Today* (Edinburgh: T. & T. Clark, 2001), 223–50.

2. An excellent, balanced account of the various ways of reading the biblical text can be found in Robert Morgan with John Barton, *Biblical Interpretation* (Oxford: Oxford University Press, 1988).

3. Exemplary in this respect are such works as Stephen E. Fowl and L. Gregory Jones, *Reading in Communion: Scripture and Ethics in Christian Life* (London: SPCK, 1991); and, recently, Ellen F. Davis and Richard B. Hays, eds., *The Art of Reading Scripture* (Grand Rapids: Eerdmans, 2003).

Part I

Approaching the gospels: context and method

1 What is a gospel?

LOVEDAY ALEXANDER

> Jesus said to his disciples: Make me a comparison, tell me what I am
> like. Simon Peter said to him: You are like a righteous angel.
>   Matthew said to him: You are like a man who is a wise philosopher.
> Thomas said to him: Master, my mouth will not at all be capable of
> saying what you are like.   Gospel of Thomas 13

What is a gospel? In many ways the question echoes the one posed by Jesus
in the gnostic Gospel of Thomas: Make me a comparison, tell me what I am
like. Peter and Matthew both take the question at its face value. They look for
points of comparison in the two intersecting cultural worlds of the gospels.
Matthew's comparison uses the categories of the Greek world: Jesus is a
philosopher, a kind of intellectual holy man, a guru. Peter's answer belongs
to the cultural world of the Bible, invoking a model of holiness that is at once
moral (faithful to the Law) and supernatural: Jesus is a righteous angel, a
messenger sent direct from God. But Thomas resists the temptation to look
for cultural analogies. For him, Jesus is *sui generis*, he is simply himself;
he is not 'like' anyone else. And Thomas's reward is to be taken aside and
given an insight into the hidden wisdom that Jesus whispers to the chosen
few. The only trouble is, the secret *gnōsis* he gains is so extraordinary, so
far removed from human categories of understanding, that he will never be
able to communicate it to anyone else: 'Now when Thomas came back to
his companions, they asked him, What did Jesus say to you? Thomas said
to them, If I tell you one of the words that he said to me, you will take up
stones and cast them at me, and a fire will come forth from the stones and
burn you up.'
   The story encapsulates neatly some of the dilemmas of contemporary
genre criticism of the gospels. There are those who stress their Jewish character, their continuity with biblical narrative patterns. There are those (in
increasing numbers) who want to locate their comparisons in the cultural
world of the Greeks and Romans, and who therefore look for analogies to

the gospels in Greek literature. And there are those, like Thomas, who stress the uniqueness of the gospels, their *sui generis* character, and refuse to make any comparisons at all with other literary genres. This means that they risk Thomas's fate of achieving understanding at the cost of cutting off channels of communication with the rest of the world; for if the gospel is to communicate, it must find some cultural common ground with those outside the charmed circle of the already convinced. But even though Thomas's solution may be risky, it is surely the right place to start. Before we can begin to ask what the gospels are *like* – that is, what literary genres they resemble – we need to make an attempt to understand them in their own terms. We need to ask what shape they are, what they are about, how they are put together, how they work. And that is where we begin.

WHAT ARE THE GOSPELS?

The four canonical gospels (which I use here as the basis for a working definition[1]) have many individual characteristics. But they also have much in common, so much so that their traditional titles present them as one gospel in four forms: *the* gospel according to Matthew, Mark, Luke and John.[2] In generic terms, it is this common core that we need to analyse, if we are to arrive at a working internal definition of gospel as a genre.

All four New Testament gospels are prose narratives of monograph length, about the amount that would fit into a single scroll in the ancient world (Luke alone adds a second volume). All are focused intensively on the person of Jesus. Mark's opening, 'The beginning of the gospel of Jesus Christ, the Son of God' (Mk 1.1) seems to be paradigmatic in this respect; later Christian texts retain the title 'Acts' for stories of apostles and other characters, 'Gospel' (*euangelion*, 'good news') for stories focused on Jesus. And the focus on Jesus is much more than skin-deep. Richard Burridge notes that an unusually high proportion of verbs in all the gospels have Jesus as their grammatical subject.[3] The proportion is even higher at the level of the pericope or individual episode. In the 'ministry' section of Mark's gospel – that is, the main narrative before the passion – Jesus is the narrative subject of virtually every episode. Where he is not the subject of the action, he is its chief object, increasingly so during the passion narrative. In Mark's gospel, there is only one episode where Jesus is completely 'off-stage' and that is the account of Herod's execution of John the Baptist, a narrative filler put in to bridge a gap where Jesus and his disciples are temporarily separated (Mk 6.14–29). Thus in structural terms, Jesus comes across as the hero of the core gospel story to an unusually high degree: he is the centre not only of the story as a whole but of virtually every individual episode.

The Herod episode illustrates another important structural feature. The presence of the disciples as observers is somehow necessary for the narrative to proceed. When the disciples and Jesus are apart, there is nothing to report. In this sense, Jesus can scarcely be said to have a 'private' existence in the gospels. Although the evangelists speak as omniscient narrators, there are relatively few points where they claim the privilege of omniscience to report the inner psychological states of their characters. Occasionally, private thoughts are externalized as overheard soliloquies (e.g. Jn 12.27–29; Lk 10.18–22). Peter, James and John sometimes function as select witnesses for the more private moments in Jesus' life (Mk 1.36; 5.37; 9.2; 14.33). But in general, the core gospel narratives concern public events, theoretically available to public view.[4]

This story is linked in specific but not detailed fashion to a particular time and place. In Mark's version, Galilee and Jerusalem, Herod and Pontius Pilate provide the barest anchor-points in the geography and history of the ancient Mediterranean world. Matthew extends the story's horizons east and south (Matt 2.1–18), and ends with a vision of worldwide mission (Matt 28.20). Luke's horizons look west, to Rome, with the consciousness of Empire providing both a political and a chronological framework for his narrative (2.1–2; 3.1–2) – a framework which becomes progressively more explicit in Acts. John adds more internal precision, both geographical and chronological. But the core gospel narrative seems to be able to subsist with a minimum of geographical and chronological information. Lk 3.23 gives Jesus' age as 'around thirty' at the point where he emerges on to the public stage as an itinerant preacher. From this point on, the narrative is episodic but continuous. Individual episodes are loosely linked, but precise time-notes are few and far between: only Luke anchors his story into world history with a real date (Lk 3.1–2).

The shape of the story is broadly biographical, tracing the hero's public ministry in a roughly chronological sequence covering three years of his life at most, and culminating in his trial and death. Only two of the gospels, Matthew and Luke, have birth stories, and neither has much information about his childhood (and the two birth narratives, though they agree in the names of Jesus' parents and the place of his birth, have little else in common). Structurally, then, we could say that the story of Jesus can be told without a birth narrative or a family history, whereas the baptism by John (with which all four canonical gospels begin) is somehow essential to the story.[5] The story itself falls into two uneven parts: Jesus' ministry (based in Galilee), and the events leading up to his death (in Jerusalem). The ministry is narrated via a loose-knit series of anecdotes of Jesus' actions (many but not all miraculous), combined with samples of his teaching: parables, sayings, discourses. The amounts and arrangements of teaching material vary: Matthew and Luke share a lot of teaching which is not in Mark (though they arrange it differently); John has fewer episodes overall and a distinctive type of meditative discourse. But it is artificial to draw too firm a distinction between action and teaching: even Mark has some teaching (chs. 4, 7, 13); and many of the 'action' stories in all four gospels are structured around a didactic or theological point (e.g. Mk 3.1–6). So Luke's description of his first volume as an account of 'all that Jesus began both to do and to teach' (Acts 1.1) is a fair summary of the content of the core gospel narrative. Finding a more precise narrative structure within that loose framework is difficult. All the synoptic gospels put the call of the disciples near the beginning, and mark some kind of turning-point at Caesarea Philippi (Mk 8.27–30 and parallels), and in all there is a noticeable increase in hostility as the narrative progresses. But individual episodes are connected to this outline in a flexible manner which suggests that the evangelists felt free to exercise a certain amount of individual licence in the overall construction of their narratives.

Things are very different when we get to the passion narratives. In all four gospels, the last week of Jesus' life occupies a disproportionate amount of narrative space – a quarter of the whole book in Luke and Matthew, up to a third in Mark and John. Here the pace slows down in an intense and highly dramatic presentation of a series of linked scenes in which Jesus progressively moves from active to passive mode until the final moment of his death. Throughout the narratives, prediction and dramatic anticipation have prepared the reader for this final scene (though dramatic and personal details may vary). And all the gospels agree that Jesus' story does not end with his death. All have descriptions of his disciples and friends visiting his tomb after his death and finding it empty, and all except Mark add stories in which the resurrected Jesus appears to his friends and talks with them.[6] The narrative focus has now moved from Jesus to his associates and their varied experiences of sorrow, disbelief and joy.

Our first definition, then, could be something like this: a gospel is a loose-knit, episodic narrative relating the words and deeds of a Galilean holy man called Jesus, culminating in his trial and death in Jerusalem, and ending with discrete and varied reports of resurrection appearances. And there is one more fact that has a fundamental impact on the way the gospels work, and that is the fact that there are four of them: four accounts of the same series of events, with large degrees of overlap and repetition, but also large degrees of variety.[7] Sometimes all four (more commonly the three 'synoptics', Matthew, Mark and Luke) tell the same episode in more or less the same words. At other times, they will narrate similar but distinct episodes, recognizably the same kind of story, but with a different location, or a different audience, or a different punchline. The order of events, particularly in the first part of Jesus' story, his Galilean ministry, seems to be flexible: episodes can be arranged in different ways without making much difference to the story; teaching can be inserted at different points. John takes more liberties with the order and selection of individual episodes, so that his gospel ends up with a quite distinct narrative texture (as well as a distinct chronology), though the overall shape is essentially the same as that of the synoptics. Whatever way we look at it, the fourfold gospel, recognized and valued by the church from early on, is a significant literary phenomenon in its own right. If the writers of the four gospels had no contact with each other, the similarities are remarkable: if they did know each other, the differences are remarkable. Either way, any analysis of the individual gospels must also take account of the relationship between them, with its peculiar combination of fluidity and fixity, coherence and individuation.

THE GOSPELS AS ORAL TRADITIONAL LITERATURE

Many of the features we have observed in gospel narrative can be paralleled in the narrative structures of the folktale. Vladimir Propp, in his analysis of the Russian wonder-tale, notes a number of ways in which the construction of folk narrative differs from that of the literary novel.[8] 'In folklore,' he suggests, 'the story is told only for the sake of the events.' Folk narrators and their audiences 'are interested only in the action and nothing more'. Descriptive details about the outward appearance of the characters or their surroundings do not form part of the story unless they play a role in the action: 'Forest, river, sea, steppes, city wall, etc., are mentioned when the hero jumps over or crosses them, but the narrator is indifferent to the beauty of the landscape.' A similar descriptive economy can be observed in gospel narrative. Mark Allan Powell, for example, notes the remarkably 'reserved' use of spatial description in the gospels: 'Spatial settings are presented with only scant notation: "Jerusalem," "a mountain," "the temple." The reader is given no information about such places that is not directly relevant to the plot.' Similarly, 'there is a paucity of sensory data. If the gospels were more like modern novels we would probably read about the sound of "waves lapping at the shore of the Sea of Galilee" and the feel of "coarse, dry sand trod underfoot in the Judean desert." Such luxury of narration is not to be found. Textures, sounds, smells, and tastes are usually left to our imagination.'[9]

As in the gospels, the narrative structure of the folktale is focused to a remarkable degree on the hero: 'Action is performed in accordance with the movement of the hero, and what lies outside this movement lies outside the narrative.'[10] This narrative focus on the 'empirical space' that surrounds the hero at the moment of action means that 'in folklore two theatres of action do not exist in different places simultaneously' (a phenomenon we have already noticed in Mk 6.1ff.). And, as in the gospels, action in the folktale is essentially public: 'Action is always performed physically, in space. Psychological novels based on the complexity of human interrelations, with dialogues, explanations, and so on, do not occur in folklore.'[11] Folklore's preoccupation with 'empirical space' means that there are no facilities to depict the hero as a romantic figure pursuing his destiny in psychological isolation. The action proceeds through a series of encounters between the hero and the groups or individuals with whom he interacts, and it is through these public interactions that his personality is defined:

> The result of the exceptional dynamic quality of action is that only those persons who contribute to the development of the plot figure in the narrative. Folklore does not deal with persons who are introduced for the sake of a milieu or a society . . . In folklore everyone is assigned a role in the narrative and there are no extra characters. All will act, and only in terms of their actions do they interest the listener. For this reason folklore tends to have only one protagonist. One character is central, and around him and his actions are grouped other people, his opponents, his helpers, or those whom he saves.[12]

Propp's distinction between the folktale and the literary novel is a helpful one because almost all our assumptions about how to tell a story are defined by the history of the literary novel – including the assumptions of film-makers and fantasists. The contrast between the two types of narrative structure can be readily illustrated from the popular English Robin Hood cycle, which exemplifies many of the structural features Propp describes in the Russian wonder-tale. At the core of the Robin Hood story lies a traditional cycle of encounter tales, building up a fluid but coherent picture of a folk hero located securely if imprecisely in time (King John) and space (Sherwood Forest). He has his trademark activity ('robbing the rich to help the poor'), and a strong popular support base.[13] He has his faithful band of followers (Little John, Maid Marian, Much the Miller's Son), and the implacable enemies who finally bring about his downfall (King John, the Sheriff of Nottingham). His story is told, in the ballads that make up the earliest surviving literary record, through a disconnected series of encounters with 'his opponents, his helpers, or those whom he saves': 'Robin Hood and Little John,' 'Robin Hood and Friar Tuck'. The connections between the individual episodes in the cycle are unclear – some naturally come near the beginning (encounter with Little John), others at the end (stories of the outlaw's death) – but for most of them, the sequence is not important. Over the last two centuries, novelists and film-makers have made numerous attempts to produce an overarching narrative of the Robin Hood story, providing the central character with precisely the features modern readers miss in this mode of narration: psychological depth, romantic interest, genealogy and family history, links with 'real' social and political history. This literary and film tradition then takes on an intertextual life of its own – as when Mel Gibson's Robin acquires a Saracen companion who completely deconstructs the Crusader theme of earlier retellings.

It is not too difficult to parallel this process in the development of the gospel tradition. Gospel films and 'life of Jesus' novels create a metanarrative which tries to supply the kind of psychological information or background detail that is lacking in the canonical gospels. This process can be seen in embryo in the gospels themselves. Matthew and Luke already feel the need to supply Jesus with a miraculous birth, a family history, and, in the temptation stories, a rare example of a private spiritual conflict. The written gospel shape comes into being by imposing order and sequence on an essentially fluid, episodic cycle of traditional units which have a life of their own, both before and after they are taken up into the literary tradition. As we have seen, narrative sequences within the gospels (apart from the obvious sequencing of the passion narratives) are treated as essentially provisional, and can be readily abandoned and re-formed by successive writers. But the core gospel tradition lying behind these varied literary forms has a strong character of its own, which imposes its own rhythms on the written gospels. It is not simply a random series of recollections but a structured oral cycle which builds up a vital and coherent picture of the hero through a series of encounters with 'his opponents, his helpers, or those whom he saves'.

The totality of the gospel tradition, with its duality between oral and written, fluidity and fixity, thus exemplifies many of the features of oral traditional literature as described by Propp and others. The study of folk-lore and oral traditional literature has been important in the development of gospel studies since the beginning of the twentieth century, and was a major influence on the pioneers of form criticism such as Gunkel and Dibelius. Such cross-cultural analogies have obvious pitfalls, but they also have great potential in allowing us to articulate and analyse the dynamics of oral tradition in a variety of cultures outside the Bible. One of the most significant is Albert Lord's 1978 study of 'The gospels as oral traditional literature', which draws on insights gained by Homeric scholars from the study of contemporary oral epic poetry from Yugoslavia, Turkey and Finland.[14] Lord points out that oral tradition should not be thought of simply as a series of unconnected units. The individual episodes presuppose the existence of a connected narrative, a cycle of tales related to a particular individual: 'If the gospels, all or any of them, in whole or in part, are oral traditional narratives, they must belong to a tradition of oral life story or biography. Such a tradition presupposes the existence of both tellers and audience as well as of stories told.'[15] As with Robin Hood, this 'life story' is rarely told in the form of a single, unidirectional narrative from birth to death: 'the separate elements or incidents in the life of the hero form individual poems or sagas'.[16] Nevertheless, the 'life' is in some sense implicit in the individual episodes – even, in broad outline, the sequence from birth to death. There are a variety of ways in which such units may be joined together in oral performance (e.g. in flashback), and different performers would tend to create their own combinations.[17] Written versions of these stories could be produced 'by people who were linked to the oral tradition either by actually being a part of it, or, perhaps more probably, by being close to it' – that is, 'by people who heard the traditional stories but did not themselves tell them: for example, a learned or semi-learned person who had heard the tales all his life but never had written the traditional stories or the traditional style'.[18]

But 'oral traditional literature' is a mode of composition and performance, not a genre, and, though cross-cultural analogies may help us to understand how such traditions tend to operate, they cannot in themselves tell us what kind of tradition the gospel is. Lord invokes a number of 'mythic patterns' from ancient epic as potential parallels to the liminal events of Jesus' life (birth, childhood, investiture, death and resurrection). But many of his closest parallels are from biblical narrative – which we know to have been a major influence on the composition of the gospels without the interposition of 'mythic patterns' – and, as he admits, the so-called 'pattern' is only imperfectly realized even in Matthew and Luke.[19] It is much harder to find parallels in epic for 'the major deeds of the mature hero, which in Jesus' case would be the events and teachings of his ministry'. In fact, as we have seen, the folktale patterns identified by Propp suggest some rather more helpful folklore parallels to the narrative structures of the gospels. Nevertheless, it remains true that 'Jesus' deeds are not like the deeds of most mythic heroes but are *sui generis*: the actions and words of a miracle worker and teacher.'[20] To find comparative material for this kind of narrative in literature contemporary with the gospels we need to look at a very different kind of tradition.

THE GOSPELS AS SCHOOL TRADITION

The earliest witnesses we have to the gospels already testify to the duality we have noticed between written and oral, between the fixed forms of the written gospels and the living voice of oral tradition. Justin Martyr, writing in Rome in the mid-second century, quotes gospel material from 'the memoirs [*apomnēmoneumata*] of the apostles, which are called gospels [*euangelia*]', and describes how these texts are used in Christian meetings:

> On the day called Sunday, all who live in cities or in the country
> gather together to one place, and the memoirs of the apostles or the
> writings of the prophets are read, as long as time permits; then when
> the reader has ceased, the president verbally instructs, and exhorts to
> the imitation of these good things.[21]

The two names Justin uses for the gospels are revealing. They are called, he says, *euangelia*, 'good news'. This word was used in a variety of secular contexts, including civic decrees authorizing the celebration of the emperor's birthday, but there is no record that it was ever the name of a literary genre anywhere outside Christian circles.[22] But Justin himself calls them *apomnēmoneumata*, that is, the reminiscences or memoirs of the apostles. It is a term which nicely encapsulates the duality of the gospel tradition. At its heart is the root *mnēmē*, 'memory': these are stories which are based (or claim to be based) on apostolic memory. But the verb *mnēmoneuein* means more than the mental act of remembering: it involves the actualizing of memory though public speech, the act of mentioning or recounting what one remembers. Thus *apomnēmoneumata* are not simply random memories but *memoirs, reminiscences*, memory codified, structured and articulated: an *apomnēmoneuma* (in the singular) is an anecdote, an oft-told tale focused on a particular individual. As a title for a written text, then, the name a*pomnēmoneumata* means a collection of anecdotes more or less artistically assembled into a unified text – though not necessarily into a unified narrative.

Papias, the bishop of Hierapolis in the early second century, displays the ambiguities of the word-group well. Papias himself is conscious that the apostolic generation is dying out, and that he himself belongs to a third generation, 'neither a hearer nor an eyewitness'. So he takes steps to bridge the gap: he seeks out and questions chance visitors, collects and passes on traditions about gospel authors and tradents (Eusebius, *Church History*, III 39.2–5). For Papias, therefore, it is important that Mark, who was not an apostle himself, is connected to Jesus at one remove via Peter. And what Mark committed to writing was Peter's *apomnēmoneumata*, his store of anecdotes, his stories of Jesus' words and actions already shaped as units of teaching material *(didaskaliai)* formulated for specific needs *(pros tas chreias)*.[23] If Papias seems slightly apologetic about this, it is precisely because Mark's written gospel preserves the essentially oral form of Peter's *apomnēmoneumata*. Mark wrote the stories up 'just as Peter recounted them', without turning them into a proper *syntaxis*, a real literary composition. Clement of Alexandria adds a few circumstantial details to the picture: it was Peter's hearers in Rome who begged Mark to put 'the unwritten teaching of the divine proclamation' into writing, 'so that they might have a written record *(hypomnēma)* of the teachings *(didaskaliai)* handed down to them in words'.[24] All Clement's language underscores the continuity between the oral tradition, shaped by constant repetition for the purposes of teaching and preaching, and the written record: *hypomnēma* is another word used of a text only one stage removed from oral composition, whether students' notes or scholar's commentary.

From the earliest recorded stages of church tradition, then, the written gospels had a dynamic, two-sided interface with oral performance. They were seen as the deposit of oral teaching and preaching; and they were used as the basis for ongoing oral instruction in the early church. The link with particular apostles (or their disciples) is not simply a claim to be recording apostolic 'memories'. It implies that behind the written gospels lies structured teaching tradition of oral material shaped by repetition and in accordance with the rhetorical needs of particular situations. In other words, the *apomnēmoneumata* already embody the gospel as *euangelion*, 'good news'. They stem from a preaching tradition focused on Jesus, honing and treasuring stories of his life and death because they conveyed the good news about Jesus, the *euangelion*. Hence the traditional titles: as soon as the gospels have titles at all, so far as we can tell, they are known as the 'Gospel *according to* Mark', or 'John', an odd phrase which seems to imply one gospel taking multiple forms.

If we take this early church tradition seriously, then, we have another answer to our question: a gospel is the written deposit of oral preaching and teaching about Jesus. It is worth noting that this early testimony reflects both a literary judgement and a historical one – that is, it embodies a claim both about the *origin* of the gospels and about their *literary form*. For anti-gnostic writers like Irenaeus, there was a clear polemical motive for linking the canonical gospels with the teaching of the apostles: which is why many scholars are inclined to be suspicious of the historical claim to apostolic origin. But the patristic testimony also reflects a literary judgement. Whether or not we accept the connection between Mark and Peter, the picture these writers paint of the transition from oral teaching to written text is entirely consistent with what we know from other ancient writers; and this in turn has some bearing on the question of genre.[25]

Papias also reveals another important fact about the gospel in the early church. Even when there were written gospels, the oral tradition continued to carry weight: 'I did not suppose', he says, 'that information from books would help me so much as the word of a living and abiding voice.'[26] There is every reason to believe that this was not just an antiquarian quirk on Papias' part.[27] It is surprisingly hard to identify clear quotations of individual gospels as written texts during the second century: Christian preachers and teachers continue to refer to 'the gospel' (or 'the Lord') as a living, unified tradition long after it is written down, and without troubling themselves too much about the viewpoints of the individual evangelists.[28] It is as if each written text represents a particular performance of 'the gospel', the good news about Jesus, and, however much it is valued and respected, it retains its 'provisional' character as a performance, as one possible instantiation of *the* gospel. Contrary to what we might expect, it is the underlying story that has solidity, while the particular performance in which it is embodied – like a particular Robin Hood film – has a more ephemeral quality.

The distinctive language used by Justin, Papias and Clement suggests that we do not have to look nearly as far afield as ancient epic to find parallels to the way the gospel tradition operates. Oral teaching was the norm in the ancient world, and the transfer of oral teaching material to written notes is well attested in a number of teaching traditions, including medicine, rhetoric and philosophy.[29] Many of the medical, rhetorical and philosophical handbooks surviving from antiquity are based on notes (*hypomnēmata*) taken by students from their teachers' lectures, and their format betrays the relative fluidity and provisionality of this form of writing: these were user-books, *Gebrauchsliteratur*, designed not as a fossilized record of a particular oral 'performance' but as a base for constant glossing and updating.

Ancient teaching methods were heavily focused on the memorization and adaptation of short, pithy tales and adages, from gnomic, one-sentence aphorisms to longer and more complex tales focused around the telling word or action of a particular teacher. The generic term for these sayings is *chreiai*, and large numbers of them survive in the rhetorical handbooks and in the biographical compilations of the philosophical tradition.[30] Justin's title *apomnēmoneumata*, in fact, belongs precisely here. The rhetorical handbooks define the *chreia* as 'a word or deed relating to a defined individual' (as opposed to a generic maxim), differing from the *apomnēmoneuma* or 'reminiscence' chiefly in length;[31] and it is these 'biographical' anecdotes that form the backbone of the ancient biographical tradition. Diogenes Laertius, writing his *Lives of the Ancient Philosophers* in the third century CE, quotes scores of them. But the existence of a vigorous tradition of biographical anecdotes does not necessarily imply the existence of a written biography. Anecdotes can be combined in an almost infinite number of ways, many of them thematic rather than 'biographical': putting them into a chronological sequence to tell a philosopher's story from birth to death is not as obvious a solution to the ancients as it is to us. What the anecdotes do imply, as Lord noted with the epic cycles, is an underlying story, acting as a mental frame of reference for assessing the significance of a particular anecdote.

This pattern can be seen particularly clearly in the anecdotal tradition relating to Diogenes and Socrates. Significantly, these are philosophers who wrote nothing (so the anecdotes are the main carriers of their teaching) and whose lifestyle was as important as their words (so the anecdotes serve an important teaching function). Significantly, too, both served as iconic figureheads for communities of disciples who had an abiding interest in modelling their own lifestyle on that of the master: so the anecdotal tradition is a focus of loyalty, with a clear ideological function in the ongoing life of a network of disciple-groups. As in the gospels, these stories tend to be structured as encounters: the teacher meets and responds to a disciple, or an enquirer, or a patron, or a hostile official. With Socrates, this anecdotal life-cycle builds up to a full-scale paradigm of the philosophic life, starting with the philosopher's divine calling and culminating with his trial and martyrdom.[32] The story of Socrates acts as a cultural hypotext which was profoundly influential in the Greco-Roman world. But there is no single 'Biography' of Socrates which tells this story 'from birth to death': iconography and lifestyle were sufficiently nourished by the anecdotal tradition, together with the *Apomnēmoneumata* of Xenophon and the Platonic vignettes of his death.

Anecdotal tradition also played an important part in the rabbinic academies. Birger Gerhardsson pioneered the study of the dynamics of oral transmission in the rabbinic schools as a possible model for the transmission of gospel tradition.[33] The rabbinic texts contain a number of significant parallels to the type of material contained in the gospels in the form of controversies and biographical anecdotes focused on particular sages.[34] Like the Greek anecdotal tradition, much of this is structured around encounters between the sages and their disciples, opponents, enquirers and (predominantly) each other: the prime locus of teaching in the rabbinic schools is the halakhic debate. The rabbinic tradition also contains a number of (rather ambivalent) anecdotes about healing encounters. But what is striking here is that, although there is ample material for putting together a life story of at least the major sages, rabbinic tradition never takes this step: there is no rabbinic 'gospel' of Johanan ben Zakkai or Eliezer ben Hyrcanus. One obvious reason is that 'neither Eliezer nor any other Sage held in Rabbinic Judaism the central position that Jesus held in early Christianity. The centre of Rabbinic Judaism was Torah; the centre of Christianity was the person of Jesus, and the existence of the gospels is, in itself, a testimony to this fact.'[35] Rabbinic tradition provides some important generic parallels to the gospel tradition, but it cannot help us to identify a genre for the written gospels.

THE GOSPELS AS WRITTEN TEXTS

So there is no shortage of material from the cultural worlds of the gospels, both Jewish and Greek, to provide generic analogues to the anecdotal gospel tradition. Justin, Papias and Clement, as we have seen, stress the continuity between tradition and text: for them, the task of the evangelists was simply to reduce the apostolic teaching to writing, and the names they choose for the gospels reflect this continuity. The form critics of the early twentieth century, though working from different premises, came to essentially similar conclusions: the gospels were little more than compilations of pre-existent units of traditional material, arranged and selected like pearls on a string. More recent narrative approaches to gospel criticism have demonstrated conclusively that the evangelists are much more than mere 'editors' or compilers. But this insight does not in itself necessarily conflict with the perception that the gospel tradition is a form of 'oral traditional literature'. Within the framework of folklore studies, it is not too difficult to understand our gospels as four individual performances of *the* gospel, each tailored with skill and artistry for an individual audience but not claiming to offer an exclusive or definitive rendition of the tradition; and in many ways this seems to be how the early church saw them. Nevertheless, writing a book is not the same thing as giving an oral performance; and, though recent studies suggest that the polarity between oral and literate modes of discourse may well have been overstated, it remains true that the move from oral performance to book is by no means inevitable, and that the literary forms it engenders are far from predictable.[36] So our final question is: what happens when we move from oral tradition to written text? What is a gospel when it is a *book*?

On the Greek side, there is an emerging consensus that the best place to look for a parallel genre for the gospels is Greek biography. In his influential 1992 study *What Are the Gospels?*, Richard Burridge points out that the Greek *bios* or 'life' is typically a monograph of similar length to the gospels, focused on the life story of a famous individual from birth to death, where (just as in the gospels) the subject of the biography is also the grammatical subject of a high proportion of verbs. Nevertheless, there are some puzzling features in the comparison. Reading the Greek biographical tradition as a whole, it is not at all obvious that if you put together a collection of anecdotes about a particular individual you will end up with something shaped like the canonical gospels, with a flowing, connected narrative tracing the hero's life from birth (or commissioning) to death. Diogenes Laertius' great collection of anecdotes about the philosophers is arranged on thematic rather than chronological lines, and there is little attempt to provide narrative coherence.[37] And what is most obviously missing in this tradition is the *good news* aspect that is essential to the gospels. Many Greek biographies are hostile, polemical or simply sensationalist: biographers are the paparazzi of the ancient world. And the encyclopaedic pattern embedded in the biographical tradition means that comparison is built into the genre; most Greek biographies bear little resemblance to cultic or kerygmatic narratives. Within the Greek philosophical tradition, the figure who best parallels the role of Jesus is Socrates, subject of innumerable anecdotes, dialogues, martyrdom stories, and fictitious letters; but no-one ever put this material together to produce a coherent biography of Socrates.

Nevertheless, the appearance of the gospels coincides with what Arnaldo Momigliano calls a 'new atmosphere' in biographical writing around the turn of the eras: 'The writers of biographies created a meaningful relationship between the living and the dead. The wise man, the martyr, and the saint became central subjects of biography, in addition to the king, the writer, and the philosopher.'[38] Signs of the new mood can be seen in second-century texts like Tacitus' *Agricola* or Lucian's *Demonax*, affectionate portraits of well-loved individuals based on personal recollection, following a broadly narrative outline, and designed to foster imitation as well as memory.[39] The shift from biography to hagiography is epitomized in the story of Apollonius of Tyana, a Pythagorean wonder-worker from first-century Syria whose life story shows remarkable parallels to the story of Jesus, and is allegedly based on the contemporary reminiscences of Apollonius' disciple Damis. A number of scholars have suggested that the *Life of Apollonius* falls into a special genre, 'aretalogy', which provides an alternative genre for the gospels.[40] But the existing biography of Apollonius was written in the third century CE by Philostratus; it is much longer and more elaborate than the gospels, and bears the rhetorical imprint of the Sophistic circles Philostratus moved in. Damis' reminiscences, on which it claims to be based, may be no more than an elaborate fiction;[41] and, by the third century, when Philostratus is writing, we have to reckon with the real possibility that the story of Apollonius is being consciously marketed as a pagan rival to the gospels.[42] Motifs found in the gospels can be paralleled with greater or lesser degrees of precision in pagan Greek literature,[43] but the precise literary form adopted by Mark's performance of the Jesus story is hard to match in the Greek biographical tradition. Indeed, a recent study of biographic writing in the classical literature of the imperial period concludes that 'the Gospels are almost unique as multiple, contemporary accounts of a single life'.[44]

Does the search for a genre for the gospels fare any better on the Jewish side? Rabbinic literature, as we have seen, offers ample parallels to the anecdotal Jesus tradition, but no connected rabbinic biography. But if rabbinic literature stops short of fully fledged biography as a literary genre, there is ample precedent for biographical narrative elsewhere in Jewish literature. The Hebrew Bible itself is much more deeply prone to 'bio-structuring' than is classical Greek historiography.[45] Much of the narrative of the Hebrew Bible is built around biographical 'story cycles' like those of Samson or Elijah, cycles in which individual tales of the hero's prowess 'are so arranged to encompass his entire life, from birth to death'.[46] Moreover, in the Hebrew Bible these tales are subordinated to the overall narrative style and goals of 'a purposeful religious, ethical, and national work' which was to determine the character of Jewish folk traditions for generations to come.[47] It is to the biblical tradition, surely, that we should look for the origins of the 'religious intensity' of the gospel narratives and their rich ideological intertextuality with the biblical themes of covenant, kingdom, prophecy and promise – all features hard to parallel in Greek biography.[48] The evangelists' move from disjointed anecdotes and sayings to connected, theologically coherent narrative is most easily explained with reference to the narrative modes of the Hebrew Bible.

Nevertheless, we still need to explain the precise narrative structure chosen by the gospel-writers; and here two contemporary developments in Jewish (specifically, Jewish-Greek) writing of the Second Temple period are worth considering. The first is in Philo, the first-century Alexandrian Jewish writer whose allegorical expositions of the Bible in Greek contain a number of single treatises devoted to individual Bible characters. Philo's *On Abraham* and *On Joseph* (and the lost *On Isaac* and *On Jacob*) are 'biographical' in the limited sense that they collect together the separate incidents related to each character in the Bible and arrange them in chronological order as a coherent narrative. The treatment of the characters, however, is allegorical rather than historical: the patriarchs represent the history of the soul, and they are described as living prototypes of the ethical principles embodied in torah.[49] Philo's *Life of Moses*, on the other hand (the only one of his works that actually bears the title *bios*: cf. *Moses* 1.1; 2.292), has a much more obviously biographical character, beginning with Moses' birth and ending with his death, and compressing into a single connected account the bulk of the biblical Moses narrative – though still arranged thematically under the headings of king, lawgiver and high priest. This is one of Philo's most accessible works, and the one that has the best claim to be addressed to outsiders. It suggests at the very least that biographical narrative provided a point of cultural contact between Greek and Jew, a flexible and readily comprehensible framework that could be moulded without difficulty to reflect the ideology and cultural values of a particular ethical tradition.

The second development is in the area of martyrology. In the Greek biographical tradition, Socrates was the model for philosophic resistance to tyranny.[50] But Jewish tradition had its own prototypes for the martyr's death, and there are a number of texts from the first century and earlier which highlight martyrdom as the proper closure to a life lived in obedience to God – and therefore allocate significant narrative space to the death of the martyr.[51] Many of the key motifs are already present in the book of Daniel, written in the period of Antiochus Epiphanes in the second century BCE, and it is this period that provides the setting for one of the most enduring paradigms of Jewish martyrdom, the Maccabean martyrs. The stories of the torture and death of the aged Eleazar and the mother and her seven sons for refusing to eat the forbidden foods pressed on them by the tyrant are told in a multiplicity of literary forms, from the plain narrative of 2 Maccabees (second century BCE) to the sophisticated philosophical encomium of 4 Maccabees (first or second century CE). Martyrology is not of itself necessarily biographical (one of the odd features of the Maccabean martyrs is that we are told nothing of the martyrs' previous lives). But the so-called *Lives of the Prophets*, almost certainly dating from pre-70 Palestine, combine intensive interest in the manner of the subjects' death with concise information about their lives.[52] These brief and schematic life stories (nothing so grand as a full biography) are subordinated to details of the manner in which the prophets died and the miracles associated with their graves. The *Lives* may have been some kind of pilgrim guidebook recounting the cult legends associated with the tombs of the saints. Whatever we call them, it is clear from a glance at these brief biographical notices that they cannot 'solve' the problem of the gospel genre by themselves. Nevertheless, their existence adds another strand to the variety of biographical forms in first-century Jewish literature, and acts as a forceful reminder of the many possibilities for cultural interchange between Jewish and Hellenistic literature in Second Temple Judaism.

THE GOSPELS AS GOOD NEWS

So are we left with Thomas's answer, that the gospels are unique? The answer in the end is probably, Yes and No. Many of the motifs that appear in the gospels can be paralleled in contemporary texts, especially in the anecdotal material which acted as a prime carrier of school traditions both in the rabbinic academies and in the Greek philosophical schools. The way the tradition works is certainly not unique: folklore studies suggest a number of fruitful analogies. But what may be unique is the particular form this tradition takes when it is written down, a form whose external shape is strongly reminiscent of the Greek *bios* but whose narrative mode and theological framework (connectives, narrative structure, use of direct speech, intertextuality) owe much more to the Bible. This could explain, incidentally, why the psychological characterization of the gospels is wholly within the biblical framework, and shows no sign of being influenced by the philosophical *ethos* tradition which so dominated Greek biography; and why the gospels show no awareness of the normal distancing mechanisms routinely employed by Greek historians and biographers to keep the supernatural at bay.[53]

If this seems inconclusive, it may be because we have been asking the wrong kind of question. Gospel criticism for most of the past century has been dominated by the search for a pre-existent genre to *explain* (or explain away) the gospels, as if we were hoping to find the mould into which Mark (or whoever was the first to write the gospel down) poured his Jesus story. Unfortunately (or perhaps fortunately), no such genre has been discovered: and that suggests that it may be time to change the way we configure the question. The gospels came into being at a time of profound cultural transformation, and were themselves active agents in that transformation.[54] That may be one reason why it is so hard to pin them down – though the same could be said of other texts and genres of the period. Certainly there is no evidence elsewhere for *euangelion* as a generic title: and for that we probably have the earliest preachers to thank. They were the ones who shaped the Jesus tradition as *good news*, focused on the encounter with the Christ whom they believed to be alive. They were responsible for giving that tradition its characteristic shape, which persists through written forms and out again into the ongoing tradition of life-giving stories carried within the community, in its iconography, its liturgy and its daily life of prayer.

Notes

1. For a full discussion of the term 'gospel' in second-century texts, see Helmut Koester, *Ancient Christian Gospels: Their History and Development* (London: SCM Press, 1990), ch. 1. Koester points out that the so-called 'Gnostic Gospels' discovered at Nag Hammadi do not claim the title 'gospel' for themselves: see especially §1.5.
2. Cf. Irenaeus, *Against Heresies* 3.11.8.
3. Richard A. Burridge, *What are the Gospels? A Comparison with Graeco-Roman Biography* (SNTSMS 70; Cambridge: Cambridge University Press, 1992).
4. The obvious exceptions are the temptation stories of Matt 4 and Lk 4, which have no human observers but are still structured as a dialogue with an external character (Satan) rather than an internal psychological process.
5. Cf. also Acts 1.22; 10.37; 13.24.
6. Mk 16.1–8; Matt 28.1–10, 16–20; Lk 24.1–11, 13–35, 36–49; Jn 20.1–10, 11–18, 19–29; 21.1–23. Luke alone has Jesus ascend to heaven: Lk 24.50–3; Acts 1.1–11.
7. Cf. Stephen C. Barton, 'Many Gospels, One Jesus?', in Markus Bockmuehl, ed., *The Cambridge Companion to Jesus* (Cambridge: Cambridge University Press, 2001), 170–83.
8. Vladimir Propp, *Theory and History of Folklore* (Manchester: Manchester University Press, 1984), 21.
9. Mark Allan Powell, *What is Narrative Criticism?* (Minneapolis: Fortress, 1990), 71.
10. Propp, *Folklore*, 22.

11. Ibid.
12. Ibid.
13. Cf. Propp's 'donors': *Folklore*, 24: 'Besides the protagonist there are helpers, donors, the hero's opponents, and persons whom he saves or rescues.'
14. Albert Lord, 'The Gospels as Oral Traditional Literature', in William O. Walker, ed., *The Relationships Among the Gospels: An Interdisciplinary Dialogue* (San Antonio: Trinity University Press, 1978), 33–91.
15. Ibid., 38.
16. Ibid., 39–40.
17. Ibid., 41–44.
18. Ibid., 80.
19. Ibid., 44–58.
20. Ibid., 45.
21. Justin, *First Apology* 67; cf. 65–6; *Dialogue* 105, 106.
22. On the history of the term, cf. Koester, *Ancient Christian Gospels*, ch.1.
23. Eusebius, *History*, III 39.15. Papias' *hosa emnēmoneusen* should be translated not 'what he [Mark] remembered' but 'what he [Peter] recounted'.
24. Eusebius, *Church History*, II 15.1–2; cf. IV 14.5–7.
25. See further Loveday Alexander, 'Ancient Book-Production and the Circulation of the Gospels', in Richard J. Bauckham, ed., *The Gospels for All Christians: Rethinking the Gospel Audiences* (Grand Rapids: Eerdmans, 1997), 71–111.
26. Eusebius, *Church History*, III 39.4.
27. Cf. Samuel Byrskog, *Story as History – History as Story* (WUNT 123; Tübingen: Mohr Siebeck, 2000), and the literature there cited.
28. Koester, *Ancient Christian Gospels*, §1.4; ch. 5.
29. Loveday Alexander, *The Preface to Luke's Gospel* (SNTSMS 78; Cambridge: Cambridge University Press, 1993).
30. Texts in Ronald Hock and Edward O'Neil, *The Chreia in Ancient Rhetoric*, I: *The Progymnasmata* (Atlanta: Scholars Press, 1986); examples in Vernon K. Robbins, *Ancient Quotes and Anecdotes* (Sonoma: Polebridge, 1989).
31. Hock and O'Neil, *Chreia*, 82–3; 109–10.
32. Loveday Alexander, 'Acts and Ancient Intellectual Biography', in Bruce W. Winter and Andrew D. Clarke, eds., *The Book of Acts in its First Century Setting*, I: *Ancient Literary Setting* (Eerdmans: Grand Rapids, 1993), 31–63.
33. Birger Gerhardsson, *Memory and Manuscript: Oral Tradition and Written Transmission in Rabbinic Judaism and Early Christianity* (repr. Grand Rapids: Eerdmans, 1998). See also now Martin Jaffee, *Torah in the Mouth* (New York: Oxford University Press, 2001).
34. P. S. Alexander, 'Rabbinic Biography and the Biography of Jesus: A Survey of the Evidence', in Christopher M. Tuckett, ed., *Synoptic Studies: The Ampleforth Conferences of 1982 and 1983* (JSNTS 7; Sheffield: JSOT Press, 1984), 19–50.
35. Ibid., 41.
36. Werner H. Kelber, *The Oral and the Written Gospel* (Philadelphia: Fortress, 1983) argues for a radical disjunction between oral and literate modes of discourse. Recent folklore studies are more inclined to approach literacy and orality as 'not incompatible but reciprocal paradigms': cf. Eli Yassif, *The Hebrew Folktale: History, Genre, Meaning* (Bloomington: Indiana University Press, 1999), ix–xi.

37. Plutarch provides better parallels to the narrative coherence of the gospels; but he shares Diogenes' conviction that the isolated saying or anecdote provides the most telling revelation of the subject's *ethos* or moral character. Suetonius prefers a purely thematic arrangement, and Arrian presents his recollections of the teachings of the Stoic philosopher Epictetus simply in the form of 'Discourses' with no narrative at all.

38. Arnaldo Momigliano, *The Development of Greek Biography* (Cambridge, MA: Harvard University Press, 1993), 104.

39. Tacitus, *Agricola* §46; Lucian, *Demonax* §2. On the new biographical mood in general, cf. M. J. Edwards and Simon Swain, eds., *Portraits: Biographical Representation in the Greek and Latin Literature of the Roman Empire* (Oxford: Clarendon Press, 1997).

40. E.g. Morton Smith, 'Prolegomena to a Discussion of Aretalogies, Divine Men, the Gospels and Jesus,' *JBL*, 90 (1971), 174–99.

41. E. L. Bowie, 'Apollonius of Tyana: Tradition and Reality', *ANRW*, II.16.2 (1978), 1652–99.

42. Edwards and Swain, *Portraits*, 28 n. 74.

43. F. G. Downing, 'Contemporary Analogies to the Gospels and Acts: Genres or Motifs?', in Tuckett, *Synoptic Studies*, 51–65.

44. Edwards and Swain, *Portraits*, 33.

45. Edwards and Swain, *Portraits*, 27: 'The Gospels obviously have close cultural connections with Jewish historiography, which is centred around prominent individuals to an extent that is alien to Greek historical writing.'

46. Yassif, *Hebrew Folktale*, 31.

47. Ibid., 37.

48. Edwards and Swain, *Portraits*, 27–8.

49. Philo, *On Abraham*, §4–5.

50. See further, Loveday Alexander, 'Ancient Intellectual Biography'.

51. Tessa Rajak, 'Dying for the Law', in Edwards and Swain, *Portraits*, 39–67.

52. D. R. A. Hare, 'The Lives of the Prophets', in J. H. Charlesworth, ed., *The Old Testament Pseudepigrapha* (New York: Doubleday, 1985), II, 385–99; Anna Maria Schwemer, *Studien zu den frühjüdischen Prophetenlegenden Vitae Prophetarum*, I, II (Tübingen: Mohr Siebeck, 1995).

53. Loveday Alexander, 'Fact, Fiction, and the Genre of Acts', *NTS*, 44 (1998), 380–99.

54. It is always worth considering the possibility that the generic influence may work in the opposite direction: cf. G. W. Bowersock, *Fiction as History* (Berkeley: University of California Press, 1994), 143. Apollonius of Tyana is a clear case in point.

Further reading

Alexander, P. S., 'Rabbinic Biography and the Biography of Jesus: A Survey of the Evidence', in C. M. Tuckett, ed., *Synoptic Studies: The Ampleforth Conferences of 1982 and 1983* (Sheffield: JSOT Press, 1984), 19–50

Bauckham, Richard, ed., *The Gospels for All Christians: Rethinking the Gospel Audiences* (Grand Rapids: Eerdmans, 1996)

Bockmuehl, Markus, and Hagner, Donald A., eds., *The Written Gospel* (Cambridge: Cambridge University Press, 2005)

Burridge, Richard A., *What are the Gospels? A Comparison with Graeco-Roman Biography* (Cambridge: Cambridge University Press, 1992).

Byrskog, Samuel, *Story as History – History as Story* (Tübingen: Mohr Siebeck, 2000)

Jaffee, Martin S., *Torah in the Mouth: Writing and Oral Tradition in Palestinian Judaism, 200 BCE–400 CE* (New York: Oxford University Press, 2001)

Kelber, Werner H., *The Oral and the Written Gospel* (Philadelphia: Fortress, 1983)

Koester, Helmut, *Ancient Christian Gospels: Their History and Development* (Philadelphia: Trinity Press International, 1990)

Niditch, Susan, ed., *Text and Tradition: The Hebrew Bible and Folklore* (Atlanta: Scholars Press, 1990)

Stanton, Graham N., *Jesus and Gospel* (Cambridge: Cambridge University Press, 2004)

Yassif, Eli, *The Hebrew Folktale: History, Genre, Meaning* (Bloomington: Indiana University Press, 1999)

2   The fourfold gospel

FRANCIS WATSON

In a famous passage in his voluminous work *Against Heresies* (c. 180 CE), Irenaeus, bishop of Lyons, reflects on the fact that the worldwide church acknowledges four gospels – neither more nor fewer.[1] The fourfoldness of the church's gospel is, he suggests, comparable to a natural phenomenon, which it would be foolish to question: for example, there are four gospels just as there are four points of the compass. Casting around for further fourfold entities in the natural order, the bishop calls to mind the four mythical living creatures of the book of Revelation – the first like a lion, the second like an ox, the third with a human face, and the fourth like a flying eagle (Rev 4.6–7). These creatures, diverse yet united in their hymn of praise to God, represent the diversity and the unity of the four gospels. The Gospel according to John opens with a declaration of the divinity of the Word that is positively lion-like in its boldness. The Gospel according to Luke opens with Zacharias the priest offering sacrifice in the temple, and is fittingly symbolized by an ox. The Gospel according to Matthew opens with a genealogy, thereby emphasizing the humanity of the Word made flesh. Finally, the Gospel according to Mark opens with a citation from Isaiah the prophet, which is said to point to the winged, eagle-like aspect of the gospel. Later, these symbolic attributions were revised: Mark and John changed places, so that Mark was identified with the lion and John with the eagle – no doubt on account of the fourth gospel's supposedly more exalted character, its capacity to soar into regions inaccessible to the earthbound synoptic evangelists.[2] In this revised form, Irenaeus' scheme has been taken up into Christian tradition, and is evident especially in artistic depictions of the evangelists. This association of the evangelists with the four living creatures serves to assimilate the fourfold gospel to the natural order, thereby putting it beyond question. It just is the case that there are four gospels, and it is as pointless to question this as to ask why there are not three points of the compass, or seven living creatures around the throne of God. That, at least, is the conclusion that the naturalistic imagery suggests.

Yet, in spite of Irenaeus, the fourfoldness of the church's canonical gospel is not a natural phenomenon. This fourfoldness was established by the collective decision of the most influential Christian communities of both east and west in the latter half of the second century. This decision was in no way inevitable or predictable; it represented a choice of one among a number of competing options. If the individual canonical gospels are all the products of the first Christian century, their gathering into a fourfold canonical form is the work of the second century: in that sense, the four gospels are a second-century artefact with a first-century prehistory. The concept of a fourfold gospel was unknown to the earliest Christians, including the evangelists themselves. Mark may have assumed that his narrative work would coexist alongside an authoritative collection of Jesus' sayings – the hypothetical Q document. Matthew perhaps imagined that his combining of the narrative and the sayings traditions would make Mark redundant (as it may have made Q redundant). Luke intended his work to be read in a form in which the first book, dealing with the life of Jesus, would be immediately followed by a second, dealing with the expansion of the early church. John may claim a uniquely privileged position for itself in its appeal to the figure of the 'disciple whom Jesus loved', supposedly its author. None of the evangelists will have been aware that they were contributing to a collection of four 'gospels'. The fourfold canonical gospel is not simply the work of the four individual evangelists. It is the (relatively) final resolution of a problem that had exercised the church's leaders for a century and a half: the problem of how to stabilize the proliferating mass of oral traditions and written texts that claimed to represent the original truth about Jesus. It is an attempt to impose order in response to the threat of chaos.

In this chapter, we will try to clarify the significance of this response by examining a number of the options that were proposed before, during and after the establishment of the fourfold canonical gospel.

THE LIVING VOICE

Jesus himself appears to have made no provision for his teachings to be recorded in writing, and it is plausible that they were originally transmitted in oral form, and that those who had heard him at first hand had a privileged role in this. In principle, then, a primarily oral transmission of tradition about Jesus might have continued indefinitely, with written texts playing only a subordinate role.

This is the possibility advocated by Papias, bishop of Hierapolis in the early second century, excerpts of whose work are preserved by Irenaeus and Eusebius. Introducing the five books of his *Expositions of the Oracles of the Lord*, Papias speaks of his eagerness to learn about the teaching of individual apostles from those who had heard them – having concluded, as he tells us, that 'what was to be got from books was not so profitable to me as what came from the living and abiding voice'.[3] This contrast between living speech and the deadness of writing is a christianized version of a theme that goes back to Plato's *Phaedrus*, and implies only a limited role for written gospels. Consistently with this, Papias offers a less than enthusiastic endorsement of the two written texts that he knows. On the authority of 'the presbyter John', he tells us that

> Mark, having become the interpreter of Peter, wrote down accurately, although not in order, what he remembered of the things said or done by Christ. For he neither heard the Lord nor followed him, but later, as I said, he followed Peter, who adapted his teaching to the needs of his hearers but with no intention of giving a connected account of the Lord's discourses. So Mark committed no error when he wrote some things as he remembered them. For he was careful of one thing, not to omit any of the things he had heard, and not to state any of them falsely.[4]

Papias is prepared to vouch for Mark's general accuracy, but not for his order. Peter's preaching appealed to individual sayings or stories, without any sense of an overarching narrative framework, and this is said to explain the absence of any such framework in Mark. Papias may refer here to Mark's reliance on relatively self-contained stories that are only loosely connected to each other; in explaining why the Gospel of Mark is as it is, Papias appears to acknowledge a definite limitation here. In principle, Mark is on a level with those 'elders' who inform Papias about 'what Andrew or Peter said, or what was said by Philip, Thomas, James, John, or Matthew, or by any other of the Lord's disciples'.[5] Yet these informants represent 'the living and abiding voice', whereas Mark's written text is regarded as so problematic that, in defending it, it is conceded that those who disparage it for its disorderliness are largely correct.

Papias also speaks of Matthew, claiming that he 'wrote the oracles [*logia*] in the Hebrew language, and everyone interpreted them as he was able'.[6] This may refer either to the Gospel of Matthew (in which case the claim about a Hebrew original is false) or to a collection of sayings of Jesus in the original Aramaic, which Papias knows only indirectly through various divergent Greek translations. On balance, the second possibility seems the more probable; this would then offer some support to the Q hypothesis, and suggest that the name of Matthew was at some point transferred from the sayings collection to the gospel in which this collection was eventually incorporated.[7] What is striking, however, is Papias' relative lack of interest in this written text, and his preference for reports about what Matthew (and other apostles) *said*, as opposed to what they wrote.

Papias' informants passed on to him sayings ascribed to the Lord, and stories relating to the apostles, which have no parallels in the gospels or in Acts. For example, he received from them the Lord's teaching about the miraculous fertility of the coming millennial age, in which genetically modified vines and wheat will bring forth in overwhelming abundance. In response to Judas' sceptical questioning, the Lord replied that those who are found worthy to attain such a time will confirm whether his words are true.[8] If Papias' preference for the living and abiding voice had been maintained, we may assume that a mainly oral tradition would have continued to develop, creating new material of its own and drawing on material derived from other sources.[9] Of course, little if any of this supplementary material would be 'authentic'.

The later establishing of the fourfold canonical gospel served to eliminate such an option – so decisively that the possibility of appealing to 'non-canonical' sayings of Jesus was drastically curtailed. Under the impact of gnostic versions of Christianity, the concept of the living and abiding voice was increasingly regarded as a recipe for chaos, and the apostolic tradition of Jesus' deeds and sayings came to be identified exclusively with canonical gospels attributed (directly or indirectly) to Matthew and John, Peter and Paul.[10] The fundamental motivation here is to preserve what is original, and to establish a critical principle by which later corruption and accretion can be identified as such. Henceforth, the living and abiding voice of the Lord is to be heard within the texts themselves. The Word made flesh receives a second embodiment: as text.

A PRIVILEGED GOSPEL

The statements of Papias derive from a time and place at which texts ascribed to Mark and to Matthew are known but not yet fully established as authoritative. In such a situation, one possibility is to give greater weight to oral tradition; another is to write a gospel that improves on these predecessors. While Luke and John may perhaps have been written with such an aim in view, the clearest statement of such an intention is to be found in the Gospel of Thomas, which in its original Greek form may have been roughly contemporary with Papias.[11]

Saying 13 of this gospel contains the following dialogue between Jesus and his disciples, which is obviously modelled on earlier accounts of the Caesarea Philippi pericope (Mk 8.27–33 and parallels):

> Jesus said to his disciples: 'Compare me to someone, and tell me whom I am like.' Simon Peter said to him, 'You are like a righteous angel.' Matthew said to him, 'You are like a wise philosopher.' Thomas said to him, 'Master, my mouth is wholly incapable of saying whom you are like.' Jesus said: 'I am not your master. Because you have drunk, you have become intoxicated from the bubbling spring which I have measured out.' And he took him and withdrew and told him three things. When Thomas returned to his companions, they asked him, 'What did Jesus say to you?' Thomas said to them, 'If I tell you one of the things which he told me, you will pick up stones and throw them at me; a fire will come out of the stones and burn you up.'

The difference implied in the questions, 'Whom do people say that I am?' and, 'Whom do you say that I am?' (Mk 8.27, 29) is here located within the circle of Jesus' disciples. It seems that the intention is to define the status of the Gospel of Thomas in relation to other known apostolic writings, ascribed to Peter and Matthew. The dialogue is primarily concerned not with individuals but with texts.[12]

Elsewhere in this work, Thomas is named only in the introductory statement: 'These are the secret sayings which the living Jesus spoke and which Didymos Judas Thomas wrote down.' The dialogue cited above serves to account for Thomas's selection as the scribe responsible for committing Jesus' sayings to writing. Thomas, it is claimed, possessed an insight into the person of Jesus that the other disciples lacked; he was therefore the recipient of esoteric teachings that were withheld from the others; and his superior insight finds expression in the gospel that bears his name. This interpretation of saying 13 explains why one of the two inadequate answers to Jesus' question is assigned to Matthew – who is not given a speaking part in any of the canonical gospels. The answer, 'You are like a wise philosopher', is assigned to Matthew as the supposed author of the Gospel according to Matthew. Similarly, the other inadequate answer is assigned to Peter as the authority supposedly underlying the Gospel according to Mark. What Peter, Matthew and Thomas have in common is that there are gospel texts that lay claim to their authority. What differentiates the text that bears the name of Thomas is the claim that it derives from a uniquely privileged insight into the person of Jesus that is lacking in the earlier gospels. If this interpretation of saying 13 is correct, the Gospel of Thomas derives from precisely the situation presupposed by Papias. Texts assigned to Mark/Peter and to Matthew are in circulation, and yet their authority is not fully established; a claim to represent a better way – whether in the form of the living voice or of another written text authored by a more insightful disciple – will therefore seem plausible.

The fourfold canonical gospel does not entirely eliminate the possibility that one gospel might be regarded as superior to the others. Clement of Alexandria speaks of the Gospel of John as a 'spiritual gospel', in contrast to the others which give only the 'external facts' (*ta sōmatika*).[13] (A preference for the fourth gospel is also found in theologians such as Augustine, Luther, Schleiermacher and Bultmann.) Yet the tendency of the canonical form of the gospel is to place the four texts on the same horizontal plane, and to resist the gnosticizing assumption that the gospels represent fundamentally different levels of insight.

A PURIFIED GOSPEL

It is possible to give precedence to oral tradition, or to a new and definitive gospel, only so long as existing gospel texts seem to lack a fully authoritative status. Once their status is established, these two options cease to be available, and a new range of possibilities comes to light. One of these is to see in the fourfold canonical gospel nothing more than a confused mass of conflicting theological positions, and to attempt by critical means to recover the original gospel of Christ from later distortions. This project would later be taken up by various forms of liberal Protestantism, and it has its ancient representative in the figure of Marcion (died c. 160).[14]

Marcion's fundamental concern is to distinguish the God of the Christian gospel as sharply as possible from the creator God of Judaism and Jewish scripture. This, he believes, is what is intended in the Pauline doctrine of freedom from the law. Confusion between these two quite distinct deities is already present even in the fourfold gospel acknowledged in the church, which represents the judaizing corruption of the pure original gospel. All is not lost, however, for criticism enables us to recover that original purity. According to Irenaeus' hostile testimony, Marcion

> mutilates the Gospel according to Luke, removing all that is written about the Lord's birth and setting aside much of the Lord's teaching, in which the Lord is recorded as most clearly confessing that the maker of this universe is his Father. He likewise persuaded his followers that he himself was more credible than those apostles who have handed down the Gospel to us, providing them not with the Gospel but merely with a fragment of it.[15]

For Marcion, the original gospel is to be found within the Gospel according to Luke alone, although here, too, judaizing corruptions such as the birth legends need to be excised. Thus the true gospel begins abruptly with the statement that 'in the fifteenth year of the reign of Tiberius Caesar . . . [Christ] came down to Capernaum, a city of Galilee' (Lk 3.1; 4.31; the intervening material is also excised).[16] While Marcion probably already assumed the traditional link between Luke and Paul, he is interested not in the Gospel according to Luke as such but in the pure original written gospel that he believes is contained within it, in among all the later accretions. According to Tertullian, Marcion's gospel presented itself as authorless, lacking a title; presumably the preface (Lk 1.1–4) was also removed.[17] The resulting text goes back to an original moment in which Christ's apostles faithfully testified to the truth of the gospel: it is not 'the gospel according to . . .'; it is simply 'the gospel', in pristine purity, preserved within the later text known as 'the Gospel according to Luke' although not to be identified with it. This original gospel is, as it were, a transparent window on its subject-matter, which is the Christ who has descended to us in the appearance of flesh, making known to us the previously unknown God of love. Where the gospel takes multiple form and is associated with particular individuals, the image becomes clouded.

In order to justify his intense suspicion of the fourfold canonical gospel, Marcion appeals to the Pauline claims that even the original apostles did not 'walk uprightly according to the truth of the gospel', and that false apostles were perverting the gospel of Christ (Gal 2.14; 1.7).[18] How can we rely even on the works attributed (directly or indirectly) to Peter, John or Matthew when we learn from Paul that even apostles can fall away from the truth, and that false apostles were also present in their midst? In the work entitled *Antitheses*, Marcion therefore 'labours very hard to destroy the reputation of those gospels which are published as genuine and under the names of apostles, in order to secure for his own gospel the credit that he takes away from them'.[19] For Marcion, the fourfold canonical gospel – apparently already established in Rome by the mid-second century – must be abandoned. We are to rely instead on a single text, purged of its judaizing accretions, in which we encounter the pure essence of the original gospel of Christ.

If Marcion opposed the fourfold gospel, the fourfold gospel represents the church's rejection of the Marcionite claim that the true gospel is absolutely independent of the Jewish scriptural texts. The true gospel is not a window enabling us to behold an unmediated event without any preparation or presupposition. Instead, the true, fourfold gospel speaks of an event

that occurs within the medium of a textuality incorporating both prophets
and apostles.

SUPPLEMENTARY GOSPELS

If for Marcion the fourfold gospel contained too much material, most
of it corrupt, for others it contained too little. For such people, the fourfold
gospel no doubt tells us all we *need* to know about Jesus, but there is much
else that we would *like* to know, especially at points where the canonical
gospel is relatively uninformative. So-called 'apocryphal' gospels were written in order to meet this demand for more than the canonical gospel is able
or willing to provide.

From Matthew and Luke we learn about the circumstances of Jesus'
birth; yet, for some early Christian readers, what they tell us merely whets
our appetite for more. How had the divine providence prepared Mary for
her role as bearer of the incarnate Son of God? What of her own parent-
age, birth and upbringing? Why did she become betrothed to Joseph, even
though he was not destined to be the father of her child? What did she and
Joseph feel about her unexpected pregnancy, and how did others respond?
Did miraculous phenomena of any kind occur at Jesus' birth? Did Mary and
Joseph begin normal sexual relations after the birth? The canonical narratives do not provide adequate answers to questions such as these, and the
text known as the *Protevangelium of James* was written – perhaps as early
as the mid-second century – in order to fill these gaps.[20]

This text has proved to be almost as influential as the canonical infancy
narratives. For example, it is the primary source for the widespread assumption that Joseph was much older than Mary. Joseph, it is said, was an elderly
widower with children of his own, who was entrusted with the guardian-
ship of Mary when it was no longer appropriate for her to be brought up
within the temple precincts. (As Origen notes, the 'Book of James' teaches
'that the brothers of Jesus were sons of Joseph by a previous wife, whom
he married before Mary'.)[21] Joseph is selected for this role because his age
makes it unlikely that he will have sexual relations with Mary, thereby ensur-
ing her perpetual virginity. And so Mary becomes 'the Virgin Mary', a title
handed down in the creeds and implying a lifelong commitment to sexual
abstinence.[22] Other, less significant but enduring additions to the canonical
narratives include the names of Mary's parents (Joachim and Anna), Mary's
riding to Bethlehem on a donkey, and her giving birth in a cave. The author
is familiar with the canonical narratives, which he seeks to harmonize, but
he has no inhibitions about supplementing them with material of his own.

Matthew tells us nothing about Jesus' childhood, and Luke has only the story about the twelve-year-old Jesus in the temple (Lk 2.41–51). Here too, the evangelists' reticence seemed to be unsatisfactory. Surely there must have been indications in Jesus' childhood that this was no ordinary child but the Word made flesh? Surely the miraculous powers he exercised during his public ministry must have been evident from the start? According to the oldest infancy gospel, ascribed to the apostle Thomas and dating perhaps from the late second century, the child Jesus performed a series of miracles which anticipate in various ways the miracles of his adulthood. Thus, at the age of five,

> he made soft clay and fashioned from it twelve sparrows. And it was the sabbath when he did this. And there were also many other children playing with him . . . And when Joseph came to the place and saw it, he cried out to him, saying: 'Why do you do on the sabbath what ought not to be done?' But Jesus clapped his hands and cried to the sparrows: 'Off with you!' And the sparrows took flight and went away chirping.[23]

The motif of the miracle on the sabbath derives from the canonical gospels (cf. Mk 3.1–6; Lk 13.10–17; Jn 5.1–18), and is here developed in a form intended to be suitable for a small child. The miracle demonstrates that, already as a five-year-old, 'the Son of man is Lord even of the sabbath' (cf. Mk 2.28). The other obvious influence here is the Genesis account of the creation of the first man, according to which 'the LORD God formed man of dust from the ground, and breathed into his nostrils the breath of life' (Gen 2.7). When the child Jesus performs a similar feat with his sparrows, this clearly discloses the presence of the Creator. Later, the child's fiery temper creates various difficulties for his adoptive father: children whom Jesus finds annoying tend to wither away or die, and he also proves impossible to educate. At other times, however, he can be very helpful. After accidentally breaking a pitcher, he brings the spilt water home in a garment he was wearing; he produces a miraculous wheat harvest in order to feed the poor; he lengthens a plank intended for a bed but too short for it; he heals James from a snake bite, incidentally causing the snake to burst; and he repeatedly raises the dead. The cycle of miracle stories concludes with the author's retelling of the Lukan story of the twelve-year-old Jesus in the Temple – indicating the author's intention to supplement canonical material whose authority is already established.

Apocryphal texts such as the *Protevangelium of James* and the *Infancy Gospel of Thomas* exploit the gaps in the canonical narratives, and respond to a perceived need to know more about the events that preceded, accompanied and followed the birth of Jesus as recounted in Matthew and Luke. One further point at which the canonical evangelists are silent occurs at the end of the story rather than the beginning: the evangelists narrate the consequences of Jesus' resurrection – the empty tomb, the appearances – but not the event of the resurrection itself. The omission is particularly striking in Matthew, where the angelic removal of the stone in front of the tomb is not, as one might have expected, the prelude to the resurrection, since this has already taken place (cf. Matt 28.1–6). No matter how early the women visit the tomb on Easter morning, Jesus has always anticipated them; and so his resurrection remains outside the boundaries of the narrative. The empty tomb may be taken to signify a gap in the narrative itself, and the *Gospel of Peter* (late second century) seeks to fill this gap in the following way:

> Now in the night in which the Lord's day dawned, when the soldiers, two by two in every watch, were keeping guard, there rang out a loud voice in heaven. And they saw the heavens opened and two men coming down from there in a great brightness and approaching the tomb. The stone that had been laid against the entrance to the tomb started of itself to roll and gave way to the side, and the tomb was opened, and both the young men entered in . . . And . . . they saw again three men coming out from the tomb, and two of them were assisting the other, and a cross followed them, and the heads of the two reached to heaven but that of him whom they led by the hand surpassed the heavens. And they heard a voice out of the heavens crying, 'You have preached to those that sleep', and from the cross there was heard the answer, 'Yes!'[24]

The author has drawn the motif of the guards at the tomb from Matthew, but has turned them into witnesses of the event of the resurrection itself, in which a gigantic Christ-figure is brought forth out of the tomb by two angelic assistants, followed by his cross. Also implied here is an answer to the question about what Jesus was doing in the interval between his death and his resurrection: he was preaching the gospel to the dead (cf. 1 Pet 3.18–20, 4.6). The canonical gospels say nothing about any such 'descent into hell'.

Thus, as early as the second century, narratives were produced which sought to fill in the gaps especially at the beginning and end of the canonical narratives. It was assumed that these gaps were an open invitation to a further proliferation of narrative material. Yet those who produced this supplementary material were clearly deviating from the idea that the four-fold canonical gospel represents a *limit*. When it was claimed that Thomas, James and Peter had also produced written accounts relating to the life of Jesus, the logic of this claim was that the number of the gospels cannot be confined to four; the canon should be reopened so as to accommodate the newer, or newly rediscovered, texts. Yet, in spite of the popularity of the newer texts, the fourfold canonical gospel remained fourfold. In the light of the supplementary apocryphal material, canonical reticence about the events at the beginning and end of the story of Jesus should be seen as integral to the evangelists' theological interpretation of these events – and not as an unfortunate deficiency which later gospels must remedy.

What the Gospel of John says about itself might be extended to the entire canonical collection: 'Now Jesus did many other signs in the presence of the disciples, which are not written in this book; but these are written that you may believe that Jesus is the Christ, the Son of God, and that believing you may have life in his name' (Jn 20.30–1). According to this statement, what is written in the fourfold canonical gospel is not intended to be comprehensive; it would take an infinite number of books to do full justice to everything that Jesus did and said and was (cf. Jn 21.25). Nevertheless, what is written within the canonical limit is *sufficient* for its purpose, which is not to satisfy curiosity but to engender life by representing Jesus in his identity as the Christ. Further books might be written, but they are not needed. The one thing that is needful is to be found only within the canonical limit.

THE HARMONIZED GOSPEL

The fourfold gospel resists both Marcionite reduction and apocryphal proliferation. Yet its plurality may still be found to be puzzling. The four gospels differ among themselves; without such differences, they would no longer be four. Yet Jesus himself is one, not four, and the fourfold gospel with its striking internal differences may appear to undermine that oneness. In response to this concern, one possible strategy is to regard the fourfold form of the gospel as accidental rather than essential, and to incorporate as much as possible of the material it contains into a single gospel or gospel harmony. This was the task undertaken by Tatian, who in the second half of the second century produced a gospel harmony known as the *Diatessaron*, which virtually supplanted the canonical gospels in Syriac-speaking contexts. The eventual elimination of this text may have owed more to the fact that Tatian was regarded as a heretic than to any convictions about the theological importance of a pluriform gospel.

The *Diatessaron* opens by connecting Mk 1.1 ('The beginning of the gospel of Jesus Christ the Son of God') to Jn 1.1–5, with its concluding reference to the light shining in the darkness. Since the Johannine prologue turns next to the ministry of John the Baptist (Jn 1.6–8), the entire Matthean and Lukan infancy narrative must be inserted in the gap between Jn 1.5 and 1.6. And so we read:

> And the light shines in the darkness, and the darkness comprehended it not. There was in the days of Herod the king a priest whose name was Zechariah, of the family of Abijah . . .   (Jn 1.5 + Lk 1.5)

This shift from John to Luke is evident, however, only to those who are familiar with John and with Luke as independent writings. For those who know the gospel only in its harmonized form, the seams are invisible, and the words derived from Mk 1.1 and Jn 1.1–5 will be perceived as an entirely appropriate prologue to the account of the birth of John the Baptist. Tatian follows the Lukan narrative until the conclusion of chapter 1, at which point he switches from Luke to Matthew:

> And the child [John] grew and became strong in spirit, and he was in the wilderness until the day of his manifestation to Israel. Now the birth of Jesus Christ was like this: when his mother was betrothed to Joseph, before they came together, she was found to be with child through the Holy Spirit. And Joseph her husband, being a just man and unwilling to put her to shame, decided to separate from her secretly.   (Lk 1.80 + Matt 1.18–19)

In its new context, the Matthean narrative invites a comparison between the reactions of Joseph and of Elizabeth to Mary's pregnancy. Elizabeth, filled with the Holy Spirit, had immediately acclaimed Mary as 'the mother of my Lord' (cf. Lk 1.43); Joseph, initially devoid of divine insight, contemplates a separation. Little attempt is made to harmonize the narratives of Lk 2 and Matt 2, which are simply set alongside each other. The confusing result is that the magi visit the Christ-child in Bethlehem after the holy family has returned to Nazareth. The Lukan story about the twelve-year-old Jesus is, however, placed logically enough after the Matthean account of the move from Egypt to Nazareth. And so the story continues, with blocks of Lukan, Johannine and Matthean material being juxtaposed in the account of the Baptist's ministry that follows.

In principle, the *Diatessaron* might have proved so successful that all independent traces of its four sources would have disappeared. If that had happened, post-Enlightenment gospel scholarship would presumably have followed a similar course to modern pentateuchal criticism, in which the contents of the Law of Moses were traced back to the four sources denominated J, E, D and P. No doubt the identification of four hypothetical sources underlying the single gospel narrative would have proved equally controversial. Unlike the final redactors of the Pentateuch, however, the redactors of the canonical gospels concluded that harmonization was inappropriate and that pluriformity was to be retained. The problem of difference was left unresolved.

As we have seen, the fourfold canonical gospel established itself in the face of a number of alternative proposals about the proper transmission of apostolic tradition relating to Jesus. It definitively rejects the claims that written texts are to be subordinated to oral tradition (Papias); that a uniquely privileged disciple was appointed to write a definitive gospel, far above the level of the others (Thomas); that the fourfold gospel has corrupted the pure original datum from which it derives, and must therefore be subjected to critical surgery (Marcion); that the fourfold gospel needs to be filled out with supplementary narrative material (apocryphal gospels); and that the four texts should be combined into a single text (Tatian). Yet the question of difference remained to be resolved.

TRUTH BEYOND CONTRADICTION

The most radical solution to this problem was proposed by Origen, the great Alexandrian theologian who died c. 250 CE. Origen's biblical hermeneutics were influenced, directly or indirectly, by the Jewish theologian Philo of Alexandria (died c. 50 CE), who had argued that the spiritual or theological truth of a scriptural text need not be undermined by its literal or historical falsehood. There was, for example, no such creature as the highly intelligent talking snake of Gen 3, and yet its non-historicity does nothing to diminish the theological value of the story. Indeed, historical implausibility serves as a positive indication of theological significance.

Origen adopts this hermeneutical theory as his own in the fourth book of his work *On First Principles*, where he extends it from Old Testament narrative to the gospels. In book x of his commentary on the Gospel of John, he applies it specifically to the issue of gospel differences. His starting-point is the observation that the Johannine account of the early days of Jesus' ministry seems to allow no room for the forty days of the synoptic temptation accounts. The attentive reader of the four canonical gospels will notice, he says, that problems of this kind are innumerable. Once one has become aware of the extent of this problem, and of the consequent impossibility of naive harmonizing such as Tatian's, only two options remain:

> The student, perplexed by the consideration of these matters, will either give up the attempt to find everything in the gospels true, and, not venturing to conclude that all of our information about the Lord is untrustworthy, will choose one of them at random to be his guide; or he will accept all four, and will conclude that their truth is not to be sought in the outward and material letter.[25]

Either we decide that one gospel alone accurately recounts the life of Jesus, or we accept that the truth of all four of them is not to be sought on the literal and historical plane alone. Origen argues that the evangelists would be fully justified

> if they sometimes dealt freely with things which to the eye of history happened differently, and changed them so as to subserve the mystical aims they had in view – speaking of something that happened in one place as if it had happened in another, or of something that took place at one time as if it had taken place at another, and introducing into what was spoken in a certain way some changes of their own. Where possible, they intended to speak the truth both materially and spiritually; and where this was not possible, they chose to prefer the spiritual to the material. Spiritual truth was often preserved, as one might say, in material falsehood.[26]

The difficulties of the gospel differences are particularly acute when relating John to the synoptics. For example, the apostle Simon is renamed as Cephas or Peter on different occasions and in quite different circumstances (Jn 1.41; Matt 16.18); the Jesus of John baptizes (Jn 4.1–2), whereas the Jesus of the synoptics does not; and the ministries of the Baptist and of Jesus overlap in John but not in the synoptics. In the face of so many difficulties of this kind, 'Who is so wise and so able as to learn all the things that are recorded about Jesus in the four evangelists, and both to understand each incident by itself, and to have a connected view of all his sojournings and words and acts at each place?'[27] For Origen, a single connected account of the life of Jesus is an impossibility. Once the futile attempt to reconcile the narratives is abandoned, however, it becomes possible to grasp the distinctive theological intentions of each of the evangelists. Their harmony is to be found not on the historical plane but in the singular though infinitely rich and diverse truth of the one Lord Jesus Christ, the incarnate Logos.

Origen's solution to the problem of gospel differences anticipates the modern (re)discovery of the individuality of the gospels and of the primarily theological orientation of their respective narratives. Arguably, modern redaction- and narrative-critical work on the gospels has recovered a sense of the *plurality* of the canonical gospel, which may be undermined where difference is harmonized away. The question remaining is whether it is still possible to interpret this diversity as a unity.

THE ONENESS OF THE GOSPEL

Modern gospels scholarship has been overwhelmingly hostile to the practice of harmonizing the gospels, with considerable justification, as we have seen. Yet it is important to see that this flawed practice is motivated by a genuine theological concern, which is to articulate the *oneness* of the fourfold gospel in its testimony to the one God and the one Lord Jesus Christ. The modern or postmodern view that in the four gospels we have no more than a plurality of diverging images of Jesus, with no principle of coherence, is totally at odds with the canonical form. To return to Irenaeus' image, the four living creatures may look different but are all praising the same Christ and the same God.[28]

As Augustine's work *On the Harmony of the Evangelists* indicates, 'harmonizing' may take various forms. In the infancy narratives, for example, Augustine follows the lead of Tatian and other predecessors and seeks to turn two stories into a single, coherent story. The Matthean account of Joseph's reaction to Mary's pregnancy here pre-dates the birth of John the Baptist (Luke); the Matthean magi follow the Lukan shepherds, after the child's circumcision; the flight to Egypt follows the presentation in the Temple.[29] In all three cases, the Matthean material is introduced at an earlier point than in the *Diatessaron*. The problem is not that the resulting narrative is incoherent, but that it destroys the integrity of the individual stories. Augustine is quite explicit about this:

> Each evangelist constructs his own particular narrative on a kind of
> plan which gives the appearance of being the complete and orderly
> record of the events in their succession. For, preserving a simple
> silence on the subject of those incidents of which he intends to give no
> account, he then connects those which he does wish to relate with

what he has been immediately recounting, in such a manner as to make the recital seem continuous.[30]

In Luke, for example, the evangelist is silent about the flight to Egypt – with the result that the return to Nazareth *seems* to follow directly from the presentation in the Temple. Once the two narratives are harmonized, however, these apparent connections dissolve away, and it becomes clear that the true order is one in which blocks of Lukan and Matthean material alternate with one another. The result is that the integrity of the individual narratives is undermined; it becomes impossible to consider each evangelist's account on its own terms. Yet the problem which this unsatisfactory harmonizing seeks to address still remains: within their canonical context, the Matthean and Lukan infancy narratives must somehow be read as complementary, and not as mutually antagonistic.

With other gospel material, Augustine adopts a range of different approaches. Where differences occur in the wording of a particular saying, he does not insist that every variant must represent an independent utterance, and finds no problem with the supposition that one version may be closer to the original than the others, and that we can speculate as to which that more original version might be. More important, however, is the need to identify *the common subject-matter* referred to in the diversity of versions, and to see that the diversity helps rather than hinders the articulation of that common subject-matter. In the case of the divine voice at Jesus' baptism, for example, Matthew presents this as a third-person utterance ('This is my beloved son . . .'), whereas Mark presents it as a second-person utterance ('You are my beloved son . . .'):

> If you ask which of these different versions represents what was actually expressed by the voice, you may fix on whichever you wish, provided that you understand that those of the writers who have not reproduced the identical form of speech have still reproduced the same sense intended to be conveyed. And these variations in the modes of expression are also useful in this way, that they make it possible for us to reach a more adequate conception of the saying than might been the case with only one form, and that they also secure it against being interpreted in a sense not consonant with the real state of the case.[31]

According to Augustine, differences may originate in accidents of transmission such as slips of memory, or in deliberate attempts to bring out the true meaning more clearly. One way or another, they must be interpreted as a necessary means of bringing out the full scope of the theological subject-matter.[32] In Augustine's reflections on gospel differences, there is no trace of an *a priori* commitment to the precise historical accuracy of every part of every gospel. Rather, this is a pragmatic, inductive approach that considers each difference on its merits, and finds the harmony of the gospels more in the theological subject-matter than in the verbal expression.

In modern scholarship, the tendency is to absolutize the differences between the gospels – in sharp reaction against the problematic harmonizing practised by a Tatian or (sometimes) an Augustine. Origen's claim that a theological truth can come to expression in a historical falsehood, and that the fourfold gospel itself falsifies the absolute historicity of its individual narratives, seems better attuned to modern scholarly assumptions about the gospels. Yet, in the end, Origen and Augustine have a great deal in common. They have both made a careful study of the gospel differences; they are both convinced that the four gospels speak in various ways of a singular though infinitely rich theological subject-matter; and they both believe that this subject-matter is articulated *in* the differences and not in spite of them. In contrast, it is not clear that modern scholarship has achieved the balance sought by these patristic theologians in their reflections on the fourfold gospel: the balance between the individual text and its plural context, or between difference and commonality.

One reason for this deficiency is the modern assumption that the four-fold canonical form is the very last place one should look for whatever theological truth the gospels may contain; truth is to be found, if at all, only in and through the individual text. Yet it is not impossible that a renewed attention to the gospels' canonical form might open up new perspectives on the theological truth that the gospels strive to communicate. This would also provide an answer to those who wish to dissolve the canonical form, whether by reduction to a pure original historical datum, or by envisioning an endless proliferation of images of Jesus with no basis in any prior truth.[33] It is, in fact, a promising time to return to the fourfold canonical form of the gospel, and to rethink its hermeneutical and theological implications.

Notes

1. *Against Heresies*, III 11.8.
2. The traditional scheme derives from Jerome, which won out over the versions proposed by Irenaeus and by Augustine – who assigned the lion to Matthew, the man to Mark, and the eagle to John (*On the Harmony of the Evangelists*, I 6.9).
3. Eusebius, *Church History*, III 39.4.
4. Ibid., III 39.15.
5. Ibid., III 39.4.

6. Ibid., III 39.16.
7. As argued by Martin Hengel, *The Four Gospels and the One Gospel of Jesus Christ: An Investigation of the Collection and Origin of the Canonical Gospels* (ET, London: SCM Press, 2000), 76–78. I am not convinced, however, by Hengel's claim that the gospel titles are as old as the gospels themselves.
8. *Against Heresies*, v 32.
9. Thus the saying about the miraculously productive vines of the millennium derives not from Jesus but from *1 Enoch* (10.19), from where it passed into the Syriac *Apocalypse of Baruch* (29.5) in a form very similar to Papias'.
10. The link between Paul and Luke is asserted by Irenaeus, *Against Heresies*, II 1.1, a passage which also contains an early ascription of the fourth gospel to John.
11. English translations of the Gospel of Thomas may be found in James M. Robinson, ed., *The Nag Hammadi Library* (Leiden: E. J. Brill, 1984); also, Stephen J. Patterson et al., *The Fifth Gospel: The Gospel of Thomas Comes of Age* (Harrisburg: Trinity Press International, 1998).
12. The possibility of a reference here to the Gospel of Matthew is noted by Stephen Patterson, *Fifth Gospel*, 42.
13. Cited in Eusebius, *Church History*, VI 14.7.
14. For discussion of Marcion in relation to modern biblical scholarship, see Francis Watson, *Text and Truth: Redefining Biblical Theology* (Edinburgh: T. & T. Clark, 1996), 127–76.
15. *Against Heresies*, I 27.2.
16. Tertullian, *Against Marcion*, IV 7.
17. Ibid., IV 2.
18. Ibid., I 20; IV 3; *On Prescription against Heretics*, 23.
19. *Against Marcion*, IV 3.
20. Along with the other apocryphal gospels discussed here, the *Protevangelium of James* is included in Ron Cameron, ed., *The Other Gospels: Non-Canonical Gospel Texts* (Guildford: Lutterworth Press, 1983); see also the standard collections of New Testament apocrypha edited by M. R. James, by E. Hennecke, W. Schneemelcher and R. M. Wilson, and by J. K. Elliott.
21. Origen, *Commentary on Matthew*, x 17.
22. The *Protevangelium* (at 19.3—20.3) also claims that Mary's virginity extends even to her physiological condition: immediately after the birth, two 'Hebrew midwives' conduct a gynaecological examination which confirms that the hymen has remained miraculously intact (compare also Clement of Alexandria, *Stromata*, VII 16.93).
23. *Infancy Gospel of Thomas*, 2.2–4.
24. *Gospel of Peter*, 35–42.
25. Origen, *Commentary on John*, x 2.
26. Ibid., x 4.
27. Ibid., x 6.
28. Compare Brevard Childs's defence of a modified form of gospel harmonization, in *The New Testament as Canon: An Introduction* (London: SCM Press, 1984), 143–209. Childs rightly argues that modern scholarship has neglected the issue of canonical unity: 'To suggest that the search [for the oneness of the canonical gospel] is of minor importance and is simply a vestige from a precritical era, is

not only to disregard the literary shape given the collection, but also to run in the face of its ancient and fully justifiable usage within the community of faith as a single corpus' (153).

29. *On the Harmony of the Evangelists*, II 5.17.
30. Ibid., II 5.16.
31. Ibid., II 14.31.
32. As Childs suggests, the fourfold gospel 'has produced a centripetal force which has contracted the original variations rather than exacerbating the differences after the model of the redaction critics' (*New Testament as Canon*, 173). The point is not to deny that differences exist, but to see them as an expression of a common subject-matter rather than as outright contradictions.
33. Currently, the fascinating and seductive Gospel of Thomas is being promoted as a 'fifth gospel', which marks not just a substitution of five for four but, above all, the ending of the canonical limit.

Further reading

Bockmuehl, Markus, and Hagner, Donald A., eds., *The Written Gospel* (Cambridge: Cambridge University Press, 2005)

Crossan, John Dominic, *Four Other Gospels: Shadows on the Contours of the Canon* (Minneapolis: Winston, 1985)

Ehrman, Bart D., *Lost Christianities: The Battles for Scripture and the Faiths We Never Knew* (New York: Oxford University Press, 2003)

Elliott, J. K., *The Apocryphal New Testament* (Oxford: Clarendon Press, 1993)

Gamble, Harry Y., *The New Testament Canon: Its Making and Meaning* (Philadelphia: Fortress, 1985)

Hengel, Martin, *The Four Gospels and the One Gospel of Jesus Christ* (ET, London: SCM Press, 2000)

Koester, Helmut, *Ancient Christian Gospels: Their History and Development* (London: SCM Press, 1990)

Lapham, Fred, *An Introduction to the New Testament Apocrypha* (London and New York: T. & T. Clark International, 2003)

Metzger, Bruce M., *The Canon of the New Testament: Its Origin, Development, and Significance* (Oxford: Clarendon Press, 1987)

Uro, Risto, ed., *Thomas at the Crossroads: Essays on the Gospel of Thomas* (Edinburgh: T. & T. Clark, 1997)

Valantasis, Richard, *The Gospel of Thomas* (New York and London: Routledge, 1997)

3 The canonical matrix of the gospels

RICHARD B. HAYS

THE STORY OF ISRAEL AS MATRIX OF THE GOSPEL STORIES

Jesus and his first followers were Jews whose symbolic world was shaped by Israel's scripture: their categories for interpreting the world and their hopes for God's saving action were fundamentally conditioned by the biblical stories of God's dealings with the people Israel. Therefore, it is not surprising that as the earliest Christian communities began to tell and retell stories about Jesus, they interpreted his life, death and resurrection in relation to those biblical stories (i.e., the texts that Christians later came to call the Old Testament). The authors of our four canonical gospels were the heirs of this tradition of storytelling, and they shared the early Christian community's passionate concern – a concern that, as far as we can tell, goes back to Jesus himself – to show that Jesus' teachings and actions, as well as his violent death and ultimate vindication, constituted the continuation and climax of the ancient biblical story. Thus, all four canonical gospels developed within the matrix of Israel's scripture: the Old Testament was the *generative milieu* for the gospels, the original environment in which the first Christian traditions were conceived, formed and nurtured.

Because each of the four gospels – different as they are – narrates the story of Jesus as the continuation and fulfillment of Israel's story, the earliest accounts of Jesus must be understood within their original scriptural environment. The point may be illustrated by comparing the parable of the wicked tenants in its canonical versions (Mk 12.1–12/Matt 21.33–46/Lk 20.9–19) to the stripped-down version that appears in the extracanonical second-century Gospel of Thomas (GosT 65). The Gospel of Thomas systematically excludes all the resonant OT allusions that appear in the canonical tellings of the tale: the details about the planting and preparation of the vineyard that vividly recall Isaiah's Song of the Vineyard (Isa 5.1–7), the description of the vineyard owner's son as a 'beloved son' (evocative of Gen

22.2; Ps 2.7; and Isa 42.1), the tenants' declaration, 'Come, let us kill him' (echoing Joseph's brothers in Gen 37.20), and the concluding citation of Ps 118.22–3, proclaiming that the stone the builders rejected has become the cornerstone.[1] Some NT scholars have speculated that Thomas's expurgated version of the parable is more historically authentic (i.e., closer to the teaching of the historical Jesus) than the canonical versions, because it is less allegorical. In fact, however, the chief effect of Thomas's exclusions is to extract the parable from its Jewish historical setting, distancing it from the cultural and religious context in which Jesus lived and taught. The canonical tellings, on the other hand, beckon the reader to recall Isa 5.7:

> For the vineyard of the LORD of Hosts is the house of Israel,
> and the people of Judah are his pleasant planting;
> he expected justice, but saw bloodshed;
> righteousness, but heard a cry!

By evoking this canonical memory, the synoptic gospels press us to interpret the parable as a word of judgement on the leaders of Israel for their failure to yield the vineyard's grapes to its rightful owner. The parable thereby places the story of Jesus within the unfolding story of Israel and presents his death as the climax of a pattern of unfaithfulness and judgement familiar to any reader of Israel's prophetic literature. At the same time, the identification of Jesus as the 'beloved son' (Mk 12.6; Lk 20.13) – linking him both to Isaac and to the Davidic king – hints that his death is to be understood not merely as a tragic episode of violence but as an event of saving significance for Israel. This intimation is confirmed by the culminating Psalm citation (Mk 12.10–11 and parallels, citing Ps 118.22–3), which looks forward to the resurrection as God's saving act:

> The stone that the builders rejected
> has become the cornerstone;
> this was the Lord's doing,
> and it is amazing in our eyes.

Thus, the canonical synoptic versions situate the parable of the wicked tenants within a larger narrative context and present Jesus' death and resurrection as the climax of the story of Israel. The canonical matrix provides both hermeneutical guidance and theological depth.

The Gospel of Thomas, by contrast, offers a colourless, enigmatic version of the parable that distances it from the story of Israel and leaves it open to be read however the reader may choose; in the case of Thomas, the parable is co-opted into a gnostic message of detachment from an evil world. Thus, Thomas's editorial de-judaizing of the parable illustrates the loss of meaning – or better, distortion of meaning – that occurs when the gospel tra-ditions are artificially removed from the canonical matrix of Israel's story.[2]

This example highlights the similarity of the three synoptic gospels to one another, in contrast to an extracanonical text. As we study the gospels more closely, however, we find significant differences; each one has a dis-tinctive manner of interpreting Israel's scripture. The number of Old Tes-tament citations and allusions in the gospels is so massive that a thorough survey is impossible. In the pages that follow, therefore, we shall focus first on the Gospel of Mark, the earliest of our canonical gospels, to see how its narrative is related to the matrix of the biblical traditions. After a close look at some representative passages in Mark, we shall more briefly consider the interpretation of the other three gospels within the canonical matrix.

THE SCRIPTURAL MATRIX OF MARK'S GOSPEL

The Gospel of Mark tells a mysterious story enveloped in apocalyptic urgency, a story that focuses relentlessly on the cross and ends on a note of hushed, enigmatic hope. Many of the key images in this mysterious narrative are drawn from Israel's scriptures; yet, unlike Matthew, Mark rarely points explicitly to correspondences between Israel's scripture and the story of Jesus. It is as though, in his deft but allusive use of scripture, Mark is whispering to his readers the same admonition delivered to Jesus' disciples as they puzzle over his enigmatic parables: 'Pay attention to what you hear; the measure you give will be the measure you get, and still more will be given you. For to those who have, more will be given; and from those who have nothing, even what they have will be taken away' (Mk 4.24–5). Precisely because Mark's uses of scripture are subtler than those of the other evangelists, it will prove helpful to examine in more detail the way in which Mark's story takes shape within the scriptural matrix.

The hope for Israel's deliverance

Although Mark, in contrast to Matthew and Luke, provides little intro-ductory framing for his narrative, his account presupposes that Israel has reached a moment of crisis. When the curtain rises on Mark's drama, we find Israel still in exile – at least metaphorically – as they are still under the thumb of Gentile powers. Despite God's past favour, the people are now in a state of powerlessness, confusion and need; they are 'like sheep without a shepherd' (6.34). There is an ill-formed but widespread hope for God to send a 'messiah' (*Christos*: 8.29; 14.61) who will restore the kingdom of David and put an end to Israel's suffering (10.46; 11.9–10).

Such a hope is by no means unprecedented; Mark finds precursors in Israel's scripture, particularly in the Psalms and prophetic literature. Near the end of the book of Isaiah, for example, the prophet appeals fervently to God to 'tear open the heavens and come down,' to bring deliverance to his people (Isa 64.1). This apocalyptic prayer sets the stage for the narrative of Mark's gospel. Although Mark does not explicitly quote this passage from Isaiah, the story of Jesus' baptism (Mk 1.9–11) alludes to it: 'And immediately as he was coming up out of the water, he saw *the heavens torn open* and the Spirit *descending* like a dove into him' (Mk 1.10). Only Mark, of the three synoptic evangelists, uses the violent participle 'torn' (*schizomenous*), offering a strong allusion to the Hebrew text of Isa 64.1 (= Isa 63.19 MT), the only passage in the Old Testament that uses the verb *qāra'* ('tear') in relation to the heavens.[3] This allusion gives us cause to suppose that Mark has Isaiah specifically in mind.[4] The gospel, according to Mark, is God's answer to Isaiah's intercessory cry: the tearing of the heavens and the descent of the Spirit upon Jesus signify that God's eschatological work of deliverance is beginning.

As the rest of the narrative will show, Mark carries forward the story of Israel by hinting that in the events of Jesus' life and death, God has at last torn open the heavens and come down, and that in Jesus the Christ both judgement and restoration have come upon Israel in a way prefigured in scripture. The announcement of God's powerful setting-right of things is the keynote of Jesus' own apocalyptic message, which Mark describes as *to euangelion tou theou* ('the good news of God'): 'The time is fulfilled and the kingdom of God has come near' (Mk 1.14b-15a; cf. Isa 40.9; 52.7–8). In effect, Mark is declaring that Israel's story has reached, in Jesus, its divinely ordained climax.

The harbinger of judgement and the new exodus

A few deft strokes in the opening lines of the gospel (at Mk 1.1–3) evoke the time of crisis and trigger a rush of hope that at last God's promised deliverance is at hand:

> The beginning of the good news of Jesus Christ, the Son of God, as it is
>   written in the prophet Isaiah:
> See, I am sending my messenger ahead of you
> who will prepare your way;
> the voice of one crying out in the wilderness:
> 'Prepare the way of the Lord,
> make his paths straight.'

The quotation is derived not from Isaiah alone; it begins with a fusion of words from Ex 23.20 and Mal 3.1. Why then does Mark attribute the citation to Isaiah? Is he simply confused? The apparent mistake has sometimes been taken as evidence that Mark is actually quoting from a primitive collection of messianic testimonies, rather than directly from the Old Testament passages. It is more likely, however, that 'Mark's use of the Isaiah ascription . . . indicates that the overall conceptual framework for his gospel is the Isaianic New Exodus'.[5] By naming Isaiah in particular, and by bringing the citation to its climax with words taken from Isa 40, Mark signals to his readers that the *euangelion* of Jesus Christ is to be read within the matrix of Isaiah's prophetic vision: God will return to Zion and restore Israel.

At the same time, however, these opening lines of the gospel also sound the theme of God's purifying judgement. The quotation ascribed in Mk 1.2 to 'the prophet Isaiah' begins with words reminiscent of the sombre warning of the prophet Malachi (Mal 3.1–5). In Malachi, the messenger sent to prepare the way for God's coming is identified with the returning prophet Elijah, whose mission will be to bring about repentance so that the coming of the Lord will not result in the cursing of the land (Mal 4.5–6).

In fact, however, the wording of Mk 1.2 is even closer to Ex 23.20 (LXX) than to Mal 3.1. In the Exodus passage, God, speaking with Moses on Mount Sinai, promises to send an angel/messenger (*angelos*) to lead Israel into the promised land of Canaan. Against this backdrop, Mark's echo of Exodus suggests that the progress of the 'gospel of God' into the world may be, like the occupation of Canaan, the beginning of a campaign against hostile forces in possession of the land. This suggestion is amply confirmed by the Markan narrative that follows, in which Jesus launches an offensive against demonic powers, who perceive immediately that Jesus has come to destroy them (e.g. Mk 1.24; cf. 3.23–7; 5.1–20).

A reader who senses the echo of the exodus/conquest[6] language in verse 2 will find the intuition immediately reinforced by what follows. The messenger sent by God is also 'the voice of one crying out in the wilderness: "Prepare the way of the Lord, make his paths straight"' (Mk 1.3, quoting Isa 40.3). The prophet's cry, in Isaiah, announces the end of exile, symbolically portrayed as a second exodus in which the power of God leads Israel through the wilderness and back to Zion.[7] Just as Isaiah drew upon the earlier exodus imagery to depict God's deliverance of Israel from the later Babylonian exile, so Mark draws on Ex 23.20 and Isa 40.3 – texts that evoke both of these past acts of God's deliverance of Israel – to introduce God's coming again in power through Jesus.

This is one of the few places where Mark alerts the reader to look for the Old Testament context for the story of Jesus. Yet these clues are so explicit and so fraught with theological significance that the reader of this gospel is invited to interpret everything that follows in relation to the narrative matrix adumbrated by these opening verses.

The future exaltation of the Son of Man

Despite Jesus' proclamation of the kingdom of God, however, Mark is under no illusion that the story of Israel has arrived at its final fulfilment. Of all the evangelists, Mark is the most sensitive to the community's continued suffering and longing for a fulfilment that is not yet seen. Mark calls his readers to remain in the same posture of expectant waiting enjoined by the conclusion of Jesus' eschatological discourse in chapter 13: 'And what I say to you I say to all: keep awake!'[8] The consummation promised in this eschatological discourse is still a future hope:

> 'But in those days, after that suffering, the sun will be darkened, and the moon will not give its light, and the stars will be falling from heaven, and the powers in the heavens will be shaken. Then they will see 'the Son of Man coming in clouds' with great power and glory. Then he will send out the angels, and gather his elect from the four winds, from the ends of the earth to the ends of heaven.'   (Mk 13.24–7)

Mark's description of cosmic portents in verses 24–5 echoes prophetic imagery for the day of the Lord's judgement, particularly Isa 13.10; 34.4 and Joel 2.10. More important, however, is the way in which the images of the coming Son of Man and the gathering of the elect (verses 26–7) are drawn directly from Old Testament antecedents. Daniel's visionary picture of the Son of Man coming with the clouds of heaven (Dan 7.13–14) is a text of great significance for Mark's narrative:

> As I watched in the night visions,
> *I saw one like a son of man*
> *coming with the clouds of heaven.*
> And he came to the Ancient of Days
> and was presented before him.
> To him was given dominion
> and glory and kingship,
> that all peoples, nations, and languages
> should serve him.

His dominion is an everlasting dominion
that shall not pass away,
and his kingship is one
that shall never be destroyed.

In its original context in Daniel, this is a vision of the vindication of
Israel. In contrast to the four strange beasts in Daniel's dream, each of
which represents a Gentile empire (Dan 7.1–8), the human figure ('one like
a son of man') in verses 13–14 symbolizes Israel, at last vindicated and
exalted by God – in accordance, we might note, with the promises of 2 Sam
7.12–16 and Ps 89.19–37 that the Davidic kingdom would be established for
ever, 'as long as the heavens endure' (Ps 89.29).[9] Mark fuses this Danielic
image of Israel's eschatological vindication with another persistent biblical
image of Israel's hope, the image of the scattered exiles being brought back
from all over the earth to reinhabit the promised land (e.g. Deut 30.3–5; Isa
11.11–12; Zech 2.6–8). Against this background of Old Testament texts it is
clear that the apocalyptic vision of Mk 13 is one not of cosmic annihilation
but rather of the restoration of Israel. The story teaches readers to look
forward expectantly to these events, with patient endurance (Mk 13.28–
37). The shape of Mark's apocalyptic hope is unintelligible apart from the
Old Testament texts that constitute the matrix for the proclamation of the
kingdom of God.

Jesus as Davidic King

Within the context of that proclamation, Mark also employs Israel's
scripture to interpret the identity of Jesus. Among the themes that Mark
persistently develops are his portrayals of Jesus as the Davidic King, Jesus as
the Son of Man (suffering and glorified), and Jesus as the Crucified Messiah.
Within the scope of the present chapter, we cannot explore each of these
motifs, but an examination of Mark's presentation of Jesus as Davidic King
will illustrate how Israel's scripture provides the canonical matrix for the
emergence of Markan christology.

The gospel's opening sentence predisposes the reader to expect an
account of Jesus as bearer of the Davidic legacy: 'The beginning of the good
news of Jesus Christ, the Son of God.' The term 'Christ' (*Christos*) is not a
proper name but a role designation: it means 'anointed one'. Mark uses the
term six more times in his gospel, and in at least five of them he understands
it as a title, 'the Messiah' (8.29; 12.35; 13.21; 14.61; 15.32).[10] The royal significance of this title is shown especially by the taunt of the passers-by in
15.32: 'Let *the Messiah, the King of Israel* (*ho Christos ho basileus Israēl*),

come down from the cross now.' This use of *Christos* as a designation for the Davidic ruler is no Christian innovation; it is illustrated, for example, by Ps 18.50 (LXX 17.51):

> Great triumphs he gives *to his king*,
> And shows steadfast love *to his anointed* (*tō Christō autou*),
> *to David and his descendants* for ever.

The synonymous parallelism of these lines shows that – in this passage, at least – *Christos* is an epithet for the Davidic king.[11] After the demise of the Davidic monarchy, such texts came to be read eschatologically, as prefigurations of the coming anointed king who would restore the kingdom to Israel. The expectation of such a king was rooted in the scriptural promise that David's kingdom would be established eternally (see, e.g., 2 Sam 7.12–14a; Ps 89.3–4; 132.11–12). The same hope is attested in a *florilegium* of messianic texts discovered among the Dead Sea Scrolls (4QFlor 1.10–13). The opening words of Mark's gospel, then, evoke the expectation for a future king who will reclaim the throne of David and set things right.

The Davidic King as God's Son

The title 'Son of God', if it belongs to the original text of Mk 1.1, reinforces the identification of Jesus as a kingly figure. In the Psalms, the king is acclaimed as God's 'son', not because of a belief about his supernatural origin but as a way of expressing the special status of election and divine favour into which the king was embraced, as in the enthronement acclamation of Ps 2.6–8:

> 'I have set my king on Zion, my holy hill.'
> I will tell of the decree of the LORD:
> He said to me, *'You are my son*;
> today I have begotten you.
> Ask of me, and I will make the nations your heritage,
> and the ends of the earth your possession.'

This passage echoes loudly in the voice that speaks from heaven on the occasion of Jesus' baptism: *'You are my Son*, the Beloved; with you I am well pleased' (Mk 1.11). Thus, whether the appellation 'Son of God' was in Mark's original text in 1.1 or not, the subsequent baptismal account explicitly links Jesus with the royal Davidic figure of Ps 2. The echo of Ps 2 in Mk 1.11 turns the baptism of Jesus into a disguised royal anointing, and

Jesus' proclamation of the kingdom follows, implicitly, as the assertion of his own claim to royal sovereignty.

Typological links between Jesus and David

This interpretation is reinforced by several other passages in Mark's gospel that posit a typological relation between David and Jesus. In Mk 2.23–8, Jesus justifies his own authority to permit his disciples to pluck grain on the sabbath by appealing to the example of David: like David in 1 Sam 21, he is the anointed king whose authority has not yet been recognized within Israel, save by his fugitive band of followers. Or again, in the first of Mark's two miraculous feeding stories, we are told that Jesus had compassion on the crowd, because 'they were like sheep without a shepherd' (6.34). This expression evokes a complex pattern of intertextual resonances. On the one hand, it suggests that Jesus is like Joshua, who was designated as Israel's leader in response to Moses' plea that God appoint a successor 'so that the congregation of the LORD may not be like sheep without a shepherd' (Num 27.17).[12] This reading is confirmed by the event that follows, a Moses-like miraculous feeding of a multitude in the wilderness (Mk 6.35–44). At the same time, however, the phrasing of Mk 6.34 recalls Ezekiel's indictment of the false shepherds of Israel who have abused and neglected the flock and left them 'scattered, because there was no shepherd' (Ezek 34.5). This allusion is significant because of the solution that Ezekiel's oracle finally promises for the plight of Israel's scattered flock:

> I will set up over them *one shepherd, my servant David, and he shall feed them*: he shall feed them and be their shepherd. And I, the LORD, will be their God, and my servant David shall be prince among them; I, the LORD, have spoken. (Ezek 34.23–4).

Thus, when Jesus feeds the multitude in Mk 6, he is not only symbolically re-enacting Moses' manna miracle of the exodus but also prefiguring the restored Davidic kingship promised by Ezekiel's prophecy. The two motifs (exodus and Davidic kingship) should be seen as complementary rather than as competing alternatives, precisely because the new exodus envisioned in the Old Testament, especially in Isaiah, has as its *telos* the restoration of God's rulership over Israel. Consequently, the Old Testament allusions in Mk 6 lead us to perceive Jesus as a kingly figure who integrates the exodus typology with Ezekiel's vision of a restored kingdom.

Acclamations of Jesus as Son of David

In keeping with Mark's fondness for dramatic irony, it is a blind man who most clearly sees and blurts out Jesus' identity as the Davidic heir (Mk 10.46–52). The blind beggar Bartimaeus hears that Jesus is coming and begins to shout out, 'Jesus, *Son of David*, have mercy on me!' The crowd tries to silence him, but he cries even more loudly, repeating the acclamation of Jesus as Son of David. The narrative effect of this repetition is to cast the resistant crowd in an unsympathetic light while creating readerly sympathy for Bartimaeus and validating his manner of addressing Jesus. Jesus reinforces this effect by calling Bartimaeus, healing him, and commending him for his faith. The final sentence of the unit is fraught with symbolic significance: 'Immediately he regained his sight and followed him on the way' (10.52). Thus Bartimaeus is portrayed as a paradigmatic disciple.

Furthermore, the immediately following story of Jesus' entry to Jerusalem (11.1–11) dramatically reinforces Bartimaeus' identification of Jesus as the Davidic king. By entering Jerusalem riding on a colt, Jesus subliminally evokes the messianic prophecy of Zech 9.9:

> Rejoice greatly, O daughter Zion!
> Shout aloud, O daughter Jerusalem!
> Lo, your king comes to you;
> triumphant and victorious is he,
> humble and riding on a donkey,
> on a colt, the foal of a donkey.

Having walked all the way from Galilee, Jesus now commandeers the colt only when he arrives at Bethany, just two miles over the hill from Jerusalem; thus, surely, his riding into the city in this manner is a staged symbolic gesture. Unlike Matthew, however, Mark offers no explicit interpretation of the gesture; those who have eyes to see will understand. They will recall Zech 9 and discern that this figure riding into Jerusalem on a donkey is the one who will 'cut off the chariot from Ephraim and the war horse from Jerusalem' and 'command peace to the nations' (Zech 9.10). As the story unfolds, Jesus' symbolic gesture is not lost on 'those who followed him', who begin a chant based on Ps 118.25–6:

> Hosanna!
> Blessed is the one who comes in the name of the Lord!
> *Blessed is the coming kingdom of our father David!*
> Hosanna in the highest!

The italicized sentence does not appear in Ps 118, but it interprets the drama being played out in Jesus' entry to the city. He is not (yet) explicitly named as king, but he is acclaimed as the one who heralds the 'coming kingdom' of David – an eschatological hope that challenges the powers now ruling Jerusalem. Some commentators suggest that the crowd's chant is merely a celebration of the festival, not an acclamation of Jesus specifically, and that 'the one who comes in the name of Lord' could apply to any pilgrim arriving in the city.[13] This reading, however, fails to account for the details of Mark's narrative, which portrays the crowd as spreading their cloaks and palm branches on the road in front of Jesus (11.8), a gesture acknowledging his royal status. Nonetheless, Mark's description of the event remains muted, and it requires the reader to listen for Old Testament texts that remain just below the surface of the narrative. Jesus' kingship is perceived only by the reader who interprets the narrated events within the matrix of Israel's scripture.

The riddle of Psalm 110

In light of the many pointers in Mark's gospel to Jesus' identity as the Davidic king, how then are we to understand 12.35–7, in which Jesus quotes Ps 110.1, apparently to refute the scribal opinion that the messiah (*Christos*) is the Son of David? The passage is sometimes understood as an outright repudiation of Davidic messianism.[14] Is Jesus now refusing the same title that he praised Bartimaeus for shouting out? Here we must read with the alert subtlety that, as we have by now learned, Mark demands of his readers. The best reading of Jesus' riddle would see it not as a rejection of Davidic messiahship but as a redefinition. David himself, speaking by the inspiration of the Holy Spirit (12.36), had foreseen a different sort of messiah – one greater than himself in being exalted to heavenly glory, one who does not fight with weapons of war but trusts God to vindicate him and give the victory. Of course, this interpretation of the riddle makes sense only in the retrospective light of the cross and resurrection. A suffering *Christos* who is enthroned at the right hand of God? No-one in the world of Second Temple Judaism expected such a thing. Jesus' riddle about David's Son comes into focus only when it is read within the larger story that Mark tells.[15]

Royal imagery in the passion narrative

The most explicit royal imagery in Mark's gospel appears in the passion narrative. Jesus is flogged and mocked as 'King of the Jews' (15.16–20), and the inscription on the cross identifies him by that title (15.26). The chief priests and scribes taunt him by calling out, 'Let the Messiah, the King of Israel, come down from the cross now, so that we may see and believe' (15.32). Yet in the midst of the mocking, the reader of the gospel discerns that the taunts are ironically true. He is the King of Israel, but he will demonstrate his kingship not by coming down from the cross but by enduring it. Jesus' death redefines his kingship but does not renounce it. Indeed, in his stunning reply to the high priest's interrogation, Jesus explicitly affirms that he *is* the *Christos* (14.61–2) – as readers of the gospel have known from its first sentence. Thus, the motif of Davidic kingship is transformed by Jesus' story, whose climax is the cross.

Overall, then, our Markan case-study demonstrates how Mark's telling of Israel's story draws pervasively on Old Testament texts and motifs, while at the same time performing a dramatic hermeneutical revision of these traditions. The story of Jesus grows out of the matrix of Israel's scripture, but that very matrix is seen in a dramatically new light because of the cross and resurrection.

MATTHEW, LUKE, AND JOHN WITHIN THE CANONICAL MATRIX

The Gospel of Matthew: reconfigured torah

Matthew is more overt than Mark in his interpretive strategies. He repeatedly gives his readers explicit guidance in understanding how Jesus is the fulfilment of Israel's scriptures. Matthew repeatedly introduces biblical proof-texts through a distinctive formula in which the evangelist addresses the reader directly in an authorial voice-over: 'This took place to fulfil what had been spoken through the prophet, saying . . .' Ten quotations in Matthew appear under this rubric, with minor variations: Matt 1.22–3; 2.15; 2.17–18; 2.23; 4.14–16; 8.17; 12.17–21; 13.35; 21.4–5 and 27.9.[16] In several cases, Matthew inserts the formula quotation to explain an allusion that was left implicit in Mark (e.g., compare Mk 11.1–7 and Matt 21.1–7). By frontloading several of these formula quotations into the opening chapters of his gospel, Matthew conditions his readers to expect that nearly everything in the story of Jesus will turn out to be the fulfilment of something pre-scripted by the prophets.

Nonetheless, Donald Senior argues convincingly that our understanding of Matthew's use of scripture will be far too narrow if we are enraptured by the 'siren song' of the formula quotations.[17] Matthew's use of scripture is considerably more diverse and complex. There are more than sixty Old Testament quotations in this gospel. That means that the formula quotations constitute, at most, only about one-fifth of Matthew's total: and that does not even begin to reckon with the hundreds of more indirect Old Testament allusions in the story.[18] Above and beyond the question of citations and allusions to particular texts, we must reckon also with Matthew's use of typology, his deft narration of tales that Senior describes as 'shadow stories from the Old Testament'.[19] Through this narrative device, with or without explicit citation, the reader is encouraged to see Jesus as the fulfilment of Old Testament precursors, particularly Moses, David, and Isaiah's Servant figure.

Matthew anchors the story of Jesus in Israel's history by opening his gospel with a genealogy (1.1–17), which periodizes the story of Israel into three great 'chapters' leading up to the birth of Jesus, each encompassing fourteen generations: from Abraham to David, from David to the exile, and from the exile to the Messiah. This way of charting Jesus' genealogy highlights his Davidic lineage – and therefore his messianic identity – and signals that the coming of Jesus portends the end of Israel's exile. The four anomalous women mentioned in the list of Jesus' ancestors (Tamar, Rahab, Ruth and Bathsheba) suggest the surprising character of God's grace and prefigure the inclusion of Gentile outsiders – a major Matthean concern.

Matthew also posits a typological identification of Jesus with Israel, so that Jesus becomes the one in whom the fate of Israel is embodied and enacted. This motif is perhaps most vividly expressed in Matthew's compressed account of the Holy Family's flight into Egypt and return after the death of Herod (2.13–15). Matthew sees in this episode a figural fulfilment of Israel's sojourn in Egypt and return to the land of promise. The key prophetic text adduced in the formula quotation of 2.15 is drawn from Hos 11.1: 'When Israel was a child I loved him, and out of Egypt I called my son.' The 'son' in Hosea is the people Israel as a whole; Hosea's metaphor evokes a tradition that goes all the way back to God's instructing Moses to tell Pharaoh that 'Israel is my firstborn son' (Ex 4.22–3). Matthew sees the fate of God's 'son' Israel recapitulated in the story of God's Son, Jesus: in both cases, the son is brought out of exile back to the land.

This example suggests that Matthew's formula quotations may have more narrative resonance and allusive subtlety than is often credited to them. Matthew cannot be unaware of the original contextual meaning of Hos 11.1 as an expression of God's love for Israel – a love that persists even through Israel's subsequent unfaithfulness (Hos 11.8–9). Indeed, Matthew's use of the quotation depends upon the reader's recognition of its original sense. The fulfilment of the prophet's words can be discerned only through an act of imagination that perceives the typological correspondence between the two stories of the exodus and the gospel and therefore discerns that Jesus embodies the destiny of Israel.

Alongside such narrative typologies, however, Matthew also envisions the fulfilment of scripture occurring through the formation of a community of Jesus' disciples who embody radical obedience to the Law, an obedience more exacting than that of the scribes and Pharisees (5.13–48). In this respect, Matthew's vision of community is thoroughly Deuteronomic (cf. Deut 30.11). Yet Matthew's strict exhortation to obedience is modulated into another key by his equally firm insistence that the obedient community of disciples must also be a community animated by mercy, love and forgiveness. The key Matthean motif of *mercy* is highlighted particularly through the use of scripture: in two places, Matthew tellingly inserts references to Hos 6.6 into narrative material taken over from Mark, in order to emphasize the hermeneutical primacy of mercy.

The first instance appears in Matthew's account of Jesus' controversy with the Pharisees over his practice of eating with tax-collectors and sinners (Matt 9.9–13). Matthew follows Mark's text closely through most of the passage, but in Jesus' climactic pronouncement Matthew adds the crucial citation of Hosea:

> Those who are well have no need of a physician, but those who are sick.
> *Go and learn what this means, 'I desire mercy, not sacrifice.'*
> For I have come to call not the righteous but sinners.   (Matt 9.12–13)

Jesus directs the Pharisees to a particular prophetic text for remedial education: if they learn what Hosea means, they will understand that God is a God of mercy (*ḥesed*) who desires to bring back the erring, not to condemn them, not even to compel them to offer the proper sacrifice. It is hardly coincidental that Matthew links Jesus' saying about the need for a *physician* to a prophetic passage that depicts Ephraim and Judah as crying out, 'Come, let us return to the Lord; for it is he who has torn, *and he will heal us*' (Hos 6.1; cf. 7.1).[20] If the Pharisees go to learn what Hos 6.6 means, they will have to read more than one verse. If they read the whole chapter, they will find there, in the midst of a judgement oracle against the people, both a call for repentance and a portrayal of a merciful, healing God who wants his people to show mercy, not contempt, to those who have gone astray.

Matthew's second pointer to Hos 6.6 appears three chapters later, in the controversy story about plucking grain on the sabbath (Matt 12.1–8).

Once again Matthew follows Mark's narrative framework[21] but inserts a reference to Hos 6.6: 'But if you had known what this means, *I desire mercy and not sacrifice*, you would not have condemned the guiltless.' Here it appears that 'mercy' and 'sacrifice' stand, respectively, for a form of piety that focuses on God's compassion towards human needs and a form of piety that focuses on ritual observances. The Pharisees are at fault because they demand punctilious observance of the Law at the expense of basic human need, represented by the disciples' hunger.

In both of these passages, Hos 6.6, with its emphasis on mercy, is put forward as a hermeneutical lens through which the Torah is to be interpreted: the Pharisees go astray in their understanding of the Law because they fail to realize that its central aim is mercy. Alongside these passages should be placed the beatitude, 'Blessed are the merciful, for they shall receive mercy' (Matt 5.7), and Jesus' pronouncement that 'the weightier matters of the Law' are 'justice and *mercy* and faith' (Matt 23.23). In such passages the quality of mercy is not set in opposition to the Law; rather, Matthew's Jesus discerns within scripture itself the hermeneutical principle – expressed epigrammatically in Hos 6.6 – that all the commandments are to be interpreted in such a way as to engender and promote the practice of mercy among God's people. Thus, the story of Israel is carried forward through a particular construal of Torah within a community called to embody the mercy of God.

The Gospel of Luke: the liberation of Israel

In the prologue to his gospel, Luke sets out to narrate 'the events that have been *brought to fulfilment* (*peplērophorēmenōn*) among us' (Lk 1.1). This weighty term suggests that Israel's long history has arrived, according to Luke, at a moment of completion and consummation. 'Theophilus', Luke's addressee, already knows about Jesus but needs further grounding and assurance (*tēn asphaleian*, 1.4), an assurance that comes from perceiving how the story of Jesus constitutes the fulfilment of the story of Israel. Thus, Luke retells the story of Jesus 'in good order' to portray it as 'the continuation of biblical history'.[22] Luke is concerned with showing the overall coherence of the epic story that runs from Adam (Lk 3.38) through Abraham to Jesus and on into the life of the church.

While Matthew's formula quotations treat the Old Testament as a book of inspired oracles fulfilled in the singular person of Jesus, Luke sees the Old Testament not merely as a collection of fragmentary predictions about a future messiah, but rather as a book of *promises* made by God to the people of Israel. Through his covenant promise, God has bound himself to this particular people and can therefore be trusted to rescue them from oppression. Further, Luke repeatedly highlights the *ecclesiological* implications of those promises: they find their fulfilment not just in the life of Jesus but in the continuing history of God's people. These themes are sounded joyfully in the songs and prophecies that dominate the first two chapters of Luke's gospel. For example, Mary's song magnifies the Lord because

> He has helped his servant Israel, in remembrance of his mercy,
> according to *the promise he made to our ancestors*,
> to Abraham and to his descendants for ever.   (Lk 1.54–5)

Similarly, Zechariah finds his tongue loosed by the power of the Spirit and declares that Israel's God

> has shown the mercy *promised to our ancestors*,
> and has remembered his holy covenant,
> the oath that he swore to our ancestor Abraham,
> to grant us, that we, being rescued from the hands of our enemies
> might serve him without fear, in holiness and righteousness
> before him all our days.   (1.72–5)

Thus, Luke interprets Israel's scripture as the medium of divine promise to Israel, and he sees that promise being brought to fulfilment through the work of the Holy Spirit in forming the church, a community that serves and glorifies God, as shown particularly in the Acts of the Apostles.

The liberating power of the Spirit is highlighted dramatically in Luke's distinctive account of Jesus' inauguration of his public ministry (4.14–30). 'Filled with the power of the Spirit', Jesus returns to Nazareth after his wilderness temptation and reads scripture in the synagogue. The passage that he selects is taken from the prophet Isaiah (actually a conflation of Isa 61.1–2 and 58.6):

> The Spirit of the Lord is upon me,
> because he has anointed me to bring good news to the poor.
> He has sent me to proclaim release to the captives
> and recovery of sight to the blind,
> to let the oppressed go free,
> to proclaim the year of the Lord's favour.

When Jesus follows this reading by declaring, 'Today this scripture has been fulfilled in your hearing', the reader of Luke's gospel has been alerted that Jesus himself is the Spirit-anointed Servant figure whose mission is the liberation of Israel. The citation of Isa 61 links Jesus' activity to

Deutero-Isaiah's hope of return from exile, and the reference to 'the year of the Lord's favour' alludes to the jubilee year (Leviticus 25), the year in which all debts are cancelled and all slaves set free. The passage also underscores the continuity between Jesus' concern for the poor – a favourite Lukan theme – and the message of Israel's prophets.

At the same time, however, Jesus encounters rejection in Nazareth. Indeed, he *provokes* rejection by citing biblical stories about Elijah and Elisha, who powerfully extended God's gracious power to non-Israelites such as the widow at Zarephath in Sidon (1 Kings 17.1–16, a story that finds an important echo in Lk 7.11–17) and Naaman the Syrian (2 Kings 5.1–14). These references prefigure the expansion of the gospel into the Gentile world – a major theme of Luke's second volume – and hint that the Gentile mission is already prefigured in Israel's scripture. Thus, Jesus' programmatic preview of his vocation already begins to undercut the assumption that Israel is the exclusive bearer of God's favour. The hostility of the Nazareth villagers to this act of subversive Bible-reading illustrates the truth of Simeon's earlier prophecy that Jesus would become the catalyst 'for the falling and the rising of many in Israel, and . . . a sign that will be opposed so that the inner thoughts of many will be revealed' (Lk 2.34–5; cf. Acts 3.22–3). At one and the same time, then, Jesus announces the fulfilment of the Isaianic hope of national restoration and challenges conventional conceptions of national privilege. No other story illuminates more clearly the way in which Luke's Jesus carries forward the story of Israel (reading Isaiah and claiming the precedent of the prophets) while at the same time transforming that story into something different and surprising.

The portrayal of Jesus as the one who completes Israel's story is brought fully into the light in Luke 24. In an exquisitely ironic narrative, the gloomy disciples on the road to Emmaus, failing to recognize the risen Jesus, lament: 'But we had hoped that he was the one to redeem Israel' (24.21). Jesus scolds them for being 'slow of heart to believe all that the prophets have declared' and, 'beginning with Moses and the prophets', he begins to expound 'the things about himself in all the scriptures' (24.27). A similar exposition is given to the gathered disciples in Jerusalem: 'everything written about me in the law of Moses, the prophets, and the Psalms must be fulfilled' (24.44).[23] Thus, Luke explicitly attributes the origin of christological interpretation of the Old Testament to Jesus himself. From the retrospective standpoint of the resurrection, Luke insists that the whole story of Israel's Bible in all its parts was, in some mysterious manner, really 'about' Jesus. The concluding chapter of this gospel, therefore, encourages the reader to undertake a comprehensive reading of Israel's scripture in light of the story of Jesus to see how this claim might be true. In any case, the resurrection definitively validates the claims made by Jesus in the synagogue at Nazareth (Lk 4): he is the one through whom the Spirit of the Lord will redeem Israel and let the oppressed go free.

For Luke, then, the canonical matrix of Israel's scripture is not merely a web of tales and images from which proof-texts may be selected at random; rather, for Luke the canonical matrix has a *plot*, and the gospel constitutes that plot's resolution. We understand the gospel rightly only when we see it as the outworking of God's purpose in history.

The Gospel of John: the temple of his body

The opening words of John's gospel echo the first words of Israel's scripture: 'In the beginning . . .' The prologue of this gospel is best understood as a midrash on Gen 1 which links the idea of a pre-existent creative divine Logos to the motif of divine Wisdom seeking a home in the world (e.g. Sir 24.1–12). In contrast, however, to traditions that identify the earthly presence of Wisdom in Israel's Law (Sir 24.23; Bar 3.35—4.4), John insists that Logos/Wisdom found only rejection in the world, even among God's own people (Jn 1.10–11; cf. *1 Enoch* 42.1–2), and therefore acted to overcome their resistance by becoming flesh in the person of Jesus.[24] Thus, the prologue of the fourth gospel immediately situates Jesus in relation to Jewish scriptural traditions while at the same time transforming those traditions through the startling claim of the *incarnation* of the Word of God.

John, like Matthew, offers a number of fulfilment citations asserting that various events happened in order to fulfil scripture (12.14–16; 12.38–41; 13.18; 15.25; 19.24; 19.36–7; cf. 2.17; 17.12; 19.28). Interestingly, John's list of citations overlaps only slightly with Matthew's (both cite Isa 6.10 and Zech 9.9); further, while Matthew clusters his fulfilment citations in the early part of the story, John focuses on texts that point to Jesus' passion and death, along with the motif of Israel's obduracy. As D. A. Carson has observed, in John 'the fulfilment motif is more forcefully stressed the closer one gets to the rejection of Jesus culminating on the cross'.[25] No doubt the purpose of these citations may be partly apologetic (justifying Jesus' rejection and death as divinely ordained), but it may be also to emphasize and illumine the mystery of Jesus' being 'lifted up' on the cross as a manifestation of divine glory. As the evangelist puts it in 12.41, 'Isaiah said this [Isa 53.1 and 6.10] because he saw his glory and spoke about him.'

The most distinctive feature of John's interpretation of scripture, however, is not his fulfilment citations but his repeated suggestion that Jesus takes up into himself the significations of Israel's Temple and its cycle of liturgical celebrations. One of the clearest expressions of this hermeneutical device appears near the beginning of the narrative, after Jesus has driven the sellers and moneychangers out of the Temple. Challenged to produce evidence of his authority for this action, Jesus replies enigmatically, 'Destroy this temple, and in three days I will raise it up' (Jn 2.19). His Jewish interlocutors, thinking that he is referring to the Herodian Temple, are understandably puzzled. The narrator, however, provides a crucial explanation: 'But he was speaking of the temple of his body. After he was raised from the dead, his disciples remembered that he had said this; and they believed the scripture and the word that Jesus had spoken' (2.21–2). The passage is of great importance for at least three reasons: (1) we are informed that right interpretation of scripture and of the traditions about Jesus could be done only retrospectively after the resurrection;[26] (2) John instructs his readers to read *figuratively*; and (3) the link between the Temple and Jesus' body is made explicit, providing a key for much that follows. Jesus now takes over the Temple's function as a place of mediation between God and human beings.[27] That is why he can later say to the Samaritan woman, 'Woman, believe me, the hour is coming when you will worship the Father neither on this mountain nor in Jerusalem' (4.21). True worship is focused on the person of Jesus himself, who is both the way to the Father and the place where the presence of God is made known (14.6–7).

The same logic applies throughout the fourth gospel to Jesus' assumption and replacement of the significance of Israel's religious festivals. For example, the rituals of *Sukkoth* (the festival of Booths or Tabernacles) involved outpourings of water and the kindling of lights in the Temple (in reminiscence of Zech 14.7–8); therefore, when Jesus proclaims on the last day of the festival, 'Let anyone who is thirsty come to me, and let the one who believes in me drink' (Jn 7.37–8), and – on the same occasion – 'I am the light of the world' (8.12), he is taking on to himself the symbolism of the occasion, claiming both to fulfil and to supplant it.

Passover symbolism is particularly pervasive in John's gospel, coming to a climax in the passion narrative, where Jesus' crucifixion takes place on the *day of preparation* for Passover (19.14), not on Passover itself as in the synoptic gospels. The effect of this chronological shift is to align Jesus' death with the slaughter of the Passover lambs, a point underscored when John tells the reader that the Roman soldiers did not break the legs of Jesus on the cross, thus allowing his death to fulfil the requirement for the preparation of the Passover lamb: 'These things occurred so that the scripture might be fulfilled, "None of his bones shall be broken"' (19.36, alluding to Ex 12.46).

Jesus, 'the lamb of God' (1.29), embodies in his death the true signification of the Passover and exodus events.

In light of this sort of figurative hermeneutic, the entirety of the Old Testament becomes allegorically available to illumine the identity of Jesus. It is not a matter of locating a few proof-texts that predict events in Jesus' life. Rather, John sees Israel's scripture as allegorically transparent to the one who became incarnate in Jesus. For example, the manna in the wilderness prefigures Jesus, who is the true 'bread from heaven' (6.31–3). This reading strategy allows John to articulate his extraordinary (and polemical) claim that all of scripture actually bears witness to Jesus:

> 'You search the scriptures because you think that in them you have eternal life; and it is they that testify on my behalf. Yet you refuse to come to me that you may have life . . . Do not think that I will accuse you before the Father; your accuser is Moses, on whom you have set your hope. If you believed Moses, you would believe me, for he wrote about me. But if you do not believe what he wrote, how will you believe what I say?'   (Jn 5.39–40, 45–7)

Thus, even more comprehensively than the other gospels, John understands the Old Testament as a vast matrix of symbols pointing to Jesus. In contrast to Luke's reading of scripture as a plotted script showing the out-working of God's promises in time, John understands scripture as a huge web of signifiers generated by the pretemporal eternal Logos as intimations of his truth and glory.

CONCLUSION

This chapter has treated only a few examples out of hundreds that could be drawn from the gospels to demonstrate how they interpret Israel's scripture. The four canonical gospels evince a striking diversity in their selection of key texts (though Isaiah and the Psalms figure prominently in all four) and in their strategies of interpretation. Yet all four evangelists agree in placing the story of Jesus firmly within the matrix of Israel's sacred narratives. A major task, therefore, for the reader of the gospels is to trace the lines of intertextual linkage between the gospel stories and their Old Testament precursors. Sometimes the evangelists make the links explicit through overt citation; more often they echo scripture subtly or highlight typological patterns of correspondence. In every case, the evangelists' presentations of Jesus emerge from the canonical matrix of Israel's Scripture.

Notes

1. Interestingly, the Gospel of Thomas retains a vestigial reduction of the imagery of Ps 118: 'Jesus said: Show me the stone which the builders rejected. It is the cornerstone' (GosT 66). The fact that this saying directly follows Thomas's version of the parable of the wicked tenants (GosT 65) – though without any narrative connection to the parable – is one significant piece of evidence that the Gospel of Thomas is actually derivative from the synoptic tradition.
2. Thomas's stripped-down text is almost certainly historically secondary. The canonical tellings bear lively witness to a controversy internal to Jewish tradition, a controversy that was alive and well both in Jesus' lifetime and in the *Sitz im Leben* of the evangelists: a controversy over who is the authentic caretaker and heir of Israel's traditions. Thomas dilutes the historical and narrative specificity of the material. Interestingly, Luke's editing of the Markan material already eliminates some of the details from Isa 5 and abbreviates the citation of Ps 118. On the other hand, Luke agrees with Matthew in adding an allusion to Dan 2.34–5, 44–5 (Matt 21.44/Lk 20.18).
3. Most of the usages of this verb in the Old Testament refer to the tearing of garments, usually as a sign of mourning. The striking echo of the Hebrew verb in Mk 1.10 is one of several instances that suggest that Mark knew either the Hebrew text of the Old Testament or a Greek version that followed the Hebrew more closely than does the Septuagint.
4. Joel Marcus, *The Way of the Lord: Christological Exegesis of the Old Testament in the Gospel of Mark* (Louisville: Westminster/John Knox, 1992), 49–50, 58.
5. Rikki E. Watts, *Isaiah's New Exodus and Mark* (WUNT, 2.Riehe, 88; Tübingen: Mohr Siebeck, 1997), 90. When the 'new exodus' theme is set alongside the actual events narrated in Mark's gospel, however, severe hermeneutical tensions arise, tensions that must be interpreted both in light of Mark's other allusions to scripture and in light of his open-ended future eschatology.
6. See Willard Swartley, *Israel's Scripture Traditions and the Synoptic Gospels: Story Shaping Story* (Peabody: Hendrickson, 1994), 95–153.
7. See Bernard W. Anderson, 'Exodus Typology in Second Isaiah,' in Bernard W. Anderson and Walter Harrelson, *Israel's Prophetic Heritage: Essays in Honor of James Muilenberg* (New York: Harper & Brothers, 1962), 177–95.
8. On Mark's eschatological perspective, see Richard B. Hays, *The Moral Vision of the New Testament* (San Francisco: HarperSanFrancisco, 1996), 85–88.
9. On this interpretation of Dan 7, see N. T. Wright, *The New Testament and the People of God* (London: SPCK, 1992), 291–7.
10. The one other case is 9.41, in which the titular interpretation is possible but not certain.
11. For other examples of this royal use of *Christos* in the Septuagint Psalms, see Pss 2.2; 19.7; 83.10; 88.39, 52; 131.10, 17. Pss 89 and 132 (LXX: 88 and 131) are particularly significant because the title *Christos* is applied to the king precisely in contexts where the promise of an eternal Davidic line is reiterated. Significant also is the designation of the hoped-for Davidic ruler as *Christos* in Pss Sol 17.32; 18.1, 3, 5.
12. The name *Iēsous* is the Greek form of the Hebrew name *yĕhōsua'* (Joshua).

13. E.g., Morna D. Hooker, *The Gospel according to Saint Mark* (Black's New Testament Commentaries; London: A. & C. Black, 1991), 256.
14. See, e. g., Richard A. Horsley, *Hearing the Whole Story: The Politics of Plot in Mark's Gospel* (Louisville: Westminster/John Knox, 2001), 20, 251.
15. For a fuller exposition and defence of this reading, see Marcus, *Way of the Lord*, 130–52.
16. At least three other Old Testament quotations in the gospel bear close affinities to this pattern of fulfilment citation: 2.5–6; 3.3; 13.14–15. Also closely related to the formula quotations are the words of Jesus at the time of his arrest in Gethsemane, affirming that 'all this has taken place so that the scriptures of the prophets may be fulfilled' (26.56; cf. verse 54) – though in this case no specific quotation is adduced. Another quotation in this format appears in some late manuscripts at 27.35, but this has apparently been interpolated by later scribes, under the influence of John 19.24.
17. Donald Senior, 'The Lure of the Formula Quotations: Re-assessing Matthew's Use of the Old Testament with the Passion Narrative as a Test Case', in Christopher M. Tuckett, ed., *The Scriptures in the Gospels* (BETL 131; Leuven: Leuven University Press, 1997), 89–115.
18. Senior ('Lure', 89) points out that 'the Nestlé-Aland appendix lists 294 implicit citations or allusions in Matthew'.
19. Senior, 'Lure', 115.
20. Modern critical readers may find in Hos 6.1–3 a depiction of an insincere or inadequate repentance, but it is doubtful that the text would have been so understood by ancient readers. Certainly Matthew offers no hint of understanding the passage that way.
21. Matthew corrects Mark by omitting the erroneous phrase 'when Abiathar was high Priest' (Mk 2.26). This is one of many editorial nuances that show how carefully Matthew was reading his sources. He does not merely take over scriptural references from Mark; he cross-checks them, either directly against the Old Testament text or against his comprehensive knowledge of that text.
22. Nils A. Dahl, *Jesus in the Memory of the Early Church* (Minneapolis: Augsburg, 1976), 84.
23. This formulation recalls the three-part division of Israel's scripture into the Law, the Prophets and the Writings. Luke surprises the reader by listing 'the Psalms' as the third member of the series. Perhaps the Psalms stand by metonymy for the Writings; even if that is so, Luke's unusual formula focuses attention particularly on the Psalms as a key to the identity of Jesus.
24. On this analysis of the Johannine prologue, see Daniel Boyarin, 'The Gospel of the *Memra*: Jewish Binitarianism and the Prologue to John', *HTR* 94 (2001), 243–84.
25. D. A. Carson, 'John and the Johannine Epistles', in D. A. Carson and H. G. M. Williamson, *It is Written: Scripture Citing Scripture: Essays in Honour of Barnabas Lindars, SSF* (Cambridge: Cambridge University Press, 1988), 245–64; quotation from 248.
26. On this point, see Richard B. Hays, 'Reading Scripture in Light of the Resurrection', in Ellen F. Davis and Richard B. Hays, *The Art of Reading Scripture* (Grand Rapids: Eerdmans, 2003), 216–38.

27. For an exposition of the pervasive allusions to the Temple motif in John, see Ulrich Busse, 'Die Tempelmetaphorik als ein Beispiel von implizitem Rekurs auf die biblische Tradition im Johannesevangelium', in Tuckett, *Scriptures in the Gospels*, 395–428.

Further reading

Allison, Dale C., Jr, *The Intertextual Jesus: Scripture in Q* (Harrisburg: Trinity International, 2000)

Bock, Darrell L., *Proclamation from Prophecy and Pattern: Lucan Old Testament Christology* (JSNTS 12; Sheffield: JSOT, 1987)

Boyarin, Daniel, *Intertexutuality and the Reading of Midrash* (Bloomington: Indiana University Press, 1990)

Carson, D. A., and Williamson, H. G. M., eds., *It Is Written: Scripture Citing Scripture* (Cambridge: Cambridge University Press, 1988)

Davis, Ellen F., and Hays, Richard B., eds., *The Art of Reading Scripture* (Grand Rapids: Eerdmans, 2003)

Evans, Craig A., and Sanders, James A., eds., *The Gospels and the Scriptures of Israel* (Sheffield: Sheffield Academic Press, 1994)

Hays, Richard B., *Echoes of Scripture in the Letters of Paul* (New Haven: Yale University Press, 1989)

Marcus, Joel. *The Way of the Lord: Christological Exegesis of the Old Testament in the Gospel of Mark* (Louisville: Westminster/John Knox, 1992)

Mulder, Martin J., ed., *Mikra: Text, Translation, Reading and Interpretation of the Hebrew Bible in Ancient Judaism and Early Christianity*, Compendia Rerum Iudaicarum ad Novum Testamentum II/1 (Assen and Maastricht: Van Gorcum, 1990; Minneapolis: Fortress, 1990)

Swartley, Willard, *Israel's Scripture Traditions and the Synoptic Gospels: Story Shaping Story* (Peabody: Hendrickson, 1994)

Tuckett, Christopher M., ed., *The Scriptures in the Gospels* (Leuven: Leuven University Press, 1997)

Watts, Rikki E., *Isaiah's New Exodus and Mark* (Tübingen: Mohr Siebeck, 1997)

4 The gospels and 'the historical Jesus'

STEPHEN E. FOWL

INTRODUCTION

No matter what their views on this subject, the phrase 'the historical Jesus' is understandable to most contemporary students of the Bible. To Martin Luther, Thomas Aquinas or John Chrysostom, however, such a phrase, rendered into their native tongues of course, would have not been immediately intelligible. For us, the phrase 'the historical Jesus' assumes that there is a gap between the gospels' portrayal of Jesus and Jesus as we come to know him in the light of various historical investigations. This is a gap that these premodern characters would not have recognized.

It may be tempting to think that the difference between Luther, Aquinas, Chrysostom and us is that they had a naively literalistic understanding of the gospels, neglecting or glossing over textual puzzles which would later provide fuel for historical study of Jesus. While the adoption of such a posture towards our premodern predecessors is very common in historical Jesus studies, it simply would not be accurate. As soon as the church recognized four canonical gospels it also recognized the extraordinary diversity of these texts and the differing things they said about Jesus. Nevertheless, attempts to harmonize the four gospels into one, such as Tatian's *Diatessaron*, have never succeeded in replacing the four gospels in all of their differences. Further, when disputes arose, it was not normally due to one side's recognition of a diversity ignored by their opponents. The difference between Ireneaus and his Valentinian opponents, for example, was not that Irenaeus refused to recognize the diversity of the New Testament texts and the Valentinians did. The difference lay in the ways they ordered that diversity.

Without repristinating the past, I want to make clear that premodern gospel interpreters were not credulous bumpkins. Nevertheless, they did not embark on quests for the historical Jesus as modern interpreters often have. In the course of this chapter I will try to explain the very modern circumstances that provoked interest in 'the historical Jesus'; I will chart some of the practices that seem to typify quests for the historical Jesus and some of the central critical debates that currently mark work on Jesus. As a way of making these theoretical matters more concrete, I will examine three contemporary voices in this debate. Finally, I will indicate that philosophical and epistemological assumptions which led to study of the historical Jesus lack the conviction they once had. In the light of this, Christians reading the gospels may be in a position to reassert the priority of theological concerns over historical ones.

THE RISE OF HISTORY

To begin, we need to explore briefly why relatively well-known textual puzzles, ruptures and obscurities began at some time in the mid- to late eighteenth century, to generate concerns that led to an interest in the historical Jesus. During this period there was a fundamental shift in the practices of biblical interpretation.[1] Prior to this shift, scripture was believed to be the most important of God's providential gifts for understanding the world and making it accessible to humans. In this light, scripture presented a unified narrative through which people could develop unified, coherent views of the world. The evident diversity and rich detail of scripture called forth a variety of reading practices, both literal and figural, that presented a common narrative. The rich variety of reading strategies characteristic of 'precritical' biblical interpretation was essential if the Bible was to provide Christians with a way of rightly ordering, understanding and living within the world.

> Since the world truly rendered by combining biblical narratives into one was indeed the one and only real world, it must in principle embrace the experience of any present age and reader. Not only was it possible for him, it was also his duty to fit himself into that world in which he was in any case a member, and he too did so in part by figural interpretation and in part of course by his mode of life. He was to see his disposition, his actions and passions, the shape of his own life as well as that of his era's events as figures of that storied world.[2]

To put the matter over-simply, premodern interpretation moved from text to world. The shift in interpretation came when this direction was reversed in the eighteenth century. When the world came to be seen as, more or less, immediately intelligible to all rational people, the 'real' world became detached from its biblical rendering. In the light of this transformation, the real events of history constitute an autonomous temporal framework of their own under God's providential design. Instead of rendering them accessible, the narratives, heretofore indispensable as means of access to the events, now simply verify them, thus affirming their autonomy and the fact that they are in principle accessible through any kind of description that can manage to be accurate either predictively or after the event. It simply happens that, again under God's providence, it is the Bible that contains the accurate descriptions.[3]

The causes of this transformation are numerous and complex. They were for the most part related to the scientific, political, economic and philosophical upheavals that accompany the rise of what we have come to call modernity. For the purposes of this chapter it is less important to explain how this transformation took place than to explain some of its consequences for the study of the Bible.

The most significant result of this was that 'history' came to be thought of as its own realm, accessible, if not immediately evident, to all. History was presumed to have a privileged access to 'the real'. Scriptural, theological and ecclesial concerns were not only separated from concerns of historical investigation, they were actively excluded from such investigation. Scholars began to inquire into the historical accuracy of the Bible. Further, as 'the historical' was now its own autonomous realm, it became important to develop independent procedures and methods for understanding and interpreting reality. Thus began a quest for a general hermeneutical method. These consequences in particular set the stage for concerns with the 'historical Jesus'.

Once this initial shift occurs in the course of the eighteenth century, three interrelated issues manifest themselves time and again in works on the historical Jesus.[4] The first issue concerns the policing of the scholar's confessional stance. Once 'the historical' was presumed to be an autonomous realm, it was a small step from presuming that the historical realm is providentially ordered (whether by the Christian God or the Deist god) to presuming that the history itself must provide its own standards of meaning and intelligibility independent of one's confessional stance. The second issue concerns the historical reliability of the biblical texts, in particular the nature and scope of evidence about Jesus. Initially, scholars focused on the character of the evangelists and their honesty. Very soon, however, the focus of this question shifted to the gospel texts themselves as scholars tried to develop a variety of methods for getting behind the final form of the gospel texts to find data about what really happened. Further, as more extrabiblical sources became available, they, too, were added to the mix of possible pieces of evidence. The third issue concerns the interpretative framework used to organize the evidence. Those interested in the historical Jesus need to develop a way of ordering and interpreting the evidence. This has tended to work in two particular ways. One strategy attempts to establish the nature of the gospels. That is, if one were able to determine what type of literature the gospels are, then one would know (by virtue of a general set of hermeneutical criteria) how to treat them. If, as D. F. Strauss, for example, argued, the gospels were myth (very precisely understood), then the way in which one treats them as evidence for the historical Jesus becomes clear. This strategy is fraught with problems, which need not concern us here. Alternatively, then, and more recently, scholars have relied on social-scientific theories about Mediterranean peasant life to provide a way of organizing and evaluating data about Jesus. Rather than focusing on the nature of the gospels, this strategy focuses on the nature of the world Jesus inhabited. In practice, these three concerns are often closely related to each other and decisions in one area tend to shape decisions in another. For purposes of explaining these issues more fully, however, I will need to treat them separately.

APPROACHING THE HISTORICAL JESUS

Of these three concerns, the latter two have been the source of the most scholarly debate and I will give them the most attention. Once the shift is made from reading scripture so as to order, understand and live within the world more faithfully, to reading scripture to see if it matched up to an already known and understood reality, a gap opened up between the 'real' world, on the one hand, and the world depicted in scripture. Such a gap manifested itself in many ways. Primarily, however, it appeared as a gap between 'the historical Jesus' and Jesus as depicted in the gospels. Instead of rendering in complex ways, a single character, Jesus, the gospels were now read as a mass of irreconcilably conflicting accounts about Jesus. Scholars then sought to distill 'the historical Jesus' from this tangle of texts. For some, like Hermann Reimarus, this was an impossible task and signalled the demise of Christianity on the grounds that there was no historical backing for Christianity's central claims. Others, like D. F. Strauss and Ernst Renan, sought to preserve the timeless essential truths of Christianity from the very confused historical particulars about Jesus.[5]

In most respects, however, by the end of the nineteenth century, scholarly emphasis shifted from attempts to separate the timeless from the contingent. In its place scholars began to treat the gospels as pieces of historical evidence coming out of specific historical situations. Two distinct sorts of critical activity result from this shift. On the one hand, there was a persistent scholarly concern with the sources lying behind or beneath the final form of the gospels. On the other hand, scholars recognized that these texts, in their various stages of transmission, reflected the concerns and interests of those who produced them. It became important to identify those concerns and interests in order to help evaluate the historical veracity of the sources. The working assumption that brings these two concerns together is that uncovering the earliest layers of the gospel traditions is likely to provide us with sources that are least tainted by the concerns of the later church. The concomitant assumption is that the earliest sources are the most reliable. As a result, relatively early in this period the Gospel of John fell into disrepute as a reliable source of historical information. The vast majority of scholarly energy was spent on the synoptic gospels and the sources behind them.

Most scholars, but by no means all, if pressed for their views, would probably say that Mark is prior to Matthew and Luke, who draw quite directly from Mark. In addition, there seems to have been material that is common to Matthew and Luke and independent of Mark. This material is generally referred to as 'Q' from the German word *Quelle* ('source'). Finally, both Matthew and Luke may each have had recourse to discrete literary or oral material, conventionally designated 'M' and 'L'.

On the hypothesis that the earliest sources are likely to be the most accurate, Mark and Q would then appear to be the best sources for 'the historical Jesus'. With regard to Mark, the work of Karl Ludwig Schmidt, followed by Martin Dibelius and Rudolf Bultmann, presumed that the written gospels were composed of discrete oral units (pericopae) that the evangelists reordered and shaped. If one could isolate these various units, describe the social function of these units in the life of the earliest church, and then peel away those elements which served to make these units functional, one would potentially have even more reliable data for reconstructing the life and ministry of Jesus. This practice comes to be known as 'form criticism'. Form criticism made numerous assumptions about orality and how traditions are transmitted and ultimately written down. Thus, form criticism depended on there being a fairly predictable pattern of growth from discrete oral units to larger oral stories which were eventually written down. Anthropological research into oral cultures and their patterns of storytelling have shown this assumption to have little basis in reality.[6] It also made assumptions about the relationship between language, the contexts in which certain phrases function, and the possibilities of separating these two things. It is now widely recognized that altering the context in which one utters a phrase can also alter its meaning.[7] In the light of the fact that the assumptions underwriting form criticism have proved untenable, it is not surprising that gospel form criticism is passing from the scholarly scene.[8]

Theories about Q have proved more resilient. Most scholars recognize that there seems to be a body of material common to Matthew and Luke and independent of Mark. Thus, Q serves as a useful hypothesis that helps account for both the priority of Mark and the evident relationship between Matthew and Luke. When pushed to say whether Q was one source or several, written or oral, discrete or part of something larger, most scholars are agnostic. This agnosticism is sufficient as long as Q remains a hypothesis related to Markan priority. A far smaller number of scholars want to go much further. They treat Q as a distinct text. Some claim to be able to discern compositional layers in Q. Not surprisingly, they posit a social setting for Q as well. Since the Q material supposedly contains little eschatological or prophetic material, it is presumed to come from a strain of Christianity shaped by notions of wisdom (either Jewish or Greek), which was suppressed. In the hands of someone like Burton Mack, Q becomes a long-lost gospel. At this point we have gone well beyond a general confidence in Q as a hypothesis in support of a larger hypothesis about Markan priority. Indeed, we have gone well beyond any available evidence. The place of Q as evidence for reconstructing the historical Jesus, in the end, seems tied to how much speculation and conjecture one is willing to entertain in one's history.[9]

As I have already noted, one of the presumptions behind attempts to dig behind the text of Mark (and the other gospels) as well as attempts to treat Q as a piece of historical evidence for Jesus is that earlier accounts are in principle more reliable than later accounts. Most historians, however, recognize that the passage of time allows the relative significance of events to become clearer. This might make later accounts preferable.[10] A theoretical preference for the earliest accounts really makes sense only if one romantically imagines some pristine early phase of Christianity, which was then systematically corrupted by institutional forces. If one makes this assumption, then one's approach to the historical Jesus will be driven by concerns about how to separate what is truly from Jesus from what has been shaped by the early church. At the same time, it is clear that the Jewish context of early Christianity might also have shaped the gospel writers' presentation of Jesus. In this light, scholars tended to treat as authentic only that material which was dissimilar from the views and convictions of the earliest church and of Judaism. This is known as the criterion of double dissimilarity. If some element of gospel material could be shown not to bear the marks of either early Christianity or first-century Judaism, then that material was likely to be authentic. Used in a consistent way, this criterion would produce a Jesus having no connection to the Judaism in which he lived and moved and no connection to the Christian movement devoted to living in the light of his life and teachings. Even in this case, there is no obvious reason to consider this Jesus 'historical'. It seems equally likely that such a criterion presents us with the idiosyncrasies of the gospel-writers.[11]

RESPONSES TO PROBLEMS OF HISTORICAL METHOD

It has become increasingly clear that all criteria which presume that the gospels are layers of tradition on top of some purer picture of Jesus are simply mistaken. There is no God's-eye perspective, a view that sees things with the immediacy God does. For the historian, there is no immediate access to Jesus. All accounts, early and late, come from people who have particular perspectives and see Jesus through their own eyes. It is simply not possible to peel away the perspectives to get at pure data.

In addition to this recognition, many scholars have become increasingly uncomfortable with relying on reconstructions of the words of Jesus as a basis for their accounts of the historical Jesus. There are two reasons for this discomfort. First, the criteria for distinguishing authentic from unauthentic words of Jesus have not yielded much fruit. Criteria of dissimilarity and multiple attestation, even when used judiciously, cannot produce the sorts of precision this quest requires. These criteria can help one make the claim that Jesus might have said something like this. They cannot further claim that Jesus said precisely this and not a similar sort of saying. Second, and more importantly, knowing precisely what someone said without knowing the specific context in which an utterance was offered is not much use. Biblical scholars have become increasingly aware of the basic philosophical notion that meaning is inextricably tied to context. Without a clear context, genuine words of Jesus cannot tell us much about Jesus.

The cumulative effect of this methodological dissatisfaction with prior attempts to recover the historical Jesus has changed the ways in which scholars have pursued the historical Jesus over the past twenty-five years. One of the pivotal works marking these changes is E. P. Sanders' *Jesus and Judaism*.[12] Sanders begins from the assumption that attempts to develop a picture of the historical Jesus based on reconstructions of Jesus' words have been an abject failure. Rather than base his reconstruction on what can be known about Jesus' sayings, Sanders begins from a (rather small) list of facts most securely known about Jesus. This list includes such things as Jesus' baptism, ministry in Galilee, controversies with other Jewish groups, crucifixion by the Romans, and the continuation of his movement by his followers.

This list of data, however, is not yet a picture of Jesus. At least it is not yet a very satisfying picture. It is a minimalist chronicle. There is no narrative ordering, no explanatory hypotheses or framework to render this data into a life of Jesus. In the light of this shift in emphasis away from the words of Jesus and from various criteria of authenticity in the gospels, critical discussion has shifted from debates about what counts as evidence and how to get at the real historical data behind the gospels, to debates about how best to order and arrange the data, about which framework to employ.

This is not to say that arguments about data have disappeared. While some still press on with refining the older debates, the more central questions about data are now focused on the relative usefulness of non-canonical and non-Christian material in reconstructions of the historical Jesus. On the one hand, there is very little non-Christian material that explicitly talks about Jesus.[13] These accounts offer some limited external testimony to Jesus, but hardly enough to generate a historical account on their own. There have been more arguments about the relative importance of non-canoncial gospels, especially the Gospel of Thomas.

The Gospel of Thomas was first discovered in a Coptic version at Nag Hammadi in Egypt. There are also some Greek fragments of Thomas which are generally dated to the beginning of the third century. In form, it is a collection of short sayings of Jesus without narrative structure. In this respect, it is similar to hypothetical versions of Q. Within the past fifteen years a few scholars have posited a very early date for an original version of Thomas and put a great deal of weight on its reliability as a historical source.[14] Even if Thomas is relatively early (and there is little reason to think it is), its value as a historical source for Jesus is very problematic because of the absence of a narrative framework within which to place these discrete sayings. Without some sort of larger context, the sayings are not particularly revealing. For some, this is an invitation to invention. For others, it is further reason to dismiss Thomas. In either case, this problem confronts us with the importance of fitting the data into some sort of interpretative framework in order to say anything about the historical Jesus.

There are three basic stances one might adopt when it comes to fitting the data about Jesus into a larger framework. One can, of course, adopt the framework provided by the canonical gospels. In a very real sense such a move abandons the historical Jesus because it rejects the initial epistemological move which generated historical Jesus work in the first place.[15]

A second possibility is to seek to fit the data about Jesus within a framework that would make Jesus recognizable to his immediate peers. This move will fit Jesus into a narrative framework that would have been recognizable to a hypothetical first-century Jewish observer. Unlike the first option, this approach will not necessarily follow the framework provided by the gospels. The canonical gospels will be treated as valuable pieces of historical evidence. Nevertheless, each of them must be subject to the larger contextual framework of first-century Judaism. This framework is not contained in any single text; rather, it is abstracted from all the relevant material. The central activity of someone taking this approach is to make the background assumptions, practices and implications of first-century Judaism, which would have been presumed but unstated in the evidence, clear to modern audiences. On the one hand, this approach risks simply repeating what the evidence says in different terms. On the other hand, if it is going to diverge from the evidence it can often have a hard time explaining why it does so. Finally, once this framework is set up, it can be difficult to make the sorts of discriminations between discrete actors within the framework that would allow one to distinguish Jesus, for example, from others.

A third possibility is to fit the data about Jesus into a framework that is primarily shaped by theoretical concerns that may not have been shared by Jesus or his peers. If one pursues such an option, the claim that such a framework would not have been recognizable to Jesus and his peers is not particularly troubling. This is because a scholar operating in this manner assumes that, despite the fact that Jesus' peers might have seen him in one particular light, our greater perspective and theoretical sophistication allow us to see better what he was really up to. While this option might seem presumptuous, it is, in fact, quite a common move.[16] One of the central questions such an approach must consistently address is whether one's commitment to an explanatory model causes one to neglect, ignore or misread evidence uncongenial to the model.

These options do not exist in any sort of pure form. Moreover, these options cannot easily be separated from ways in which one notes and evaluates the evidence. They do, however, represent dispositions and tendencies within a scholar's work. As a way of making these descriptions less abstract I would like to conclude by briefly examining three contemporary influential works on Jesus as representative of each of these approaches.

JOHN DOMINIC CROSSAN'S JESUS

I take John Dominic Crossan's *The Historical Jesus: The Life of a Mediterranean Jewish Peasant*[17] to be paradigmatic of the third option mentioned just above. By contrast with most books on the historical Jesus, in the first half of Crossan's 426-page text Jesus does not really play a central role. The first 200 or more pages are devoted to the development of several sociological and anthropological models for understanding peasant life in occupied Palestine in the first century. Crossan clearly understands the difficulty in this task. All of the sociological and anthropological models come from relatively modern studies where subjects can be interviewed, where demographic, economic, agricultural and other data abound. The primary issue for Crossan or anyone else trying to employ such schema to explain the life of Jesus or anyone else in the first century concerns the legitimacy of applying models derived from life in the nineteenth and twentieth centuries to life in the first century. To help with this, Crossan relies on archaeological data and a relatively large store of papyri detailing peasant life in Egypt during the relevant time period.

Crossan recognizes the amount of synthetic interpretative work involved in formulating a set of sociological and anthropological categories for explaining the data about Jesus. His reading is broad and his judgements are reasoned. Central issues for Crossan concern individual honour (and its obverse, shame), and political power – how it is managed, deployed and disputed. Crossan uses the commercial metaphor of brokerage to characterize the Roman Empire as one of 'brokered power', in which networks of master and slave and patron and client operate. Palestine was a site of 'embattled brokerage'. Patronage networks broke down, causing social disruption as peasants in Galilee, for example, struggled against the centralization of wealth in urban centres such as Jerusalem and Sepphoris. Within such turmoil, various forms of religio-political protest emerged, culminating in the revolt of 66–70 CE. Crossan's account is detailed, clear and erudite. As yet, however, it has said little about Jesus. Rather, it has provided a set of sociological considerations in the light of which the data about Jesus can be ordered in a coherent way.

Within this matrix Crossan presents Jesus as a peasant Jewish Cynic.[18] Jesus' mission was to present a 'brokerless' kingdom of God. This was a form of extremely inclusive and egalitarian Judaism in contrast to more exclusive versions. The archetypal practice of Jesus was his open commensality in which all are called and welcomed to a common table. This practice, along with Jesus' magical works, subverted the broken patronage system in Palestine, offering a 'shared egalitarianism of spiritual and material resources'.[19] Such a picture accounts for any opposition Jesus might have faced from entrenched power interests. As a matter of history, however, Crossan thinks we can know very little about Jesus' crucifixion. Further, resurrection is a highly unlikely explanation for what happened to Jesus' body.

Crossan claims that he comes to his picture of Jesus by applying his sociological lenses to the bedrock evidence of the earliest forms of the traditions about Jesus. It is here, at the level of data, where Crossan tends to adopt mystifying positions. Crossan insists on relying primarily on the very earliest data. To do this in a way that maximizes the data available, he has to solve numerous puzzles in gospel source criticism and redaction criticism. Virtually all of his solutions are highly contestable and, taken as a whole, become extremely speculative. Most problematic is his willingness to treat the Gospel of Thomas as a very early text (he situates the earliest version of Thomas between 30 and 60, along with the *Gospel of the Hebrews* and the Cross Gospel and Q, among others). At certain points in the recent past, scholars might have followed Crossan in these matters. Today there is more scholarly debate, disagreement and uncertainty about issues of dating material, tracing sources and the validity of our assumptions about how these sources were transmitted than at any point in the past fifty years.[20] This does not mean that Crossan is wrong about these matters. His are, however, highly contestable judgements which the vast majority of scholars either seriously question or reject outright.

In addition, although Crossan regularly identifies Jesus as a Jew, this does not seem to play a major role in his account of the historical Jesus. For example, in his account of Jesus' open commensality he notes, 'I emphasize most strongly . . . that such egalitarianism stems not only from peasant Judaism, but even more deeply, from peasant society as such.'[21] He further argues that Jesus' kingdom language is not limited to Jewish apocalyptic or to specifically Jewish interests at all.[22] In part, Crossan sees first-century Judaism as such a diverse collection of convictions, practices and concerns that calling something Jewish does not really provide many clear parameters for a description. Again, this is a highly contestable account of first-century

Judaism. Any alternative account of Judaism would certainly require a reshaping of Crossan's account.

N. T. WRIGHT'S JESUS

N. T. Wright's *Jesus and the Victory of God*[23] is an example of an account of the historical Jesus that seeks to be recognizable to a first-century observer. 'If we are to be historians of Jesus' own period we must think our way back from those subsequent rereadings to the very historically concrete worldview of the second-Temple period itself.'[24]

Wright, who is a strident critic of Crossan, begins with a very thorough survey of previous quests for the historical Jesus. Wright argues that over the previous twenty years what he calls a 'third quest' has started.[25] Wright situates himself within this third quest. As Wright sees it, there are several things which participants in the third quest have in common. They treat textual material from various strands of first-century Judaism (e.g. Josephus, the Dead Sea Scrolls, various apocalyptic and pseudepigraphic writings) as valuable historical evidence for understanding the gospels. Behind this attention is a commitment to fitting Jesus as fully as possible into an understanding of first-century Judaism. Following E. P. Sanders, Wright places little emphasis on recovering words of Jesus and a greater emphasis on establishing what Jesus did and how it would have been understood by first-century Jews. As a result, Wright does not emphasize the recovery of the earliest layers of the gospel traditions. Instead, the synoptics, in particular, are treated as discrete witnesses to and interpreters of Jesus' activities. Nevertheless, Wright is quite clear that in sifting through, organizing and ordering the work of these discrete witnesses, he is acting as a historian and not as a theologian. Theological activity is secondary to and dependent upon prior historical activity.[26] Thus, Wright treats the gospels as sources of reliable evidence for Jesus on the one hand, but as a much less reliable framework for interpreting the evidence, on the other hand.

In this light Wright approaches his task with a particular set of questions in mind. For understanding the historical Jesus, the three questions which are most significant are: How does Jesus fit within Judaism? What were Jesus' aims? Why did Jesus die?[27] He then brings these questions to bear on events in Jesus' life. In the course of answering these questions, Wright presents Jesus as a prophet announcing the onset of the kingdom of God. Such an announcement anticipated God's decisive intervention to restore the fortunes of Israel. This would include the expulsion of all foreign occupation and influence over the land, thus unequivocally ending Israel's exile, God's final triumph over all evil powers, and the glorification of Zion. In this respect Jesus' prophetic vocation was continuous with a wide range of contemporary Jewish expectations. Alternatively, through his symbolic acts of judgement on the Temple, his open fellowship with sinners and his rejection of armed resistance to the Romans, Jesus called Israel to a radically different way of living, thinking and worshipping as the elect of God. Thus, it is quite plausible that such activity would have generated hostility among Jesus' contemporaries.

Wright's historical reconstruction is quite close to the synoptics in most respects. The most significant deviations are his treatment of the parables and the crucifixion. The parables are an excellent way to display important elements in Wright's method. According to Wright, the vast majority of the parables are all about Israel. They are 'Israel's story in miniature'.[28] Clearly, some of the parables fit this without much difficulty. The parable of the vineyard and the wicked tenants (Mk 12.1–12 and parallels) comes immediately to mind. Some are much harder to see in this light. The parable of the prodigal son (Lk 15.11–32) is a case in point. Wright treats this parable of a son's rejection of his father, departure from his home, and penitent return to a welcoming father and resentful brother as a story about Israel's return from exile as related in Ezra and Nehemiah.[29] Taken in literary isolation, Wright's account of the parable has a measure of plausibility. Even here, however, the primary problem is that the prodigal initiates his own departure and return whereas God exiles and calls Israel back from exile. Be that as it may, the larger issue has to do with the context of the parable. Within Luke's gospel this parable fits nicely within a series of stories and examples of God's yearning for and welcoming of those who repent. In the larger context of Lk 15.1 to at least verse 32, and arguably through chapter 16, we have a series of sayings, examples and stories all ordered around the theme of sin, forgiveness and repentance. In this context Wright's exilic reading is much less plausible. Moreover, Luke's is the only context we have for this parable.

The context in which one reads or hears a parable is the decisive factor in what one takes as the force and intelligibility of the parable. Rather than follow Luke's framework, Wright places this parable into a framework provided by his reconstruction of the mindset or worldview of first-century Judaism. If one grants the adequacy of this reconstructed worldview, one would have to say that first-century Jews such as Jesus might plausibly have understood this parable in the way Wright does. The question is: did one particular Jew, Jesus, utter this parable in the sort of context Wright presumes, or in something much more like the context Luke provides, or not at all? Even if we leave the sceptical response aside, there seems to be no way to decide historically between Wright's context and Luke's, unless one argues, against the evidence, that a first-century Jew would not have understood Luke's account.

Another question arises with regard to events surrounding Jesus' death. The gospel-writers and Paul all portray the death of Jesus through a series of allusive, interpretative invocations of Old Testament prophetic themes. Wright's reconstruction of a first-century Jewish mindset renders a plausible account of how these can be held together in order to provide a very particular sort of intelligibility and force to an account of Jesus' death. Wright goes on, however, to assert that this was Jesus' own particular mindset. 'I propose, then, that we can credibly reconstruct a mindset in which a first-century Jew could come to believe that YHWH would act through the suffering of a particular individual in whom Israel's sufferings were focused; that this suffering would carry redemptive significance; *and that this individual would be himself.* And I propose that we can plausibly suggest that this was the mindset of Jesus himself.'[30] Most scholars, including those far less sceptical than Crossan, presume that such a complex interpretative framework is more likely to be due to the gospel-writers than to Jesus himself. In this case, the question is: what historical reasons are there for locating this mindset within Jesus rather than, for example, Matthew? Once you have a general mindset for a particular group at a specific time, how do you make the move to the mindset of distinct individuals within that group?

The larger question here is: given Wright's reconstruction of a worldview, how does the historian make further discriminations between specific actors all holding their own particular versions of this worldview? Wright's method will be much better at telling us what is *un*likely to have happened in the life of Jesus. This can be argued on the grounds that an action would not have been a plausible option for a first-century Jew. It is much less likely that this approach can show what a specific actor said and did.

For all of their disagreements, both Wright and Crossan are examples of attempts to order the data about Jesus by fitting it within a framework other than the frameworks provided by the canonical gospels. Although the frameworks they develop are very different from each other, they produce such frameworks because of the demands of history. Thus, in this crucial respect Wright, Crossan and those in between perpetuate that late eighteenth-century shift in reading practices wherein history understood in a particular way is given priority over theology.

LUKE TIMOTHY JOHNSON'S JESUS

One final approach to this question of how to order the data about Jesus is to privilege the framework provided by the canonical texts. There are a variety of reasons for doing this, some theological, some literary. The example I want to focus on, Luke T. Johnson's *The Real Jesus* (and his companion volume, *Living Jesus*), relies for the most part on theological reasons.[31] While Johnson aims to talk about the real Jesus rather than the historical Jesus, he often has much to say about various approaches to the historical Jesus. A significant part of *The Real Jesus* is designed to deflate the over-inflated claims of various contemporary participants in the historical Jesus work. The chief among these is Robert Funk and his claims about the achievements of the Jesus Seminar.[32] Further, Johnson aims to show the severe limits placed on historical work on Jesus by virtue of the fact that the data are both extremely limited and tied to the explanatory framework of the gospels. Moreover, contrary to the claims of many biblical scholars, Johnson's work indicates that such historical work is not essential for the Christian life.[33]

Johnson's work indicates the difficulties in pursuing the historical Jesus by showing the problematic nature of history and historical knowing. 'Perhaps the most problematic aspect of the spate of Historical Jesus books is their authors' assumption that "history" is unproblematic.'[34] As noted above, questions about the historical Jesus really begin once history is seen as an autonomous realm of knowledge with privileged access to the real world. This assumption easily leads both to work on the historical Jesus and to presumptions about the priority of history over theology. Once this assumption is made, historical work on the Bible becomes necessary for understanding. Johnson points out that such an assumption about 'history' is largely unfounded. Historical knowing is one mode of knowing among many. This is not to say that all modes of knowing are equally adequate for understanding and ordering the world. Rather, it means that there is no *a priori* reason for assuming that historical knowing is or ought to be the primary one.

Further, those who pursue historical Jesus research face three significant limitations. First, we have very little evidence for the earliest period of Christianity from outside observers. Secondly, the vast majority of the data we have comes from Christians who are primarily writing out of 'experiences and convictions concerning the ultimacy of Jesus as the revelation of God'.[35] Finally, 'the writings now found within the New Testament are, for the most part, impossible to locate precisely either geographically or chronologically'.[36]

He concludes:

> The problem is real and insoluble: the majority of the sources on
> which any historical reconstruction of early Christianity must be
> based are themselves impossible to locate historically because of the
> lack of firm geographical and chronological controls. History is more
> than chronology, of course, but it is deeply dependent upon
> chronology. If the very sequence of events cannot be determined,
> questions of causality or even influence can scarcely be raised.[37]

As Johnson indicates, the reality of the problem is that one must have
some sort of framework in order to turn chronicle into history. The insol-
ubility of the problem seems to lie in the fact that this dearth of evidence
makes the adoption of any framework somewhat arbitrary.

Finally, Johnson notes that, traditionally, Christians have never based
their faith on a historically reconstructed Jesus. Moreover, for Christians,
any framework other than that provided by the canonical gospels read in
the light of the Rule of Faith will not be able to give a theologically sufficient
account of Jesus, an account that both rightly identifies Jesus as Lord and
properly accounts for Christian claims about Jesus' continued presence in
the lives of believers and the church.[38] This becomes clear in Johnson's
account of the resurrection.

Critics often misunderstand Johnson's assertion that 'the Christian
claim concerning the resurrection in the strong sense simply is *not*
historical'.[39] His point is not about the resurrection. Rather, it is about the
limitations of historical knowing. Historical knowing is confined to events
in space and time. A fully Christian understanding of Jesus' resurrection as
his defeat of death and his passage into the life of the triune God occurs
outside of space and time. Therefore, it is outside the scope of historical
knowing. Those scholars who attempt to give a historical account of the resurrection will, by definition, either give an account that is not adequately
Christian (by focusing on the historicity of the empty tomb), or end up
accounting for the experience of the first followers of Jesus (an account
which says nothing directly about Jesus).[40]

Johnson's criticism of historical Jesus work brings us face to face with
the manifest failure of 200 years of critical scholarship to present a widely
agreed-upon account of the historical Jesus. In and of itself this failure is not
a reason to abandon work on the historical Jesus. Under certain conditions
it might even be a reason for scholars to redouble their efforts. When such
manifest failure is coupled with profound disagreement about the nature
and scope of the evidence and about the ways in which that evidence should

be interpreted historically, however, it does not bode well for future work in this area.

CONCLUSION

I initially raised the question of why long-recognized textual irregularities and puzzles began to fuel a quest for the historical Jesus only in the modern period. The key to this seems to be the rise of history as an autonomous realm of inquiry and the assumption that history, rather than theology or anything else, provides privileged access to reality. Once this shift was made, various trends and practices devoted to uncovering the historical Jesus began to take shape. As a way of showing particular movements within this quest of the historical Jesus I surveyed the works of J. D. Crossan and N. T. Wright.

In addition, I surveyed the work of L. T. Johnson. Johnson's work exposes the numerous internal problems confronting historical work on Jesus. Most significantly, however, Johnson's work implicitly questions the necessity of the priority of history over theology. The foundations of modernity have shifted sufficiently so that it is no longer self-evident that 'history' should be treated as an autonomous realm with a privileged place when it comes to ordering and accounting for reality. 'History' no longer aspires to offer a God's-eye conspectus on the past.[41] In this light, it may now be possible to revisit the issues that led to quests of the historical Jesus and to begin to argue for the priority of theology over history when it comes to reading the gospels. If, for Christians at least, theological concerns take priority over historical concerns, several things might follow. First, it will be important for Christians to relearn the ways in which scripture (theologically read) must be allowed to render the world in which they live. To quote Johnson on this point, 'If Scripture is ever again to be a living source for theology, those who practice theology must become less preoccupied with the world that produced the Scripture and learn again to live in the world Scripture produces.'[42] This will, among other things, require a reinvigoration of forms of premodern reading practices. Recall that what marked these practices was the presumption that scripture, theologically read and interpreted, provided the resources one needed to understand, and live faithfully within, the world. Adequately unpacking this notion would take more than my available space. I will simply indicate a brief example of what might be involved when theological concerns are given priority when it comes to reading scripture. For example, when Christians read Gen 1–3 (among other texts), they recognize creation as the peaceable donation flowing from the superabundant love of the triune God. This, then, should lead Christians to conceive of their wealth very differently from those who understand wealth in terms of global market forces. Of course, Christians cannot ignore historical and scientific findings and claims. These can and must be engaged. They can be engaged only in *ad hoc* ways that are driven by theological concerns. If there comes a point at which sufficient scientific or historical data cannot be comprehended by Christian reading practices and Christian accounts of the world, then the answer is not historical Jesus research, but the abandonment of Christianity.[43]

Science, history, astrology, market forces and other elements will continue to provide alternative ways of comprehending, ordering and living within the world. Some of these visions will compete directly with Christianity; others will run side by side with Christianity. Christians will, no doubt, rub up against all of these competing visions in the course of living in the world. Since, however, none of these accounts (and that includes Christianity) will be able to offer immediate and self-evident access to reality, decisions between competing visions will often come down to whether Christians or others can live together peaceably, justly and charitably such that the beauty of the lives they lead compels others to join them in reading the gospels of the crucified and resurrected Lord.

Notes

1. I am following the story told by Hans Frei in his book *The Eclipse of Biblical Narrative* (New Haven: Yale University Press, 1974). Most biblical scholars stumble over Frei's somewhat confusing characterization of the gospels as 'history-like narratives'. As a result they miss the much more significant shift in reading practices he displays.
2. Ibid., 3.
3. Ibid., 4–5.
4. This period begins with D. F. Strauss's *The Life of Jesus Critically Examined* (ET, Philadelphia: Fortress, 1972; original German, 1835–6).
5. Reimarus' views were so incendiary that his *Fragments* were published posthumously and anonymously by G. E. Lessing between 1774 and 1778. An English version edited by C. H. Talbert was published by Fortress Press in 1970. Ernst Renan's 1863 *La Vie de Jésu* can be found in English as *The Life of Jesus* (Buffalo: Prometheus Books, 1991). Early work on the historical Jesus was chronicled by A. Schweitzer, *The Quest of the Historical Jesus* (London: A. & C. Black, 1906). N. T. Wright's *Jesus and the Victory of God* (Minneapolis: Fortress, 1996) has a more recent history of scholarship.
6. The foundational work in this area was done by Milman Parry and his student Albert B. Lord. See Lord's *The Singer of Tales* (Cambridge, MA: Harvard University Press, 1960).

7. One of the best ways to become acquainted with some of these issues is to read J. L. Austin's *How to Do Things with Words* (Oxford: Clarendon, 1962).

8. For the most probing and critical account of gospel form criticism see Erhardt Güttgemanns, *Candid Questions Concerning Gospel Form Criticism*, tr. W. Doty (Pittsburgh: Pickwick Press, 1979).

9. See Burton Mack, *The Lost Gospel: The Book of Q and Christian Origins* (San Francisco: HarperCollins, 1993). Mack relies on work by John Kloppenborg. See his *Q Parallels: Synopsis and Critical Notes and Concordance* (Sonoma: Polebridge Press, 1988). Lest anyone think that there is widespread agreement among Q scholars, one should also look at Christopher Tuckett's article on Q in the *Anchor Bible Dictionary* v 567–72.

10. Those acquainted with Arthur Danto's *Analytic Philosophy of History* (Cambridge: Cambridge University Press, 1965) might claim that the earliest account is the least likely to be accurate. See also Ben Meyer's *The Aims of Jesus* (London: SCM Press, 1980), 38, for similar sentiments.

11. In addition to the criterion of double dissimilarity, scholars also argued that if words of Jesus or an event in Jesus' life receive multiple attestation in various gospels, then this should count as evidence of the words' or event's authenticity. On the one hand, this seems to be a plausible criterion. If a variety of independent sources, who may disagree on other matters, all present an event or saying, then that should weigh in its favour. A problem arises when there are significant questions about the nature and scope of the independence of the sources.

12. London: SCM Press, 1985.

13. See the discussion of these data in Luke T. Johnson's *The Real Jesus* (San Francisco: HarperCollins, 1996), 112–17.

14. Interestingly, while the Pauline literature is undoubtedly early, it seems to play little role in current debates. This would seem to be because the discrete Pauline data about Jesus presume the framework provided by the canonical gospels. See the discussion in Johnson, *The Real Jesus*, 117–20.

15. I will not cover here those who adopt the framework of the gospels for largely literary reasons. While literary readings of the gospels are an alternative to historical Jesus approaches to the gospels, they are different from theological interpretation of the gospels.

16. Here is a small example: when contemporary scholars speak of various texts as 'apocalyptic' – in a technical scholarly sense of the term – they are explaining something about these texts that their authors themselves would not have recognized.

17. San Francisco: HarperCollins, 1991.

18. Crossan describes Greco-Roman Cynics as 'hippies in a world of Augustan yuppies' (421). The primary connection between Jesus and Cynics seems to be a shared commitment to living out a counter-cultural point of view.

19. Ibid., 341.

20. In contrast to this, see Luke Johnson's almost complete agnosticism with regard to the date, author and place of composition for the gospels in ch. 5 of *The Real Jesus*.

21. Crossan, 263.

22. Ibid., 287.
23. Minneapolis: Augsburg Fortress, 1996.
24. Ibid., xviii.
25. As Wright himself recognizes, whether this is a third quest or a thirty-third quest is not as important as characterizing ways in which scholars both share certain characteristics and differ from others. While this is correct, I would also point out that Wright and others continue in the basic eighteenth-century shift noted by Frei, establishing the priority of history over theology.
26. See, for example, *Jesus and the Victory of God*, 16, 107, 117–24.
27. See Ibid., 89–109.
28. Ibid., 179.
29. Ibid., 125–31.
30. Ibid., 593.
31. *The Real Jesus* (San Francisco: HarperCollins, 1996); *Living Jesus* (San Francisco: HarperCollins, (1999).
32. See *The Real Jesus*, ch. 1.
33. One often hears the argument, usually attributed to Ernst Käsemann, that historical research is necessary to protect us from docetism. Andrew K. M. Adam thoroughly demolishes this view in his essay 'Docetism, Käsemann, and Christology: Why Historical Criticism Can't Protect Christological Orthodoxy', *SJT* 49 (1996), 391–410.
34. *The Real Jesus*, 81.
35. Ibid., 88.
36. Ibid., 89.
37. Ibid., 91.
38. The Rule of Faith regulates Christian reading of the gospels so that, amid the plurality of four canonical gospels, Christians can articulate claims about Jesus which are necessary to the practice of Christianity. For a similar point see Stephen C. Barton, 'Many Gospels, One Jesus?', in Markus Bockmuehl, ed., *The Cambridge Companion to Jesus* (Cambridge: Cambridge University Press, 2001), 181–2.
39. *The Real Jesus*, 136.
40. See *The Real Jesus*, 132–6.
41. It may be that certain sorts of science aspire to do this for us. That is, however, a separate issue beyond the scope of this chapter.
42. Luke T. Johnson, 'Imagining the World Scripture Imagines', *Modern Theology* 14 (1998), 165.
43. This is one of the points of William Placher's very fine account of historical research and the Bible in 'The Gospels' Ends', in *Narratives of a Vulnerable God* (Louisville: Westminster/John Knox Press, 1994), 87–108.

Further reading

Allison, Dale C., *Resurrecting Jesus* (London: T. & T. Clark International, 2005)
Bockmuehl, Markus, ed., *The Cambridge Companion to Jesus* (Cambridge: Cambridge University Press, 2001)
Borg, Marcus J., *Jesus in Contemporary Scholarship* (Valley Forge: Trinity Press International, 1994)

Crossan, John Dominic, *The Historical Jesus: The Life of a Mediterranean Peasant* (San Francisco: HarperCollins, 1991)

Dunn, J. D. G., *Jesus Remembered* (Grand Rapids: Eerdmans, 2003)

Frei, Hans, *The Eclipse of Biblical Narrative* (New Haven: Yale University Press, 1974)

Johnson, Luke T., *The Real Jesus* (San Francisco: HarperCollins, 1996)

Sanders, E. P., *Jesus and Judaism* (Philadelphia: Fortress, 1986)

Schweitzer, Albert, *The Quest of the Historical Jesus* (1906; London: A. & C. Black, 1954)

Strauss, D. F., *The Life of Jesus Critically Examined* (1836; Philadelphia: Fortress, 1972)

Witherington, Ben, *The Jesus Quest* (Downers Grove: InterVarsity Press, 1995)

Wright, N. T., *Jesus and the Victory of God* (Minneapolis: Fortress, 1996)

5 The Gospels and the reader

SANDRA M. SCHNEIDERS

FROM OBJECT TO SUBJECT IN NEW TESTAMENT STUDIES

From at least the eighteenth to the mid-twentieth century the prevailing understanding of history and of texts and their meaning was almost exclusively object-centred. The reader of the text seldom came into view, and if she or he did, the exegesis was suspect. History was understood as a free-standing state of affairs which existed 'in the past' independently of the reader. Texts were free-standing semantic containers in which a single, stable meaning was intentionally embedded by the author. The meaning in the biblical texts was presumed to be primarily information about history. Thus, the task of the biblical scholar was primarily if not exclusively to extract from the text what it had to say about history. The primary concern was, at first, to discover 'what really happened' in the past; for instance, who Jesus really was and what he really said and did.

Gradually, as source criticism gave rise to redaction criticism in gospel scholarship, the interest shifted to what each evangelist contributed to the presentation of this historical material and how that contribution both influenced the data about Jesus and his message (e.g., through selection and emphases) and gave the reader access to another sphere of historical data, viz., the *Sitz im Leben* or the community context in which the oral tradition about Jesus was transmuted through practice into text. However, the interest still focused on the information that was embedded in the text, either explicitly or implicitly. The ideal was still historical objectivity, but now less focused on 'what really happened' and more on 'what the author intended to say' about what really happened.

This move from concern with what was presumed to be objectively behind the text to what the evangelist intended to communicate precipitated a shift in perspective among New Testament scholars. The text, which had been virtually invisible because it was understood as a kind of clear window through which the scholar examined first-century realities, had now become visible as an object of study itself.[1] 'New Criticism', which had developed in secular literary scholarship in the 1950s, began to influence New Testament studies in the 1970s and 1980s. New Criticism focused directly and exclusively on the text itself as a 'closed world' which was completely independent not only of authorial intention but also of the context and genetics of the text's production or the existence and/or significance of its extra-textual referent. Such an approach could never have become absolute in New Testament studies because the significance of the subject-matter of the text, the story of Jesus, was dependent on the actual existence of its historical referent. It did, however, precipitate a new focus on the received text in its final form. Methodological interest shifted to text-oriented approaches such as structuralism, narrative criticism and rhetorical criticism, which challenged the hegemony of historical concerns in the field.

The emergence of this new, predominantly literary interest positioned New Testament scholarship to experience the impact of what has been called, in both philosophical and literary studies, the 'turn to the subject'. From a virtually exclusive concern with history, attention turned first to the text itself as a literary entity rather than simply as a source of historical data, and then, inexorably, to the subject, the reader of the text. The path of New Testament scholarship from the 1950s into the 1990s was from exegesis as the extraction of a single valid authorially established meaning *from* the text, to attention *to* the text itself as a literary structure, to interpretation *of* the text, now understood as a mediation of meaning *by* a real reader engaged in a unique process of reading.

This development gave rise to a number of new questions. What is meaning? How is it achieved? What does it mean to interpret a text? Can a text have more than one valid meaning, and, if so, how is validity determined? Can the text 'change' in the process of interpretation, and, if so, what does this imply about the authority and normativity of the biblical text as scripture in and for the Christian community? Who is the competent reader and what kind of responsibility does the reader have to the text on the one hand and to the community on the other? And who is served by various interpretations?

In this refocusing of attention on the reader and the reading process, the historical referent and the text retained their importance even as the understanding of them was modified. History was now seen not as a free-standing, objective reality but as an aspect of the subject-matter of the witness of the evangelists emerging from the experience of the Jesus event in real communities. The text was seen, not as a window through which to see something else (viz. the first-century world and the theological concerns of the evangelist, or as a closed literary object detached from any context or content outside itself), but as a dynamic literary structure which mediates the interaction between the subject-matter of the text and the reader. The reader, once virtually invisible, and the activity of reading, once thought to be an exclusively methodological operation on an inert textual object, had become the primary focus of attention.

This new perspective has given rise to a number of new approaches to the study of the New Testament involving new historical, literary and theological methods.[2] The new approaches with which this particular chapter is concerned belong to the field of *hermeneutics*, or theories of interpretation and the practices of reading. The engagement of the text by the contemporary reader is the focus of attention. In what follows, three clusters of subject-matter will be discussed: first, a group of approaches to interpretation which are primarily concerned with the reader and which I will call 'pragmatic'; second, hermeneutics as a global philosophical theory of interpretation which grounds particular approaches to reading, whether historical, literary, theological or pragmatic; third, particular questions about the text, the reader and reading which arise from a reader-oriented approach to interpretation. The interaction among the topics discussed in the third section will suggest the effect of interpretation in the reader, in the community and in the world.

PRAGMATIC APPROACHES TO THE TEXT

Hermeneutics as a global theoretical enterprise is concerned with the interpretation of 'texts', which includes not only literary texts such as the gospels but also any meaningful material such as oral discourse, actions or artefacts. It asks about the meaning and conditions of possibility of human understanding, the process of meaningful engagement with texts, the effects of understanding, and the criteria of validity of the whole enterprise. In other words, hermeneutics is an ontological and epistemological inquiry into understanding through interpretation.

Most biblical scholars leave this global enterprise to philosophers while they operate within and in terms of certain intermediate hermeneutical frameworks which allow them to address their particular interests in regard to the texts (e.g., the gospels) with which they are concerned. Many scholars have a preferred hermeneutical framework, (e.g., historical, literary or theological) within which they tend to apply a particular set of methods to all the texts they interpret and to select for interpretation texts amenable to this framework. But other scholars, especially those involved in what I am calling 'pragmatic interpretation', will move back and forth among a number of hermeneutical frameworks, using methods from all of them. Pragmatics is the theory of how texts and their users are related. Reading, in this perspective, is concerned not exclusively with the knowledge obtained through interpretation but with the way that knowledge and life, both personal and social, affect each other.

Although the earliest interpreters of the NT understood biblical interpretation primarily as a life-transforming activity (i.e., as a dimension of their spirituality), contemporary pragmatic hermeneutics has no real antecedents in the precritical or Enlightenment periods. The starting-point of pragmatic interpretation, unlike that of traditional historical, literary, or theological interpretation, is not the text but the present situation of the reader. Furthermore, the various forms of this type of interpretation are asymmetrical in relation to each other so that even grouping them together is problematic. I am calling them 'pragmatic' approaches because of the emphasis in all of them on enlisting New Testament resources in a conscious and structured project of action for social or personal transformation. I will discuss several such approaches without attempting to be exhaustive.

Liberation hermeneutics

Liberation hermeneutics has arisen in the communitarian context of the oppressed poor. The biblical text read in these communities, whether in Latin America, Asia, Africa, or among people of colour or native peoples in first-world countries, is seen first and foremost as being about the readers and their present situation rather than about the first century. Often these readers lack academic training in biblical studies and their approach to the text is not linguistically, historically or literarily sophisticated. They read from their own place addressing to the text the survival questions of their everyday life. Often they are aided by trained biblical scholars who have articulated the hermeneutical framework for this kind of reading and who can be especially helpful in maintaining a critical appreciation of the 'otherness' of the text, but the real work of interpretation is done by the poor themselves.[3]

The oppressed find in the biblical text resources for their struggle. Liberation interpreters, both the lay people participating in the reading and the scholars who have made the liberation of the oppressed their primary academic agenda, read the biblical text through the lens of grinding poverty, rampant disease, premature death and socio-political powerlessness. In the text they find the assurance that their suffering is not willed by God but unjustly imposed by those in power and that God is on the side of the oppressed. They are concerned not primarily with what the text means intellectually but with what it means for transformative action in their own situation.

Characteristic of this and other pragmatic approaches is the emphasis on praxis. Praxis is not simply the application to behaviour of the understanding of the text. Rather, it is an ongoing spiralling process in which the interpretation is incorporated into action and the lived experience is then brought back into dialogue with the text, which, in turn, is reinterpreted in light of the experience as the basis for further action.

Feminist hermeneutics

Although feminist hermeneutics is rightly considered a form of liberationist hermeneutics, it is marked by distinctive features it does not share with the former. Like other forms of pragmatic interpretation, it begins in the experience of oppression, specifically the gender-based oppression of women. Patriarchal oppression, however, is not the oppression of a particular group (e.g., people of colour in a particular society), but of half the human race. It cuts across all races, ethnic groups, social classes and religions. This lends numerical strength to the feminist cause but it also makes it more difficult for feminists to come together around biblical interpretation or the action to which it gives rise, because different women (e.g., poor and middle-class, educated and illiterate, black or Asian or white, married and single women) experience their oppression in vastly different ways around very different foci of urgency.

In contrast to other forms of liberationist interpretation which can appeal to the biblical testimony to God's preferential option for the poor, feminists often confront a biblical text in which God is in league with the male oppressor. In the biblical text, women are often marginalized or even invisible; their suffering is regarded as acceptable collateral damage within male projects; their agency is devalued or subverted. Thus, feminist interpreters see the need not only to liberate the oppressed, namely women, *through* scripture, but also to liberate the biblical text itself *from* its own androcentric perspective, patriarchal assumptions, and tolerance or approval of sexist practice. Furthermore, the biblical academy must be liberated from its collusion, conscious and unconscious, with the patriarchy and sexism in the text.

A final distinctive feature of feminist hermeneutics is its universalist perspective. The liberation of women is one dimension of an agenda of social transformation which envisions the definitive dismantling of all forms of domination through the subversion of their foundation in the ideology of hierarchical dualism.[4] The domination of women by men is the paradigmatic instance of this dominative ideology which justifies myriad systems of oppression of the weak by the powerful extending even to the rape by humans of nature itself. Consequently, the feminist agenda is indeed liberationist, but its ultimate aim is more universally transformative. Christian feminists interpreting scripture in the service of this agenda have, as their ultimate objective, the modelling of human society on the egalitarianism, dialogical mutuality and interdependence of the triune God revealed in Jesus. In short, the universality and radicality of the feminist agenda, the problems of the biblical text in regard to women, and the diversity of the social situations of many women who are oppressed not only because of gender but also because of race, class, and other factors, put feminist hermeneutics in a unique position among liberationist interpreters.

Ethical interpretation

Ethical interpretation can mean either interpreting the biblical text ethically or using the biblical text to address ethical problems. Biblical scholars are increasingly aware that there is no neutral or innocent reading of 'what the text says'. Liturgical reading, preaching, commentary, the determination of the structure and content of the lectionary, translation, are all political; that is, they respond to and serve the interests of those who engage in them. Therefore, they are ethical enterprises. Objectivity in dealing with the text is an illusion, and the claim to such objectivity is often, deliberately or not, in service of the powerful. To read historically anti-Jewish texts in Matthew or John without attending to their antisemitic potential is not objectivity but racism. The particular texts that never (or always) appear in the liturgical cycle, where they begin and end, and on what liturgical occasions certain texts are (or are not) read, as well as sexist and racist translations, are not fidelity to the text but strategies of exclusion and oppression.

A second form of ethical interpretation concerns the use of the biblical text in the effort to act ethically, personally and socially. The globalization that has increased steadily since the Second World War has raised heretofore unimagined and seemingly intractable ethical problems in the areas of social life, politics, economics, medicine and technology. This has led politicians, scientists, educators, cultural critics and ethicists within the Christian tradition to turn to the Bible, and especially to the New Testament, for resources in facing these challenges. Because these problems were inconceivable in first-century Palestine, contemporary readers must choose between declaring the New Testament irrelevant to the Christian quest for moral wisdom in these times or finding a way to read the text that will go beyond the search for objective answers and enable present-day Christians to confront new problems with what Paul called 'the mind of Christ'.

Ethical interpretation shares with liberationist and feminist hermeneutics the starting-place in the situation of the reader(s) rather than in the engagement of the reader with the text, the high practical stakes of its success or failure, and its agenda of social transformation. Like much feminist interpretation, it is located primarily in the academy. Its practitioners are trying to develop hermeneutical understandings that can integrate biblical and especially New Testament perspectives into moral theories and reasoning in ways that will be genuinely enriching and transformative of those theories. However, since most ethical theories current in the academy were developed within philosophical rather than theological or biblical frameworks, if the project of integrating New Testament perspectives into ethical discourse is to be taken seriously a biblical hermeneutical theory which can facilitate a dialogue with this secular synthesis is needed.[5]

Spiritual hermeneutics

Spiritual hermeneutics is closely related to ethical interpretation, but its focus is on the transformation of the individual and/or community in relation to God, self and world. It, also, is pre-eminently a reader-centred approach to scripture. Christian spirituality is the lived experience of Christian faith. Within this overall project the practice of interpreting the Bible, especially the New Testament, as a resource for personal transformation began in the patristic period, was thematized in the medieval practice of *lectio divina*, was the backbone of the spiritualities of the Reformation, and has seen a renewed flowering among Catholics since Vatican II. The challenge today is to integrate appropriate critical strategies into an engagement of reader and text in such a way that the transformative participation of the reader is fostered while a relapse into a precritical naivety is forestalled.[6] In regard to spiritual as well as liberationist, feminist and ethical interpretation, the urgent agenda is the development of an adequate hermeneutical framework for an appropriately critical, post-Enlightenment, personally and socially transformative, non-alienating engagement of the reader with the text.[7]

A HERMENEUTICAL FRAMEWORK FOR READING
THE NEW TESTAMENT AS SACRED SCRIPTURE

Whether or not the interpreter attends to the fact, all particular approaches to interpretation, including those which focus on the reader, imply a philosophically based hermeneutics or global theory of what it means to understand, how the human subject achieves understanding, and what understanding effects. In other words, there is some ontological-epistemological theory operative, at least implicitly, in all interpretative processes. Contemporary interpreters who attend to this fact appeal to a variety of hermeneutical theories and theorists from deconstructionism to the thought of Mikhail Bakhtin. Discussing this array of competing theories is beyond the scope of this chapter. However, by drawing on the contribution of two twentieth-century hermeneutical philosophers, Hans-Georg Gadamer and Paul Ricoeur, I will attempt to supply a (not the only possible) workable hermeneutical framework for New Testament reader-centred interpretation.

A theory of text

Ricoeur's hermeneutical theory involves a nuanced analysis of text. He argues that a text is not simply a written form of oral discourse.[8] The text is a different kind of being from speech. Rejecting the Platonic argument that discourse 'dies' in writing and must be 'revived' by oral proclamation, Ricoeur contends that writing is an enriched form of discourse. Inscription not only stabilizes and preserves meaning but also liberates discourse from its producer. The effects of this transformation are extremely important for the process of interpretation.

First, the encoding of discourse in writing creates a text which is *semantically autonomous*, which has a 'life of its own'. It can outlive its author and interact with audiences its author may never have envisioned. The meaning of written discourse – unlike that of oral speech, which is controlled by the intention of the speaker, who can correct misinterpretations in the actual experience of dialogue – is in the public forum, available to any competent reader, and meaning whatever it actually means no matter what might have been intended by the author.

Second, the autonomous text can be *re-contextualized*. The meaning is no longer completely conditioned by, nor restricted to, the socio-historical context and specific ostensible references of the original speaking event. A speaker speaks to one audience in one place and time, can indicate by pointing, physically or verbally, to what she or he intends, and can correct misunderstandings by the hearers if these are expressed. But the written text can be read in entirely different situations which might profoundly alter its original meaning. A judicial verdict which originally applied to a single specific case, once it becomes written text, may serve as precedent in subsequent cases that have very little in common with the original one. Writing not only preserves the memory of the original case but creates a text which becomes a source of judicial wisdom for future situations which the original judge could not have imagined. In short, writing does not impoverish the meaning of discourse, but enhances it by both stabilizing it and endowing it with a certain degree of semantic autonomy in relation to its originator and to its situation of composition.

Gadamer contributed to a usable theory of text by his reflection on the nature of the *classic*.[9] Some texts, because of the universality of their subject-matter, their compositional effectiveness and their stylistic beauty, transcend their own time and circumstances and address the human situation as such. They continue to be meaningful, within their own tradition and beyond, down through the ages. Because of both their semantic autonomy as written, and their intrinsic worth as classics, such texts have a 'surplus of meaning' that emerges as they are interpreted in new and different circumstances. Such texts, composed long ago but recognized as important in the present, raise the genuinely hermeneutical, as opposed to the purely historical, question. How can such texts be 'actualized', rendered contemporary with and meaningful to the present reader?

Gadamer evoked the analogy of the work of art to explain both the mode of existence of the classic and the role of interpretation in actualizing it in the present. Just as great art (e.g., the *Mona Lisa*) exists, even when it is not being aesthetically appreciated as an art object, but comes into the fullness of being as a work of art only when it is actually engaged by the viewer, so the classic text exists physically as potentially meaningful until it is actualized by a competent reading. The stability of the text as artefact grounds the continuity and family resemblance of subsequent interpretations, which will all be different because of the different circumstances, interests and capacities which individual interpreters bring to the task.

The eminent scholar of religions, Wilfred Cantwell Smith, came to a complementary conclusion about the nature of the Christian Bible as scripture.[10] Comparing the Bible to the sacred texts of other world religions, he located their 'scriptural' character not in some ontological feature of the text as such but in their historically demonstrated role of mediating the engagement of their respective communities with the transcendent. In other words, the biblical text has a sacramental character arising from the conjunction of the classic religious text with the interpretative practice of the community.

A theory of textual meaning

Ricoeur devoted considerable attention to the meaning of meaning. Given that the meaning of the text is not reducible to the intention of the writer, how and what does a text mean? Ricoeur distinguished between meaning as *propositional content* and meaning as *event*. Our concern for the moment is the former. A text, said Ricoeur, is a dialectical reality in which sense and reference mutually interact to constitute meaning. The *sense* of discourse is established by the grammatical and syntactical integrity of the sentences and their relation to each other. 'A dog is a feline' makes sense. In fact, we can judge that it is false only because we can understand it. *Reference* is the sentence's intention to reach reality. The referent in this case is not properly accessed because dogs are not felines but canines. Of course, literary discourse is much more complex than this simple example, and the referent is often not mere fact but truth: about humanity, history or God. Furthermore, literary discourse often has a 'split reference', referring not only to extra-discursive reality but reflexively to the discourse itself. The gospel accounts of the resurrection of Jesus, for example, refer to the fate of Jesus after his death and the experience of that reality by the first disciples (i.e., to facts and events 'outside' the discourse), but they also refer to the theology of resurrection developing within the early Christian community precisely through and in the writing of these texts. Ricoeur's theory of textual meaning as a dialectic between sense and reference allows for focus either on what the text itself says (its sense), or on the reality about which it speaks (its reference), which may include its extratextual, intratextual and intertextual reference.

Gadamer's most important contribution to the theory of textual meaning is his conception of *effective history* and *effective historical consciousness*. History is not composed of stable events which, once they have occurred, remain frozen in their facticity in the past, able to be observed by the historian from some objective and a-historical point of view. An event, such as the Second World War, is part of the process of history, and not only continues to affect all subsequent history but continues to be affected by subsequent history. Thus, the 'meaning' of the war has changed as subsequent events have manifested, magnified or relativized its significance. The meaning of the war in 2006 is different from its meaning in 1945 because its effective history is now part of the meaning of the event itself.

Texts also have an effective history. The meaning of the crucifixion of Jesus today includes everything that that event unleashed in history: for example, theologies and spiritualities of redemptive suffering, the Eucharist as sacrament of the paschal mystery, and heroic self-sacrifice; but also controversies over its meaning, Jewish–Christian antagonism, and contemporary feminist repudiation of a God who is placated by the shedding of innocent blood, all of which is part of the effective history of the crucifixion and part of the meaning of the text which recounts it.

The interpreter who faces this text today does so, not with objective consciousness, but with a consciousness profoundly affected and shaped by all that the text has produced which is now part of its meaning. As the reader interprets, he or she will contribute to the history of interpretation of this text, further expanding its effective history. In other words, Gadamer brilliantly captured the dynamic character of meaning, not only as process or event but also as content. Textual meaning is never simply static, residing in an inert text. It is being constantly transformed by the incessant interaction of the text with its context, including the interpretative activity of readers.

A theory of interpretation

Ricoeur's ultimate purpose in establishing the nature and characteristics of texts as written discourse and of textual meaning as content was to ground a theory of interpretation that could account for both the similarity and the difference among interpretations of a single text and allow the development of criteria to adjudicate among interpretations. How does the potential meaning (the *ideal* meaning created by the dialectic of sense and reference in a text) emerge as *real* meaning? This occurs as event in the interaction between a reader and the text in the act of interpretation. Just as real music occurs only when a musician plays the score, so real meaning occurs only when a reader interprets the text. And just as the real music is normed by the score (the ideal music encoded in the notation) but not constrained by it to wooden repetition, so the interpretation of a text is normed by the text (the ideal meaning created by inscription) but can and must be original and fresh in the hands of each reader. The same score can be played beautifully by a virtually infinite number of talented performers, each of whom contributes with originality to the body of interpretation of the piece, which itself remains identical. Similarly, the integrity of the text is not threatened by the potentially infinite variety of interpretations by readers whose interpretations are creatively diverse but faithful to the text. And just as it is possible to grade musical performances as good or better, flawed or totally inadequate, so it is possible to distinguish good textual interpretation from bad.

How does the event of meaning occur? According to Ricoeur, all interpretation begins with the educated guess, a provisional hypothesis about what the text might mean arising from whatever familiarity with the subject-matter or contextual clues might be available. This hypothesis must then be tested in a process of oscillating between *explanation* and *understanding* until the reader achieves a certain 'rest' or satisfaction in the meaning achieved. The text not only 'makes sense' in that one knows what it says (e.g., 'Jesus rose from the dead') and to what it refers (viz., that Jesus, who really died, is now alive), but has some understanding of what this means, not just notionally but really (i.e., that in the personal experience of Jesus the ultimate power of death over all humanity has been definitively broken). The reader, in short, has come to some understanding of the meaning of the text. Meaning has emerged as event in the experience of the reader.

Explanation includes the use of whatever investigative tools of biblical criticism seem appropriate. Each methodological move increases the understanding of the interpreter, thus deepening and widening the basis and framework for the next methodological move. This back-and-forth between explanation and understanding, which could (and historically in the community does) continue indefinitely, will halt for the reader when she or he is satisfied that a certain level of understanding is adequate for the moment. This understanding is not total or exhaustive, and it will be supplemented, corrected, challenged, expanded in dialogue with other understandings, both those achieved by the same interpreter in subsequent encounters with the text and those of other interpreters approaching the text in other times, places, circumstances. Interpretation is a never-ending process of engagement and re-engagement with a text whose real meaning is always developing through the work of interpretation.

Gadamer's treatment of this ongoing process of interpretation of a classic text within a community of shared life experience highlighted the *role of tradition* in the process. This is an important contribution to understanding the interpretation of the New Testament in the Christian community because the biblical text arose within and from the ongoing experience (i.e., the living tradition) of the church. Tradition preceded the production of the biblical text and is enshrined within it. The eventual selection of the texts which make up the Bible (i.e., the process and product of canonization) was part of that lived experience of the faith. And tradition provides the normative context within which the text is interpreted in the church down through the centuries.

Nevertheless, as Gadamer's critics have pointed out, tradition is a potentially oppressive category. Not everything that has been thought, done, or taught in the history of the church is worthy of or even minimally faithful to the gospel. The church's establishment of the canon was a deliberate choice to norm its life and faith (i.e., its tradition) by this foundational text. Consequently, a unilateral appeal to tradition as authoritative in the interpretation of scripture is as wrong-headed as treating the text as if it emerged full-blown from the hand of God independently of human context. Tradition and scripture must mutually interpret each other, or, more exactly, function dialogically and dialectically in the work of interpretation.

A theory of understanding

Understanding, as both Ricoeur and Gadamer insisted, is not simply an epistemological process of arriving at new knowledge. Rather, in the ontological sense of the word understanding denotes the specifically human way of being-in-the-world. Understanding integrates us into reality. Consequently, to come to new understanding is to expand one's existential horizon (and thus to see not only more but also to see everything differently) and to deepen one's humanity. Gadamer talked about application and Ricoeur about appropriation, but essentially they both intended to designate the transformation of the subject that is effected by an enriched encounter with reality.

The interpreter of a gospel is not merely trying to grasp what happened in the first century or what the evangelist intended to say or what the text actually does say about what happened. The interpreter is undergoing the kind of transformative experience that the person listening to great music undergoes. One emerges from the experience somehow different. Gadamer called understanding a 'fusion of horizons' or an expansion of existential context. This metaphorical expression captures well the experiential character of understanding as well as its transformative effect. Through understanding one becomes understanding. This is a comment not on the quantity of a person's knowledge but on the quality of the person.

THE INTERACTION OF TEXT AND READER IN THE HERMENEUTICAL PROCESS

Text

Because the Christian reader of the gospels regards these texts as sacred scripture, as somehow 'authored' by God for the sake of our salvation and therefore marked by such theological notes as inspiration, revelation and normativity, certain contemporary notions concerning texts, all clustered around *the issue of 'objectivity'*, raise serious questions. If all texts are relatively indeterminate, constructed by the reader, non-objective, and changing in and through the process of interpretation, how can the biblical text be considered authoritative for the believer and the community?

Although the Enlightenment notion of objectivity as the independent condition of the free-standing non-subject which confronts the knower as self-enclosed and non-negotiable is rightly rejected, the concept of objectivity itself cannot be simply abandoned if the New Testament reader's engagement with the text is not to be reduced to an exercise in pure projection. The text is not simply an object. The process of reading involves a co-constructing of the text by the reader. But that construction is a response to an 'other' which places demands on the reader. In other words, the text is not a subject in the same sense in which the reader is. The reader must come to terms with the reality of the text which is neither absolutely determined nor totally indeterminate.

The text pre-exists the reader and it has a certain form and content united according to the demands of a particular genre and within the style of a particular 'author' (individual or collective). Nevertheless, it remains somewhat indeterminate. It speaks in its own voice but, like any speaker, it cannot say everything. There are 'gaps', areas of indeterminacy, which the reader must resolve and which can be resolved in a number of different ways. The concepts borrowed from narrative theory of 'implied author' and 'implied reader' are an attempt to acknowledge both the claim of the text on the reader and the reader's relative autonomy in responding to that claim.

The implied author and implied reader are distinguished from the real author and reader as constructs of the text rather than actual actors. The point of view, convictions and intentions encoded in the text (which are not necessarily those of the real author) are implicit in the way it treats the subject-matter. And the text encourages the reader to respond in certain ways, to identify with certain characters, to care about certain outcomes, to struggle with certain issues, to arrive at certain conclusions, and so on. In other words, the text attempts to construct its reader, to guide the reader's responses. Although these rhetorical strategies have always been operative in texts, the contemporary reader is explicitly conscious of them and therefore in a position to respond more freely to this subtle manipulation by the text. The real reader may choose to respond as the text suggests but may also choose to resist or to transgress this textual programme.[11] Consequently, the interaction between reader and text becomes not simply a passive acquiescence of the reader but an active engagement in which the text may be welcomed, challenged, questioned, even rejected. The text, like real speech, often says what it means (both positively and negatively) rather than what its author meant to say. For example, a feminist reader may refuse the textual invitation of the gospels to see women as auxiliary or marginal to the Jesus story and may, through the interpretative process, 'force' the text to yield more of the submerged history of women in early Christianity than the evangelists intended to recount.[12] The liberationist reader may call into question the inevitability of having the poor always with us (cf. Mk 14.7).

Such an understanding of reading requires a revision of simplistic notions of the *authority* and *normativity* of the text as scripture. Scripture is not purely declarative or prescriptive. Its authority is not that of apodictic statements which demand unquestioning submission. Rather, the authority of scripture (like any real authority) arises from the recognition of truth. As Gadamer pointed out, interpretation is a dialogical process in which the reader attempts to discern the question that gave rise to the text as 'answer'. If the question (e.g., of slavery) is properly discerned, then the answer a particular text (e.g., Eph. 5.5–8) offers might be questioned, modified, or even rejected in terms of the truth about the subject-matter (slavery) as it has become increasingly clear over the centuries of Christian experience (i.e., that slavery is never acceptable). The reader who resists Paul's support of slavery as an institution is not rejecting the authority of scripture. She or he is identifying the question raised by the text but recognizing that the text can play a different role (e.g., showing how uncritical acceptance of cultural realities can betray the gospel) in answering that question today than it did when it was written. If the text were not authoritative the reader would not take seriously either the question itself or the responsibility to help shape a genuinely Christian answer in the current situation. Thus the normativity of the text has more to do with the *questions* the Christian must engage and the *co-ordinates of appropriate responses* that the text offers (e.g., that masters have no right to lord it over slaves because both master and slave have one master, God) than with apodictic prescriptions that would lock Christian experience into the past.

Such an approach, of course, raises the question of whether the biblical text 'changes' as it goes through history. The preservation of the New Testament text in its original language in the most critically correct version possible is vital. It is equivalent to preserving the original manuscript of a Beethoven sonata even though the instruments for which he composed are no longer played today and a vast body of arrangements and interpretations has modified what was originally considered the optimal performance. The art object must remain stable in order that the work of art, that is, the subsequent performances of the sonata, may be faithfully and creatively realized.

The New Testament text is the unchanging 'art object'. But, as performed text, as 'work of art', it changes and develops. The narrative content, structures and dynamics of the text continue to norm every valid reading and thus maintain an organic continuity in the effective history of interpretation. But what a text like Jn 20.11–18 (the appearance to Mary Magdalene) means today, especially in respect to the apostolic vocation of women in the early and contemporary church, has certainly changed dramatically since the modern period, in which it was read as a purely private, ecclesially insignificant story of Jesus consoling a woman.

Reader

As the role of the reader in co-creating textual meaning has achieved greater prominence, the once simple question of who the reader is and how he or she functions has been problematized. Protestants since the Reformation and Catholics since Vatican II have recognized that official ecclesiastical authority cannot, either in theory or in practice, reserve to itself the role of legitimate reader. The church as community, the individual believer and the well-disposed outsider are all legitimate readers of the New Testament text who have genuine and complementary, if not equal, contributions to make to the task of ongoing interpretation. And the trained biblical specialist has a unique, although limited, contribution to make not only to interpretation itself but to the reading of all the others.

The *church as community of faith*, as Spirit-empowered subject of tradition, is the primary reader of the New Testament text as sacred scripture. This community 'reads' not only by actually proclaiming the text but by enacting it in liturgy, incarnating it in the spiritualities of its members, and living the gospel in the world. Church authority, whether pastoral or academic, plays a significant role in this ongoing process in virtue of both leadership and learning, but history testifies eloquently that unless the community as a whole appropriates the interpretation of the gospel, official definitions of the meaning of the text are ineffectual.

Individual believers, both scholars and lay, are also readers of the text. Although they read within the context of the church as community, it is precisely as individuals studying, praying and living the gospel that they contribute to the ongoing task of interpretation. Several factors have changed the role of the individual reader in recent history. Printing and widespread literacy have made possible not only personal reading of the text but also a different kind of engagement with the text. The person reading a written text can reread, read intertextually, read in various orders, read selectively, compare translations, and otherwise move about in the text in a way that is not possible when one hears the text chosen and segmented by another, in relation to certain other texts, and so on. The potential for new connections and insights, different perspectives and original interpretation is greatly increased, as is, of course, the potential for aberrations in interpretation.

However, contemporary readers are more self-aware about their reading activity than were their predecessors. They know that there is no such thing as presuppositionless reading or purely objective interpretation. All reading, no matter how highly placed or well-endowed the reader, is done from some 'place', from some particular and circumscribed social location that is influenced by cultural situation, gender, race, age, ethnicity, education, religious tradition and social class. Acknowledging the situated character of all reading has both subverted the claims of the elites (ecclesiastical, academic, economic or political – and virtually always male) to control of the process of interpretation, and has greatly enriched the interpretative enterprise with the perspectives and insights of those whose voices have heretofore seldom been heard.

The New Testament text is also read by *well-intentioned outsiders*, those who are neither believers nor opponents. By 'well-intentioned' is meant the reader who does not share the faith of the Christian community but is not antagonistic to it. Just as a Christian can read with profit the *Bhagavad Gita* or the Qur'an, so the prepared non-Christian can competently read the New Testament. Its role in the pacifist commitment of Mahatma Gandhi, for example, is well known. Furthermore, such readers sometimes bring forward a fresh perspective, new questions, the unexpected insight or even the serious challenge, which long habituation to the text might have obscured for the community itself.

This possibility raises the question of the *role of faith* in the reader and the reading of the New Testament as scripture. Is Christian faith indispensable, an obstacle, or irrelevant to valid interpretation of the biblical text? If it were indispensable, then the non-Christian, no matter how well disposed, could not be a competent reader, and this is plainly contrary to experience. And if faith were an obstacle, then only the non-believers, or scholars who agreed to bracket their Christian commitments while working on the text, could achieve valid interpretations. Again, this is clearly contrary to the community's experience as articulated by some of its more eminent interpreters from Origen to Bultmann and beyond. But it is also counter-intuitive to hold that in reading a text written from faith for faith, the faith of the reader is irrelevant. This is equivalent to maintaining that experience as an actor is irrelevant to the appreciation of Shakespeare.

Faith may denote either that saving openness to revelation which Jesus often recognized in non-Jews as a sufficient disposition for healing, or a thematically articulated participation in a particular religious tradition. The former is certainly necessary for any fruitful engagement of the biblical text. Only a person open to the truth-claims of a text is properly disposed to understand it. On the other hand, thematized and active participation in the Christian tradition which produced the text and has lived it through the centuries familiarizes one with the underlying story, sensitizes one to its religious perspective and symbol system, enriches one with the history of its interpretation, and thus generally increases the reader's competence. Just as an American, other things being equal, is better equipped to understand the US Constitution than someone who has never lived in the United States but reads the document in school, so a participant in the Christian tradition has the immediate context for competent reading that the non-Christian must access vicariously. Of course, if faith is understood in fundamentalist terms as a blind submission of intellect to a literalistic reading of the biblical text as prescriptive, faith might indeed be an obstacle to interpretation, but intelligent and critical faith commitment is neither irrelevant nor an obstacle but an asset.

Finally, there is the special case of the reader who is a trained *biblical scholar*. The person who commands the languages in which the biblical text was written, who has studied the history of the subject-matter of the text as well as of the text itself, who is competent in the theology and spirituality that come to expression in the text, and who is equipped with an articulated hermeneutical framework within which to engage in the interpretative process in a critical way is obviously in a different relation to the work of interpretation than is the lay reader. The difference is neither hierarchical nor moral. It is a difference in competence. The professional biblical scholar has access to resources specific to the academic specialty not available to most readers, including many church officials.

Situating the biblical scholar in the reading community has often been a problem. In some traditions which have weak (or no) central authority and a limited sense of tradition, there can be a tendency to absolutize biblical scholarship so that faith itself is tied to developments in the field, with either fundamentalistic or secularizing results. In other traditions which have strong (or even 'monarchical') central authority, biblical scholarship can be marginalized or ignored in the interests of ecclesiastical control.

Ordinary lay readers can be so overwhelmed by scholarly virtuosity that they feel totally incompetent to read the text and thus consign themselves to mere absorption of academic results. Others can arrogantly claim the competence of a faith that can dispense with learning and ignore developments in scholarship. Biblical scholars, on the other hand, can see themselves as the only competent readers, unanswerable to the church's office-holders, its pastors, or its lay members, and restrict themselves to conversation with other 'experts'. This usually leads to a practical agreement to bracket faith considerations while engaged in biblical work. Others can see themselves as mere employees of church authority, enlisting the text to promote hierarchical agendas or protecting the weak faith of the laity. This obviously subverts any real scholarly contribution to the church's understanding of the biblical text as well as the contribution of faith to scholarship and vice versa.

The attitudes of a culture towards expertise in any field are likely to influence how biblical scholars view themselves and are viewed and allowed to function in the community of the church. Only if biblical scholarship is seen as a special kind of competence in the reading of the normative texts of the community will the place of the biblical scholar in the community be properly discerned and valued. Like all the members of the community, the scholar is the servant, not the master of the word of God. But both pastoral leaders and lay believers need the contribution of trained and committed biblical scholarship if the community as a whole is to deepen its grasp of revelation.

Reading

From all that has been said, the question 'What is reading?' should suggest its own response. Reading is not blind submission to a text conceived as self-enclosed, objective and absolutely authoritative. The biblical text is not a divinely dictated tissue of assertions, declarations or prescriptions requiring unquestioning acceptance. On the other hand, reading, especially of a sacred text which functions as scripture in a believing community, cannot be a free-wheeling and cavalier, nihilistically deconstructive 'play' with a totally indeterminate linguistic artefact. If the text and the reader have been well described in this chapter, reading must be understood as a disciplined engagement with a mediator of meaning that is neither 'objective' in the Enlightenment sense of that term nor a Rorschach inkblot that is susceptible to any and all projections. In the oscillation between *explanation*, carried out with all the competence to which the reader has direct or vicarious access, and an ever-expanding and deepening *understanding*, the reader actualizes the text in the transformative event of meaning.

Meaning, appropriated as and in understanding, is always *meaning for someone*, not some body of objective intellectual data. This means that it is located, limited and partial. Whether the scholar is interpreting to increase the understanding of the text, the pastor to foster the faith of the community, or the individual believer for personal growth in commitment, the reading process is a particular and limited engagement with transcendent reality through a mediating text susceptible of a wide range of valid interpretations. There is no one 'right' interpretation, although there may well be wrong ones. The ideal is not to achieve a dominant interpretation which will exclude all other possibilities but to achieve a valid interpretation which commands conviction by virtue of its explanatory power, its fidelity and/or healthy challenge to the tradition, and its potential for transformative influence in the world. No interpretation is final, definitive or irreformable, although the progress of the community in interpretation is, in some matters, irreversible (e.g., its realization that Eph 6.5–8 cannot be used as a justification for slavery).

Understanding, as has been said, is both a *process* of coming to clearer perception of reality and the *existential condition* of the person as human-being-in-the-world. The former increases, deepens, broadens and enriches the latter. Biblical interpretation reaches its ultimate goal when it actually promotes and nourishes the transformation of the reader (whether the individual or the community) in relation to God, self, world and society. In other words, spirituality as the lived experience of the faith is the ultimate goal and final fruit of the engagement of the reader with the gospel message which is mediated by the gospel texts.

Notes
1. Edgar V. McKnight in *Post-Modern Use of the Bible: The Emergence of Reader-Oriented Criticism* (Nashville: Abingdon, 1988) provides a good history of these developments.
2. See Joel B. Green, ed., *Hearing the New Testament: Strategies for Interpretation* (Grand Rapids: Eerdmans, 1995), for explanations and examples of most significant contemporary methods.

3. See Gerald West, *The Academy of the Poor: Towards a Dialogical Reading of the Bible* (Sheffield: Sheffield Academic Press, 1999).
4. This term refers to the dividing of reality according to various dualistic schemes, e.g., humans/nature; whites/people of colour; young/old; clergy/laity; royalty/commoner; wealthy/poor, etc., and assigning superior value to one of the terms which implies its right to dominate the other.
5. See Richard B. Hays, *The Moral Vision of the New Testament: A Contemporary Introduction to New Testament Ethics* (San Francisco: HarperSanFrancisco, 1996), esp. part III, 'The hermeneutical task: the use of the New Testament in Christian ethics'; John R. Donahue, 'Biblical perspectives on justice', in *The Faith that Does Justice: Examining the Christian Sources for Social Change*, ed. John C. Haughey (New York: Paulist, 1977), 68–112, for attempts in this direction.
6. See the special issue of *Interpretation* 56 (April 2002), devoted to biblical spirituality which includes both Protestant and Catholic contributions on both Testaments with emphasis on both personal and social spirituality.
7. I have treated this subject at some length in *The Revelatory Text: Interpreting the New Testament as Sacred Scripture*, 2nd ed. (Collegeville: Liturgical Press, 1999), 157–79.
8. The following treatment of Ricoeur's thought is most readily available in Paul Ricoeur, *Interpretation Theory: Discourse and the Surplus of Meaning* (Fort Worth: Texas Christian University Press, 1976).
9. The hermeneutical theory of Gadamer is set forth in his *Truth and Method*, 2nd, rev. ed., tr. by Joel Weinsheimer and Donald G. Marshall (New York: Crossroad, 1989).
10. Wilfred Cantwell Smith, *What is Scripture? A Comparative Approach* (Minneapolis: Fortress, 1993). See especially 212–42.
11. An excellent example of a real gospel-reader dealing consciously with the implied author and reader is Adele Reinhartz, *Befriending the Beloved Disciple: A Jewish Reading of the Gospel of John* (New York and London: Continuum, 2001).
12. This is the expressed agenda of Elisabeth Schüssler Fiorenza in *In Memory of Her: A Feminist Theological Reconstruction of Christian Origins* (New York: Crossroad, 1983).

Further reading

Adam, A. K. M., *What is Postmodern Biblical Criticism?* (Minneapolis: Fortress, 1995)
Green, Joel B., ed., *Hearing the New Testament: Strategies for Interpretation* (Grand Rapids: Eerdmans, 1995)
McKnight, Edgar V., *Post-Modern Use of the Bible: The Emergence of Reader-Oriented Criticism* (Nashville: Abingdon, 1988)
McKnight, Edgar V., and Malbon, Elizabeth Struthers, eds., *The New Literary Criticism and the New Testament* (Valley Forge: Trinity Press International, 1994)
Tompkins, Jane P., ed., *Reader-Response Criticism: From Formalism to Post-Structuralism* (Baltimore: Johns Hopkins University Press, 1980)
Ricoeur, Paul, *Interpretation Theory: Discourse and the Surplus of Meaning* (Fort Worth: Texas Christian University Press, 1976)

Schneiders, Sandra M., *The Revelatory Text: Interpreting the New Testament as Sacred Scripture*, (2nd ed. (Collegeville: Liturgical Press, 1999)

Schüssler Fiorenza, Elisabeth, *In Memory of Her: A Feminist Theological Reconstruction of Christian Origins* (New York: Crossroad, 1983)

Smith, Wilfred Cantwell, *What is Scripture? A Comparative Approach* (Minneapolis: Fortress, 1993)

Thiselton, Anthony C., *New Horizons in Hermeneutics* (London: HarperCollins, 1992)

Part II

The gospels as witnesses to Christ: content and interpretation

6 The Gospel according to Matthew

STEPHEN C. BARTON

A NEW GOSPEL FOR A NEW PEOPLE

Written later than the Gospel of Mark (on which it almost certainly draws), in all likelihood at some time towards the end of the period 70–100 CE, the Gospel of Matthew came to be given priority of place among the four canonical gospels and therefore, subsequently, priority of place as the first book of the New Testament.[1] From a theological point of view, this way of ordering the canon is suggestive. It conveys the conviction, held from early on, that Matthew's presentation of Jesus as the fulfilment of scripture and the hope of humankind is true and authoritative. Beginning as it does with a genealogy which displays Jesus' messianic identity as 'the son of David, the son of Abraham' (1.1), Matthew's gospel picks up, as it were, where Malachi, the last book of the Old Testament in its Septuagintal form, leaves off. Malachi ends with the prophecy of the return of the prophet Elijah 'before the great and terrible day of the LORD comes' (Mal 4.5). In Matthew, the end-time Elijah duly appears in the person of John the Baptist, preparing the way for 'the Lord', one whose identity is revealed at his baptism as Jesus, God's 'beloved Son' (3.17). The Gospel of Matthew, in other words, is a fulcrum between the Testaments in a traditional Christian reading. It expresses the fulfilment of the Old Testament (or 'covenant') and the beginning of the New.

The encounter between old and new gives to Matthew its *dynamic* quality. In Matthew's story of Jesus there is continuity with the past and discontinuity, profound indebtedness to the scriptures and traditions of Judaism, but also rupture and innovation. The fundamental continuity has to do with God. The God whose grace to humankind in times past was shown above all in the deliverance of Israel as God's chosen, covenant people is *the same God* whose grace is shown now in the person of Jesus whose life, death and resurrection constitute the inauguration of a new covenant people. Jesus, therefore, is 'God with us' (1.23). He is the one in whom God is 'well pleased' (3.17; 17.5).

The discontinuity has a theological rationale also. God, in Matthew's story, is doing something new. The signs are manifold. Above all, *God's Spirit* is active. The conception of the one who is named Jesus is 'of the Holy Spirit' (1.18, 20), and at his baptism, the Spirit of God descends from heaven and, like a dove coming to earth – an image evocative of creation (Gen 1.2) – alights on him (3.16). John the Baptist, furthermore, speaks of the coming one as he who 'will baptize you with the Holy Spirit and with fire' (3.11), a prophecy which anticipates the cleansing, purifying judgement which will characterize Jesus' words and actions as Israel's messiah (cf. Isa 4.4; 4 Ezra 13.8–11). Nor is the creative presence of God's Spirit evoked only at the story's beginning. It is evoked in the middle of the story as an interpretation (drawn from Isaianic prophecy) of Jesus' compassionate ministry of healing (12.18). It comes at the end as well. The disciples of Jesus are to continue the work he began. They too are to make disciples. They too are to baptize – 'in the name of the Father and of the Son *and of the Holy Spirit*' (28.19).

Matthew's gospel, then, seeks to bring together and hold together the old and the new. In a revealing passage, where Matthew modifies Mark's account of Jesus' parabolic teaching about the kingdom of God, the Jesus of Matthew adds a parable which is wonderfully indicative of the dynamic that runs through the gospel as a whole: 'Therefore every scribe who has been trained for the kingdom of heaven is like a householder who brings out of his treasure *what is new and what is old*' (13.52). The order is significant: the new has priority over the old. But the conjunction is significant also: the old retains its fundamental worth. Furthermore, the creative tension between the old and the new is embodied in the leading metaphor itself: the discerning disciple of Jesus is like a 'scribe' (who honours and preserves the tradition), but a scribe 'trained for the kingdom of heaven' (the eschatological reality revealed in Jesus and his teaching).[2]

It is worth adding that the 'old' for Matthew appears to refer, not just to the scriptures and traditions of Judaism, but also to more primitive (i.e. earlier) *Christian* tradition, whether we are speaking of the Gospel of Mark or other pre-Matthean tradition such as the (hypothetical) sayings source which scholars designate 'Q'. Matthew's relation to Mark, for example, can hardly be explained otherwise. On the one hand, Matthew incorporates most of Mark (approximately 80 per cent) and follows his Markan source closely. On the other hand, Matthew composes a gospel which is distinctively his own.[3] For example, he augments the beginning of Mark's story of Jesus with a genealogy and birth narrative; reshapes the ending of Mark by adding resurrection appearances and the sending of the disciples on mission; introduces scriptural 'formula quotations' to enhance his portrayal of Jesus as the fulfilment of Israel's eschatological hopes (e.g. 1.22–3; 2.15, 17–18; 4.14–16; etc.); and massively expands the teaching of the Markan Jesus while at the same time imposing on it a distinctive structure, organizing it, broadly speaking, into five major discourses (cf. Matt 5–7; 10; 13; 18; 24–25). So Matthew is both conservative of the old (in the shape of his Markan and other sources) and innovative as well – which is why his gospel is so dynamic.

What is at the heart of this dynamic tension between the old and the new in the Gospel of Matthew, and in what terms is it elaborated? One way of answering this question is to appeal to the historical circumstances that are likely to have influenced Matthew's writing. Of particular importance here is the relationship between Jews and Christians in the period after Easter, particularly (so most scholars hold) the period after the defeat of the Jews by the Romans and the destruction of Jerusalem and the Temple in 70 CE.[4] On this view, Matthew's story of Jesus can be read as reflecting the tensions of a later period, tensions between the church and the synagogue, where the church is composed largely of Jewish Christians (but with a growing number of Gentile adherents as well), and the synagogue is made up of Jews seeking to redefine their identity and re-establish a common life based on renewed dedication to torah in the wake of the loss of Temple and cult. Such a setting for Matthew is historically very plausible. After all, tensions between Jews and Christians (both Jewish and Gentile) were ubiquitous in the latter half of the first century and are reflected in most of the New Testament texts. As Graham Stanton puts it, 'for much of early Christianity, and for Matthew in particular, the relationship between Christianity and Judaism was the central problem for Christian theology'.[5]

In the first instance, however, Matthew's gospel, like all the canonical gospels, is a life of Jesus, closest in literary genre to an ancient biography (or *bios*). We do well, therefore, to read it as such. On this level, the dynamic of the narrative is to be sought in the innovations, tensions, surprises and conflicts generated by Jesus himself in his own time and place as Matthew tells it. To read Matthew's life of Jesus primarily as a mirror of the church in its relations with the synagogue in the period after Easter certainly helps to throw historical light on how and why the evangelist has shaped and developed the Jesus tradition in the distinctive ways he has. But of overriding importance for the interpreter of Matthew's gospel *as scripture* must be the evangelist's central preoccupation: the revelation of the divine presence ('the kingdom of heaven') in the coming of Jesus as messiah, in fulfilment of scripture, to call Israel to repentance and through a renewed Israel to bring God's blessing to the nations of the world.

THE BIRTH OF THE MESSIAH (MATTHEW 1–2)

The story of Jesus' beginnings is carefully crafted and artfully told. In the first two chapters, the messianic credentials of Jesus are displayed to powerful effect. As Krister Stendahl has shown,[6] Matt 1, with its genealogy and birth story, is dominated by *personal* names and answers the question, 'Who is the Messiah?' Matt 2, with its story of the coming of the magi, the massacre of the innocents in Bethlehem, the flight into Egypt, the return to Galilee and the settling in Nazareth, is dominated by *place* names and answers the question, 'Where is the Messiah from?' In answering the first question, Jesus is shown to be Israel's long-awaited Davidic Messiah ('the Son of David'), the hope also of all the nations ('the son of Abraham'), and pre-eminently, the divine Son of God, whose conception is miraculous and whose birth is accompanied by heavenly portents in the shape of dream-revelations and angelophanies. In answering the second question, Matthew shows Jesus to be, like King David, of the tribe of Judah and the town of Bethlehem.

What is more, his story is told in such a way as to recapitulate the story of Moses and the people of Israel. The threat to the life of God's 'son' Israel and of the infant Moses at the hands of Pharaoh is played out again in the threat to the life of God's Son, the infant Jesus, at the hands of King Herod. And as Moses the delivered becomes the deliverer of Israel, so Jesus the delivered becomes the saviour of Israel (and beyond) also.[7]

From the outset, the stakes are high and the drama profound. Events on earth are being directed by a heavenly hand. As God has acted in the past to save his people, so God is acting again, as the elaborate scriptural 'formula quotations' ('Then was fulfilled what was spoken by the prophet . . .') show. But the divine initiative, the divine grace, is not coercive. Two responses are possible. In the 'righteous' (*dikaios*) man Joseph we see the response of obedience to God's will, the outcome of which is the preservation of the infant Messiah's life. In King Herod we see the response of resistance and paranoia, the outcome of which is the vindictive and self-defeating slaughter of the children of his own people. Contrasted with Herod is not only Joseph but also (and surprisingly) the Gentile magi from the east, probably astrologers from the royal house of Persia. Where they offer the infant Messiah gifts and obeisance, Herod offers violence and death. There are, in other words, *two ways*: obedience to the divine will, shaping human affairs and offering salvation, or disobedience, leading to disaster.

There is a clear narrative pattern here which recurs throughout the story: not least at the end, in the narrative of the trial and passion, where the Roman governor's wife testifies on the basis of a dream-revelation to the innocence of Jesus – and again the term used is *dikaios* (27.19; cf. 1.19) – in stark contrast to the way of false witness and duplicity chosen by the group identified as the 'chief priests and elders' (e.g. 26.3–4, 14–16, 47–8, 59; 27.1–2), who seek only Jesus' death. The clear message of Matthew is that the coming of Jesus the Messiah and the revelation in him of God's kingly rule ('the kingdom of heaven') creates conflict and division. This pattern is reinforced by a pervasive irony: those who should know better, especially the leaders of the Jews like Herod or the chief priests and elders of the people, reject him, and those on 'the outside' in one way or another (Gentile magi, the centurion at the cross, for example) respond positively.

THE TESTING OF THE MESSIAH (MATTHEW 4.1–11)

The story of Jesus' baptism by John in the Jordan River, mentioned already, is followed immediately by the story of his testing in the wilderness.[8] The sequence is important. At the baptism, and in consequence of his willingness in baptism to 'fulfil all righteousness (*dikaiosunē*)', Jesus receives a double blessing from heaven: he sees the Spirit descend upon him and he hears the voice of God name him (in scriptural terms – cf. Isa 42.1 and Ps 2.7) as 'my beloved Son, with whom I am well pleased' (3.16–17). But the call is incomplete without the testing: is Jesus' divine sonship genuine? Noteworthy is the fact that the Spirit who comes upon Jesus at his baptism is the same Spirit who leads him into the wilderness to be tested by the devil (4.1).

There is a biblical pattern here. The obedience of Adam and Eve to the restriction placed by God on the tree of the knowledge of good and evil in the Garden of Eden is tested by the serpent (Gen 2.15–17). The loyalty of Job is tested by the Satan acting with God's permission (Job 1–2). But of particular relevance to the story of Jesus is the testing of Israel. Just as Israel, God's 'son', is tested for forty years in the wilderness, having first been 'baptized' in the waters of the Red Sea, so Jesus, God's Son, is tested after forty days in the wilderness, having first been baptized in the Jordan. Once again, therefore, the story of Israel is being recapitulated in the story of Jesus. But with the continuities, there are the discontinuities also. Above all, where Israel repeatedly falls into temptation, Jesus shows his true sonship by his repeated refusal to succumb.

In fact, the story, with Jesus quoting three times from Deut 6–8, resonates against the backdrop of the covenant theology of the book of Deuteronomy. More specifically, the testing of Jesus is a midrash on Deut 8.2–3: 'And you shall remember all the way which the LORD your God has led you these forty years in the wilderness, that he might humble you, *testing you to know what was in your heart*, whether you would keep his commandments, or not. And he humbled you and let you hunger and fed you with manna, which you did not know, nor did your fathers know; that he might make you know that man does not live by bread alone, but that man lives by everything that proceeds out of the mouth of the LORD.'

Israel's filial loyalty to God in the wilderness was tested by hunger (cf. Ex 16), physical dangers (cf. Num 13–14) and the temptation to fall into idolatry (the Golden Calf episode of Ex 32). Now, Jesus' loyalty to God as God's Son is tested likewise. And in resisting the three temptations, Jesus shows true covenant obedience: that, in the words of the Shema (Deut 6.4–5), there is one Lord, and that he loves the Lord God three ways – with all his heart, with all his soul, and with all his might.

Thus, first, in refusing to use his power to satisfy his personal need for food and instead placing his existence under the word and will of God, Jesus shows wholehearted love of God. Significantly, when he does use his power to make bread, it is to meet the needs of others, the hungry crowds of 14.13–21 and 15.29–38. In refusing, second, to presume on God for protection from physical danger or, alternatively, in refusing to force God's hand instead of trusting that God will save in God's good time, Jesus shows that he loves God with life itself (all his soul). Here is foreshadowed his acquiescence to the will of God in Gethsemane (26.36–46) and his subsequent refusal during the crucifixion to use his power to come down from the cross and save himself (27.39–44). Finally, and climactically (noting the setting on a 'very high mountain'), in refusing to accept prematurely the authority that was rightfully his – 'all the kingdoms of the world and the glory of them' (4.8) – but at the cost of exclusive covenant loyalty to the one true God, by worshipping Satan, Jesus shows that he loves God with all his might (or possessions). And his love is rewarded. When Jesus appears from heaven to the disciples after his resurrection (again on a mountain), he announces that God has given him even more than what the devil had offered: 'all authority *in heaven and on earth*' (28.18).

The wilderness is a place of testing. It is also a place of preparation. In fact, the testing is an essential part of the preparation. Israel's forty years' wandering in the wilderness was a preparation for entry into the promised land as God's covenant people. The Qumran covenanters made their community in the wilderness to purify themselves in preparation for the end time and the coming of God (cf. 1QS 8.13–16). In similar fashion, Matthew's story of the testing of Jesus in the wilderness is a story of preparation: Jesus' fasting for forty days and nights prepares him for the testing by the devil; and the testing itself prepares him for what is to come. But it also shows who he is: God's true Son, who shows by his example how God's people are to live in the light of the coming of the kingdom of heaven.

THE TEACHING OF THE MESSIAH (MATTHEW 5–7)

Having been called and tested, Jesus is ready to begin his public ministry. Significantly, following hard upon his initial preaching, the nucleus of a new community is established. Jesus 'calls' two pairs of brothers to 'follow' him and, in obedience and faith, they do so (4.18–22; cf. 8.18–22; 9.9–10; 10.1–4). The brothers become the core of a brotherhood of disciples (cf. 23.8). The fishermen become apprentices in the business of 'fishing' for people. There is, in other words, a fundamental orientation in the work of Jesus on the building and renewing of community – in the first place, the community of God's people Israel, and then, through a renewed Israel, the renewal of all the nations of the world.

Critical to the work of building and renewing the common life of God's people Israel is the task of *teaching God's Law*: for the Law is the revelation of God's will for how his people are to live in righteousness. Thus, in a further recapitulation of the story of Moses and Israel, and recalling in particular the giving of torah by God through Moses on Mount Sinai (Ex 19ff.), Jesus ascends a mountain and teaches the disciples (as the nucleus of the renewed community) and the crowds (5.1–2; 7.28–9).

How is the so-called 'Sermon on the Mount' (Matt 5–7) to be understood? Apart from the obvious point that it is not a 'sermon' at all, what are we to make of this remarkable and carefully structured collection of blessings, parables, torah interpretation, teaching about the practices of traditional piety (almsgiving, prayer and fasting), wisdom sayings, and apocalyptic warnings?[9] Given that, like the gospel as a whole, the sermon owes its final form to the evangelist Matthew, it is fair to suppose that the situation in which Matthew wrote helped to shape its purpose and meaning. If, therefore, as suggested earlier, the gospel comes from a period in the life of the early church when the often fraught relations between Christians and Jews were being worked out and 'formative Judaism' was developing its identity in the wake of the destruction of Jerusalem and the Temple, it is likely that the sermon has both a constructive aspect and a polemical aspect. The *polemical* aspect lies in the claim that it is Jesus (not Moses) who authoritatively and finally reveals the will of God, that what he offers in his teaching is the way to a 'greater righteousness' (than that taught by the Pharisees), and that God will judge the people on the basis of their response to that teaching (cf. 5.20; also 7.28–9). The *constructive* aspect lies in the fact that the sermon offers followers of Christ divine wisdom about how to live in the light of the drawing near of God with the coming of God's Messiah. It is about how to 'enter the kingdom of heaven', how to be a citizen in the new, eschatological community (cf. 5.3–10; 7.13–14).

This constructive aspect is by far the most important. In the flow of the narrative from the genealogy and birth story on, the sermon comes as one more act of divine revelation: the teaching of the Messiah is all part of the gift of the Messiah as 'God with us'. This is important. It helps us to recognize that the sermon is not law as a preparation for the gospel (as in classic Lutheran doctrine), nor is it some kind of radical, unsustainable 'interim ethic' to fill the gap until the kingdom of God finally comes (as in some forms of liberal Protestantism). Rather, the sermon is intrinsic to the gospel as utterly realistic teaching on the virtues and practices that make true human community under God possible.

Here, attention may be drawn to just a few points. First, the sermon begins with words of blessing (the Beatitudes) and ends with words of warning, as if to say: God's grace, understood as blessing, is not 'cheap grace' – revelation of the way to life brings with it the serious responsibility to respond in obedience. What is important is not just to hear the teaching of Jesus, but to do it as well (7.21–7). The one who hears but does not act lacks integrity. His is the type of character identified as that of the 'hypocrite' (e.g. 6.2, 5, 16; 7.5; etc.).

Second, that it begins with words of blessing on 'the poor' and 'those who mourn' is significant. This is an allusion to the prophecy of Isa 61.1–2, 'The Spirit of the Lord God is upon me, because the Lord has anointed me to bring good tidings to the afflicted [poor], he has sent me to bind up the brokenhearted, to . . . proclaim the year of the Lord's favour . . . to comfort all who mourn.' In other words, the Beatitudes (along with the sermon as a whole) have an eschatological thrust: they represent the fulfilment of God's promise to redeem Israel. They make clear also that readiness to respond requires hearts, minds and wills that are appropriately prepared.

Third, the sermon as a whole has three main parts: a preamble, which includes the Beatitudes (5.3–16); a central section, which begins and ends with the claim that the teaching Jesus offers fulfils 'the law and the prophets' (5.17—7.12), and a conclusion (7.13–27). Arguably, at the heart of the central section, is the Lord's Prayer (6.9–13).[10] Seen in relation to the Lord's Prayer, therefore, the sermon is teaching about how to live, both inwardly and outwardly, for all who call God 'Father' and who live in God's presence as God's 'children'. It is about how to 'hallow' or sanctify God's name, how to anticipate in the present the life of God's kingdom still to come, how to do God's will on earth as it is done in heaven.

Fourth, the fundamental precept underlying the exposition of what it means to do God's will is the love commandment. Elsewhere, in response to a lawyer's question, Jesus replies that the 'great commandment' is love of God and love of neighbour, and that 'On these two commandments depend all the law and the prophets' (22.40). Here in the Sermon on the Mount, the 'law and the prophets' (5.17; 7.12) are expounded and elaborated also in terms of love. So, for example, the first 'Antithesis' (so called because it takes the form, 'You have heard that it was said . . . But I say to you . . .') prohibits anger against one's 'brother' (as the best way to observe the prohibition on murder in the Decalogue) and advocates reconciliation (5.21–6). The sixth and final Antithesis goes further: from love of one's 'brother' to love of one's enemy (5.43–7). In between, the other Antitheses advocate the practice of love in disciplines relating to sexual relations and marriage, truth-telling and retaliation (5.27–42). Furthermore, the principle Jesus enunciates at the end of the central section of the sermon is a form of the Golden Rule – 'So whatever you wish that men would do to you, do also to them' (7.12a) – itself a version of the command to 'love your neighbour as yourself'.

There is no doubt that the Sermon on the Mount is a demanding articulation of what it means to be the 'salt of the earth' and the 'light of the world' (5.13, 14), what it means to practise a 'righteousness' greater than that of the scribes and Pharisees (5.20). But in Matthew's understanding, this is necessarily the case. Practice of the 'greater righteousness' is a corollary of the revelation of the Son of God and the coming of the kingdom of God. It is an expression of what it means to be 'blessed' (5.3–12). It also offers a warrant for the claim that Jesus, even more than Moses and those who follow Moses, shows the way to life (cf. 7.13–14, 15–20; also 12.6, 41, 42). Nor are readers of Matthew left wondering how on earth such righteousness might be possible. As we saw earlier in the account of the temptation, the life of Jesus is exemplary in this very respect. Jesus, according to Matthew, embodies the 'greater righteousness', and it is Jesus who, according to the word of promise with which the gospel ends, is 'with' his people always (28.20).

THE DEEDS OF THE MESSIAH (MATTHEW 8–9)

If, according to the teaching of Jesus, the righteous person is the one who not only hears God's will but also puts it into practice (cf. 7.21–3, 24–7), then Matthew shows us that this is supremely true of Jesus himself. Thus, immediately following the account of Jesus' teaching in Matt 5–7 comes an account of Jesus' deeds of mercy in Matt 8–9. Nor is the sequence of the narrative the only tell-tale sign of how word and deed are uniquely present in Jesus' ministry. The entire block of material is bracketed by essentially identical statements which summarize Jesus' activity as one of teaching/preaching and healing: 'Jesus went throughout Galilee, teaching in their synagogues and proclaiming the good news of the kingdom and curing every disease and every sickness among the people . . . Then Jesus went about all the cities and villages, teaching in their synagogues, and proclaiming the good news of the kingdom, and curing every disease and every sickness' (4.23; 9.35).

The healing stories themselves are drawn from Markan and non-Markan source material: but Matthew organizes them into three groups (8.2–15; 8.23—9.8; 9.18–34) and interprets them in his own way.[11] For example, in 8.2–4, he takes over from Mk 1.40–5 the story of the healing of the leper, but abbreviates the ending significantly in order to leave the emphasis on the authority of Jesus' word of command and his conformity with torah (cf. 5.17–19). Elsewhere, paradoxically, he shows a fondness for expansion and repetition: the healing of the dumb demoniac in 9.32–4 is repeated in a modified form in the healing of the blind and dumb demoniac in 12.22–4; and the healing of the two blind men in 9.27–31 is recapitulated and expanded in the healing of the two blind men – in Mark's parallel there is only one blind man, named Bartimaeus (Mk 10.46–52)! – in 20.29–34.

Like the teaching, the healing miracles are revelatory both of Jesus' authority as Messiah and Son of David and of God's gracious presence to Israel and the nations in and through him. As part of this general framework of understanding, a number of Matthean tendencies are evident. First, there is a heightening of Jesus' dignity and authority: he is addressed as 'lord' (*kurios*) (e.g. 8.2, 6, 8, 25; 9.28; etc.) and 'Son of David' (e.g. 9.27; 12.23; 21.9, 15); suppliants kneel before him (e.g. 8.2; 9.18; 14.33; 15.25); *all* who come to him are healed (e.g. 4.23–4; 8.16; 12.15; 14.35; 15.37); and his healings take place 'from that hour' (8.13; 9.22; 15.28; 17.18). Second, the theme of faith is highlighted in the recurring imperative, 'according to your faith be it done to you' (8.13; 9.29; 15.28) and in the attention drawn to the problem of those of 'little faith' (in 6.30; 8.26; 14.31; 16.8; 17.20). Third, the healings are interpreted as the fulfilment of scripture, as in the summary statement, 'That evening they brought to him many who were possessed with demons; and he cast out the spirits with a word, and cured all who were sick. This was to fulfil what had been spoken through the prophet Isaiah, "He took our infirmities and bore our diseases"' (8.16–17; cf. Isa 53.4). Fourth, there are intimations in the miracle stories of the privileges and demands of life in the Christian community. Interesting in this connection is the way Matthew concludes the healing of the paralytic: 'When the crowds saw it [i.e. the paralysed man walking], they were afraid, and they glorified God, *who had given such authority to men*' (9.8; contrast Mk 2.12). Even more interesting is the episode, unique to Matthew, of the story of Peter walking on the water to Jesus (14.28–33), with its intimations of the need of disciples for faith in times of crisis.

At the same time, however, as well as their essentially positive role, the acts of healing also play a role in the growing division over Jesus between those who believe and follow and those who remain in unbelief. A significant intimation of this is the jarring intrusion into the story of the healing of the centurion (8.5–13) of the word of warning that 'many will come from east and west and will eat with Abraham and Isaac and Jacob in the kingdom of heaven, *while the heirs of the kingdom will be thrown into outer darkness*' (8.11–12; contrast Lk 7.9–10). Another intimation of the same are the sayings about the homelessness of the Son of Man and the warnings of the cost of discipleship (8.18–22). Indeed, it is noticeable that the calling of disciples and teaching about discipleship is intertwined with the healing miracles (cf. also 9.9–13, 14–17) just as dissent with the Pharisees escalates (9.11–13, 34).

It is evident, then, that a parting of the ways is taking place. The ministry of Jesus in word and deed manifests God's salvific presence, and this ministry is to be continued and expanded in the mission of the disciples (cf. 10.1, 7–8a); but this represents, at the same time, a rebuke to Israel's failed leadership. As the evangelist, alluding to Ezekiel's prophetic condemnation of Israel's leaders in an earlier time (Ezek 34), puts it: 'When he saw the crowds, he had compassion on them, because they were harassed and helpless, *like sheep without a shepherd*' (9.36). Not surprisingly, therefore, in the episodes that follow, Jesus' words of revelation and acts of compassion take place against the backdrop of growing resistance led especially by the Pharisees.

THE TRANSFIGURATION OF THE MESSIAH (MATTHEW 17.1–9)

As if to show how misplaced such resistance is, the evangelist provides, at the heart of his gospel, the remarkable account of the transfiguration of Jesus, which he takes over from Mark (Mk 9.2–8) and develops in his own way.[12] Prominent again is the implicit and polemical (for the Pharisees in particular!) claim that Jesus is greater than Moses. For example, Matthew adds to Mark's version the striking detail that Jesus' face 'shone like the sun' (17.2), an obvious reminder of the testimony about Moses in Ex 34.29 that 'the skin of Moses' face shone because he had been talking with God' (cf. also Philo, *Life of Moses* 2.70; and Paul, in 2 Cor 3.7–18). So Matthew makes the connection clear: what happened to Jesus on the mountain is comparable with nothing less than the revelation to Moses on Mount Sinai.

However, it is also the case that Jesus' shining face and glistening white garments are a reminder of traditions in Jewish and Christian apocalyptic that, at the end of time, the righteous will be transformed gloriously and clothed in white. For example, in the interpretation of the eschatological parable of the weeds, Jesus says that, after the wicked have been thrown by the angels into the fiery furnace, 'the righteous will *shine like the sun* in the kingdom of their Father' (13.43). Later on, in Matthew's version of the parable of the great feast, attention is drawn to the hapless wedding guest who has no (presumably white) wedding garment (22.11–14). And at the resurrection, the angel who appears to the women at the tomb is described thus: 'His appearance was like lightning, and his raiment white as snow' (28.3). So a good case can be made for the view that Matthew, like Mark, understands the transfiguration of Jesus in apocalyptic terms as a disclosure in the present, and to a select few, of Jesus' glory as God's Son, a glory hidden for the most part but soon to be revealed at the resurrection. The 'greater than Moses' theme is subordinate, therefore, to what for Matthew is even more important: the theme of Jesus as the divine Son of God.

The revelation of Jesus' heavenly glory (in the presence of the two heavenly beings, Moses and Elijah) at this midpoint in the gospel does not stand in splendid isolation. Rather, it is part of the larger central section which begins with Peter's declaration at Caesarea Philippi that Jesus is 'the Christ, *the Son of the living God*' (16.16; contrast Mk 8.30b). It also resonates with the baptism and the temptation earlier on in the gospel, and with Gethsemane, the passion and the resurrection, at the end of the gospel. So, for example, Matthew more than Mark makes the alignment of the transfiguration and the baptism quite explicit. The words of the heavenly voice are verbatim the same: 'This is my beloved Son, *with whom I am well pleased*' (3.17; 17.5; contrast Mk 9.7b). And at the temptation, it is Jesus' divine sonship which Satan puts repeatedly to the test. Significantly, Jesus' refusal of the (premature) glory Satan offers him at the temptation is shown now to be vindicated in this disclosure at the transfiguration of the greater glory given him by God.

The transfiguration is also an anticipation of the testing and vindication of Jesus' sonship in the events of the passion. Just as, in the middle of the gospel, Caesarea Philippi is the testing ('Get behind me, Satan! You are a stumbling-block to me', 16.23) and the transfiguration the proleptic vindi-cation, so at the gospel's end, Gethsemane and the events of the passion are the final testing and the resurrection the ultimate vindication. And, as at the transfiguration, the vindiction is displayed in the language and imagery of apocalyptic: the presence of God is manifest in apocalyptic events presa-ging the end of the age – the rending of the Temple curtain, the earthquake, the opening of the tombs, the resurrection of the saints, the angelophany at the empty tomb and, of course, the appearances of the risen Son of God himself.

THE RESURRECTION OF THE MESSIAH (MATTHEW 28.1–20)

If the way Matthew begins his gospel is significant, so also is the way he ends it. And just as he modifies and augments his Markan source at the beginning, so he does also at the end.[13] For example, where Mark has the women wondering who would roll the stone from the tomb, Matthew obliges with an earthquake and a strong and dazzlingly bright angel; where Mark has the (three) women fleeing in terror from the mysterious 'young man' and saying nothing to anyone, Matthew has the (two) women departing 'with fear *and great joy*' and going in obedience to tell the disciples; where Mark shows no concern that the empty tomb might be explained away as a case of body-snatching, Matthew provides guards at the tomb and, subsequently, a cover-up plot by a perfidious Jewish leadership; most striking of all, where Mark has no appearances of the risen Christ, Matthew has two, the first to the women as they leave the tomb, the second to the eleven disciples on a mountain in Galilee.

It is as if, where Mark wants to emphasize the mystery of the divine action, such that concealment on God's side and misunderstanding on the human side are part of the very essence of things, Matthew wants to provide sure grounds for faith.[14] His motivation is likely to be a reflection, at least in part, of his historical and social context. In response to hostility and disbelief from his compatriots in Judaism given expression in denials of the resurrection and in social and religious ostracism, Matthew offers clear warrants both for resurrection faith and for mission beyond Israel to all nations. At the same time, Matthew ends his gospel in a way that skilfully draws together themes running through the gospel as a whole.

This is especially true of 28.16–20, the account of the resurrection appearance to the eleven disciples.[15] Here, we note first that this appearance story has the form of a biblical commissioning. Like the commissioning of Moses in Ex 3.1—4.16, for example, there is a mountain setting, an encounter with a heavenly being, a reaction (typically of awe and fear), the giving of a commission to lead the people, and a reassuring promise of God's enabling presence. This form-critical observation is important. On the one hand, it provides us with clues about the kinds of literary influences which shaped the Matthean tradition. On the other hand, it makes the theological point that the resurrection is not an end in itself: rather, it is characteristic of how God acts. As in times past God has acted to save his people by calling and sending deliverers (like Moses), so now the risen Son of God continues that work by sending on mission those whom he himself has called and trained.

Second, there is the significance of the location. Galilee is significant because it takes the reader back to the very beginning of Jesus' ministry, as if to say that the disciples – who themselves were called in Galilee – are to continue what Jesus began (cf. 4.12–25). It also looks forward, because, identified at the first as 'Galilee *of the Gentiles*' (4.15), it speaks of the mission to all nations yet to come. The reference to 'the mountain' functions similarly. It speaks of revelation and of Jesus' authority as the Son of God. It points back to the mountain of temptation where Jesus rejects demonic authority; also to the mountain where Jesus teaches the people as a kind of 'new Moses'; also to the mountain where Jesus is transfigured and his heavenly glory proleptically revealed. It also points forward to the ministry which the risen Jesus now is commissioning them to do. What is being conveyed overall is a strong sense that the end of the story is like its beginning – because it is a *new* beginning. The disciples are to do what Jesus has done and shown them to do. They are to recapitulate in their lives what Jesus taught and did in his. Matthew's understanding of discipleship, therefore, has at its heart *the imitation of Christ*.[16]

Noteworthy, thirdly, are the encounter and the reaction: 'And when they saw him, they worshipped him; but some doubted [or, and they hesitated]'

(28.17). Worship as the appropriate response to the presence of the God-with-us in Jesus is a favourite theme of Matthew: the magi worship (2.2, 8, 11); so does a leper (8.2), a ruler of the people (9.18), the disciples, when Jesus comes to them walking on the water (14.33), the Canaanite woman (15.25), and so on – not forgetting the two Marys, who meet the risen Jesus at the empty tomb (28.9). Disciples are to be worshippers, for in Jesus they have encountered God.

But Matthew also says, 'and some doubted' (NRSV): or we should probably translate the Greek, 'and they hesitated. And [i.e. in response to their hesitation] Jesus came . . .'[17] Like Peter, who also 'hesitates' (same word, *distazō*) when walking on the water to Jesus (14.31), the disciples are unsure. They do not know what to do next, what the resurrection means for them. So Jesus offers gracious clarification in the form of a final word of revelation.

This brings us to the so-called 'great commission' itself. It begins with the Risen One's testimony to the status God has bestowed on him in virtue of his obedience even unto death as God's Son and in fulfilment of the messianic hope of Israel (cf. Dan 7.13–14): 'All authority in heaven and on earth has been given to me' (28.18b). What has been a point of temptation and a source of controversy during his ministry has now been settled definitively. Jesus now has '*all* authority' – and not only on earth (which is all that Satan could offer him, 4.8–9), but in heaven as well, since it has been given him by God. Significantly, the adjective 'all' occurs four times: '*All* authority . . . *all* nations . . . *all* that I have commanded you . . . *all* the days'. What it conveys is the comprehensiveness of Jesus' authority, the universal scope of his ongoing mission, the completeness of the teaching he has given them to pass on, and the constancy of his protecting and guiding presence with them.

Then comes a threefold sequence of imperatives: go and make disciples; baptize in the threefold name; and teach all that Jesus has commanded. The disciples (*mathētai*) are themselves 'to disciple' (*mathēteusate*) others just as Jesus has made disciples by calling them. They are to bring new disciples into the Christian brotherhood through the rite of baptism, just as Jesus himself was baptized, except that now, baptism is baptism into the threefold name of Father, Son and Holy Spirit – a 'name' which sums up the message and story of the gospel as a whole. And they are to teach new disciples all that Jesus has taught them, both in what he said and in the way he lived and died.

This is a tall order. That is why the words of commissioning end, not on the note of command, but of promise: 'And behold! I am with you all the days, to the close of the age' (28.20). Just as the gospel begins with the revelation that Jesus is Immanuel, God with us (1.23), and as in the middle it contains the promise of the presence of Jesus 'where two or three are gathered . . .' (18.20), so too at the end there is the great word of promise and encouragement in the revelation of the ongoing presence of the risen Son of God with his people.

So Matthew's gospel, in distinct contrast to the Gospel of Mark, ends on a very positive note. But – and in this respect it is not so unlike Mark – it also ends in a way which is *open-ended*. Yes, there is the resurrection of the Son of God and the saints (27.52–53); but the general resurrection has not taken place, and the news that the new age is breaking in needs urgently to be proclaimed abroad. Yes, in fulfilment of Israel's messianic hopes the Son of God has come and has received from the Father 'all authority'; but that authority is not yet acknowledged among the nations. Yes, the disciples have been taught by Jesus and have learned from him; but it remains to be seen whether they will do what they have been commissioned to do once they come down from the mountain.

It is this openendedness that makes the gospel ending both a conclusion to what has gone before and a beginning to all that is yet to come and all that is yet to be done. And for some readers and hearers, at least, this will constitute something of an invitation: to make the ending of the gospel a point of new departure.

Notes

1. For a discussion of the complex textual and historical data concerning the canonical gospels, see Martin Hengel, *The Four Gospels and the One Gospel of Jesus Christ* (London: SCM, 2000). On Matthew's acceptance as the first gospel of the fourfold gospel see especially 76–8.
2. See further David Orton, *The Understanding Scribe: Matthew and the Apocalyptic Ideal* (Sheffield: JSOT Press, 1989).
3. See most recently Richard C. Beaton, 'How Matthew Writes', in Markus Bockmuehl and Donald A. Hagner, eds., *The Written Gospel* (Cambridge: Cambridge University Press, 2005), 116–34.
4. See, for example, J. Andrew Overman, *Matthew's Gospel and Formative Judaism* (Minneapolis: Fortress, 1990); also, David L. Balch, ed., *Social History of the Matthean Community: Cross-Disciplinary Approaches* (Minneapolis: Fortress, 1991). For an excellent overview of scholarly opinion, see Donald A. Hagner, 'The *Sitz im Leben* of the Gospel of Matthew', in David R. Bauer et al., eds., *Treasures New and Old: Recent Contributions to Matthean Studies* (Atlanta: Scholars Press, 1996), 27–68.
5. Graham N. Stanton, *A Gospel for a New People: Studies in Matthew* (Edinburgh: T. & T. Clark, 1992), 168.
6. Krister Stendahl, '*Quis et Unde*? An Analysis of Matthew 1–2', in Graham N. Stanton, ed., *The Interpretation of Matthew* (London: SPCK, 1983), 56–66.

7. For a full exploration of the influence of Moses tradition on Matthew's story of Jesus, see Dale C. Allison, *The New Moses: A Matthean Typology* (Minneapolis: Fortress Press, 1993).

8. See further Birger Gerhardsson, *The Testing of God's Son* (Lund: Gleerup, 1966); also Jeffrey B. Gibson, *The Temptations of Jesus in Early Christianity* (Sheffield: JSOT Press, 1995).

9. Among a considerable literature, see Ulrich Luz, *The Theology of the Gospel of Matthew* (Cambridge: Cambridge University Press, 1995), 42–61; also Dale C. Allison, *The Sermon on the Mount: Inspiring the Moral Imagination* (New York: Crossroad, 1999).

10. So Luz, *Matthew*, 49.

11. Foundational are the essays by Gunther Bornkamm and H. J. Held in Gunther Bornkamm et al., *Tradition and Interpretation in Matthew* (ET, London: SCM Press, 1963). For a recent discussion, see Luz, *Matthew*, 62–80.

12. See further Stephen C. Barton, 'The Transfiguration of Christ according to Mark and Matthew: Christology and Anthropology', in Friedrich Avemarie and Hermann Lichtenberger, eds., *Auferstehung – Resurrection* (Tübingen: Mohr Siebeck, 2001), 231–46.

13. See further Morna Hooker, *Endings: Invitations to Discipleship* (London: SCM Press, 2003), 31–47.

14. This point is explored nicely in J. L. Houlden, *Backward into Light: The Passion and Resurrection of Jesus according to Matthew and Mark* (London: SCM Press, 1987).

15. Famous on this is Otto Michel, 'The Conclusion of Matthew's Gospel: a Contribution to the History of the Easter Message', in Stanton, *The Interpretation of Matthew*, 30–41.

16. Valuable on discipleship in general is Terence L. Donaldson, 'Guiding Readers – Making Disciples: Discipleship in Matthew's Narrative Strategy', in Richard N. Longenecker, ed., *Patterns of Discipleship in the New Testament* (Grand Rapids: Eerdmans, 1996), 30–49.

17. So, too, R. W. L. Moberly, *The Bible, Theology, and Faith: A Study of Abraham and Jesus* (Cambridge: Cambridge University Press, 2000), 191–193.

Further reading

Allison, Dale C., *The New Moses: A Matthean Typology* (Minneapolis: Fortress, 1993)

Aune, David, ed., *The Gospel of Matthew in Current Study* (Grand Rapids: Eerdmans, 2001)

Balch, David L., ed., *Social History of the Matthean Community* (Minneapolis: Fortress, 1991)

Bauer, David R. et al., eds., *Treasures New and Old. Recent Contributions to Matthean Studies* (Atlanta: Scholars Press, 1996)

Howell, David B., *Matthew's Inclusive Story* (Sheffield: Sheffield Academic Press, 1990)

Luz, Ulrich, *The Theology of the Gospel of Matthew* (Cambridge: Cambridge Universtiy Press, 1995)

Overman, J. Andrew, *Matthew's Gospel and Formative Judaism* (Minneapolis: Fortress, 1990)

Saldarini, Anthony J., *Matthew's Christian-Jewish Community* (Chicago: Chicago University Press, 1994)

Sim, David C., *The Gospel of Matthew and Christian Judaism* (Edinburgh: T. & T. Clark, 1998)

Senior, Donald, *What Are They Saying About Matthew?*, rev. ed. (New York, Paulist, 1996)

Stanton, Graham N., ed., *The Interpretation of Matthew* (London: SPCK, 1983)

Stanton, Graham N., *A Gospel for a New People: Studies in Matthew* (Edinburgh: T. & T. Clark, 1992)

7 The Gospel according to Mark

JOEL B. GREEN

THE GOSPEL OF MARK: INTRODUCTORY QUESTIONS

More than one hundred years ago, Martin Kähler spoke of the gospels as 'passion narratives with extended introductions'.[1] Although directed at all four of our New Testament gospels, subsequent research took this as a description especially of the Gospel of Mark. This label is now dismissed as overly simplistic, and rightly so, given the importance of Mk 1–10, chapters too easily marginalized when relegated to the status of mere introduction. Nevertheless, Kähler's formulation helpfully underscores the centrality of the cross of Christ to the Gospel of Mark at the same time as drawing attention to the fact that Mark's narration from Jesus' entry into Jerusalem to the empty tomb occupies fully one-third of the gospel. Indeed, there is no coming to terms with this gospel – its spirituality, christology, theology, ethical vision and so on – without giving maximal consideration to Jesus' ignominious demise at the hands of Roman justice. Perhaps more importantly, we have in Kähler's statement a reminder that the cross of Christ is cast within a larger plot, from which it draws its profound significance. How it does so is perhaps the central question confronting those who read and study Mark's narrative.

This is not only because the crucifixion of Jesus is woven so pervasively – sometimes with subtlety, often explicitly – into the fabric of the narrative. It is also to recognize that the cross is capable of multiple interpretations, and that Mark's gospel presses its readers in a particular direction as they seek both to make sense of Mark's perspective on Jesus of Nazareth and to embody his vision of discipleship. As Paul Veyne rightly observes, the execution of Christ is worth mentioning at all, and so gains its interpretative significance, only within a narrative sequence, a plot.[2] And this means that, in reading this gospel, we will want to take with seriousness that this narrative, like all narratives, is the fruit of selectivity and arrangement. Assuming that Mark's gospel comes to an abrupt conclusion in 16.8 ('So they went out and fled from the tomb, for terror and amazement had seized them; and they said nothing to anyone, for they were afraid'),[3] what purpose is served by Mark's decision not to recount, as the other gospels do, scenes depicting the resurrection and appearance of Jesus? Why has Mark chosen to give fear the last word, so to speak, when the existence of communities of Jesus' followers at the time of Mark's writing and, indeed, the very fact that he has written his gospel, bear witness to the eventual faithfulness of these witnesses of the empty tomb and angelophany? With regard to Mark's ordering of events, what purpose is served by the plentiful references to the impending death of Jesus that seem to spoil the terrain of the gospel's early chapters, which otherwise evidence the growth of Jesus' popularity, the acclaim he attracts as a teacher, healer and wonder-worker? The juxtaposition of these images, popular acclaim and the shadow of heinous execution, raises early in the narrative the irony that surfaces explicitly in the voices of his tormenters at the end, 'He saved others; he cannot save himself' (15.31). Finally, every narrator struggles with the problem of a beginning: How to indicate the logic whereby initial events are shown to be the product of forces within the discourse itself rather than a given reported by the narrative.[4] If narratives are characterized by their being constituted by a beginning, a middle and an end, then the question, 'Where does Mark's narrative begin?' becomes all the more crucial.

That such questions might be addressed to the Gospel of Mark may seem wrongheaded, given the contours of the history of its interpretation. Only very recently has the particular narrative quality of this text (and with it, the other gospels, and Acts as well) been taken seriously. Voicing what was already a prevalent view, Augustine concluded that the Gospel of Mark was an abridgement of Matthew (*Harmony of the Gospels* 1.2.4), effectively relegating Mark's narrative to the margins of the church. Backed by a tradition associating the narrative and its author with the apostle Peter, Mark remained in the gospel collection, but only to dwell in the shadows of Matthew and Luke, on the one hand, with which Mark shares the substance of all but some two dozen of its verses, and, on the other hand, of John, a gospel that was deemed theologically superior. The early church has provided us with no real commentary on the Gospel of Mark, for example. In the latter half of the eighteenth century, Mark began to be rediscovered, and by the end of the nineteenth it was widely regarded as the earliest of the four gospels. Its importance was assessed along quite divergent lines, however. For some, Mark's gospel was the oldest and presumed therefore to be the most trustworthy, with the result that it was examined primarily as a source book for constructing the many 'lives of Jesus' that stocked bookshelves of the late nineteenth century. The narrative quality of Mark's achievement was not considered, however. Instead, his gospel was imagined as a depository of raw materials from which modern folk could draw as they wove their own narratives concerning Jesus. For others, the gospel was regarded as tendentious through and through, devoid of historical content but nonetheless of interest as a window into first-century religion. In the twentieth century, the second evangelist moved into the limelight of critical scrutiny, but this new-found fame was not necessarily welcome. His Greek was often dismissed as barbaric, his potential contribution to the New Testament disparaged as a scissors-and-paste job. Reflecting the modern dichotomy segregating 'facts' and 'interpretation', which continues to plague much of the ongoing research on the historical Jesus, this early work on Mark could not conceive of Mark the evangelist as a narrative theologian. When interest in *narrative* did enter the world of gospels study, it did so first with reference to the Gospel of Mark, but only in the twilight years of the last century.[5]

What of the traditional association of the Gospel of Mark with the apostle Peter? Like the other New Testament gospels, this one is anonymous. The author makes no self-reference within the narrative by which we might identify him, nor has he 'signed' his account. The title, 'The Gospel according to Mark', was added subsequent to the gospel's completion. This anonymity may be the result of a deliberate decision on the part of the author – who thus directed attention away from his own creative contribution and toward the subject of his work, the coming of God in Jesus of Nazareth. It might signal as well the degree to which the material woven into the gospel narrative, and perhaps even the basic framework of the gospel itself, was traditional by the time of its being recounted in this fashion. Alternatively, it might be that the author would simply have assumed that his audience knew who he was. These choices are not mutually exclusive, of course. At the same time, we should remind ourselves in the case of this last possibility that 'authorship' was not so closely guarded a practice in antiquity as it has become in the last two or three centuries, especially in the west. Even if we should attribute the completion of the Gospel of Mark in its final form to one person, this would not preclude the heavy influence of tradition nor the role of the author's own worshipping community in the unfolding of the narrative.

According to the earliest available tradition, this gospel was written by 'Mark', the interpreter of Peter – thus Eusebius quotes Papias, who himself credits 'the Elder' as the source of this information (Eusebius, *Church History* III 39.15):

This also the elder says: Mark, who was the interpreter of Peter, wrote down carefully, but not in the right order, everything that he remembered, both what had been said by the Lord and also what had been done by him. For he had neither seen nor had he followed the Lord, but later (he followed) . . . Peter, who shaped his teachings to the needs (of the hearers), however, not in such a way that he gave an orderly account of the sayings of the Lord. So Mark did not make a mistake in writing down some things as he remembered them. For he had one concern, not to omit anything that he had heard or to falsify anything in it.

This tradition, which probably dates back to the turn of the second century CE, is picked up and echoed in the latter part of that century by Irenaeus and Clement of Alexandria. What do we learn? First, although it can be read as a defence of the gospel in terms of accuracy and with reference to apostolic authority, this statement is also critical of Mark. He was not an eyewitness and his account is not 'orderly' – presumably, in contrast to what was judged to be the superior work of Luke (Lk 1.1–4). Second, it opens the way for us to consider Mark's creative contribution, since 'the Elder' reports that Peter passed on to his interpreter only anecdotes while Mark has provided a full-blown narrative. This encourages the view that Mark's innovation consisted above all in the choice of episodes to recount and in the way he has woven them together to signal causality and purpose, rather than in the wholesale creation of episodes apart from the tradition available to him.

This is consistent with the literary form of Mark's gospel, which conforms most closely to the genre of biography, a form of Greco-Roman literature that grew out of the practice of historiography as particular persons became the focus of study and writing. Early on, biographies, like historiography, proceeded along roughly chronological lines, as is the case with Mark. This is not to say that the literary efforts of Mark were shaped under the influence only of contemporary Greco-Roman literature. A complete accounting for the character of this work cannot overlook the important influence of Old Testament and subsequent Jewish historiography, not least in their shared undertaking to represent the outworking of the divine will in historical narratives. Even if no Old Testament books have the look of the Gospel of Mark, parts of some of those books, such as the Abraham-cycle or the Elijah narrative, are suggestive precursors, and this is a reminder of the potential debt Mark has to Old Testament faith.

In referring to Mark as 'biography', we should remember not to conceive of Mark's book on the analogy of those biographies with which we are most familiar today. Psychological motivations, childhood influences, physical appearance, date of birth – these and other data figure prominently in our expectations of contemporary biography, but have little or no role to play in the Greco-Roman world. In antiquity a biography related the significance of a famous person's career, rarely focusing on his childhood but often including reference to the way he died (for how a person dies was regarded as a measure of his character). Moreover, 'famous' persons acquired their fame not so much through their individuality, their standing out from the crowd, since the modern, western conception of individuality had little place in Roman antiquity, where the identity and importance of persons were determined in relation to their groups of reference. Thus, an individual might be represented in a biography because he exemplified the qualities valued by society. An initial reason for regarding the Gospel of Mark as having been written primarily for Christian communities rather than as an evangelistic tool for non-Christians is the degree to which it assumes that its readers would have admired and begun already to adopt the unconventional values proclaimed and lived by Jesus.

Returning to the report of Eusebius, we may add that there is no reason to reject out of hand the association of the Gospel of Mark with Peter, even if the picture painted by Eusebius must be regarded as simplified. Mark, after all, is not providing a record of events for the sake of posterity, as though the written word would have been put forward to supplant oral tradition. Rather, he is presenting a narrative whose intent would have been persuasive, oriented as it is to encourage a particular understanding of Jesus' ministry and execution, together with particular responses to this Jesus. But who is this 'Mark'? *Markus* was a common name in the Roman world, so, again, we owe it to popular tradition that the 'Mark' who came to be associated with the production of this gospel is none other than the 'John Mark' of Acts 12.12, 25; 13.13; 15.37–9; Phlm 24; Col 4.10; 2 Tim 4.11; 1 Pet 5.13 – and, thus, a sometime companion of both Paul and Peter.

In the end, however, little is gained for the interpreter by identifying the author of Mark's gospel as 'Mark', even if this person was in fact 'John Mark'. This is because we know next to nothing about this Mark *except what we can glean from the gospel itself.* In the terminology of literary study, the 'author' of the Gospel of Mark to whom we have most direct access, then, is the 'implied author'; this is the implicit image of the author that shines in and through the narrative text itself. The author of Mark, for example, would thus clearly be one who could work in Common (*Koinē*) Greek, trafficked in regions where Latinisms have entered his vocabulary (perhaps Italy, even Rome, though other areas of the Empire marked by the heightened military or commercial presence of Rome would also be candidates), and who possessed intimacy with the Old Testament, particularly in its Greek version, and especially the Psalms, Isaiah and Zechariah. The evangelist seems to have a developed understanding of Judaism and Jewish practices, even if he writes to an audience which repeatedly requires that these be explained (e.g., 7.3–4; 12.18).

Nor can we speak with certainty about the date of the Gospel of Mark. Early tradition urges a date after Peter's death in Rome, usually assumed to be in 64 or 65 CE.[6] For further evidence, scholars often turn to the text of Mark itself. Mk 13.14, with its instructions 'to flee to the hills' at the destruction of Jerusalem, makes little sense in light of the historical realities of the Roman siege on Jerusalem. The Roman army had completely surrounded the city with a seamless blockade, making such an attempt at escape inadvisable and probably impossible. Similarly, that mention of the 'abomination of desolation' is not more directly related to the pillaging of the Temple by Titus, the Roman commander, suggests that Mk 13 was written prior to the fall of Jerusalem in 70 CE. Consequently, many date the completion of the Gospel of Mark to the latter 60s, during the Jewish War but before the destruction of Jerusalem itself. As we shall see, even this range of dates is helpful for grasping the purpose of Mark's gospel.

FINDING A BEGINNING: MARK AS THE STORY OF GOD

Having just referred to Mark's gospel as a biography of Jesus, it is necessary now to nuance that description in an important way, for there is a crucial sense in which Mark's foremost concern is not with sketching the career of Jesus. Instead, he has framed his work as a story about God. This assertion is not grounded in any claim that God enters Mark's story repeatedly as a major character. In fact, God is active only indirectly: he speaks, but his voice comes 'from heaven' or 'from the cloud' (1.11; 9.7); his will is evident through the scriptures (e.g., 14.21) or through Jesus' appeal to divine necessity (e.g., 8.31); and that the Temple curtain was ripped, as Mark puts it, 'from top to bottom' might suggest to some readers the work of divine hands (15.38). As interesting as this line of evidence might be, this is not the primary basis on which we might be led to read the story of Jesus as the story of God. Rather, Mark has framed his biography of Jesus in theological terms, in a way that structures this sequence of scenes as the emplotment of God's own story, which puts on display God's character and purpose. By 'framing', I refer to the larger mural within which Mark has included his portrait of Jesus – a mural, then, that is presumed by Mark's narrative and within which it has its significance.[7] The nature of this larger mural is signalled at the very beginning of Mark's book, in the way he has resolved 'the problem of a beginning'.

For Mark, the problem of a beginning is the need for a point of departure capable of supporting, even funding, the significance allocated to Jesus and the mission of his followers in his narrative as a whole. This issue is raised by the opening verse of the Gospel of Mark, *Archē tou euangeliou Iēsou Christou huiou theou*, usually rendered, as in the NRSV, as a kind of title or heading: 'The beginning of the good news of Jesus Christ, the Son of God.' Such a translation is potentially misleading, since it suggests that Mark's own narrative, or some part of Mark's opening chapter, is this 'beginning of the good news' – a reading that violates both the grammar and the theology of the second evangelist, as recent commentators have observed. Robert Guelich helpfully translates, 'The beginning of the gospel concerning Jesus Messiah, Son of God, as written by the prophet Isaiah.' R. T. France adopts a more traditional translation, analogous to the NRSV, but underscores nonetheless, with Guelich, that the beginning of the good news does not lie with the advent of Jesus, but with the prophet Isaiah.[8] The ongoing story within which the Gospel of Mark is located, which helps to give the story of Jesus' ministry its significance, and which is itself shaped by Mark's presentation of Jesus, has its roots in the divine promise of the liberation of Israel from the bondage of exile as this is related by the prophet Isaiah.

Throughout the scriptures of Israel, we hear that God's people understood that the activity of God, definitively expressed in the exodus, resides at the forefront of God's own memory and is a transparent window into God's own character. Images of the exodus abound. Exodus is God's own signature: 'I am the LORD your God, who brought you out of the land of Egypt, out of the house of bondage' (Ex 20.1). The exodus is celebrated annually in the festival of Passover. The exodus is the ground and warrant of torah, and the giving of torah at Sinai marks nothing less than the creation of a people whose corporate vocation was to reflect God's own character. In these and countless other texts, the scriptures of Israel weave the story of Israel's life with strands of yarn spun out of the exodus.[9]

Efforts at casting the hope of Israel in the well-formed patterns of exodus reach their zenith in Isaiah, and especially Isa 40–66. Israel is now in exile on account of its drawing back from its life as a people formed by the exodus, its having withdrawn from covenant partnership with God. What hope remains? As God had warred against Egypt so as to deliver Israel, so, when Israel patterned its life after oppressive Egypt, God had clashed with Israel. Yet, God's judgement against Israel would not be the last word. And the promise of restoration is patterned after the living memory of the exodus. In the exodus, God delivered the Hebrew people from Egyptian subjugation, forming them into his own people and leading them to the land of promise. In the new exodus, God would deliver his people from captivity and exile, restoring them as his people. In the hands of Isaiah, the exodus story is transformed for its role in the service of new exodus hope.

Locating 'the beginning of the gospel' in Isa 40, Mark lays bare his presupposition that the narrative he is about to develop has as its conceptual framework that larger story of exodus, exile and new exodus. This observation is grounded not only in the citation of Isa 40.3 in Mk 1.2–3, but in the other ways, already in his preface, in which Mark interprets the importance of Jesus within the contours of Isaianic hope: the coming of John in the wilderness (compare Mk 1.4–8 with Isa 40); the baptism of Jesus (compare Mk 1.9–11 with Isa 42.1; 61.1); Jesus in the wilderness (compare Mk 1.12–13 with Isaiah 40; 65); and Jesus' proclamation of the gospel of God (compare Mk 1.14–15 with Isa 40.9; 52.7; 61.1–2). Indeed, the boundaries of Mark's prologue are set by matching references to 'gospel' (*euangelion*) in verses 1, 14–15:

> the beginning of the gospel of Jesus Christ, the Son of God, is as it was written in the prophet Isaiah (1.1)
> Jesus came to Galilee proclaiming the gospel of God (1.14)
> 'Repent and believe the gospel' (1.15)

This intertextuality, Mark's writing his narrative into Isaianic expectation, gives substance to the 'gospel'. From one point of view, 'good news' among the Romans is the message brought from the battlefield, announcing Roman victory. 'Gospel' or 'evangel' was also used with regard to the celebration and veneration of Rome's emperor. By indicating that the story of Jesus cannot be understood except that story be read with reference to the ancient-now-present hope of Israel as this is articulated in Isaiah, Mark develops his use of 'gospel' along a different route. Longing for the age of promise, the Isaianic herald speaks of the 'good news' as the coming of God (40.9), the saving reign of God in peace and justice (52.6), the work of God on behalf of the outcast (61.1–2). On display here are Israel's hopes for divine intervention and rule, and for the restoration of God's people. At the same time, even if the narrative context Mark provides in the opening of his gospel urges the importance of reading 'evangel' in an Isaianic context rather than in strictly Roman terms, we should not too easily dismiss the juxtaposition of images that would result from hearing the reverberations of both: the sovereignty of God over against the sovereignty of Rome. Authentic peace, the promised good news of God, comes not through the subjugation of people but through their release by God, and through the restoration of God's people under God's banner of salvation.

Writing his gospel into the hope of Isaiah, and setting in parallel the two phrases 'gospel of Jesus Christ' and 'gospel of God' (1.1, 14–15), Mark indicates that the story of Jesus is at a more significant level the story of God's project coming to fruition. Mark's gospel is thus concerned with God's intervention in history to actualize the promises of scripture and to inaugurate God's reign and rule, his kingdom. In an ultimate sense, then, the Gospel of Mark is about God.

As the gospel unfolds, Mark's presentation draws on the theological and literary repertoire of the new exodus in dozens of ways. Healings and exorcisms, feeding the thousands, mastery of the sea, the motif of journeying – in these and a myriad other ways, Mark clothes Jesus in the cloth of Yahweh's servant who liberates the exiles and restores the people.[10]

This observation intimates something important about Mark's gospel – namely, that Mark's primary objective, and the primary basis of the authority of his narrative, rest in its capacity to speak on behalf of God. Historical events, even events whose central character is Jesus of Nazareth, do not generally contain within themselves their own interpretation. Mark's narrative is a presentation of Jesus' public career, to be sure, but it is one oriented toward providing a divine perspective on that career. The story of Jesus is the continuation and actualization of the story of God.

INTERWEAVING CHRISTOLOGY AND DISCIPLESHIP

Who is Jesus? A biography might be expected to address the question of the identity of its main character, and, in the Gospel of Mark, this question is front and centre. It breaks out into the open in 8.27, 29, where Jesus asks of his disciples, in turn, 'Who do people say that I am?' and 'Who do you say that I am?' By the time we reach this midpoint in the narrative, however, this issue has already become pivotal, and baffling. The crowds ask of one another, 'What is this? A new teaching – with authority!' (1.27). Demons do not ask, but seem to perceive already who Jesus is: 'I know who you are, the Holy One of God!' (1.24); 'What have you to do with me, Jesus, Son of the Most High God?' (5.7; cf. 1.34). Yet Jesus silences these voices. Though diabolical spirits recognize him, their acclamations are empty: they serve another.

Jesus' human adversaries, too, worry over his identity. In particular, they wonder about the basis of his authority: 'Where did this man get all this? What is this wisdom that has been given to him?' (6.2). 'By what authority are you doing these things?' (11.28; cf. 2.7, 16, 24; 3.21–2; 6.14–16).

Most puzzling to the reader and frustrating to Jesus is the failure of Jesus' own disciples to comprehend his identity. Even after having received private instruction (e.g., 4.34) and having 'been given the secret of the kingdom of God' (4.11), they are stunned by his mastery of the storm and sea: 'Who then is this, that even the wind and the sea obey him?' (4.41). When he comes to them walking on the sea, they take him for a ghost (6.49).

God, on the other hand, is clear about Jesus' identity. Twice God claims Jesus as 'my Son, the beloved' (1.11; 9.7), and Jesus affirms this relationship in his Gethsemane prayer: 'Abba, Father' (14.36; cf. 13.32). Moreover, when he is asked by the high priest at his trial before the Jewish Council, 'Are you the Messiah, the Son of the Blessed One?', Jesus replies, 'I am' (14.61–2). This perspective is also shared by the narrator, Mark (1.1), so it is surely of consequence that it is shared by no other human being until the very end of the story. It is true that Peter acclaims Jesus as Messiah (8.29), but his understanding of this title is manifestly deficient (8.27–33). In effect, the question of Jesus' identity is clearly central to Mark's portrayal, but just as clearly the true nature of his identity is privileged information, known only to Mark and his readers, and within the story itself only to God, Jesus, the demons, and finally the centurion at the cross: 'Truly this man was God's Son!' (15:39).

Who is Jesus? Various titles are used to name him – especially Son of Man, Son of God, and Messiah – but Mark does not depend on these to fill out Jesus' identity and significance. Rather, Mark weaves a narrative, and in doing so evidences his conviction that only a 'storied' christology will do, that our capacity to grasp the significance of Jesus in a way that can be transformative is dependent on the story of Jesus, and the embeddedness of Jesus in the story of God. In this way, the identity of Jesus must be interwoven with the character of his disciples; their story is shaped by, draws its character from, his story.

If we were to stand too close to the Markan narrative, we might be baffled by the ambiguity of Mark's portrayal of Jesus. It is precisely the genius of narrative that it can hold in tension seemingly antagonistic claims, and readers or hearers of the gospel might be forgiven for imagining that, in composing his narrative, Mark struggled with how to present two, apparently conflicting images of Jesus. When the gospel is viewed as a whole, most noticeable is its concern to portray the ministry of Jesus as a relentless progression of events leading to the crucifixion of the Messiah. One-third of the gospel is given over to the events of Jesus' last days, marked by repeated prophecies of his coming suffering and death and a detailed and dramatic presentation of his passion. More than this, in the earlier chapters of the Gospel of Mark one already encounters intimations, implicit and explicit, of swelling malice against Jesus. As early as Mk 2.18–20, Jesus anticipates his sudden, unexpected departure, and by Mk 3.1–6 antagonism has progressed to the point that Mark can record: 'The Pharisees went out and immediately conspired with the Herodians against him, how to destroy him.' This is not unanticipated, since Mark had already noted the arrest of John, who spoke on God's behalf, and would go on to relate his execution under Herod (Mk 1.14; 6.14–29). Clearly, from Mark's vantage-point, the ministry of Jesus cannot be understood apart from the cross that casts its shadow back across its entirety.

Even as it follows the Messiah's journey to Golgotha, the Markan narrative is punctuated again and again with evidence of Jesus the popular miracle-worker, powerful healer and authoritative teacher. He casts out demons, astounds his own followers by walking on the Sea of Galilee, feeds the thousands, heals the blind and lame, and confounds those who listen to him by the nature of his teaching. Throughout especially the first half of the gospel, the evangelist often prefers to *tell* his audience about Jesus the powerful teacher rather than *show* them. Early on in his gospel, Mark begins to use the literary device of summary to tell his audience what is typical of Jesus' ministry. 'The whole town gathered at the door,' he writes, 'and Jesus healed many who had diseases of various kinds. He also drove out many demons' (1.33–4). Again, 'thus he travelled throughout Galilee, preaching in their synagogues and casting out demons' (1.39). The effect is an apparently pervasive emphasis on Jesus the healer, juxtaposed with statements concerning the overwhelmingly positive and pervasive support Jesus attracted from the general populace. Evidence of Jesus' powerful ministry abounds, so that we are left with the impression that Jesus is the authoritative teacher who manifests the power of God, the herald of God's rule in whose ministry the power of God is made available.

Mark's audience is left to wonder: powerful teacher and rejected Messiah – how can Jesus be both? The key to Mark's narrative is to take it as a narrative, and this narrative *both* affirms that these two presumably competing portrayals are true *and* insists that Jesus' true identity cannot be grasped apart from the correlation of these two. Jesus not only demonstrates power but also experiences the powerlessness of rejection, suffering and death. Indeed, Jesus' activity as authoritative teacher and agent of miraculous power is the immediate cause of the hostility directed against him. He forgives sins by way of healing a paralytic, with the consequence that he is charged with blasphemy (2.1–12). He breaks the boundaries of conventional piety – eating with tax-collectors and sinners, refraining from teaching his followers to fast, and failing to keep the sabbath according to generally prescribed views – and on this basis is censured by those Pharisees who monitor his behaviour (2.13–28). He heals on the sabbath and this serves as the impetus for the first recorded organized conspiracy against him (3.1–6). Even those who admit his power attribute it to the devil (3.22), while others request a sign in order to test him (8.11). Evidently, for Mark, wondrous demonstrations of divine beneficence and hostile response do not constitute competing storylines. One folds into the other as Jesus' adversaries assert their alternative rendering of God's will, their alternative interpretations of what conduct is congruent with torah.

The integration of these two images of Jesus is demonstrated in another way as well. At the gospel's centre-point in chapter 8, Jesus asks his disciples, 'Who do you say that I am?' (8.29). Taking account of the Markan narrative from its beginning to this point, we might agree with Peter in his profession of Jesus as the Messiah of God, and mean by it that Jesus is the long-awaited deliverer, the one through whom the power of God had come to visible expression. If Jesus the authoritative, power-working teacher constitutes the melody of Mk 1–8, however, the counter-melody consists of those numerous anticipations of Jesus' passion to which we have already called attention. Mark's portrait in these first chapters is not as univocal as it might at first appear, then. Similarly, once Jesus attempts to qualify Peter's understanding of his identity by drawing together into one whole the profession of messiahship with the plain prediction of the rejection and suffering he would experience (8.31–3), suffering and death enter the conversation regularly (especially 9.31; 10.31–4). But this does not signal the end of the miraculous in Mark's narrative. Even these prophecies are indicative of Jesus' status as God's agent, supernatural portents accompany the crucifixion (see 15.38), and the gospel closes with an account of the empty tomb (16.1–8). Even in the latter half of the gospel, hostility and suffering run together with works of power and wonder.

For Mark, powerful wonder-worker and suffering servant do not form two contradictory portraits of Jesus, nor does the one correct or exclude the other; rather, together they disclose a single, integrated portrait of Jesus and his mission. *It is precisely as the worker of powerful deeds and authoritative teacher that Jesus goes to the cross.* These merge together in order to signify the full nature of his redemptive mission. 'The Son of Man came not to be served but to serve, and to give his life a ransom for many' (10.45).

To urge that these two images of Jesus are woven into a single cloth is not to remove the scandal of Mark's portrait. There is something powerfully unsettling about Mark's affirmation that powerful deeds and messianic status *and* rejection and execution are, in the case of Jesus, *both* outworkings of the divine will. There is something profoundly disturbing about the juxtaposition of Gethsemane and Golgotha, this portrait of Jesus' awareness of his filial relationship to God and faith that, for God, 'all things are possible', set in tandem with his cry of divine abandonment at his death. He who has taught that 'whatever you ask for in prayer, believe that you have received it, and it will be yours' (11.24), and who knows that God *can* rescue him from death (14.36), nevertheless gives himself to discerning and conforming to the divine will.

Swirling around the fundamental issue of Jesus' identity are two motifs: conflict and discipleship. Simply put, the disciples do not understand. They may hold the mystery of the kingdom, they may be witnesses of Jesus' powerful deeds, and they may have heard his predictions of rejection and death, but they have not been able to put these pieces together. Hence, they are stunned by Jesus' mastery of the storm and sea (4.41; 6.49). Failing to understand the identity of Jesus and the nature of his message, they reject plain talk about his suffering (8.32), puzzle over his expectation of vindication (9.10), and repeatedly fail to comport themselves as befits those who follow a Messiah who resists the status quo on issues of honour and shame and even presents himself as a servant (see 9.33–41; 10.35–45).

The Markan story of the disciples, then, is repeatedly one of disappointment, with the disciples not only lacking in understanding but actually standing in opposition to Jesus and his teaching. Instances of the motif of conflict branch out beyond the circle of Jesus' followers, though, to include diabolic forces and, especially, the Pharisees and the Jewish and Roman authorities in Jerusalem. Indeed, the disciples, like Jesus' adversaries, can be characterized by their hardness of heart (e.g., 3.6; 6.52) – that seat of evil intentions and fear – or of love and faith (e.g., 7.21; 11.23; 12.30, 33). Particularly in Galilee, the Pharisees, together with supporters of Herod, are cast consistently in the role of Jesus' opponents. The Pharisees monitor his behaviour and question his teaching and ministry practices. They plot against him and seek to entrap him (see 2.1—3.6; 12.13). Within Mark's account of Jesus' passion, their role is taken over subsequently by the chief priests, scribes and elders, who form a kind of triumvirate responsible for orchestrating Jesus' final demise. Pilate participates in these affairs so as to do the crowds a favour, according to Mark, who thus underscores again the inexorable animosity of the Jewish elite in Jerusalem.

Mark's interest in the identity of Jesus is thus not a speculative affair, as though he was concerned merely with passing on a correct understanding of the Messiah. Instead, Mark's narrative braids together these two strands, christology and discipleship, in order to show that one flows into the other. Against this backdrop, the motif of conflict serves a number of important roles in addition to adding suspense to the narrative. For example, the fact that the Jewish elite actually sides with the devil and his minions in opposing Jesus' mission signals how far the institution of the Temple and its supporters have departed from their role in God's redemptive purpose. Moreover, Mark uses the motif of conflict in order to demonstrate that even persons within the community of Jesus' followers are capable of misunderstanding and, on this basis, opposing Jesus. And Mark demonstrates that conflict is only to be expected when one identifies as Jesus had done with God's redemptive purpose.

This last point may be the most pressing. In his passion predictions, Jesus writes his expectation of suffering and death into the will of God (*dei*, 'it is necessary'), but just as quickly observes that, for those who would be his disciples, there are certain consequences that follow. 'If any want to become my followers, let them deny themselves and take up their cross and follow me. For those who want to save their life will lose it, and those who lose their life for my sake, and for the sake of the gospel, will save it' (8.34–5). 'The cup that I drink you will drink; and with the baptism with which I am baptized, you will be baptized' (10.39). The way of the Messiah is thus paved in order to serve as the way of discipleship as well, with opposition only to be expected for those who give themselves to the imitation of Christ. This is not the result of their masochistic tendencies, as though suffering were the red badge of authentic discipleship, but because the disciples are to give themselves entirely into the hands of God, to serve his purpose in a world that opposes him – and, thus, them.

What are we to make of the motif of discipleship failure in Mark's gospel? Often enough, and especially as the narrative unfolds, the disciples seem distant from Jesus in their commitments and behaviours. They receive authority to heal and to exorcize demons (3.14–15; 6.6b–13), they receive special instruction (4.11, 34), but they go on to prove themselves impotent in the face of human need (9.14–29), generally inept at grasping his message (e.g., 9.32) and full more of fear than faith (e.g., 4.40), and finally they betray, deny or abandon him (14.27–31, 43–5, 50, 66–72). They are negative examples within the narrative. At the same time, it is worth noting that Jesus' words to (potential) followers are often cast as general statements, invitations directed not only to persons within the narrative but also those outside it, Mark's own readers: 'If any want to become my followers . . .' (8.34); 'If anyone is ashamed of me and my words . . .' (8.38); 'Whoever wants to be first . . .' (9.35); 'Whoever welcomes one such child in my name . . .' (9.37). The contours of faithful discipleship are written into the fabric of the gospel, even if we find little by way of exemplars in its pages.

These images of discipleship point to the ambiguity resident in Mark's first readers, followers of Jesus, it would seem, familiar with trials of faith and persecution. The courtroom scene portrayed in 8.34–8 intimates the existence of situations in which disciples might be called upon to disavow their association with Jesus. According to 13.9, legal interrogations by both Roman and Jewish authorities are the lot of Jesus' followers. In addition, in 10.38–9 there is the surprising addition of a reference to 'persecutions' in the list of 'gifts' received by those who give up everything to follow Jesus. Trouble and persecution are anticipated in 4.17, and in 13.13 we read the stark prediction, 'You will be hated by all on account of my name.' Affliction and unrest seem to characterize the experience of Mark's audience. Indeed, the progression of Jesus' instruction in Mk 13 makes good sense within the difficult historical circumstances of the late 60s CE, circumstances that would have fuelled doubts and temptations of various kinds among disciples distant from Jesus in time and space. Such experiences of duress would naturally have raised questions about the nature of Jesus' 'victory', the character of his power and the shape of the kingdom he had proclaimed.

Some might have found in these exigencies the impetus for a retreat into end-time speculation. Others might have heard the rebel call to take up arms and to join the cause against Rome. Still others might have been tempted to leave their faith in disillusionment. Jesus advises an alternative route: 'The end is still to come. This is but the beginning of the birth pangs' (13.7). Such trials provide the arena for wakefulness, alertness, watchfulness (13.5, 9, 23, 33, 37). They furnish opportunities for discerning the presence of the kingdom of God (Mk 4) and for extending the mission to all nations (13.10). The measure of Jesus' ministry embraces powerful acts of healing and authoritative teaching, to be sure, but also service, even death, on behalf of others.

The message of Mark's gospel might have been especially welcome among persons who had already failed in the context of duress. Struggling with present, concrete expressions of discipleship failure, they may have been encouraged by the striking emphasis Mark places on the failure of

Jesus' inner circle of followers within the narrative. On the one hand, the failure (and anticipated restoration) of Jesus' own disciples would have softened the blow of parallel instances of failure in later Christian communities. Failure need not be the most resounding or final word. On the other hand, the Gospel of Mark would allow its audience to locate the perplexity and pain of persecution against a wider interpretative horizon. Suffering, according to Mark's narrative, is not a denial of one's status before God or among the people of God. Jesus, as a part of his divine mission, journeys to Jerusalem with the full knowledge that entry into Jerusalem could lead only to his shameful death.

Of course, neither does Mark attempt to glorify suffering, or urge that duress is the indisputable trademark of the faithful disciple of Jesus. Clearly, he envisions the possible death of disciples on account of their faithfulness in identifying with Jesus. But the fundamental issue for Mark is not one's capacity or willingness to embrace suffering and death. Jesus' central commitment is to fulfilling God's purpose for him, to serve the will of God foretold in the scriptures. Relying utterly on God, he becomes the object of controversy and hostility. So too must Jesus' disciples reckon with the cost of living a life radically oriented toward God in the midst of this 'sinful generation' (8.38).

MARK'S CONCLUSION

Readers of Mark face a knotty problem, created by an uncertainty in the manuscript tradition, concerning the extent of the narrative. As most contemporary translations indicate, the ending of the Gospel of Mark has been an issue of considerable concern. Given the evidence currently available, Mk 16.8 offers the most probable original ending of the Gospel of Mark: 'They went out and fled from the tomb, for they were trembling and astonished. They said nothing to anyone, for they were afraid.' None of the various endings that have been supplied are strongly attested in the manuscript tradition, nor do their style, content and vocabulary cohere with the body of the Gospel of Mark. Already in the early centuries after the publication of the Gospel of Mark, however, the possibility of closing the narrative at 16.8 proved unsatisfactory. Its apparent abruptness undoubtedly contributed to a sense of dissatisfaction, and the location of the Gospel of Mark alongside the Gospels of Matthew, Luke and John pressed this issue even further. This is because Mark alone among the New Testament gospels has failed to provide a witness to the appearances of the risen Lord. Among the attempts to address this void are the shorter and longer endings provided in most recent

English translations of the Gospel of Mark, typically separated from the end of the gospel by appropriate headings and explanations. Of course, the evidence cannot prove decisively that the gospel ended with verse 8, but, taken together, the external evidence drawn from the extant manuscript tradition and the internal evidence based on Markan style and language favour our rejecting the authenticity of the other endings proposed by the manuscript tradition.[11] Some scholars, agreeing that the current endings found in some manuscripts are non-Markan additions to the gospel, postulate that the final page or pages of Mark's narrative have been lost. This is possible, of course, but speculative and, perhaps, unnecessary.

What are we to make of the ending of Mark's gospel? If the women 'said nothing to anyone, for they were afraid', how do we know the gospel story? Most contemporary readers of Mark make sense of this strange ending by observing that the gospel anticipates the resolution of its crises outside of the narrative itself. The regathering of the disciples and their faithful witness to Jesus' person and mission (see 14.28; 16.7) are promised and fulfilled. In the same way, Jesus' promise of the Spirit's presence in the midst of persecution (13.9–13) and, indeed, the promise of his own glorious return (13.24–27; 14.62) are also to be trusted. But they will happen in the ongoing story of the good news, not within the pages of the Gospel of Mark itself.

If Mark's ending emphasizes and depends on the trustworthiness of Jesus' prophetic words, it also addresses the issue of faithful discipleship. The failure of these women disciples, who 'said nothing to anyone', matches the earlier failure of the male disciples Mark had underscored in chapters 14–15. Jesus had predicted, 'You will all fall away, for it is written, "I will strike the shepherd and the sheep will be scattered"' (14.27), and, only a short while later, Mark notes that 'everyone deserted him and fled' (14.50). To the degree, then, that Mark's own readers had identified themselves with the disciples in the Gospel of Mark, to this degree they have walked into a trap. In the end, none of the disciples – not even those faithful women who had followed Jesus from Galilee, cared for his needs, witnessed his crucifixion and prepared his body for burial (15.40–1; 16.1) – provide a model of discipleship worthy of emulation. Only one exemplar worthy of imitation remains: Jesus. Leaving his gospel open-ended in this way, Mark presses his audience of Jesus-followers to an accounting of their own participation in faithful discipleship. In the face of opposition, in bewildering and troubling times, will they, in imitation of Jesus, persist in their pronouncement of the good news of God? Will the good news of God be written in their lives, with their story taking as its point of departure this announcement, 'He has risen!' (16.6), and Jesus' promise to go before them in mission?

Notes

1. Martin Kähler, *The So-Called Historical Jesus and the Historic Biblical Christ* (ET, Philadelphia: Fortress, 1964), 80 n. 11.
2. Paul Veyne, *Writing History: Essay on Epistemology* (Middletown: Wesleyan University Press, 1984), 42.
3. The problem of the ending of Mark will be discussed below.
4. See Aristotle, *Poetics* 23.1 §1459a.17–29; Edward W. Said, *Beginnings: Intention and Method* (New York; Basic, 1975). More generally, cf. Dennis E. Smith, 'Narrative Beginnings in Ancient Literature and Theory', *Semeia* 22 (1991), 1–9; Mikeal C. Parsons, 'Reading a Beginning/Beginning a Reading: Tracing Literary Theory on Narrative Openings', *Semeia* 22 (1991), 11–31.
5. For a brief history of interpretation of the Gospel of Mark, see William R. Telford, 'Mark, Gospel of,' in *A Dictionary of Biblical Interpretation*, ed. R. J. Coggins and J. L. Houlden (London: SCM Press; Philadelphia: Trinity, 1990), 424–8. The turn to narrative in gospels study was signalled especially by the publication of David Rhoads and Donald Michie, *Mark as Story: An Introduction to the Narrative of a Gospel* (Philadelphia: Fortress, 1982).
6. See Irenaeus, *haer.* 3.1.1; and the anti-Marcionite prologue.
7. Thus Deborah Tannen, 'What's in a Frame? Surface Evidence for Underlying Expectations', in Deborah Tannen, ed., *Framing in Discourse* (New York: Oxford University Press, 1993), 14–56.
8. Robert A. Guelich, *Mark 1—8.26* (Word Biblical Commentary 34A; Dallas: Word, 1989), 3—14; R. T. France, *The Gospel of Mark* (New International Greek Testament Commentary; Grand Rapids: Eerdmans, 2002), 49–53. See also Joel Marcus, *Mark 1–8* (Anchor Bible 27; New York: Doubleday, 2000), 141–9.
9. Cf. Rikki E. Watts, 'Exodus', in T. D. Alexander and Brian S. Rosner, eds., *New Dictionary of Biblical Theology* (Leicester: Inter-Varsity Press; Downers Grove, Illinois: InterVarsity Press, 2000), 478–87.
10. See Rikki E. Watts, *Isaiah's New Exodus and Mark* (WUNT 2.88; Tübingen: Mohr Siebeck, 1997).
11. For a recent analysis, see Paul L. Danove, *The End of Mark's Story: A Methodological Study* (BIS 3; Leiden: E. J. Brill, 1993), 119–31.

Further reading

Broadhead, Edwin K., *Teaching with Authority: Miracles and Christology in the Gospel of Mark* (Sheffield: Sheffield Academic Press, 1992)

Donahue, John R., and Harrington, Richard A., *The Gospel of Mark* (Collegeville: Liturgical Press, 2002)

France, R. T., *The Gospel of Mark* (Carlisle: Paternoster Press; Grand Rapids: Eerdmans, 2002)

Garrett, Susan R., *The Temptations of Jesus in Mark's Gospel* (Grand Rapids: Eerdmans, 1998)

Horsley, R. A., *Hearing the Whole Story* (Louisville: Westminster/John Knox, 2001)

Malbon, Elizabeth Struthers, *In the Company of Jesus* (Louisville: Westminster/John Knox, 2000)

Marcus, Joel, *Mark 1–8* (New York: Doubleday, 2000)

Marshall, Christopher D. *Faith as a Theme in Mark's Narrative* (Cambridge: Cambridge University Press, 1989)

Rhoads, David, and Michie, Donald, *Mark as Story* (Philadelphia: Fortress, 1982)

Telford, W. R., *The Theology of the Gospel of Mark* (Cambridge: Cambridge University Press, 1999)

  ed., *The Interpretation of Mark* (London: SPCK, 1985)

Watts, Rikki E., *Isaiah's New Exodus and Mark* (Tübingen: Mohr Siebeck, 1997)

8 The Gospel according to Luke

JOHN T. SQUIRES

THE NATURE AND PURPOSE OF LUKE'S GOSPEL

Of the four canonical gospels, only the Gospel of Luke begins with a direct explanatory declaration (Lk 1.1–4). The first sentence is a concentrated statement, constructed in an aesthetically pleasing style, drawing on the complexities of Greek syntax. This sentence has been carefully crafted, the vocabulary has been judiciously selected, and distinct literary conventions from the Hellenistic period have been employed to disclose the intentions of the author. In this sentence – the only time the authorial first person singular is used in this gospel – the author articulates his view of the literary nature of the work, the method used in writing it, his main purpose in writing, and the audience he had in view. (The similar first-person style of Acts 1.1–5 stamps it as an additional authorial declaration at the start of the companion volume to the gospel.)

Literary nature

What kind of literature does the author write? Earlier claims that the canonical gospels are *sui generis*, being comparable to no known literature of the time, have given way to discussions of the gospels in relation to other forms of Hellenistic literature. Lk 1.1–4 bears many formal similarities to prefaces found in ancient scientific and technical manuals. The use of the term 'narrative' (*diēgēsis*) in the first clause indicates that the work is written with a definite historical purpose in mind. Certainly, many of the formal characteristics of Luke-Acts resonate with the way that 'history' was presented in the Hellenistic world; a comparison with ancient biography is particularly fruitful. Also within the very first clause, reference is made to 'the events that have been fulfilled among us' (*peplērophorēmenōn*), pointing to the motif of the fulfilment of prophecy. Implicit in this phrase is the sense of some form of divine guidance behind the story; precisely the kind of thematic centre which shaped not only the Hebrew Scripture, but also many Hellenistic histories.[1]

Method

How does the author proceed as he writes Luke-Acts? First, there is an acknowledgement that the author is aware of previous attempts to tell the same story (1.2). Modern source critics have identified such material as the Gospel of Mark, the Sayings Source (*Quelle*, or Q), and other material unique to this gospel (labelled by some as L, or Special Lukan material). The language used (*paredosan*, 'handed on') implies a faithful transmission of this material which is claimed to stretch back through early Christian preachers ('servants of the word') to individuals actually present at some of the events ('eyewitnesses').

However, the author implies some dissatisfaction with these earlier attempts to tell the story of Jesus, when he indicates that, 'after investigating everything carefully', he proceeded 'to write an orderly account' (1.3). The language used suggests a critical evaluation of the sources (*akribōs*, 'carefully'), and a deliberate reshaping of the material according to the author's design (*kathexēs*, 'orderly'). Once again, modern redaction critics observe that the Lukan treatment of the Markan material, and comparisons with Matthean material in the Q material found in Luke, are suggestive of certain theological perspectives being brought to bear on the material. The inclusion and arrangement of much of the so-called L material corroborates these perspectives; despite the chronological arrangement of its opening and closing chapters, the majority of the gospel is structured thematically. Furthermore, the technique of acknowledging but critically evaluating previous efforts is explicitly described in the prefaces of many Hellenistic histories, as well as being implicitly observable in the historical works of Hebrew scripture and of the late first-century Jew Flavius Josephus. Thus, the preface indicates that the author of Luke's gospel employs the familiar techniques of history-writing of the time, in order that he might provide his fellow believers with a clear and comprehensive account which has been carefully and critically assembled so as to be of maximum benefit for those who hear or read it.[2]

Purpose

Why does the author write? The final clause of the preface declares that this work is designed to provide 'assurance' or 'certainty' (*asphaleian*, 1.3). The NRSV translation, 'truth', evokes the sense of correct dogma or irrefutable historical fact, but points beyond this to the notion of truth as an interpretation of the material collected in the work which is pertinent and applicable to the context in which those who hear or read it are located. Hellenistic writers were explicit in noting that a good history must be for the benefit of its audience, by instilling the truth in those who read their works. The preface thus expresses the purpose of the work in terms of the historical enterprise, indicating that the author writes to encourage his fellow believers in their faith, and to equip them to bear witness to their faith in the circumstances of their daily lives.[3]

Audience

To whom does the author write? Alone among the canonical gospels, this work names its intended recipient: Theophilus (1.3; also Acts 1.1). The symbolism of this Greek name is attractive; could the work be a general treatise, directed towards all those who are 'lovers of God'? Yet Theophilus is addressed as 'most excellent', a term of respect used when addressing one's social superior. Further, the conventions of Hellenistic history dictated an acknowledgement of one's sponsor, or patron, in the introductory sentences of a work. It is most likely that Theophilus was a real person, who functioned as Luke's patron for the period of research that he undertook prior to the writing and publication of his two volumes. While dedicated to this one individual, the work was intended for lodging within the patron's library and for reading among gatherings of his friends.

Theophilus is further described as being already 'instructed' about the matters included in the work (1.4); he was thus a believer, possibly seeking more understanding or deeper insight into the story of Jesus and his followers. So the preface signals the orientation of the work to insiders; as the story of Jesus is retold, the intention appears to be to demonstrate more fully how to live as a faithful follower of Jesus.

And yet, being a Latinized Greek name, Theophilus indicates that the audience is part of the wider Hellenistic world; once more, the broader focus of Luke's gospel is in view. Discipleship takes place within the realities of life in the Roman Empire; the worldview set forth in this gospel takes its place in the marketplace of competing religious and philosophical options of the day. So, the aim of conveying 'certainty' includes providing the resources to equip the believers who hear or read the gospel with the means to explain and, if necessary, defend their beliefs within this wider world. We may call such an aim apologetic, in the sense of 'speaking forth' one's point of view. Historians often wrote with an apologetic purpose in mind, to reinforce the self-understanding of their designated audiences, and to enable them to hold to their beliefs and proclaim them with vigour as a viable option.[4]

Author

One other matter remains for consideration in this section: who wrote this work? By tradition, the author is known as 'Luke'. But this name is not to be found in the text; it first appears in a later ecclesial heading to the gospel. As the tradition develops, the author is designated as the beloved physician, a companion of Paul, referred to in Col 4.14 (see also Philm 24; 2 Tim 4.11). But there is no specific indication in the gospel that this figure is its author. Thus, the name 'Luke' is used purely by convention to designate the unknown author of this gospel. At the very least, we can say that 'Luke' was an educated person of the Hellenistic world; the relatively high literary style of Greek, the knowledge of Roman chronology, the presentation of Jesus at table in the manner of a teacher at a symposium (or drinking party), and the allusions to classical Greek sayings and proverbs, point to such a conclusion. The fact that the author also appears to be most knowledgeable about Judaism and familiar with the Hebrew scriptures indicates that he may have been a Gentile God-fearer, or, more likely, a Hellenized Jew.[5]

THE SHAPE OF THE LUKAN STORY OF JESUS

Each canonical gospel testifies to God's actions within human history, telling the story of how God relates to human beings especially through the life of Jesus of Nazareth. The Gospel of Luke (as also the Gospel of Matthew) follows the basic outline of the story of Jesus which is found in the Gospel of Mark, as table 8.1 (on page 162) indicates.

Yet the story told in this gospel is significantly reshaped from the Markan account, with notable differences in the opening chapters, in a lengthy middle section, and in the closing chapter. Luke sets the story of Jesus within a far-reaching framework, emphasizing that in Jesus, God relates to the creation in its totality. Numerous details of the story of Jesus are reshaped in the light of the author's stated purpose. This author makes further distinctive contributions by continuing the story of Jesus forward in time into the story of the early church, in the Acts of the Apostles, and by frequently indicating how this story links back in time to the story of Israel, in references to passages from the Hebrew scriptures. An overview of these aspects will illustrate how this gospel offers a distinctive vision of God's special relationship with all humanity through Jesus.

Table 8.1 *The Gospels of Mark and Luke*

	Mark	Luke
Jesus is baptized by John	1.9–11	3.1–22
and tested in the desert in Judea.	1.12–13	4.1–13
He then moves to Galilee,	1.14–15	4.14–15
where he preaches, teaches, heals and exorcises	1.16—9.50	4.16—9.50
On his return to Judea	10.1–52	18.15—19.27
he comes to Jerusalem and enters the Temple,	11.1–25	19.28–48
engages in controversy with the authorities	11.27—12.44	20.1—21.4
and instructs his disciples.	13.1–37	21.5–38
After sharing a last supper with his disciples,	14.1–25	22.1–38
Jesus is arrested, tried and crucified.	14.26—15.41	22.39—23.49
Then he is buried in a tomb	15.42–7	23.50–6
which is subsequently found empty.	16.1–8	12.1–12

Beginning the story of Jesus

The opening section of the gospel (Lk 1.5—2.40) carefully sets the story of Jesus in the historical, religious and cultural context of the time. Whereas Mark begins with the adult Jesus in the desert, alongside the marginal Jewish prophet, John (Mk 1.1–13), Luke begins three decades earlier in time, 'in the days of King Herod of Judea' (1.5), with an account of the conceptions and births of both John and Jesus (1.5—2.40). The location of the story is highly symbolic: from the start, Jesus is found at the heart of the people of Israel, in the Temple precincts in the centre of Jerusalem. In this Temple the faithful Zechariah, serving as priest, receives a message from 'an angel of the Lord' concerning his wife's surprise conception and the expected birth of his son (1.5–23). In the same Temple the faithful parents of Jesus present him, as their firstborn son, to God (2.22–4). The opening chapters include vignettes of a number of faithful Jewish people who reveal their trust in God and his promises of redemption: Elizabeth (1.24–5, 39–45, 57–66), Mary (1.26–38, 46–56; 2.19, 21–4), Zechariah (1.5–23, 59–80), some shepherds (2.8–20), the Spirit-inspired Simeon (2.25–35), the prophet Anna (2.36–40), followed by the unique Lukan picture of the twelve-year-old Jesus, fully engaged in discussion with the Temple teachers (2.41–52). These chapters set the scene with a note of confident expectation, and ground the story of Jesus firmly within the hopes of pious Israel. God's ancient promises appear set to be fulfilled.

Activities in Galilee

Luke's account of Jesus' activities in Galilee (Lk 4.14—9.50) closely parallels Mk 1.14—9.50. Jesus is portrayed as an itinerant preacher who seeks out 'sinners' and invites them to follow him. He prays to God, heals those afflicted with illnesses and casts out demons from those who are possessed. He teaches followers and crowds, using ethical exhortations and rabbinic-style parables, and debates the interpretation of torah with Pharisees and scribes. Jesus amazes his followers by performing other miracles; he enjoys widespread popularity across Galilee and is 'praised by everyone' (4.14–15). He attracts large crowds and disperses his message by sending out those he has called as disciples (9.1–6).[6] Distinctively in Luke, Jesus is acclaimed as one who does 'wondrous things' (5.26), 'a great prophet' (7.16a) and the one who brings 'God's favour' (7.16b). He comes to the attention of an interested John the baptizer (7.18–19; cf. Matt 11.2–3) and a perplexed Herod (9.7–9, only in Luke).

The section is introduced with a characteristic Lukan dating (3.1–2; cf. 1.5; 2.1), an expanded account of the baptism of Jesus by John (3.1–22) and an emphasis on the role of the Spirit (3.16, 22; 4.1, 14, 18). The genealogy of Jesus (3.23–38) verifies the important pedigree of Jesus; while he is a descendant of David and Abraham (cf. Matt 1.1–17), his lineage reaches back as far as 'Adam, son of God'. Even though this gospel has begun firmly within Jerusalem, the ultimate universal horizons of the story are set forth at an early stage.

The scene recounting Jesus' visit to his home town (Mk 6.1–6) is brought forward to an earlier place in the Lukan narrative (Lk 4.16–30) and functions as a manifesto setting forth Jesus' mission 'to proclaim the year of the Lord's favour' (4.19). It is expanded by the inclusion of key Lukan motifs: a scripture citation, reference to the Spirit and to the fulfilment taking place 'today', a mention of faithful Gentiles (4.25–7) and early signs of opposition to Jesus (4.24, 28–9). This rejection of Jesus, reiterated later by his family (8.19–21; see also 11.27–8), points to the looming conflict that will dominate the later sections of the gospel. Towards the end of this section, in the account of his transfiguration, a heavenly voice declares Jesus to be 'my Son, my Chosen' (Lk 9.35; cf. Mk 9.7; Matt 17.5), matching the similar declaration at his baptism ('my Son, my Beloved', Lk 3.22; cf. Mk 1.11; Matt 3.17). These declarations of the ultimate significance of Jesus frame the Galilee section.

Journey to Jerusalem

The brief Markan comment that Jesus went to Judea (Mk 10.1) forms the basis for a major Lukan reworking of the story of Jesus. Using language replete with prophetic symbolism (9.51), Jesus signals his intention to journey to Jerusalem. In a lengthy middle section of the gospel, Jesus and his followers are portrayed as being 'on the way', heading slowly but inexorably towards the capital city (Lk 9.51—19.48). Drawing almost exclusively from the Q source shared with Matthew's gospel, and sources used only in Luke's gospel,[7] this section reports Jesus' encounters and debates with various people, the parables, exhortations and teachings he uttered, the meals he shared and the healings he performed.

Interwoven throughout these scenes is a refrain providing regular reminders of the journey towards Jerusalem (9.52–60; 10.38; 13.31–5; 14.25; 17.11; 18.35). The tension mounts in the final stage of the journey (18.35—19.46) as Jesus draws near to the city, climbs the Mount of Olives, weeps for the city as he surveys it, and then swiftly enters the temple to enact his prophetic message. He remains teaching 'in the temple' for some days (19.47–8; 20.1; 21.37–8), yet his presence in Jerusalem puts Jesus in threat of his life (19.47b; 20.19; 22.2). Indeed, the city where Jesus will soon meet his fate has cast a long shadow back over Luke's report of Jesus' long journey there (9.22, 31; 13.33; 18.31–4). The road to Jerusalem is a road towards suffering and death; Jesus walks this road with his followers, who must share in his fate (9.23; 14.27). Once again, the location of the Lukan story, 'on the road', is symbolic. The intertwining of exhortations and instructions within this extended journey signal the necessity of counting the cost of following Jesus (9.57–62; 12.49–53; 13.22–30; 14.25–35).

Last days in Jerusalem

The Lukan account of Jesus' last days in Jerusalem largely follows the Markan account. Within the Temple precincts, Jesus debates with various authorities (20.1—21.4) and instructs his disciples (21.5–38). To distance Jesus from fanatical apocalyptic speculation, Luke's version of these instructions clearly distinguishes the time of Jesus from the end times (21.9, 12, 20, 24, 28). The account of Jesus' last supper contains an extended version of Jesus' words over the meal (22.14–20, including two cups) and more of his teachings (22.21–38). After Jesus' prayer, betrayal and arrest on the Mount of Olives (22.39–53), he is denied by Peter (22.54–62), taunted, then interrogated by Jewish authorities (22.63–71). Jesus' appearance before Herod is reported only in this gospel (23.6–12), linking back to Herod's interest in Jesus (9.7–9; but cf. 13.31). When Jesus is brought to trial before Pilate (23.1–5, 13–25), Luke's version (with an eye to the Roman authorities?) particularly emphasizes his innocence (23.4, 14, 22).

The crucifixion scene in Luke's gospel (23.26–43) includes unique reports of Jesus' words to 'the daughters of Jerusalem' (23.27–31) and to one of the criminals crucified with him (23.43); some versions include his words of forgiveness to those who carried out this crucifixion (23.34). Jesus' death (23.44–9) is reported with distinctive Lukan touches: Jesus dies not with a cry of agony (cf. Mk 15.34) but with a serene confidence (23.46); the centurion declares him to be *dikaios*, translatable as 'innocent' or 'righteous' (23.47); the crowds who are present (23.33) mourn what they have observed (23.48); and those watching from a distance are identified as 'all his acquaintances' (23.49), including, but not limited to, women from Galilee (cf. Mk 15.40–1). All these Galilean women also witness his burial (23.55–6). Jesus is buried by Joseph (23.50–6), a man identified as 'good and righteous' (23.50), harking back to the similar description of Zechariah and Elizabeth (1.6) in such a way as to place Jesus, even in his death, back within the heart of faithful Judaism.

Ending the story of Jesus

All four canonical gospels end with a scene at the empty tomb near Jerusalem (Mk 16.1–8; Matt 28.1–10; Jn 20.1–18; Lk 24.1–12). The appearance of the risen Jesus to his followers in Galilee (Mk 16.7; Matt 28.16–20; Jn 21.1–14) is omitted from Luke's gospel, for Jesus appears only on the road to Emmaus (24.13–32, only in Luke) and in Jerusalem itself (24.33–49; cf. Jn 20.19–29). The focus on Jerusalem and environs brings the gospel back to where it started, at the heart of Judaism. As Jesus' birth is located, symbolically, in the centre of Judaism, so his resurrection appearances occur only in this strategic location. The focus on Jerusalem has a dual purpose. It looks back in time, to evoke the prophetic traditions concerning the significant role of Jerusalem on the Day of the Lord.[8] It points forward in time to underline that the movement which will emerge from Jesus remains in continuity with Judaism.

Three canonical gospels report that the risen Jesus explicitly directs his followers to continue the mission he has begun (Jn 20.21; Matt 28.19; Lk 24.47). In the Lukan narrative, the universal earthly horizon of the command ('all nations', 24.47) is mirrored by the heavenly horizon ('into heaven', 24.51). The final phrase in the ascension narrative indicates that, despite the arrest and crucifixion of Jesus on the instigation of the Jewish authorities in Jerusalem (22.2, 52–3; 22.66—23.1; 23.13–25), a positive relationship continues to exist between the followers of Jesus and the Jerusalem Temple (24.52–3).

The Lukan version of Jesus' parting charge specifies that Jerusalem is to be the springboard for missionary activity: 'beginning from Jerusalem' (24.47). What follows in the account of this mission must be seen as a consequence of the events in Jerusalem; the movement to 'all nations' has its genesis in this central site. Luke's gospel is unique in insisting on the symbolic primacy of Jerusalem in the midst of the universal scope of Jesus' mission. Jerusalem, the holy place, of key importance in the prophetic traditions, is now the place where Jesus was crucified and yet was raised. The Jewish foundations of the story of Jesus and his followers remain important throughout the Lukan story.

Continuing the story into the future

Only Luke's gospel, among the canonical gospels, continues on from the story of Jesus, into a second volume, the Acts of the Apostles. In addition to the appearances of the risen Jesus recounted in the gospel (Lk 24.13–49), Acts refers to many additional appearances by Jesus during the forty days after his passion (Acts 1.1–3) and underlines the significance of remaining in Jerusalem at this stage (Acts 1.4–5). The gospel's brief report of his ascension into heaven (Lk 24.50–1) is repeated in expanded form (Acts 1.6–11) and the mission charge of Jesus (Lk 24.47) is articulated with more geographical detail ('in Jerusalem, in all Judea and Samaria, and to the ends of the earth', Acts 1.8). The community of followers established by Jesus (Lk 6.12–16) continues in an enlarged form (Acts 1.12–14) and the reconstituted leadership of the group ensures that their witness to Jesus continues (Acts 1.15–26).

The Holy Spirit has been at work from early in the gospel (Lk 1.15, 17, 35, 41, 47, 67; 2.25–7; 3.16, 22; 4.1, 14). Luke's account of Jesus' visit to his home-town synagogue in Nazareth (4.16–30) highlights the prophetic claim which Jesus appropriates for himself: 'the Spirit of the Lord is upon me' (4.18a). This Spirit enables Jesus to perform striking deeds (4.18b; 7.21–2) and continues to be active in similar fashion in Acts, beginning in a spectacular way on the day of Pentecost when the Spirit gives rise to portentous signs and speaking in tongues (Acts 2.1–4). The Spirit brings into being new communities of God's faithful people (Acts 2.37–47; 4.32–7; 10.44–8), empowers these people to testify to Jesus (Acts 2.5–13; 4.31; 10.45–6), and initiates important new stages in the story (Acts 8.29; 9.17–18; 10.19–20; 13.2; 15.28–9; 16.6–7; 19.21; 21.11).

The Spirit also inaugurates the last days (Acts 2.16–21), bringing to fulfilment elements of Jesus' preaching about the coming kingdom, for the heavenly portents and earthly signs taking place (Lk 17.20–37; 21.9–11, 25–6) form the prelude to the Day of the Lord (Lk 21.27–8; Acts 2.20b–21). The vision of God's relationship with 'all flesh', already prefigured in the gospel (Lk 3.6), takes on more explicit dimensions in Acts (Acts 2.17; cf. 2.39; 9.15; 10.34–6; 15.17; 17.30–1; 22.15; 26.20). Strong lines of continuity are thus drawn between the narrative present of the Gospel of Luke (the story of

Jesus) and future events subsequent to Jesus which are narrated in Acts (the story of the early church).

Connecting the story to the past

Strong lines of continuity are also drawn between this narrative present (the story of Jesus) and past events prior to Jesus (the story of Israel, reported in Hebrew scripture). On many occasions, Luke's narrative looks back in time, to draw explicit links with scriptural texts. The unique Lukan prophecies uttered by faithful Jewish characters in the opening chapters (1.46–55, 68–79; 2.29–32) draw strongly from the language and ideas of the Hebrew scriptures; God's promises are now coming to fulfilment. The Spirit which has rested upon Jesus (3.21–2) is interpreted by the Lukan Jesus with reference to the prophetic oracle concerning the promised eschatological action of God inaugurating the era of 'the Lord's favour' (4.18–19, citing Isa 61.1–2a). Later, Jesus articulates the full prophetic understanding, balancing the blessings brought by God (6.20–3) with the curses that accompany them for those who are unjust (6.24–6; see also 19.11–27).

Later events in Jerusalem are similarly interpreted in the light of scripture. As Jesus enters the city (19.38), crowds sing out Ps 118.26; as Jesus clears the Temple forecourt (19.46), he cites Isa 56.7. He foresees his betrayal by Judas (22.37), in fulfilment of Isa 53.12, and various details at his crucifixion evoke scriptural texts.[9] Jesus' final words from the cross (23.46) repeat Ps 31.5a. The risen Jesus identifies the basic hermeneutical principle, interpreting 'the things about himself in all the scriptures' (24.26–7; see also 18.31; 24.44–6; Acts 26.22b–23). This principle recurs throughout the apostolic testimony of Acts 1–13, when Peter, Stephen, Philip and Paul each preach about Jesus with frequent references to scriptural texts. The consistent Lukan perspective is that the story of Jesus is a continuation, indeed a fulfilment, of God's way of relating to Israel in the past. The clearest statements of the connection between the story of Jesus and Israel's story are articulated in key speeches by Stephen (Acts 7.2–53) and Paul (Acts 13.17–41). Stephen locates Jesus, the prophesied Righteous One, in an unbroken line of God's dealings with Israel, from Abraham to Moses to Solomon. Paul moves seamlessly from Egypt to Canaan to David to Jesus, the promised Saviour, appropriating the story of Israel as the model for understanding the story of Jesus.

The intimate connections drawn between Luke's story of Jesus and the Hebrew scriptures signify that God's relationship with Israel flows on in a continuous line into God's relationship with humanity through Jesus. This Lukan understanding is strongly influenced by Isaianic traditions: God has related to the world through Israel, a 'chosen' one (Isa 42.1; 61.1) who is a 'light to the nations' (Isa 42.6; 49.6), bearing witness to the 'salvation' wrought by God (Isa 43.3; 45.15, 17; 49.6, 8–12; 62.1). Now God continues that relationship through Jesus, another 'chosen' one (Lk 9.35; 23.35) who, as a 'light to the nations' (Lk 2.32), plays a fundamental role in bringing God's 'salvation' (Lk 2.30; 19.9–10; Acts 4.12; 5.31), since he is 'Lord of all' (Acts 10.36). The picture developed throughout Luke-Acts reveals that God's relationship with people perseveres, broadens and develops across a large span of time. The story of Jesus performs a strategic role in this development; it may well be characterized as 'the midpoint in time' in God's dealings with humanity.[10]

LUKE'S KEY THEMES

In reworking his sources about Jesus and crafting a literary work oriented to encouraging faithful discipleship within the Roman Empire, Luke takes on a major interpretative task. As he retells the story of Jesus, he highlights the key theological motif of the sovereignty of God which is now at work in Jesus. Such an emphasis provides a firm basis for the subsequent followers of Jesus to live with confidence in their world. Despite the trials that Jesus faced, culminating in his crucifixion, Luke understands that Jesus has brought about a tangible expression of God's salvation. Jesus has sought to restore the fullness of the covenant to Israel, the people of God, and to begin the process that will incorporate the Gentiles into this renewed covenant community. In this way, Jesus both inaugurates the kingdom promised by the prophets and announced by Jesus himself, and by his Spirit establishes and guides the church as it lives in faithful obedience to the way of God in the world of the early Roman Empire.

The sovereignty of God

The Gospel of Luke particularly emphasizes the guidance of God throughout the twists and turns of the narrative, no matter how unexpected. The narrative begins with the emphasis that 'the Lord God of Israel' is at work among 'the house of his servant David' (Lk 1.68–9). The miracles which occur (1.22, 24, 34–7, 57–8, 64–5; 2.7), the appearance of angelic messengers (1.11–20; 1.26–38; 2.8–14), the activity of the Spirit (1.15, 35, 41, 67; 2.25–7) and the proclamation of prophetic oracles (1.67; 2.36–8) each point to God being active. In response, God's actions are praised in the series of scripture-like songs (1.46–55; 1.68–79; 2.14; 2.29–33). The main story of the gospel is set within such a context of God at work among the people of Israel; Jesus was 'the message [God] sent to the people of Israel' (Acts 10.36).

In the Lukan account of the activity of Jesus in Galilee and Judea, people acclaim that God has been at work when Jesus forgives sins (5.21, 25), raises the dead (7.16), casts out demons (8.39; 11.20), heals people (9.43; 13.13; 17.15, 18; 18.43) and performs deeds of power (19.37). Jesus proclaims the standard Jewish message of God's ultimate sovereignty ('the kingdom of God', 4.43; 8.1; 16.16; 17.20–1; 22.16, 18) and instructs his followers to do likewise (9.2, 60; 10.9, 11). His attitude to life is grounded in the certainty of God's providential care (12.22–31), which presents the assurance of the promised kingdom (12.32; 22.28–30). Even his death reveals God at work (23.47), for it takes place in accordance with what the prophets of Israel had foretold (18.31; 22.37; 24.26–7, 44–6).

As the story of Jesus is proclaimed in Acts, at the heart of Peter's preaching stands the simple declaration: 'God was with him' (Acts 10.38). He continues the interpretation of Jesus' death as having taken place in accordance with God's plan (Acts 2.23)[11] and especially emphasizes that 'God raised him from the dead' (Acts 2.24; 3.15; 4.10; 5.30; 10.40; cf. 13.30). As the Sanhedrin opposes the preaching of Peter and John (Acts 4.1–3, 5–6; 5.17–18, 27–8, 33) and that of Stephen (Acts 6.12—7.1, 54–60), believers can be encouraged by recalling the fatal confrontation between Jesus and the Jerusalem authorities (Lk 22.66–71; 23.13–23; Acts 2.23; 3.14–15; 4.10, 27–8; 5.30; 7.52; cf. 13.27–29). The divine vindication experienced by Jesus provides them with hope and strength in their sufferings. God's sovereignty remains the governing element in the narrative when Gentiles in Caesarea join the (Jewish) believers (Acts 10.44–8; 11.15–18) and when Jews and God-fearers respond positively to Paul's preaching (Acts 13.43, 48; 17.4, 12, 34; 19.26); this pattern is described as being God's doing (Acts 14.27; 15.12). Luke peppers his narrative with explanations that the offering of the gospel to the Gentiles is in accord with God's intentions, for it is as scripture testifies (Acts 13.47; 15.15–18), the Spirit guides (Acts 13.2; 16.6–8; 19.21) and God directly instructs (Acts 15.7–9; 16.9–10; 18.9–10). The universal scope of God's sovereignty will be fully revealed on the day of judgement, when God will deal with 'all people everywhere' (Acts 17.30–1). The extensive reach of such all-encompassing divine sovereignty is consistently demonstrated throughout the story reported in Luke-Acts. This emphasis serves to encourage those who hear (or read) Luke's gospel, with the assurance that the community to which they belong is integral to the divine plan.[12]

The salvation of God

The specific quality of God's sovereignty is manifested in actions which bring salvation, or redemption. These terms had long been used to describe God's way of relating with the people of Israel (Lk 1.68–71, 77) and a traditional Israelite way of praising God was with the title 'Saviour' (1.47).[13] From early in the story of Jesus, however, it is clear that God's salvation is now to be prepared 'in the presence of all peoples' (2.30–1) and is intended to encompass 'all flesh' (3.6). The particularly Lukan emphasis that 'this salvation of God has been sent to the Gentiles' (Acts 28.28) is, in fact, derived from the prophetic tradition that Israel is set as 'a light for the Gentiles . . . to bring salvation to the ends of the earth' (Acts 13.47, quoting Isa 49.6; see also Lk 2.32; Acts 1.8).

The story of Jesus is set in the heart of this story of universal salvation. Jesus is presented as the faithful agent, chosen by God, to carry out God's actions. The gospel portrays God at work in Jesus, bringing salvation, or redemption, to all people. (The same theme continues to be prominent in Acts.) Jesus acts as God's agent to restore the fullness of the covenant to Israel and to begin the process that will incorporate the Gentiles into this covenant community. In this way, Jesus will both inaugurate the kingdom long promised by the prophets and establish guidelines for the church as it continues his mission in subsequent years.

This key role which Jesus plays is signalled in some of the titles assigned to him in Luke's gospel. As in each of the gospels, he is acclaimed as *Messiah*, or Chosen One (Mk 8.29; Matt 16.16; Lk 9.20; Jn 1.41). The apostolic preaching continues this claim (Acts 2.36; 9.22; 17.3; 18.5). Jesus is the one chosen by God to implement this crucial stage of the divine plan. In like fashion, the Jewish invocation of God as *Lord* is applied to Jesus in each of the gospels (Mk 11.3; Matt 21.3; Lk 19.31, 34; Jn 6.68), although Luke's gospel intensifies this by including many more such occurrences, continuing on throughout Acts. As Lord, Jesus is accorded the same qualities as God; the universal scope of God's actions is thus also applicable to Jesus. So it is that Peter is reported as declaring that Jesus is 'Lord of all' (Acts 10.36).

Distinctive to the Lukan writings is the claim that, as Jesus is the one who brings God's salvation, he is to be honoured as *Saviour* (2.11). The mission of Jesus is 'to seek out and to save the lost' (19.10), so salvation can be seen in him (2.27–30) and God's redemption becomes a present reality through him (2.38; 21.28; 24.21). In his parables, the message of salvation is implicit (8.12), and in reflecting on his deeds, he can declare that 'salvation has come to this house' (19.9). Sometimes, when Jesus heals sick people, he declares that the person's faith has saved them (8.50; 18.42; cf. 7.50). Questions regarding salvation can rightly be put to Jesus (13.23; 18.26). To the careful reader of this gospel, then, the taunting of Jesus as he hangs on the cross, to 'save himself' (23.35, 37, 39), is full of irony, for Jesus is the Saviour![14] The apostolic preaching in Acts presents the view that Jesus occupies a fundamental position in God's salvation (Acts 4.12), as he is, indeed, Saviour (Acts 5.31; 13.23). Those who proclaim him offer 'a way of salvation' (Acts 16.17, 31; cf. 13.26; 15.11). So the prophetic word of potentially universal salvation is fulfilled: 'everyone who calls on the name of the Lord shall be saved' (Acts 2.21, quoting Joel 2.32).

Thus, Luke is emphatic in presenting Jesus as the Messiah who is sovereign Lord and redeeming Saviour. He portrays the salvific work of God, begun in Israel, offered afresh in Jesus, empowered by the Spirit, proclaimed by the apostles (including Paul), and enacted in the life of the community of faith. All of this is focused in the story of Jesus, the 'Saviour who is the Messiah, the Lord' (Lk 2.11). Luke writes in the belief that the saving actions of Jesus will manifest the sovereignty of God in his own time under the Roman Empire, and will thereby point towards the kingdom which is promised in all its fullness.[15]

THE GOOD NEWS OF THE KINGDOM OF GOD

The message of Jesus can be succinctly summarized: 'the kingdom of God'. The focus on the kingdom runs consistently throughout the gospel; Jesus both proclaims the kingdom in his teachings and parables and embodies the kingdom in his exorcisms and healings. As he speaks and acts, his life is devoted to manifesting 'the good news of the kingdom of God'. As a response to this good news, Jesus calls on those who hear him to express their repentance and to follow him as disciples. Such discipleship is costly; however, this commitment is always met by the expression of God's grace. The implications of discipleship are especially demanding in terms of the stewardship of material possessions. Jesus invites people to share in table fellowship as a sign of the promised kingdom. He shares his table with people marginalized by society, welcomes women into the inner core of his followers, and points approvingly to the place which Gentiles will have in the coming kingdom.

Proclaiming the kingdom

In each synoptic gospel, Jesus proclaims that God was about to intervene in ordinary life in Israel, establish his kingdom and institute a new order of justice (Mk 1.14–15; Matt 4.17; Lk 4.43). As in other gospels, in Luke's account Jesus proclaims this message as he travels the countryside (8.1) and declares the mysteries of the kingdom in parables (8.9–11). Jesus compares the kingdom with a mustard seed (13.18) and with yeast (13.20); it belongs to such as children (18.16–17) but is difficult for the rich to enter (18.24–5).

Luke's particular presentation of Jesus' preaching holds together two views about the kingdom. One view, authentic to the historical Jesus, is that its arrival is imminent (9.27; 10.9, 11; 21.29–32). Jesus prays for the kingdom to come (11.2; cf. Matt 6.10). Luke intensifies this with Jesus' claim that the kingdom is already present (16.16, modifying Matt 11.12; 17.20–1, found only in Luke), with a key role in this being played by the Son of Man (9.26; 17.22–37; 21.27; 22.69). The other view, developed in the early decades after Jesus, is that there will be a significant delay before the kingdom is present (12.45; 19.11; Acts 1.6–7), so it is important to watch and prepare for its coming (12.35–48; 21.34–40). Luke reshapes his portrayal of Jesus to emphasize the importance of being faithful and thus being prepared; it may well have been that this was precisely the message of encouragement and exhortation which the contemporaries of Luke needed to hear within their own situation.[16]

Embodying the kingdom

Each gospel reports that Jesus performed a number of miraculous deeds during his adult life, healing the sick and casting out demons (Mk 1.32–4; Matt 8.16–17; Lk 4.40–1; Jn 11.47; 12.37). As well as repeating the six Markan occasions of how Jesus healed the sick, Luke adds five reports of similar healings.[17] Among ordinary people of the ancient world, the ability to effect healing was attributed more to religious capabilities than to medical knowledge. Also part of this worldview was the notion that good and evil forces at work in the world were personified 'demons'. Luke reports three of the four Markan instances when Jesus cast out demons, or unclean spirits, from possessed people (4.38–9; 8.27–35; 9.38–43). As Jesus thereby confronts, and defeats, the powers of evil, his followers perceive Jesus to be inspired by a divine power. They applaud his miracles as acts of God and understand them to be signs that, in some way, the kingdom was already present in him (10.9; 11.20). Yet not everyone viewed things in this way. Some of his contemporaries claimed that Jesus was acting under the influence of Beelzebul, the prince of the demons (11.14–15). (The same debate can be found, in relation to the followers of Jesus, in Acts.) Luke's version of the story of Jesus provides a clear interpretation of Jesus as a divinely empowered healer (11.19–22).[18]

Responding with repentance and faith

In each synoptic gospel, Jesus emphasizes the need to follow the Law as spelt out in the scriptures (Ten Commandments: Mk 10.19; Matt 19.17–19; Lk 18.20; the two great commands: Mk 12.28–34; Matt 22.34–40; Lk 10.25–8). However, Jesus clashes with the religious leaders of the time – especially when he criticizes the way that they interpreted Jewish law and proposed his own interpretations. In debating with these religious authorities, the Lukan Jesus makes no claim that they are set outside the covenant which existed between God and Israel (cf. Matt 21.43). He seeks a renewal of the covenant through faithful living in accordance with the Torah, since obedience to this Law was integral to the way of the kingdom (16.16–17; cf. Matt 5.17–20; 11.11–13). Jesus envisages that the kingdom would be ordered in a familiar Israelite pattern (22.28–30) and characterized by the prophetic vision of the messianic feast (13.29; 22.15–18, 30a; cf. 14.15). The prophetic call for repentance[19] is integral to the programmatic proclamation of Jesus (Mk 1.15; Matt 4.17; Lk 5.32); the Lukan Jesus issues this call with greater frequency (11.32; 13.3, 5; 15.7, 10 (and see 15.18, 21, 32); 17.1–4; 24.47). John the baptizer had declared that repentance would issue forth in good fruit (3.8–9); the Lukan Jesus preaches the same message (6.43–44; 8.11–15; 13.6–9) and encourages those whose encounter with him leads them to express their faith in practical, constructive ways (5.18–20; 7.6–9; 7.36–50; 8.43–8; 17.11–19; 18.35–43; cf. 18.8).

Discipleship: preparing for the kingdom

Jesus' exhortation to 'seek the kingdom' (Matt 6.33; Lk 12.31) is modelled as he lives out the radical values of the kingdom in life on earth. In each synoptic gospel, he calls people to follow him in this way of life, as his disciples.[20] The call to discipleship is highlighted in the teachings of the Lukan Jesus, especially as he journeys towards Jerusalem. This journey stands as an extended parable of what it means for others to follow Jesus. He reveals to those who would be his followers precisely what it will cost them to follow him, particularly at the start of this journey (9.57–62) and further along the way (14.25–33). He exhorts them to live as he lives, as if the kingdom were already present, adopting the radical renunciation of family (12.49–53; 14.26; 18.28–30), possessions (9.3; 10.4; 12.22–3; 14.33; 18.22) and securities (9.24; 12.22–3).

As this journey nears its end, Jesus speaks in detail of the fate in store for him in Jerusalem – he will be 'handed over to the Gentiles, mocked, insulted, spat upon, flogged, and killed' (18.32–3). The implication is clear. This is what the journey will cost Jesus; those who 'go up to Jerusalem' with him (18.31) face a similar fate. They will go out 'like lambs into the midst of wolves' (10.3), and when they visit places where they are not welcome, they will be advised to 'shake the dust off their feet' and move on (9.5; 10.10–11). They will know what it means to be 'hated, excluded, reviled, defamed' (6.22). Indeed, they will know the experience of arrest, persecution, trial, betrayal, hatred and even death, as the Lukan version of Jesus' apocalyptic discourse puts it (21.12–19).

In such a context, Jesus advises his followers, 'Do not worry' (12.22, 29) and encourages them with the words, 'Do not be afraid' (12.32). He reminds them of God's unending grace towards them (for instance, in the parables of 15.3–32) and assures them that 'not a hair of your head will perish' (21.18).

Yet it is not only those who 'go to Jerusalem' with Jesus who share this fate, for Luke's second volume contains numerous instances of how these prophetic words are fulfilled. As people are persecuted, imprisoned, brought to trial and put to death, the true cost of faithfulness is made known. The charge given to Paul summarizes what all faithful followers of Jesus might expect: 'how much he must suffer for the sake of my name' (Acts 9.16). Yet Paul, too, is given the encouragement of God's gracious presence (18.9–10) and is assured of safety in the midst of danger (27.24). The cost of faithfulness is met by God's abundant grace.[21]

Stewardship of material possessions

The Lukan Jesus has a message of good news particularly for those who are described as 'the poor' (4.18, citing Isa 61.1; 7.22). His preaching is marked by his reassurance to the poor that 'yours is the kingdom of God' (6.22); he promises the hungry, 'You will be filled' (6.23). Such teachings are reminiscent of the hymn sung by Mary, before the birth of Jesus: '[God] has filled the hungry with good things, and sent the rich away empty' (1.53). Jesus tells parables in which the poor are reassured of their invitation to share in the feast of the kingdom (14.21; 16.19–31); he contrasts the arrogant scribes (20.45–7) and rich people (21.1) with the humble, poor widow (21.1–4). Again, these teachings recall Mary's hymn: '[God] has brought down the powerful from their thrones, and lifted up the lowly' (1.52). The nexus between the good news and the poor is strong throughout Luke's gospel; any of 'the poor' who heard this gospel soon after it was written would have rejoiced at its implications for them.

Alongside these references to the poor, Luke's gospel includes many encounters which Jesus has with people from the upper classes of society, and the parables of Jesus reported only in this gospel include a number of upper-class people.[22] This interest in people towards the apex of the social pyramid continues in Acts.[23] Theophilus was one such person; it is highly likely that others of similar status came to know of Luke's writings. The message confronting them was direct: Jesus warns against greed and a single-minded focus on the abundance of possessions (12.13–21), advises against storing up treasures on earth (12.33–4) and issues the blunt command to sell everything (12.33; 18.22). Only the Lukan Jesus admonishes his Pharisee host to invite 'the poor, the crippled, the lame and the blind' to his meals (14.13), and tells a parable about inviting these groups when a banquet is held (14.21). He urges the shrewd use of resources (16.1–13) and cautions about the punishments that can be expected for failing to share material goods with poor neighbours (16.19–31). To the beatitude spoken to the poor (6.22; cf. Matt 5.3), the Lukan Jesus adds a strong warning to the rich (6.24).

Jesus' encounter with Zacchaeus, found only in Luke's gospel (19.1–10), provides a positive role model for the wealthy to consider how they might effect restitution for any unjust financial practices they have committed (19.8). Luke's report of Jesus' encounter with a wealthy torah-observant ruler (18.18–25) is carefully edited, so that, instead of leaving, grieving at his inability to enter the kingdom (Mk 10.22–3), the man stays put and continues to grapple with the implications of the confronting words spoken by Jesus (Lk 18.23–4). Similarly, Luke revises the Markan story of the woman who has anointed Jesus with perfume prior to his death (Mk 14.3–9), omitting Jesus' words to the woman, 'you always have the poor with you' (Mk 14.7). His version of the incident (Lk 7.36–50) includes a parable in which Jesus specifically enjoins the cancellation of large debts (7.41–3), in the manner of the Israelite institution of the Jubilee (Lev 25.8–55). This theme is given added weight because of the way it is developed in the portrayal of the early Christian community in Jerusalem (Acts 2.44–5; 4.32–7). Such stewardship is advocated as the model for the church of Luke's time.[24]

Table fellowship

Luke appears to take particular delight in reporting frequent scenes of Jesus at table. In addition to being the guest of Pharisees (7.36–50; 11.37–54; 14.1–24), Jesus in Luke's gospel is renowned for sharing a table with people who were considered by others to be outcasts and undesirables (5.30;

7.37–9; 15.1–2); people readily labelled him 'a glutton and a drunkard' (7.34). Yet such table fellowship becomes a way for Jesus to enact his vision of the kingdom, which he sees as being like a feast, where all would be welcome and there would be plenty to eat and drink (13.29). This vision is put into practice in the meals which Jesus shares with his followers (22.14–20; 24.28–30, 36–2; cf. 9.12–17). As Jesus calls people to follow him, he invites them to share in table fellowship as a sign of the promised kingdom (14.15; 22.29–30). It is in these table-fellowship scenes that Luke prepares for the ideal of inclusive Christian community, presented in full in his second volume (Acts 10.1—11.18), and traces its origins to the practices of Jesus.[25]

The marginalized

In Luke's gospel, as we have seen, the followers of Jesus are drawn from across the range of social classes. Just as Jesus shares at table with people marginalized by society ('sinners') as well as those with high status (Pharisees), so within the community of faith, the poor are as welcome as those with wealth – indeed, the rich are responsible for using that wealth for the benefit of the poor. Luke particularly emphasizes Jesus' solidarity with the marginalized and outcast, repeating Markan accounts of Jesus healing the sick (4.38–9, 40–1; 8.40–56) and encountering outcasts such as a leper (5.12–16), a paralysed man (5.17–26), tax-collectors (5.27–9), a man with a withered hand (6.6–11), some demon-possessed individuals (8.2, 26–39; 9.37–43), and a blind man (18.35–43). To these reports, Luke adds Jesus' encounters with a crippled woman (13.10–17), a man with dropsy (14.1–6), and ten lepers (17.11–19); and he repeats the accusation that Jesus consorts with 'sinners' (5.30; 15.1–2) in order to provide Jesus with an opportunity to tell three parables which justify his practice (15.3–32).

That Jesus would be found in the company of outcasts had already been signalled early in Luke's gospel, when the newborn Jesus is visited by shepherds (2.8–16), characters despised for their lowly and unworthy occupation.[26] Furthermore, the Lukan Jesus is deliberate in his acceptance of those most hated of outsiders, the Samaritans. He stops his disciples from bringing harm on the Samaritans (9.52–6), uses a Samaritan as an example of neighbourliness (10.29–37), and commends a Samaritan leper for his faith after he had offered thanks to Jesus for being healed (17.15–19). The Samaritan motif continues into the story of the early faith communities; it was the people of Samaria who first accepted the gospel when it was preached outside of Judea (Acts 8.5–25).

Men and women

Luke also indicates that the followers of Jesus are not only male, but also female, and so each gender stands on an equal footing within the community of faith. Luke's distinctive beginning to the story of Jesus introduces faithful characters of both genders: Zechariah and Elizabeth (1.5–25, 57–80), and Simeon and Anna (2.25–38), as well as Mary, 'the servant of the Lord' (1.38). Only Luke specifically notes that during Jesus' activities in Galilee, women travelled around with the group of male disciples of Jesus (8.1–3). Only this gospel includes the story of Mary and Martha, sisters who gave Jesus hospitality, and reports Jesus' commendation of Mary for her desire to learn from Jesus as a disciple (10.38–42). At the end of the gospel, the strategic role of the first witnesses to the empty tomb is delivered to women (23.55–6; 24.1, 10). This emphasis on female discipleship continues in Acts. The Spirit is poured out upon males and females alike (Acts 2.17–18) and a number of significant women are presented as positive models of faithfulness (9.36; 12.12; 16.15; 18.26; 21.9). Thus, both males and females will become disciples of Jesus and, later, members of the early church communities. Discipleship is inclusive in gender terms; women enjoy equal status within the group of Jesus' followers.[27]

Jews and Gentiles

Luke clearly conceived of the community of Jesus' followers as bringing Jews and Gentiles together in table fellowship. He reports Jesus' approval of the place which Gentiles will have in the coming kingdom (13.29). The motif of the inclusiveness of the community comes to dominate Acts; in the story of Peter and Cornelius (10.1—11.18), the Jewish Peter declares that the Gentiles in Caesarea 'have received the Holy Spirit just as we have' (10.45), that 'the Holy Spirit fell on them just as it had upon us at the beginning' (11.15), and that 'God gave them the same gift that he gave us when we believed' (11.17). The council in Jerusalem concludes that 'God has given even to the Gentiles the repentance that leads to life' (11.18). For Luke, there is no doubt that the community of believers incorporates Gentiles on an equal footing with Jews.

Pointers to such universal implications of Jesus' message appear early in Luke's gospel. When Simeon holds the infant Jesus in his arms, he speaks of God's salvation as being 'a light for revelation to the Gentiles and for glory to your people Israel' (2.32; cf. Isa 49.6). In Luke's report of the preaching of John the baptizer, the prophetic vision is already declared: 'all flesh shall see the salvation of God' (Lk 3.6, citing Isa 40.5). Luke alone reports that crowds from Tyre and Sidon (that is, Gentile territory) listen to the adult Jesus (6.17). The mission of the seventy-two disciples (10.1–20) may allude to the Gentile mission begun in Acts. Gentile centurions exhibit great faith (7.1–10) and express sympathetic understanding of Jesus at the moment of his death (23.47). The course has been set by the Lukan Jesus for the ultimate inclusion of Gentiles into the people of God (cf. Acts 15.7, 14, 17). Indeed, Luke has carefully shaped the sermon of Jesus preached in the synagogue in Nazareth so that it prefigures the faith community which is revealed in Acts – a community in which Jews and Gentiles belong together (Lk 4.25–7). Such an inclusive community is what Luke desires for the church of his time; he reshapes the story of Jesus in order to validate this vision.[28]

CONCLUSION

Luke's gospel exercises a powerful effect in the contemporary Christian church. By portraying Jesus as Lord of all, it underlines the sovereignty of God, even in the midst of upheavals, trials and despair, and encourages those who hear or read it to live in that reality. By representing Jesus as Saviour, it emphasizes the ever-present possibility of salvation for all, and stimulates those who read or hear it to bear witness to those opportunities. By emphasizing the inclusion of all within the community of faith – Jew and Gentile, rich and poor, male and female, insiders, those on the margins, and outcasts – it offers a tangible vision of the hope of the kingdom. The gospel is both a resource for equipping believers to engage with those among whom they live, and a challenge to communicate the good news in ways relevant to those to whom they speak.

Luke's gospel thus presents a beacon of hope for the contemporary world. As the church seeks to shape itself as a redemptive community of faith, inclusive in its membership and responsible in its stewardship, filled with confident hope and living with joyful trust, as the Lukan writings envisage, it offers glimpses of the kingdom as a tangible present reality. This is surely good news: a clear witness to God's compassionate and just providential concern for the entire world.

Notes

1. Scientific treatises: Loveday Alexander, *The Preface to Luke's Gospel* (Cambridge: Cambridge University Press, 1993). History: David Aune, *The New Testament in Its Literary Environment* (Cambridge: James Clarke, 1988), chs. 3, 4; Gregory E. Sterling, *Historiography and Self-Definition* (Leiden: E. J. Brill, 1992). Biography: Charles H. Talbert, *What is a Gospel?* (Philadelphia: Fortress, 1977); Richard A. Burridge, *What Are the Gospels?* (Cambridge: Cambridge University

Press, 1992). Fulfilment of scripture: Hans Conzelmann, *The Theology of St Luke* (ET, London: Faber, 1960); Charles H. Talbert, *Luke-Acts: New Perspectives* (New York: Crossroads, 1984). Providence in history: John T. Squires, *The Plan of God in Luke-Acts* (Cambridge: Cambridge University Press, 1993); Joel B. Green, *The Theology of the Gospel of Luke* (Cambridge: Cambridge University Press, 1995), ch. 2.

2. Luke's historiographical techniques: Squires, *The Plan of God*, ch. 2; Sterling, *Historiography*.

3. Robert Maddox, *The Purpose of Luke-Acts* (Edinburgh: T. & T. Clark, 1982), chs. 1, 7; Green, *Theology of Luke*, ch. 6.

4. Squires, *The Plan of God*, ch. 8.

5. Green, *Theology of Luke*, ch. 1.

6. Preaching: 4.31, 42–4; 5.1; 6.17; 8.1; 9.10–11. Sinners: 5.30–2; 7.34; 15.1–2. Followers: 5.1–11, 27–8; 6.12–16; 8.1–3. Prayer: 3.21; 5.16; 6.12; 9.18, 28. Healings: 4.38–40; 5.12–16, 17–26; 6.6–11, 18–19; 7.1–10, 11–15, 18–23; 8.40–56. Exorcisms: 4.31–7, 41; 7.21; 8.26–40. Teaching: 4.15, 31; 5.17. Exhortations: 6.20–42. Parables: 6.43–9; 7.40–8; 8.4–18. Torah interpretation: 5.29–32, 33–9; 6.1–5. Other miracles: 8.22–5; 9.10–17. Crowds: 5.1, 19; 6.17; 8.4; 9.11, 37.

7. Material unique to Luke's gospel is found at Luke 9.51–6; 10.17–20, 29–42; 11.5–8, 27–8; 12.13–21, 47–8; 13.1–9, 31–3; 15.11–32; 16.14–15, 19–31; 17.7–19; 18.1–14; 19.1–10. Only Luke 18.15–43 parallels Markan material. The remainder is Q material.

8. Most fully in Zech 14.1–21; see also Isa 40.9–11; 62.1–12; 65.17–25; 66.5–13, 18–24; Joel 2.32—3:2; Zeph 3.14–20; Zech 1.14–17; 2.10–12; 8.3–7, 20–3; 12.1–5.

9. Luke 23.32, crucified with criminals (Isa 53.12); 23.34, casting lots to divide clothes (Ps 22.18); 23.35, the scoffing leaders (Ps 22.17); 23.49, friends watch from afar (Ps 38.11).

10. Conzelmann, *Theology of St Luke*.

11. See also Acts 4.28; 5.38–9; 13.36; 20.27; and Squires, *The Plan of God*, ch. 3.

12. Squires, *The Plan of God*, chs. 3–7; Green, *Theology of Luke*, ch. 2.

13. Salvation of God: Gen 49.18; Ex 15.2; 2 Sam 22.36, 47, 51; 1 Chron 16.35; 46 times in Pss; 25 times in Isa; Jer 3.23; Mic 7.7; Hab 3.18. God as Saviour: 2 Sam 22.3; Pss 17.7; 106.21; Isa 43.3, 11; 45.15, 21; 49.26; 60.16; 63.8; Jer 14.8; Hos 13.4. Note also, redemption of God: Ps 111.9; God as redeemer: Job 19.25; Pss 19.14; 78.35; Isa 41.14; 43.14; 44.6, 24; 47.4; 48.17; 49.7, 26; 54.5, 8; 59.20; 60.16; 63.16; Jer 50.34.

14. Of the references to salvation cited in this paragraph, all are unique to Luke's gospel except for the healings (8.50; 18.42), the question of 18.26 and the crucifixion scene (23.35, 37).

15. I. Howard Marshall, *Luke: Historian and Theologian* (Exeter: Paternoster, 1970), 103–15; Green, *Theology of Luke*, ch. 3.

16. Maddox, *The Purpose of Luke-Acts*, ch. 5; John T. Carroll, *Response to the End of History* (Atlanta: Scholars Press, 1988).

17. From Mark: Luke 4.38–9; 5.12–13, 18–25; 6.6–10; 8.43–8; 18.35–43. From Q: 7.1–10. Unique to Luke: 13.11–13; 14.1–4; 17.11–19; 22.50–1.

18. John J. Pilch, 'Sickness and Healing in Luke–Acts' in Jerome H. Neyrey, ed., *The Social World of Luke-Acts* (Peabody: Hendrickson, 1991), 181–209; Ben Witherington, 'Salvation and Health' in I. Howard Marshall and David Peterson (eds.), *Witness to the Gospel* (Grand Rapids: Eerdmans, 1998), 145–66.
19. Isa 6.10; 31.6; 45.22; 59.20; 63.17; Jer 9.5; 15.19; 18.11; 25.5; 31.19; 34.15; 35.15; 36.3; Ezek 3.19–20; 14.6; 18.21–32; 33.8–19; Jon 3.8.
20. Mk 1.16–20; 2.13–14; 8.34; 10.21, 28, 5, each of which is paralleled in Matthew and Luke; Matt 8.18–22, paralleled in Lk 9.57–62.
21. Green, *Theology of Luke*, ch. 5.
22. In the parables: a rich man (12.13–21), a tower-builder (14.28–30), a king at war (14.31–2), a rich father (15.11–32), a steward of a wealthy man (16.1–13), a rich man (16.19–31), a farmer with slaves (17.7–10) and a judge (18.1–8). In the narrative: a wealthy centurion (7.1–10); a synagogue leader (8.40–2, 49–56); a rich chief tax-collector (19.1–10).
23. Converts are drawn from women of high standing (Acts 13.50; 17.4, 12, 34), communities of believers meet in the houses of people of means (2.46; 5.42; 8.3; 10.5–6, 32; 10.24, 48; 11.12; 12.12; 16.14–15, 29–34; 17.4; 18.7, 8; 20.20; 21.4,7, 8, 10; 21.16) and other wealthy or powerful people are favourably disposed towards the gospel (6.7; 8.7; 10.1; 13.7, 12; 16.14; 18.24, 34; 19.31).
24. Luke T. Johnson, *Sharing Possessions* (London: SCM Press, 1981); Philip F. Esler, *Community and Gospel in Luke-Acts* (Cambridge: Cambridge University Press, 1987), ch. 7; Halvor Moxnes, *The Economy of the Kingdom* (Philadelphia: Fortress, 1988).
25. Esler, *Community and Gospel*, ch. 4; Green, *Theology of Luke*, ch.4.
26. *Mishnah* (*m.Kidd*. 4.14) classifies shepherds among those who practise 'the craft of robbers'.
27. Turid K. Seim, *The Double Message* (Edinburgh: T. & T. Clark, 1994).
28. Esler, *Community and Gospel*, ch. 2.

Further reading

Alexander, Loveday, *The Preface to Luke's Gospel* (Cambridge: Cambridge University Press, 1993)

Carroll, John T., *Response to the End of History: Eschatology and History in Luke–Acts* (Atlanta: Scholars Press, 1988)

Conzelmann, Hans, *The Theology of St Luke* (New York: Harper & Row, 1960)

Esler, Philip F., *Community and Gospel in Luke-Acts: The Social and Political Motivations of Lucan Theology* (Cambridge: Cambridge University Press, 1987)

Green, Joel, B., *The Theology of the Gospel of Luke* (Cambridge: Cambridge University Press, 1995)

Johnson, Luke T., *Sharing Possessions: Mandate and Symbol of Faith* (Philadelphia: Fortress, 1981)

Maddox, Robert, *The Purpose of Luke–Acts* (Edinburgh: T. & T. Clark, 1982)

Moxnes, Halvor, *The Economy of the Kingdom: Social Conflict and Economic Relations in Luke's Gospel* (Philadelphia: Fortress, 1988)

Neyrey, Jerome H., ed., *The Social World of Luke-Acts: Models for Interpretation* (Peabody: Hendricksen, 1991)

Seim, Turid K., *The Double Message: Patterns of Gender in Luke and Acts* (Edinburgh: T. & T. Clark, 1994)

Squires, John T., *The Plan of God in Luke-Acts* (Cambridge: Cambridge University Press, 1993)

Sterling, Gregory E., *Historiography and Self-Definition: Josephos, Luke-Acts and Apologetic Historiography* (Leiden: E. J. Brill, 1992)

9 The Gospel according to John

MARIANNE MEYE THOMPSON

As the fourth of the 'fourfold gospel' of the New Testament canon, the Gospel of John relates a selection of the words and deeds of its central figure, Jesus of Nazareth, so as to present his identity and significance. And while many of those deeds, such as the healing of the sick, teaching disciples and confronting the religious and political authorities of his day, are familiar to readers of the other gospels, the terms, images and titles through which John characterizes Jesus are often unique to John. In this gospel, Jesus is the incarnation of God's own Word, the embodiment of God's glory, truth and will, and the way to life with God. Although the other gospels speak of the manifestation of God's kingdom and the presence of God in Jesus, it is the fourth gospel which boldly declares that the one who became flesh was with God 'in the beginning' and indeed 'was God' (1.1). As one who came from God, not just as a prophet or authorized teacher, but as the embodiment in human history of God's Word and the revelation of God's glory, truth and life, Jesus makes God known to humankind, not by conveying information about God, but rather through the personal, incarnate revelation of God. That is the daring and foundational claim of the fourth gospel and the key to Jesus' identity in it.

JOHN AMONG THE GOSPELS: SIMILARITIES AND DIFFERENCES

In advancing its claims for Jesus, John shares both similarities and differences with the other canonical gospels. An enormous amount of scholarly ink has been spilled in assessment of the similarities and differences between John and the synoptics, and in efforts to account for them. Here 'theology' and 'history' have sometimes been played off against each other, so that some scholars see John as a theologically shaped narrative of Jesus' life, with doubtful claims to historicity, while others have argued that John had access to an independent fund of traditions about Jesus.[1] Even granting that supposition, most scholars nevertheless also acknowledge that John has left a significant creative impression on his material, reworking it more thoroughly than do any of the synoptic evangelists. In order to assess these options, we do well to have some data before us. We may first look briefly at some of the similarities which John shares with the other canonical gospels, similarities which go a long way towards explaining why John was included in the canon of the New Testament.

In agreement with the other gospels, John presents Jesus as the Messiah of Israel, who heals, teaches and dies and rises. Furthermore, the basic outlines of the four gospels share a number of similarities. Jesus first appears in public ministry in connection with the baptizing ministry of John; he teaches, calls disciples and heals the sick; he confronts other Jewish teachers, particularly the Pharisees, about the interpretation of God's will; he is put to death on a Roman cross; and subsequently appears to his disciples alive after his death. Within this framework there are other incidents which find a place in all the gospels, including the feeding of the 5,000; a public entry into Jerusalem and a demonstration in the Temple; a closing discourse to his disciples warning about what will come after his death; a last meal eaten with them prior to his betrayal by one of his own disciples; and his arrest, trial and crucifixion by the Romans.

There are also important points of contact between John and the other gospels in the characterization of Jesus. Although, as indicated, John does use some distinctive imagery and terms for Jesus, the gospels share in common the designation of Jesus as the Messiah. Mark opens with this designation of Jesus (Mk 1.1), and it is found in the summary purpose statement of the Gospel of John (20.30–1). Throughout the gospels people wonder whether Jesus might be the promised Messiah, and all the gospels state that to his cross were affixed the accusatory words, 'King of the Jews'. Yet in spite of the importance of the term to all the gospels, none of them shows Jesus himself regularly or publicly using this term. This shared reticence appears in sharp relief in John, where, in the first chapter alone, he is designated Lamb of God (1.29, 35), Messiah (1.41), the one written of in scripture (1.45), King of Israel and Son of God (1.49), and the Son of Man (1.51). John makes Jesus' identity known early on. In keeping with the other gospels, Jesus' preferred self-designation is 'Son of Man' a term which neither his disciples nor his opponents use with respect to him. Both John and the synoptics speak of the Son of Man as exercising God's authority on earth (Mk 2.10; Jn 5.27).

But the synoptic gospels place the accent on the Son of Man as one who lives a lowly and humble existence (Lk 9.58), who suffers and dies

(Mk 8.31), and who will come again in glory (Mk 8.38), whereas John speaks of the Son of Man in a distinctively Johannine image as coming from above to reveal the glory of his Father (Jn 1.51).

In spite of the many similarities, the striking differences between John and the synoptics have generated a great deal more discussion, leading to characterizations of it as 'the maverick gospel' and 'an enigma'. These differences may be catalogued briefly here. The characters and incidents in John are often distinctive to John. Figures such as Nicodemus, the Samaritan woman and Lazarus appear only in John. Miracle stories including the changing of water to wine at the wedding in Cana (2.1–11), the healing of the man at a pool in Jerusalem (ch. 5), the healing of the blind man (ch. 9) and the raising of Lazarus (ch. 11) are only in John, although Jesus does similar miracles in the other gospels. One sort of miracle notably missing from John is demonic exorcism, which in the synoptic gospels demonstrates Jesus' divinely given power and mission (Mk 3.27; Lk 11.20; Matt 12.28).

The Jesus of the gospels is a teacher. But while the synoptic gospels present Jesus as teaching the crowds in parables (Mk 3.34), John contains none of the most familiar parables. In John, Jesus does teach using symbols and metaphors, but he does not use the classic story parables or short pithy illustrative sayings familiar from the other gospels. Similarly, while a number of the synoptic parables have as their subject the kingdom of God, and the synoptic gospels sometimes summarize Jesus' teaching in terms of his proclamation of the kingdom of God (Mk 1.14–15; Lk 4.42), this phrase appears only twice in John. Instead, John presents Jesus as teaching often in lengthy discourses, typically introduced with the majestic 'I am' statements, such as 'I am the bread of life' and 'I am the light of the world', none of which are found in the synoptic gospels. Thus while it is sometimes said that in the synoptic gospels Jesus points away from himself to God's kingly rule and, in John, points to himself as the source of life, John also presents Jesus as seeking the glory of his Father (5.44; 7.18; 8.49), doing his Father's will (5.30), and teaching what the Father has given to him (7.16; 8.28), for 'the Son can do nothing on his own' (5.19, 30). But it is fair to say that in John Jesus calls attention to his own identity and role, and that the fourth gospel is particularly explicit in characterizing Jesus in relationship to God. Indeed, Johannine christology would be unthinkable if it did not characterize Jesus first and foremost in his intimate and unique relationship with the one God, creator of all. As one who 'was in the beginning with God', who exercises the divine powers of judgement and life, Jesus can in fact be called 'God' (1.1; 20.28).

There are other significant differences in the content of the teaching in the synoptics and John. The synoptic gospels contain instructions and exhortations regarding such matters as the use of money, giving of alms, anger, lust, adultery, divorce, forgiving others, and justice, so that the Jesus of the synoptic gospels often sounds a good deal like the Old Testament prophets. But in John, Jesus' teaching has been distilled into a single 'new command', to love one another (13.34–5). A final distinguishing marker of Jesus' teaching in John is found in his choice of vocabulary. Love, truth, light, darkness, life, world, see, look, know, believe, have faith, send, abide, hour, glory, Father, and Son are words common to John, and appear in this gospel more often than in the rest of the gospels combined. In short, in John Jesus addresses different topics and uses both a different vocabulary and a different teaching style.

This brief overview of the differences between John and the other gospels suggests that, in recounting the life of Jesus of Nazareth, John often goes its own way, narrating incidents and using terminology and imagery which are distinctive to it. No single factor can account for John's distinctiveness. Although in earlier days John was sometimes thought to be essentially a creative, theological reworking of one or more of the synoptic gospels, that theory has largely been supplanted by the view that John has access to independent traditions of the ministry of Jesus.[2] These traditions are the foundation of the gospel. Additionally, John's gospel has likely been shaped in part by the rising tensions between synagogue and church, or between those who did not hold that Jesus was the Messiah and those who did.[3] Traces of such conflict can be found in other writings of the New Testament, but they have left a distinct stamp on certain chapters of John, particularly Jn 8. John therefore emphasizes those elements in his portrait of Jesus which show him to be the embodiment of God's presence and the fulfilment of God's promises. At this point, John's approach differs from that of Matthew or Luke. While John does quote the Old Testament to speak of promises fulfilled in Jesus, more often he draws out the significance of Jesus' deeds or words by explaining them in terms of motifs and imagery drawn from the pages of the Old Testament and from Jewish interpretative traditions.[4] But John also seeks to present Jesus to a wider readership, and scholars have sometimes pointed to the universal appeal of its imagery and to the contacts John has with Hellenistic expressions and thinking to suggest that John's ultimate purpose is to paint the portrait of Jesus on a universal canvas.[5]

Some of the most memorable images, which have exerted enormous influence on subsequent Christian theology, are found in its opening eighteen verses, the so-called prologue of the Gospel of John. But before turning to a closer examination of this prologue, we may note briefly the outline of the gospel:

(1) 1.1–18: The prologue introduces the central figure of the gospel, Jesus of Nazareth, and foreshadows response to him.

(2) 1.19—12.50: The first main section of the gospel narrates seven of Jesus' miraculous signs, including the mixed response to him, his deeds and his words.

(3) 13.1—21.22: The second main section recounts the events surrounding Jesus' death, including his last supper, last words to his disciples, trial, arrest, crucifixion, and resurrection appearances to his disciples.

(4) 21.23–5: Epilogue, a brief closing statement.

As we shall see, all the prologue and the two major parts of the gospel bear the stamp of John's distinctive presentation of Jesus.

'IN THE BEGINNING WITH GOD': JOHANNINE CHRISTOLOGY

Each gospel opens with a preface or prologue of some sort, introducing Jesus in a manner in keeping with the portrait of him in the rest of that gospel. John opens with a pithy, confessional summary of Jesus' identity, which also notes both the positive and negative responses to his ministry (1.1–18). In this prologue, John calls Jesus 'the Word of God', adding that he was 'in the beginning with God' (1.2). The Greek for 'word' is *logos*, which in ancient Greek philosophy was used to designate the rational principle of the universe. In earlier generations, scholars tended to see John as the presentation of the gospel to the Greek world. To designate Jesus as the Logos, the Word, would woo such an audience from the outset. But John's description also recalls the opening words of the Old Testament, for in the Greek translation of the Old Testament, the Septuagint, Gen 1.1 and Jn 1.1 begin with the same prepositional phrase, 'in the beginning'. Echoes of Gen 1.1 are deliberate, for John immediately describes the Word as the one through whom God created all things (1.3), the one in whom life is to be found (1.4). In characterizing the Word as one who existed prior to creation and, indeed, the agent of God's creation of all the world, John attributes to Jesus the divine prerogative of creating and giving life and thus identifies him without hesitation as 'God' (1.1).

In the Old Testament, 'word of God' refers not only to the word by which the world was created (Gen 1.1; Ps 33.6) but also to the word given to the prophets (Hos 1.1; Joel 1.1) and to the scriptures (Ps 119:105, 130).

But while John refers to Jesus as 'the Word,' in many ways it is the figure of Wisdom which provides the specific imagery used with reference to Jesus (see Prov. 8.22–31; Sir 24; Wis 7). Wisdom existed in the beginning, prior to the creation of the world; indeed, wisdom was God's agent in creation (Prov 8.21–30; Wis 7.21). Coming forth from the mouth of God (Sir 24.3; Wis 7.25), from its dwelling with God in heaven (Sir 24.4), Wisdom brings life and light to those who accept it (Prov 8.35–6; Sir 24.27), growing into a tree with 'branches of glory and grace' (Sir 24.16). Sir 24.23 equates wisdom with the Law given through Moses, which enlightens and instructs people, giving them knowledge of God and God's ways (Prov 8.32–3; Sir 24.26–7, 33). Wisdom invites people to eat and drink (Sir 24.19–21). John's point is that now God's word, wisdom, glory, grace, life and light are embodied in the person of Jesus of Nazareth, whose revelation of God is definitive, ultimate and personal. While Jesus is sent, teaches, and works miracles, not unlike the prophets of old, ultimately his origin and identity are most intimately bound up with the eternal God. The Word of this God has become a human being (1.14), Jesus of Nazareth, a first-century Jewish figure, who lived and worked among the people of Israel. Because the Word of God is incarnated as Jesus of Nazareth, Jesus manifests the very glorious presence of God. In the Old Testament 'glory' attends God's presence with Israel in the wilderness (Ex 25.8–9), and the prophets hoped for a new 'encampment' of God with his people (Joel 3.17; Zech 1.10). John indicates that this hope is fulfilled in the 'encampment' of the Word of God in the person of Jesus of Nazareth, with the consequent revelation of divine glory (2.11; 11.40).

Thus the prologue spells out Jesus' identity in terms that link him to the self-manifestation of God, and that do so specifically in vocabulary which sets him both in continuity and contrast with God's wisdom as manifested in creation, but also in the Law given to Israel. There is thus an apologetic edge to the prologue, making Jesus known *vis-à-vis* Israel's God and Israel's peculiar possessions. In serving as something of an *apology* for or defence of Jesus, the prologue also anticipates the mixed response to Jesus. On the one hand, revelation implies visibility, suggesting that it should lead to seeing, understanding, knowing and believing. In keeping with that expectation, some who see the revelation of God's glory in and through Jesus come to believe in him as God's Word of revelation, as the Son of God, who perfectly embodies his father (1.12–13). But, on the other hand, the revelation of God in Jesus also meets with unbelief and rejection, both from the world which was made through him (1.10) and from his own people (1.11). Although rejected by his own, Jesus gathers around him a new circle of 'his own', a group which will eventually consist of 'all people', Jew, Samaritan and

Gentile who believe and become children of God (1.12–13; 11.48–52; 12.32). When, upon seeing the risen Lord, Thomas, one of Jesus' own, confesses Jesus as 'My Lord and my God!', the gospel has come full circle, back to the opening confession of the prologue, 'the Word was God'. The prologue thus contains the gospel in a nutshell, summarizing for the reader this gospel's beliefs about Jesus. Having read the prologue, the reader always has the distinct advantage of knowing what the characters in the gospel do not know.

'HE MANIFESTED [GOD'S] GLORY': THE NARRATIVE OF JESUS' LIFE AND DEATH

Following the prologue, John presents a selective series of incidents designed to reveal Jesus as the Messiah, the Son of God, the way to God, and the truth and life from God. These various incidents are typically built upon the miraculous deeds of Jesus, which in John are referred to as *sēmeia* or signs. While *sēmeia* does not mean 'miracles', in the Gospel of John it refers to the various miracles which Jesus did. They are signs which reveal him to be the life-giving Son of God and, as such, they call for faith in him (Jn 20.30–1). The signs are also called 'the works of the Father', precisely because they both symbolize and confer God's life graciously given to human beings. Jesus' various discourses and dialogues typically explicate the significance of a particular miracle. Thus when he feeds 5,000 people, he proclaims to the people, 'I am the bread of life' (6.35). 'I am the light of the world' frames the healing of a blind man (8.12; 9.5). Prior to raising Lazarus from the tomb, he announces to Martha, 'I am the resurrection and the life' (11.25–6). Deed and word together summarize Jesus' identity as the one who does the work and carries out the will of God, thus making manifest the unity of Jesus with God, a constant if not central theme of John's christology. Because Jesus' miracles bring life to people, they manifest his union with the living God who alone gives life.

Perhaps the most important terms in John to express the relationship of Jesus to God, which the signs reveal, is their respective designations of Jesus as Son and of God as Father. Although the other gospels use the language of 'Father' and 'Son', that language occurs far more often in John – over 120 times in John, compared with four uses in Mark – where to a large extent it carries the freight of Jesus' identity in relationship to God. This personal language is drawn from the sphere of the family, and shows that God and Jesus have their identity in relationship to each other. 'Father' indicates especially that God is the source of life, the 'living Father' (6.57) and that the Son has both his identity and origin as Son from his Father.

Because of their relationship as Father and Son, they share an intimate and reciprocal knowledge, mutual love, and unity of will and work. As Son, Jesus perfectly expresses the will of his Father in all things, doing only what the Father commands him (5.19; 10.18; 14.31). The Father has entrusted 'all things' to the Son (3.35), including the power to judge and to give life (5.25–6). Indeed, as the 'only Son', Jesus stands in a unique relationship to God. Because of the Son's relationship to the Father, he can bring others into a similar relationship. But only Jesus is called the Son (*huios*), whereas all others are spoken of as 'children' (*tekna*) of God. Although, like the Son, these children have the life of God, the Son has 'life in himself', even as God does, while the children of God always have eternal life mediated through the Son and in dependence upon the Son.

As indicated earlier, one of the other most notable aspects of the characterization of Jesus is his self-revelation through a series of 'I am' statements typically, although not always, coupled with one of Jesus' signs. The 'I am' sayings of John draw on the scriptural self-revelation of God to Israel. In Ex 3.14, God reveals himself to Moses with the mysterious assertion, 'I AM WHO I AM'. And in Isaiah God frequently asserts his sovereignty, uniqueness, and divinity with statements such as 'I am the first and I am the last; besides me there is no other' (44.6). Jesus' use of words which resonate with Scriptural statements of divine revelation show particularly his unique identity as the Son of the Father, through whom life is given to the world.

Each of seven statements offers a picture of Jesus' life-giving work. He is the bread of life (6.35); the light of the world, who shows the way out of darkness (8.12; 9.5); the gate to life-giving pasture for the sheep (10.9); the good shepherd, who lays down his life for the sheep (10.11); the resurrection and the life (11.25); the way, the truth and the life (14.6); and the vine who gives life to the branches (15.1, 5). As one who has 'life in himself' (5.26), and has the power to lay down his life and take it again (10.17–18), he has the power to give life to others. Indeed, he embodies this life, and he gives it to others, not as something abstracted from his own person, but precisely to those who align themselves with him, finding in him the 'life of the world'. While the Gospel of John is written in order to bring people to a particular understanding of Jesus – namely, that he is the Messiah, the Son of the Father, the Word who became incarnate, embodying the glory of God, and so also the way to God – response, whether positive or negative, to God's revelation is response to a person, not to a set of ideas, and that response is depicted in personal terms. The gospel calls upon people to follow Jesus (1.39, 43) because he has the words of life (6.66) and is the light which illumines the pathway (8.12); and to depend upon him for life (15.1, 5), because he is the life (14.6).

Even as John's portrayal of Jesus' life has numerous distinctive features, so also does his presentation of Jesus' death. Because through Jesus' self-giving death on the cross God brings life to the world, the cross does not spell failure and defeat, but rather constitutes the victory of God over the forces of darkness and evil. It is in fact the means through which the King of Israel (1.49; 19.3, 19) assumes his sovereignty over a kingdom 'not of this world' (18.36–37). Even in his death, 'the light shines in the darkness, and the darkness has never overcome it' (1.5). Jesus, who raises Lazarus from the dead and is himself the resurrection and life, dies on the cross, but he is raised to life by his Father. Therefore Jesus' death is his 'glorification', the means whereby God glorifies him and he brings glory to God. John also speaks of the cross as Jesus' being 'lifted up'. On one level this refers to the physical elevation of a body on a painful instrument of death, but on another level it signals an elevation, an exaltation, to the glory that Jesus had with his Father 'before the world was made' (17.5). Once again it is clear that nothing can separate Jesus from his Father, and nothing can darken his revelation of the Father. Finally, John particularly stresses that the cross shows forth the love of Father and Son for all the world. John introduces the account of Jesus' last meal with his disciples with the words, 'having loved his own, he loved them to the end' (*eis telos*). In playing on the word 'end', John means both that Jesus loved his disciples to the very end of his life, as demonstrated on the cross, and that he loved them with the fullest, ultimate love one can love. Indeed, Jesus lives out the example which he commends to his followers, 'No one has greater love than this, than to lay down his life for his friends' (15.13). On the cross, Jesus dies, having uttered the statement, 'It is finished!' or, 'It has been brought to completion!' (*tetelestai*; 19.30). Jesus' work of revealing the Father, of calling people to himself, of bringing the light that leads to God and offering the life that comes from God, has been completed in his death on the cross and his return to his Father. He is now 'with God' (1.1), 'ever at the Father's side' (1.18).

THE MISSION OF JESUS

The mission which Jesus has accomplished, which has been brought to completion on the cross, can be summarized in a number of ways. Jesus' mission is to make God known through the fully embodied revelation of God's glory, truth and life (1.18). Because Jesus reveals God, 'seeing' becomes an important image of salvation, where mere physical 'sight' is distinguished from true 'insight' into and understanding of what one has seen. The gospel calls for discernment of the divine identity of Jesus and of the divine origin of the gifts offered through him. One may 'behold his glory'; Jesus invites enquirers to 'come and see'; he gives sight to those who are blind that they may see the truth; he is a light to guide one on the pathway to God. While the revelation of God cannot simply be read off the surface of the historical figure of Jesus, nevertheless, with divinely given insight one may see in the person of Jesus more than a Galilean rabbi; one may see the manifestation of the glory of God.

Jesus' mission can also be summarized as bringing knowledge of God. Because Jesus is the unique embodiment of God's Word and presence, he offers knowledge of God, and the gospel is replete with a number of terms for hearing, knowing and believing, which suggest both a cognitive and personal dimension in the kind of knowledge which John has in view. It has often been pointed out that while the gospel says Jesus came to make God known, relatively little 'content' is involved in that revelation. There is no strikingly new characterization of God when compared with either the Old Testament or contemporary Jewish sources. But what does distinguish John is the emphasis that God is now known, and known distinctly and uniquely, through the manifestation of his Word in Jesus of Nazareth. One must attend to the word of Jesus as the Word of God, and respond to the Father through the Son (14.6). The embodied revelation of God calls for a response to the one in whom that revelation is embodied.

Jesus' mission embodies God's love for the world. Throughout the gospel the term 'world' (*kosmos*) has a primarily negative connotation. Though made by God, through the agency of his Word, the world rejects the love of God offered through the Son. Even more strongly, the 'world' is said to hate both Jesus and his followers. But John underscores the depth of God's love by noting that, although the world was made through the agency of the Son, the world rejects the Son and thus also God's love given to it. Jesus reveals the depth of this love in giving his life for his own.

One of the most distinctive features of the gospel is the formulation of his mission in terms of giving 'eternal life' to those who believe (3.16–17; 20.30–1). While the other gospels use the phrase 'eternal life' (Matt 19.16–17; Mk 10.29–30; Lk 18.29–30), in John it has the prominence which 'kingdom of God' has in the other gospels, perhaps even serving as a restatement of the hoped-for 'kingdom of God'. What the two phrases have in common is that both are theocentric: the kingdom Jesus offers is the kingdom of God; and the life which he brings is eternal life, the kind of life which God has. For as the 'living Father,' the source and creator of all that is, God alone has eternal life. But through the Son, one may see and know God and so participate in the life of God. As John writes in 17.3, 'This is eternal life: to know God and Jesus Christ whom [God] has sent', indicating that 'eternal life' is not some possession which one may attain, but rather precisely what one has in knowing God through Christ. And thus because one may know God in the present, 'eternal life' refers not only to what one has at some future time, after the present life, but also to what one receives in the present (5.24–6). One may experience 'eternal life' in the present because one can have the knowledge of God and enter into the relationship of life-giving dependence, such as is pictured in the image of the vine which gives life to the branches, through the mediation of the Son.

Thus John emphasizes the present possession of eternal life precisely because the Son mediates the Father's gift of life. A key statement at this point is Jn 5.25–6: 'Truly, truly, I say to you, the hour is coming, and now is, when the dead will hear the voice of the Son of God, and those who hear will live. For as the Father has life in himself, so he has granted the Son also to have life in himself.' Here John underscores that the hour, expected in the future, when God would give life to the dead, has now come through the life-giving mission of the Son. John's eschatology has sometimes been labelled a 'realized eschatology', because it presents the blessings of the future – namely, eternal life with God – as 'realized' in the present time through faith. Some interpreters of John have seen little future hope remaining: all is embodied in Jesus in the present. There is still, however, a future resurrection of the dead, when they 'come out of the tombs' and enter fully into eternal life with God (5.28–9; 6.44). Jesus is both the resurrection, the one who was raised to life by God and through whom the dead will be raised from the tombs at the last day, and the life, God's means of giving eternal life to all who have faith (11.25). John thus maintains the hope of resurrection, but stresses the present possession of eternal life for those who remain in union with the source of life, the Son who comes from the Father.

SYMBOLISM IN THE GOSPEL OF JOHN

One does not need to read much of the Gospel of John to note that its depiction of Jesus depends greatly on the use of metaphor and imagery. Some of the images used for Jesus include 'lamb of God', 'temple', 'bread of life', 'gate', 'shepherd', 'vine', 'light', and 'path'. Much of this imagery and many of the themes in John have a widespread religious appeal. Metaphors incorporating light, life, water, eating and drinking, new birth, shepherds and sheep, vines, seeds and growth are common to Judaism and Christianity, but also to other religions, for they are fundamentally images of and about life. For this reason, John has sometimes been dubbed a 'universal gospel,' directed to the widest possible readership, including believers and non-believers, Jews and Gentiles. As we noted earlier, the opening designation of Jesus as the Logos would serve well to capture both the Greek and the Jewish imagination.

But while the various Johannine images do indeed have a universal flavour, most, if not all, also have particular resonances with Old Testament imagery and the Jewish traditions of Jesus' own day. To take one example, bread may be the 'staff of life,' but to designate Jesus as 'bread of life' also recalls the manna with which God sustained the wandering Israelites in the wilderness (Deut 8.1–4), the unleavened loaves subsequently eaten at celebrations of Passover, and both wisdom and the Torah (Jn 6; Sir 15.3; 24.19–21). To picture Jesus as the 'bread of life' uses an image of food, fundamental to human sustenance, but also compares him to the particular gifts of God to Israel which nourished them physically and spiritually. The duality of this symbolism fits with John's presentation of Jesus as the Word, through whom the world was created, in whom 'was life' (1.13), and who became incarnate in particular historical circumstances to bring knowledge of God which is eternal life (17.3; 3.16). To understand him properly one must understand him against the universal canvas of creation, as well as against the Jewish canvas of scripture.

Particularly when John portrays Jesus *vis-à-vis* his Jewish heritage, there is an emphasis on the surpassing abundance of grace and truth which is embodied in and through him. The gift of bread given through him surpasses the manna given through Moses (6.32–3), even as the grace and truth which come through the incarnate Word provide a fullness, an abundance, not known even through Moses (1.14, 16–18). Torah was described not only as bread to be eaten, but as a path to follow so that one may live (Deut 5.32–3) and a light for the path (Ps 119:105). But now Jesus is the living bread, and also the light, not only for Israel, but for the whole world (8.12; 9.5), and the very pathway to life (14.6). The shepherd was used both for God (Pss 23; 78.70–2; Jer 31.10) and for the king of Israel (Ezek 37:24). Now Jesus is the ideal shepherd and king, who is willing to give his life to protect his flock. Israel was sometimes portrayed as a vine or vineyard (Isa 5.1–10; Jer 2.21; Hos 10.1; Ezek 15, 17, 19), but now Jesus and his followers are the 'true vine' of God who bear much fruit. The banquet used to picture future salvation is now already being served with an abundance of wine (2.1–11) and bread (6.12–13).

John uses references to various feasts of the Jewish calendar to provide movement to the narrative, and draws upon imagery important in the celebration of these feasts to further portray the significance of Jesus *vis-à-vis* his Jewish heritage. On the day of rest commanded for Israel, Jesus does the 'work' of his Father when he heals one man and opens the eyes of another. After healing a man at the pool of Bethesda on a sabbath (5.1–11), Jesus justifies his apparent violation of the Law by claiming that he has the right to do God's work of giving life and judging, and that he has the authorization to work on the sabbath day, a prerogative which the later rabbis, as well as Jewish authors such as Philo, thought reserved for God. Thus, in doing the sort of life-giving, saving work which God does, and in doing so on the day intended for human rest, Jesus shows himself to be 'equal with God' (5.18). John sets Jesus' feeding of the 5,000 and his death at Passover, a feast commemorating God's great act of deliverance of his people from Egypt to the promised land, and his provision for them in the wilderness. Jesus feeds the people in the wilderness, offering them the sustaining food of his life-giving death (6.51), which delivers them from slavery to sin (8.31–6). Chapters 7–9 are set in Jerusalem at the feast of Tabernacles, and include the healing of the blind man, the promise to give the Spirit, who will be like a well of water of eternal life, as well as the revelatory saying, 'I am the light of the world.' Tabernacles provides an important context for the narration of these events, because water and light were both important symbols in its celebration. On the last day of the feast, a golden candelabra, said to give light to all Jerusalem, was lit in the Temple, and water drawn from the pool of Siloam was poured over the altar in the Temple. It is likely that John wishes to present Jesus as the one who brings light to the blind and water to the thirsty, and to do so with respect to Law, Temple and other aspects of Jewish ritual, suggesting that God now offers through him what was previously offered in other ways.

JOHN'S DUALISTIC WORLDVIEW

Johannine symbolism has been called dualistic, setting the realities it pictures in stark opposition to each other. Jesus brings light to darkness, freedom from slavery, and life out of death, and reveals love in the midst of hate. He is 'not of this world', whereas his opponents are. In such statements, to 'be of' (*ek einai*) something refers both to origin and destiny. That Jesus is not 'of this world' means that ultimately he comes from God, in whom his destiny also lies. He himself is the Son of Man, who comes from above, whereas his adversaries are 'from below'. Only the life-giving Spirit can bring the birth from above to give new life to the flesh without which it otherwise remains dead (3.6; 6.63). Dualism, as its name implies, is the view that the world is divided into two realities. But Johannine dualism is not absolute, in that the two realities are not co-equal or co-eternal. Sometimes scholars speak of such dualism as 'modified' or 'qualified', because in Jewish and Christian thought God is the ultimate creator and source of all that is, hence the dualism does not inhere in the created order. Rather, Johannine dualism describes, in the sharpest categories, what is at stake in following Jesus. Since he is the light, life and truth which come from above, to follow him means to align oneself with those realities found only in him.

Johannine dualism also underlies the frequent misunderstandings in the gospel, instances in which individuals misunderstand Jesus' words or deeds because they have not understood them 'from above' but rather 'from below'. Often these misunderstandings play on dual meanings of words. Jesus tells Nicodemus that he must be 'born from above' (*anōthen*), a word which may also mean 'again'. Misunderstanding Jesus' point that he needs the Spirit of God to bring new birth to him so that he may enter into the life of God, Nicodemus incredulously asks how a person can enter into his mother's womb to be born a second time. When Jesus tells the woman at the well in Samaria that he can give her 'living water', she thinks he is promising her some kind of running stream which would spare her the long trek to Jacob's well. When Jesus feeds the crowds in the wilderness and promises that he can give them bread from heaven, they think he is talking about a perpetual source of bread to eat (6.33–4). Having healed the man born blind, Jesus says that he has come into the world 'so that those who do not see may see, and that those who see may become blind' (9.39), leading the Pharisees to wonder whether he is calling them blind. Caiaphas ironically prophesies that Jesus must 'die for the nation', by which he means that Jesus must be offered up as a scapegoat to prevent the Roman destruction of the Jewish people. But John calls this a prophetic statement, for Caiaphas did not in fact know that Jesus would indeed die 'not only for the nation, but to gather together the children of God who are scattered abroad'. Even the disciples misunderstand Jesus' reference to Lazarus as one who is 'asleep' (11.13).

The failure to understand Jesus illustrates the need for the Spirit's work to give insight into the identity of Jesus and to understand the realities of which he speaks. Those who are 'of the world' cannot understand the one who comes from the Father, who is from above, apart from a divine act of spiritual birth (3.3, 5) and God's instruction (6.44–5). Without such divine initiative and intervention, there is misunderstanding, confusion and rejection of Jesus. When some of Jesus' followers fail to understand how he will give them his flesh to eat, and perhaps think he is talking about an act of cannibalism, they no longer follow him. Similarly, when he makes the bold claim, 'Before Abraham was, I am', even those who had believed in him (8.31) pick up stones to throw at him (8.59). His inner core of disciples often does no better, but nevertheless they have an essential trust that Jesus is the Messiah, the holy one of God, who has 'the words of eternal life', and so they continue to follow after him in discipleship.

DISCIPLESHIP AND SPIRIT IN THE GOSPEL OF JOHN

John's symbolic portrait of Jesus highlights both the personal and the corporate dimensions of faith. On the one hand, response to Jesus is response to a person, rather than adherence to a set of ideas or a movement. The first words which Jesus speaks in the gospel are an invitation to follow after him: 'Come and see' (1.39; cf. 1.46) and 'follow me' (1.43). And the last words which he speaks are the same invitation, 'follow me' (21.19, 22). John thus underscores that discipleship in the post-resurrection situation remains essentially the same as before, in that it entails following after a person. In calling people to follow him, Jesus promises them light so that they may see, and speaks of himself as the path to the Father, and a gateway for entry into life. The prominence of imagery of Jesus as a path to follow points to discipleship as an act of personal commitment which requires steady persistence. There is a particularly negative view of disciples who make an initial commitment to Jesus but subsequently cease to walk with him or, worse, betray him altogether, like Judas. By contrast, John alone describes one of Jesus' followers as 'the disciple whom Jesus loved', and this disciple follows Jesus even to his death on the cross, and is still faithfully following the risen Jesus. Perhaps, then, it is no accident that John always uses the verb 'believe', rather than the noun 'belief'. Belief, or faith, is an ongoing commitment, a persistent trusting. Indeed, John sketches the perils of being a follower of Jesus, warning of hatred, persecution and martyrdom (15.19–23). In such situations, discipleship requires faithfulness, constancy and commitment.

Coupled with this dynamic view of discipleship as a steady, persistent following after Jesus are images of dwelling in safety and security. The original Temple, built by Solomon, son of David, was destroyed, even as the Temple built after the return from the Babylonian exile was also destroyed; but Jesus is a temple, a dwelling-place of God, which is eternal (2.21–2).

As the good shepherd, Jesus gathers the sheep together into a sheepfold where he protects them from wolves and thieves (10.11–16). He holds them securely in his hand, a picture which once again calls upon Old Testament images of God as holding his sheep. Thus when the man born blind is virtually disowned by his parents (9.21–3) and ridiculed and repudiated by others, Jesus seeks him out (9.28–35). Aware of his imminent death, Jesus promises his disciples that he is going to prepare a place where they may be with him and with God, but he also promises them that he is not abandoning them (14.18). Instead, he and his Father will 'dwell with them' (14.23). Jesus' promise here echoes the earlier affirmation of the prologue that in him the Word had become flesh and 'dwelt among us' (1.14). There is a constancy of Jesus' presence with his own, making it possible for them to remain united with him, clinging to him as a branch to a vine, in order that they may continue to have life (15.4–5). Because disciples have a secure dwelling-place, they also have peace, joy and assurance.

John's metaphors also underscore the corporate dimensions of discipleship. As a shepherd, Jesus gathers the sheep together into a sheepfold (10.16). His death will serve to 'gather together the children of God scattered abroad' (11.52). As a seed must first be buried in the ground, Jesus must die so that he will not remain alone (12.24). On the cross, he designates his mother and the disciple whom he loved as mother and son to each other, thereby establishing the family of the children of God (19.26–7). Throughout the gospel he had spoken of his death as the act whereby 'all people' are drawn to him (12.32); the new family gathered by him is the result of his death. Jesus also commands the disciples to love each other (13.34–5), praying for their unity, even as he and his Father are one (17.21).

Whereas in the synoptic gospels Jesus admonishes his disciples to love their enemies, in John the primary command given to them is to love each other. Both the synoptic and Johannine traditions base these commands on the model of divine love. According to Matthew, disciples are to love their enemies because they are children of the heavenly Father, who 'makes his sun rise on the evil and on the good, and sends rain on the just and on the unjust' (Matt 5.43–5). In the Gospel of John, it is the love of God in Christ which lays the foundation for the identity and communal life of the community of disciples after Jesus' death. Even as the Father demonstrates his love for the world through the giving of the Son (3.16), so the church witnesses to the love of God as it strives to live together in the kind of self-giving love for each other which Jesus had for them.

Jesus equips his followers for this mission by sending them the Spirit, even as he had promised. John's gospel presents a somewhat fuller picture of the Holy Spirit than do the synoptics and, not surprisingly, John's portrait of the Spirit has numerous distinctive features. Most notably, John refers to the Spirit as 'the Paraclete', the only book in the New Testament to do so. The term most likely refers to the Spirit as an advocate on behalf of the disciples. The Spirit defends the disciples, serving as an advocate for them, by convicting the world of sin, thus proving the disciples to be in the right in their commitment to Jesus (Jn 16.7–8). Within the community itself, the Spirit has the role of making Jesus and the Father present to the disciples, in part by continuing the role of teaching and revealing truth. Clement of Alexandria spoke of the synoptic gospels as presenting *ta sōmatika*, the 'bodily' or 'physical' facts about Jesus, whereas John wrote a 'spiritual' (*pneumatikon*) gospel.[6] Whatever Clement may have meant, John views the Spirit of God as guiding the disciples into understanding and remembering the truth, and undoubtedly believed that the portrait of Jesus found in the gospel was the product of just such guidance.

The Spirit also seals the disciples in eternal life, effecting the new birth promised by Jesus (3.3–5). In keeping with John's accent on Jesus as the one who exercises divine prerogatives and power, Jesus 'breathes' the Spirit to his disciples (20.22–3). This scene recalls Gen 2.7, where God breathes the breath of life into humankind so that they become 'living beings'. The prophet Ezekiel uses this imagery to speak of God's re-creation and renewal of his people after their sojourn in the Babylonian exile, for God will breathe life into them, and make their dry, dead bones live (Ezek 37). So too Jesus breathes the Spirit of life into his disciples. And thus the gospel comes full circle, for the one through whom God created the world now breathes the renewing Spirit of God to his followers.

CONCLUSION

The distinctiveness of John's gospel has never gone unnoticed in the church. Clement's dictum that John was a 'spiritual gospel' acknowledges, but does not attempt to explain fully, that distinctiveness. Perhaps no amount of scholarly effort can ever achieve that goal; John, for whatever reasons, has simply penned a distinctive account of the life and ministry of Jesus of Nazareth. And yet this is clearly an account of that same Jesus, an account framed by the ministry of the Baptist at the beginning and the crucifixion and resurrection at the end, with overlapping if not identical incidents recounted in between. Moreover, virtually all of the themes and imagery in John have counterparts in the synoptic tradition, but these very themes are also developed more much extensively in John. If in the synoptic gospels God is named as 'Father' and Jesus as 'Son', what is merely sounded as a theme in the first three gospels becomes a full-blown symphony in John. Not every theme is picked up and developed in that way; some are simply left untouched. But those which are picked up, elaborated and introduced from other material or from the evangelist's own creativity are used to present Jesus as the embodiment of God's presence in the world for its life and salvation. More than any other gospel-writer, John wishes his reader to see that what Jesus is for believers in the present, he was for his disciples during his own lifetime, the life and light of God for the world.

Notes

1. The commentaries of C. K. Barrett (*The Gospel According to St John*; 2nd edn; Philadelphia: Westminster, 1978) and Raymond E. Brown (*The Gospel according to John*; Garden City: Doubleday, 1966, 1970) might be taken here as representative of these two different approaches.

2. For a judicious discussion of the issues, which argues for John's independence from the other gospels, see D. Moody Smith, *John Among the Gospels: The Relationship in Twentieth-Century Research* (Minneapolis: Fortress, 1992).

3. The work of J. Louis Martyn (*History and Theology in the Fourth Gospel*; 3rd edn; Louisville: Westminster/John Knox, 2003), more than any other recent work in Johannine studies, has sharpened the focus on the relationship of the 'church' and 'synagogue' as shaping the Gospel of John. But, for some caveats, see the various essays in Richard Bauckham, ed., *The Gospels for All Christians: Rethinking the Gospel Audiences* (Grand Rapids: Eerdmans, 1998).

4. The ways in which John has drawn upon the Old Testament and diverse Jewish interpretative traditions have been the focus of numerous recent studies; see, for example, the work of Peder Borgen, including *Bread from Heaven* (Leiden: E. J. Brill, 1965); and 'God's Agent in the Fourth Gospel', in John Ashton, ed., *The Interpretation of John* (Edinburgh: T. & T. Clark, 1997).

5. For the potential diversity of the influences which have shaped John, see the still valuable and suggestive work by C. H. Dodd, *The Interpretation of the Fourth Gospel* (Cambridge: Cambridge University Press, 1953).

6. Eusebius, *Church History*, VI 14.

Further reading

Ashton, John, ed., *The Interpretation of John* (2nd edn, Edinburgh: T. & T. Clark, 1997)

Ashton, John, *Understanding the Fourth Gospel* (Oxford: Clarendon, 1991)

Barrett, C. K., *The Gospel according to St John* (2nd edn, Philadelphia: Westminster, 1978)

Brown, Raymand E. *The Community of the Beloved Disciple* (London: Goeffrey Chapman, 1979)

Dodd, C. H., *The Interpretation of the Fourth Gospel* (Cambridge: Cambridge University Press, 1953)

Hill, Charles E., *The Johannine Corpus in the Early Church* (Oxford: Oxford University Press, 2004)

Koester, Craig R., *Symbolism in the Fourth Gospel: Meaning, Mystery, Community* (2nd edn, Minneapolis: Fortress, 2003)

Lincoln, Andrew T., *Truth on Trial* (Peabody: Hendrickson, 2000)

Martyn, J. Louis, *History and Theology in the Fourth Gospel* (3rd edn, Louisville: Westminster/John Knox, 2003)

Painter, John, *The Quest for the Messiah: The History, Literature and Theology of the Johannine Community* (2nd edn, Nashville: Abingdon, 1993)

Smith, D. Moody, *The Theology of the Gospel of John* (Cambridge: Cambridge University Press, 1995)

Thompson, Marianne Meye, *The God of the Gospel of John* (Grand Rapids: Eerdmans, 2001)

Part III

The afterlife of the gospels: impact on church and society

FRANCES YOUNG

THE GOSPELS IN THE EARLY CHURCH

Before we examine what impact the gospels had on the development of doctrine, we need to explore the place of the gospels in the church in the first centuries. By the end of the second century an established pattern had clearly developed: the four gospels that we know as part of the New Testament canon were accepted as authoritative and read liturgically in most of the churches recognized by what would become the Christian mainstream. However, it is also clear that this was the result of some struggle over the issue, and that there were groups designated as heretical which preferred gospels other than the four we know, or fixed on one of the four, or sought to create one out of the four. Irenaeus, bishop of Lyon at the end of the second century, provides us with the arguments for the fourfold gospel and against other positions. Examining what he has to say, and what lay behind it, is instructive, if somewhat strange, to our ways of thinking.

For Irenaeus,[1] the fourfold gospel is providential, corresponding, first, to the fourfold nature of the created universe: there are four regions of the world and four winds (using the same Greek word as for 'breath' and 'spirit'), so, as the church is scattered all over the world and her 'pillar and ground' (1 Tim 3.15) is the gospel and the Spirit of life, it is fitting that she should have four pillars, breathing out immortality and reviving people in every place. Secondly, the fourfold gospel corresponds to the cherubim with four faces – the lion, the calf, the human, the eagle – each representing an aspect of the Logos (Word), namely, his kingship, his sacrifice, his first advent, and his gift of the Spirit. Irenaeus relates each gospel to one of these, so beginning a long tradition of artistic and exegetical symbolism. Finally he notes the four covenants given to the human race: with Adam, with Noah, with Moses, and the new covenant in Christ.

These analogies imply that the fourfold-ness relates to underlying unities: the unity of the one church throughout the world, the unity of the one God who is enthroned upon the cherubim (Ps 80.1), the unity of the Son of God, the Logos, and finally the unity and continuity of God's 'economy', that is, the way God orders his relations with the world in covenantal dispensations. But, for Irenaeus, such unities do not imply one gospel text, since there is a kind of given-ness about the four. So firm is the ground on which the four gospels rest, he says, that even the heretics start from these documents, as each tries to establish his own doctrine but is confuted by the gospel text itself. He claims that the Ebionites use only Matthew, and Marcion only a Luke he has mutilated; that adoptionists prefer Mark, and Valentinians exploit John. Later he refers to Valentinian use of a work called the Gospel of Truth, which he roundly rejects, claiming that the four gospels alone are reliable and true, and that they represent God's harmonious arrangement of everything.

All of this discussion presupposes that there is a close link between correct doctrine and the proper use and interpretation of the four gospels together; yet it uses arguments which are extraneous to the gospels themselves. It also implies the reception of the four gospels as authoritative, while providing evidence that that reception was contested. Irenaeus indicates that the fourfold gospel is established as scripture alongside the Apostle (a collection of epistles), and matching the Fivefold Law and the Prophets. But, as we shall see, his assumption that that was originally the case and that the heretics challenged an existing canon cannot be right. The status of the gospels earlier in the second century needs to be investigated.

If we go back to the beginning, we enter what has been termed a 'tunnel period', in which it is far from transparently clear what was happening to the Jesus traditions or the gospels as such. New Testament scholarship has exercised much ingenuity in trying to piece together clues about the origins of the gospels, the debates betraying how little is really certain. By Irenaeus' time there was a general consensus that two were written by apostles, Matthew and John, and two by close associates of the apostles, Mark and Luke, but it is doubtful how secure the apostolic attributions are. Determining the dates of their composition is even more speculative, given the absence of any traditions and the evidence of mutual interaction in the composition of the first three gospels, if not also of the fourth. Tradition had it that Matthew was the first to be written, but the biblical criticism of the modern period generally reached the consensus that Mark had priority. At what date the gospel texts were known and used is likewise contested, and this is the issue that we need to focus on for the purpose of this chapter. If the gospels were not widely disseminated and known, how could they have influenced the development of doctrine at the time under discussion?

The evidence we can muster is sparse and its interpretation contested. Apart from the writings of the New Testament itself, we have a group of works known as the Apostolic Fathers, variously dated to the late first and early second centuries, but their dating is subject to the same difficulties as dating the gospels themselves. Like the New Testament epistles, these writings never explicitly quote from or even refer to written gospels, though sayings and phrases often seem like allusions to them. So debate has raged[2] as to whether these parallels arise because of a common oral tradition, or whether they imply direct knowledge of one or other of the gospel texts. The matter is not easily settled. Our conventions about acknowledging sources and quoting accurately were not operative in the ancient world – indeed, rhetorical textbooks advised a rather freer and more creative use of literary allusion. The reader can easily see the nature of the problem by turning to Rom 12–14. Paul never says that any of the sayings he uses come from Jesus, and the majority of scholars now dismiss the idea that he knew the Sermon on the Mount or other written gospels, yet time and again his words recall familiar gospel material. The case is much the same in the writings known as the Apostolic Fathers. Clearly, if the original reader knew that the author was alluding to the written gospels, this would make a difference to the way the text was understood. But it could be that they were sharing the 'in-language' of the community they belonged to, sayings current among them, phrases from their gatherings for worship, as seems most likely in the case of Paul. As indicated, scholars can be found arguing the case on either side, and we should not forget that Papias, bishop of Hierapolis and contemporary of Polycarp, the aged bishop who is reported to have known the apostle John, is said to have preferred the 'living and abiding voice' to things written in books.[3] It would seem that, despite apparently knowing the gospels of Mark and Matthew, he regarded highly any kind of contact with the apostles, even if second-hand and mediated by oral tradition. So the debate is not easily settled.

We remain, then, in the 'tunnel period', further tantalized by the discovery in Egypt of a papyrus fragment of the Gospel of John which is dated to the first quarter of the second century, though it should more likely be placed at or somewhat before mid-century. This certainly challenged some extreme theories about the late date of this gospel, especially given the time needed for dissemination from wherever it was composed (probably Asia Minor or Syria) to the place where this fragment was found. It also suggests that the process of dissemination was remarkably fast. Maybe the churches in the major cities of the Mediterranean did generally have copies of the gospels rather earlier than the actual evidence can prove. On the other hand,

John's gospel in particular appears to have been problematic; for the discussion in Irenaeus' work rather suggests that he had to rescue it from the heretics, dispelling reservations about its use because gnostics had found it congenial. He provides it with a pedigree, tracing back tradition through the aged bishop Polycarp: Polycarp had known the apostle John, and Irenaeus himself knew Polycarp.[4] As for Papias, written material needed to have its authenticity confirmed by living contact, however indirect. The heretical use of the fourth gospel is confirmed by Origen's *Commentary on John*, which repeatedly refutes the exegesis of a gnostic named Heracleon, who seems to have been the first to create a commentary on the Johannine text.

The earliest reference to what could be gospel reading in church comes around mid-second century in the first *Apology* of Justin Martyr.[5] Justin outlines a Christian meeting, largely to show how innocuous such meetings were. He refers to 'memoirs' composed by the apostles, 'which are called gospels'. These indicate that Jesus took bread and when he had given thanks, said, 'Do this in remembrance of me.' Later he mentions that these memoirs of the apostles or the writings of the prophets are read as long as time permits at the Sunday gathering. It seems most likely that it is to some or all of the four gospels that Justin refers here, but which gospels did he know? In an earlier section of his *Apology*[6] where he is explaining what Christ taught, he seems to be quoting the Sermon on the Mount, or sometimes the Lucan version of the same teaching. So in Justin's time written texts of Christian origin are already being used within the church's liturgical setting alongside the Greek version of the Jewish scriptures (the Septuagint), and these seem to include at least Matthew and Luke. It might be all four: for Tatian was a pupil of Justin, and it was Tatian who composed the *Diatessaron* (c. 175 CE), a harmony of the four gospels.

The existence of the *Diatessaron* is important from two different angles. On the one hand, it shows that the four were widely known and accepted as the authoritative texts; on the other hand, it demonstrates a certain embarrassment about this, and awareness of discrepancies – should not 'the gospel' be one and consistent? By the time of Irenaeus there was resistance to the kind of tampering with the four that Tatian undertook, perhaps reinforced by the fact that by then he had been identified as a heretic. But meanwhile he had conducted missions in the Syriac-speaking areas on either side of the eastern border of the Roman Empire, and there the Syriac version of the *Diatessaron* became the most widely used gospel. In the fifth century we find the bishop of Cyrrhus, Theodoret, trying to establish the use of the four gospels and stamp out the *Diatessaron*. But to return to the mid-second century, it is interesting that, though the four have primacy, there seems little inhibition about revising the texts into one harmonious whole.

Indeed, Tatian's disquiet about the four, together with his willingness to be creative, is representative of attitudes in the mid-second century. For gospels, along with other narrative material, were multiplying in this period, while some groups, as indicated by Irenaeus, were restricting themselves to one gospel. It may be objected that such developments were largely countenanced among heretics, but it is not quite as simple as that. Hindsight so often provides the classifications – at the time it must have been much more difficult to discern where the truth lay. Indeed, orthodoxy often emerged in reaction to teaching that was rejected, and notorious heretics like Valentinus and Marcion were members of the church in Rome for some time before being excommunicated. The boundaries were not clear – they were being clarified. Besides, some of the narrative literature that was produced continued to have influence in the church even if not received into what became the canon of scripture: in particular this is true of the *Protevangelium of James*, which provided details about the Holy Family and the birth of Jesus, especially affirming Mary's perpetual virginity. Other lost gospels, such as the *Gospel of the Hebrews*, were known to the church fathers and attributed to groups such as the Ebionites, who were probably Jewish Christian groups marginalized by the predominantly Gentile mainstream, and mistakenly vilified. Scholarship now knows more about the many eventually proscribed gospels because of the rediscovery of gnostic material at Nag Hammadi, and some scholars[7] believe that the rediscovered Gospel of Thomas may well contain reliable traditions that are older than the canonical gospels. Hindsight did indeed tend to label alternatives to the four as unorthodox.

If we put ourselves back into the second century, then, there is a real question as to whether emerging doctrine determined which gospels were acceptable, or whether acceptable doctrine was derived from the gospels regarded as most reliable. The interaction was probably complex, though one suspects that the former trend was dominant, not least because we have evidence of the use of the *Gospel of Peter* being discouraged after the bishop of Antioch, Serapion, discovered that it was not the innocent document he had supposed, but that the heretical doctrines of the docetists were to be found in it.[8]

DOCTRINE AND GOSPEL

One reason why there was an instinctive sense that the gospel should be one must have been that the word did not originally suggest a written text at all. In the New Testament the word means 'good news', and there is only one gospel, that of Jesus Christ. This is what Paul repeatedly claims he preaches, condemning those who preach 'another gospel' (Gal 1.6). In a number of places he provides a confessional summary of his gospel: to take but one example, 'the gospel of God, which he promised beforehand through his prophets in the holy scriptures, the gospel concerning his Son, who was descended from David according to the flesh, and was declared to be Son of God with power according to the spirit of holiness by resurrection from the dead, Jesus Christ our Lord . . .' (Rom 1.1–4). Interestingly, such confessions can be found, not only in the New Testament, but also in the Apostolic Fathers.[9] This kind of summary provided the kernel of the one gospel, which, as Irenaeus would eventually argue, came in a fourfold form. It would appear that such statements are the distant precursors of creeds. What I want to suggest is that, particularly in the earliest stages, such statements were in practice more important for doctrinal development than the gospels themselves.

What is doctrine? The word comes from the Latin, and both the Latin word *doctrina* and the Greek word *dogma* simply mean 'teaching'. Teaching was not characteristic of religion in the ancient world. Naturally it belonged to the world of education, and the climax of education for the elite was philosophy. So it is highly significant that Justin Martyr dressed and behaved as a Christian philosopher. In its socio-historical context, the early church was more like a school than a religion.[10] Jews had already attracted some approval as philosophers with a high moral standard. Synagogue and church alike were analogous to schools, teaching from a body of literature other than the classics of the Greco-Roman tradition, namely the Jewish scriptures.

For the second-century church the significant body of literature remained the Septuagint. So it is particularly telling that Justin tells the story of Jesus Christ through prophecies in the Jewish scriptures, not from the gospels.[11] This might seem less generally important in light of an assertion of Ignatius, the early second-century bishop of Antioch (whose writings are included among the Apostolic Fathers): against those who would not believe a thing unless it was found in 'our ancient records', he had affirmed, 'My records are Jesus Christ, and my sacrosanct records are His cross and death and resurrection, and the faith that comes through him'.[12] But in fact that protest proves the point: the only recognized scriptures were the Jewish scriptures, and they were interpreted as containing the gospel. Christian teaching (=doctrine) was exposition of those scriptures so as to identify the one to whom they pointed.

That exposition was shaped by those summary confessions about Jesus Christ, malleable as they were. Ignatius, indeed, shows how they were easily adapted to exclude what was regarded as false teaching: 'Be deaf when anyone speaks to you apart from Jesus Christ, who was of the stock of David, who was from Mary, who was truly born, ate and drank, was truly persecuted under Pontius Pilate, was truly crucified, and died in the sight of beings heavenly, earthly and under the earth, who was also truly raised from the dead, His Father raising him . . .'[13] As in Paul's summaries, the birth, death and resurrection are far more important than the teaching or miracle-working; but there is an added dimension – for apparently in some sense the reality of the incarnation is being contested, treated as a mirage or sham, perhaps. So the emphasis on that reality is reinforced. The summaries are becoming ways not merely of confessing the faith but of safeguarding the principles at its heart.

In this first stage of doctrinal development, then, the gospel texts seem to play little part, but the gospel in the form of confessional summary is key. In the following section we will explore the continued outworking of this as we look at creeds and the gospels. We shall find that even when the four gospels had been accepted as canon, and their texts quoted for doctrinal proof, the overarching sense of what scripture as a whole is about remains the most significant factor for doctrine, that sense being summed up in creeds – the successors to these confessions. However, after Irenaeus we can discern a new stage in doctrinal development. For now there is a recognized literary collection articulating the 'New Covenant/Testament', and balancing the 'Old Covenant/Testament' enshrined in the Septuagint. This has become a 'canon' or 'benchmark', the standard to which appeal will be made in future debate and controversy. Although the precise contents of that canon would remain fluid for a couple of centuries more, the place of the four gospels within it would not be controversial again.

Controversy about doctrine, however, would continue. Increasingly, as people were engaged in defending and making sense of the faith, all sides would claim to represent the tradition and would appeal to the text of scripture, including the gospels. Doctrine would become increasingly defined in formulas directed at excluding what were judged to be erroneous interpretations of these benchmarks. The origin of creeds probably lies in the context of baptismal instruction and liturgy, but their precursors included statements used specifically for the purpose of safeguarding orthodoxy, and as time went on this function became increasingly important. If we are to consider how the gospels affected the development of doctrine we must examine how they relate to the creeds.

CREEDS AND GOSPELS

The clearest statement about the relationship between scripture and creed is to be found in the *Catechetical Orations* of Cyril of Jerusalem in the fourth century. By this date learning a creed by heart and reciting it back to the catechist was a recognized element in the process of preparing for baptism. Cyril introduces the creed his catechumens are to learn by commenting: 'Since all cannot read the scriptures, some being hindered from knowing them by lack of education, and others by want of leisure . . . we comprise the whole doctrine of the faith in a few lines.' He adds that these were to be committed to memory, treasured and safeguarded, because 'it is not some human compilation, but consists of the most important points collected out of scripture'.[14]

Close inspection of the creeds, however, hardly suggests that that was literally how they took shape. The relationship with scripture is more problematic than that – there is nothing, for example, about the history of Israel as God's chosen people, though God does appear as the creator of everything there is, and there is reference to the prophets. The relation with the gospels is even more problematic. To all intents and purposes, there is nothing about the life and teaching of Jesus, the proclamation of the kingdom of God, or even the miracle-working. In fact the common elements in the various creeds of this date seem closer to the summary points in the early Christian confessions we were discussing before: they refer to Mary's virginal conception, to the crucifixion under Pontius Pilate, to death, burial and resurrection, to ascension, sitting at God's right hand in heaven, and future judgement. They are coherent with the gospels, but hardly derived from them. Prime emphasis is laid on the birth, death and exaltation of Christ Jesus, the Son of God.

Irenaeus again provides us with key evidence. In his various works he offers us several summaries of the faith which he designates as 'the Canon of Truth'. Slightly later we find similar material, often referred to as the 'Rule of Faith', in the works of Tertullian and Origen – these two represent both east and west in the early third century. All of them regard these summaries as statements of core Christian doctrine to be defended against heretics. Origen insists that all his theological explorations are consistent with this fundamental core. Yet the way these writers set out the Rule of Faith is remarkably flexible. No two accounts of it are identical. At the same time they often carry the set phrases familiar from the creeds and already traced in earlier second-century confessions, if not in the Pauline epistles. All of this suggests a continuous tradition which originated independently of written texts, and which ultimately became the criterion whereby the written texts of scripture, including the gospels, were interpreted.

Irenaeus' doctrinal arguments demonstrate how and why this was important. Let us consider one of his descriptions of how scripture is distorted by the heretics:

> Such then is their system, which the prophets did not announce, the Lord did not teach, and the Apostles did not hand down; but which they boastfully declare that they understand better than others . . . As the saying is, they attempt to make ropes of sand in applying the parables of the Lord, or prophetic utterances, or Apostolic statements to their plausible scheme, in order that they may have foundation for it. But they alter the scriptural context and connection, and dismember the truth as much as they can. By their perversions and changes, and by making one thing out of another, they deceive many with their specious adaptations of the oracles of the Lord. It is just as if there was a beautiful representation of a king made in a mosaic by a skilled artist, and one altered the arrangement of the pieces of stone into the shape of a dog or a fox, and then should assert that this was the original representation of a king. In much the same way they stitch together old wives' tales, and wresting sayings and parables, however they may, from the context, attempt to fit the oracles of God into their myths.[15]

Later on, Irenaeus uses another analogy, the custom of composing 'centos' of Homer – selected lines were taken out of context and strung together to make a new poem with a different plot. As Irenaeus points out, 'Anyone who knew Homer would recognize the lines but not accept the story.' He implies that this is what heretics do with the scriptures. So he not only needs to argue for the unity of all the scriptures, holding together the gospel and the books of the Old Covenant; he also needs a framework which demonstrates what the storyline is, what is the overarching sense of scripture. The 'Canon of Truth' provided the criterion of interpretation.

The same principle applies with respect to creeds in the later period. During the Arian controversy, some complained that the term *homoousios* was not scriptural, but the use of the term in the Nicene creed was defended on the grounds that only this term would guarantee the right reading of scripture.[16] It was necessary to have a grasp of what the whole gospel was about in order to read the gospels appropriately.

Many of the clauses which eventually found their way into the classic creeds are there because they incorporate traditional phrases which became prominent in the second century when the need was to defend, against the gnostics and Marcion, first, the oneness of the one true God, who is creator of all as well as Father of our Lord Jesus Christ, and, secondly, the reality of Christ's human birth of Mary the Virgin and of his suffering and death by crucifixion. Indeed, not just the creeds but the very text of the gospels betrays the effects of these second-century struggles, as Bart Ehrmann has demonstrated in his book *The Orthodox Corruption of Scripture*:[17] the state of flux in the second century explains some of the classic gospel variants, which emerge as the struggle with adoptionists, separationists and docetists was played out, subtle textual changes reinforcing the points that Jesus did not 'become' Christ at the baptism by adoption, the divine Christ did not 'forsake' the human Jesus on the cross, and the whole thing was no sham. These changes dominate the manuscript tradition. Yet it is more likely than not that they arose in the second century and were retained because they suited the emerging orthodox position.

So again we find that, in the earliest period, doctrinal formulations shaped the gospels rather than vice versa, and, even when the received text was fundamentally fixed, it remained true that interpretation of the gospels was affected by doctrinal considerations. Now, however, the gospels were themselves exploited to support positions argued for in doctrinal debate, and creeds provided both the criteria by which orthodox interpretation was identified and the overarching perspectives within which the gospels were read.

THE GOSPELS AND DOCTRINAL EXEGESIS

Systematic exegesis of scripture, in the form of commentaries or continuous homily series, does not appear until the emergence of Christian scholarship in the third century. Of the earliest biblical scholars, only the work of Origen survives in sufficient quantity to provide us with much access to methods and interests. From the fourth and fifth centuries, however, a mass of material is available, and eventually excerpts from the great patristic commentators were collected in *catenae*. This is not the place to explore such systematic exegesis as such. But discussion of the exegetical exploitation of the gospel texts in doctrinal controversy needs to be balanced with some observations about the interests of those for whom exegesis was the prime aim.

Christian scholarship adopted the methods of exegesis developed in the schools of antiquity (grammatical, rhetorical and philosophical), where the reading of the classics was the medium of instruction. Learning to read texts written without word division or punctuation, and often composed in archaic language, meant that initially much attention was paid to the details of construal and vocabulary. Such attention to the text rapidly led to the identification of metaphors and figures of speech, meanings not 'according to the letter'. For rhetorical purposes it was important to identify how the author had clothed his subject-matter in appropriate verbal dress, and to identify the use of allusion, explaining the classic myths, gods, heroes, events, places, etc. All of this generated the typical commentary note to assist the reader. But there was a universal interest in moving on from that to discuss the moral implications of the text, and, in the philosophical schools, to find their 'dogmas' about life, the universe and everything, hidden in the classic texts, often by means of allegory. It is hardly surprising that Christian scholars, such as Origen, approached texts in the same way, transferring these methods to the body of literature adopted by the Christian church, namely the scriptures. Moral and doctrinal reading was entirely natural. Such reading was reinforced by the inherited tradition of reading the Old Testament prophecies as referring to the Christ or the new dispensation inaugurated by him. Christian teaching about God, Christ, the Holy Spirit, salvation and the way to live was the real meaning of the whole Bible, clothed in narratives and metaphors.

Exactly how dogma was read out of scripture varied. There was a reaction against allegory in some quarters in the fourth century, but moral and doctrinal reading continued despite that. It is instructive to compare the exegeses of the feeding narratives by Origen (third-century allegorist) and John Chrysostom (late fourth-century anti-allegorist).[18] Origen[19] took the story of Christ's feeding of the multitude as symbolic of spiritual feeding. The desert place represented the desert condition of the masses without the law and the word of God, and the disciples were given power to nourish the crowds with rational food. The five loaves and two fish symbolized scripture and the Logos. Chrysostom[20] notes that Christ looked up to heaven to prove he is of the Father, and he used the loaves and fish, rather than creating food out of nothing, to stop the mouths of dualist heretics like Marcion and Manichaeus. He let the crowds become hungry, and gave them only loaves and fish, equally distributed, to teach the crowd humility, temperance and charity, and to have all things in common. He wanted to ensure that they did not become slaves to the belly.

Gospel commentaries from the fifth century are full of statements that we would regard as dogmatic. The atmosphere after Arius was such that commentators had to ensure that the texts were not being read wrongly. Indeed, Cyril of Alexandria's commentary on John's gospel is avowedly

looking for a 'more dogmatic exegesis', as he propounds orthodox interpretation and opposes heretical readings. This affects the whole approach
adopted in the commentary. It was written prior to his bitter controversy
with Nestorius over christology and the appropriateness of calling Mary
Theotokos, yet the issues that were to be focused then were already arising
as the implications of the Nicene reaction to Arius were taken to heart. An
example makes the point most easily. On Jn 14.16–17, Cyril's first comment
arises from the promise of Jesus to pray to the Father:

> He mingles again the human with the divine and neither returns to
> the pure glory of the Godhead nor indeed dwells wholly on the human
> dimension, but in a manner which transcends reason yet at the same
> time is consistent with the union of the natures operates through
> both, seeing he is simultaneously both God and man. For he was God
> by nature, in virtue of being the fruit of the Father and reflection of
> his essence. On the other hand he was man in virtue of having become
> flesh. He therefore speaks both as God and as man at the same time,
> for in this way it was possible to observe properly the form of words
> appropriate to the dispensation of the flesh.[21]

Clearly, doctrinal controversy shaped the questions that arose in relation
to the gospel texts. With awareness of the impact of doctrinal controversy
on exegesis of the gospels in general, it is time to look at the use of the
gospels in the controversies which shaped such dogmatic exegesis. To what
extent are the gospels quoted and referred to? Did their overall narrative of
the life and teaching of Jesus play any role?

There is a sense in which the great arguments about christology that took
place in the fourth and fifth centuries were essentially exegetical debates.
But it is important to realize that they were not focused exclusively on
the gospels, but rather on the whole of scripture. The core proof-text for
Arius seems to have been Prov 8.22: 'The LORD created me a beginning
of his ways.' Everybody agreed that this passage was about the pre-existent
Christ, the Logos, the Word or Wisdom of God, through whom God created
all things. Arius argued on the basis of this text that the Logos was a creature.
Athanasius countered by trying to discern the 'mind' of scripture as a whole
and the general use of language in scripture as a whole. We can see gospel
proof-texts figuring alongside others in this debate, but they appear far from
dominant. Irenaeus' legacy seems to remain fundamental. The unity of the
Bible, the fact that the Word of God speaks about himself in the prophecies of
the Old Testament, the Rule of Faith as the criterion for interpretation – all of
these contribute to the way texts are used, together with the intertextuality

developed by the scholarly exegetes for discerning the underlying sense of scripture as distinct from its surface meaning.

We can see how these factors operate if we explore some of Athanasius' anti-Arian writings. There is a brief treatise on the Nicene decrees (*Defence of the Nicene Definition*) which summarizes the arguments. There are the first two books of *Against the Arians* which systematically deal with key Arian claims and the texts on which they are based. Book III may not be authentic, and book IV certainly is not, though the third book is important whether Athanasian or not, and we will take it into consideration later. We may observe three general points:

(1) The controversial texts that Athanasius sets out to discuss in *Against the Arians* I and II are Phil 2.2–10; Ps 45.7–8; Heb 1.4; 3.2; Acts 2.36; and Prov 8.22 (at great length). All these texts, as read by the early church, were about the pre-existent Logos or Son of God. The problem was they seemed to imply that the Son of God was 'made' or appointed or exalted or created, not eternally and really Son of God. None are gospel texts. The *Defence of the Nicene Definition* discusses the different scriptural senses of the word 'son', drawing up collages of texts to distinguish between real sonship (Isaac being the son of Abraham), and the kind of sonship attributed to those who are obedient to God, or adopted by God, a sonship open to human creatures. The object is to establish the Logos's real sonship of the Father, while explaining the texts that favour the Arian position as applying solely to the conditions of the incarnation. Gospel texts are not the principal focus in this general discussion about the meaning of the word. Scripture as a whole is the issue.

(2) Athanasius has a series of favourite gospel texts that appear again and again, sometimes in collages of texts from all over scripture, sometimes singly in developing his argument. These are mainly Johannine. References to the prologue appear 4 times in the *Defence*, 12 times in book I of *Against the Arians* and 15 times in book II, various verses being called upon at differ-ent times. Other Johannine texts that appear in the *Defence* and repeatedly in *Against the Arians* are Jn 10.30 ('I and the Father are one') and Jn 14.9, 10–11 ('whoever has seen me has seen the Father'; 'the Father who dwells in me'; 'I am in the Father and the Father is in me'). In the more expansive exegetical discussions of *Against the Arians*, many more Johannine texts appear, notably some of the 'I am' sayings, quotations from chapter 17 and references to other Johannine discourses about who Jesus is, such as appear in chapters 5 and 8. Favourites in the synoptics are sparser, but include reference to the baptismal voice, to Peter's confession, to the address of the Lord's Prayer ('Our Father'), and to the passage in Matthew known today as the 'Johannine thunderbolt' (Matt 11.27).

(3) There is little reference to the details of Christ's human life apart from summary statements about his being hungry and thirsty, needing to ask questions like where Lazarus lay, and his suffering. Arians had clearly used the human life to argue that the Son was a creature; so the implications of these things are debated. The general picture presented in the gospels is implied by this, though the gospels themselves play little part.

The third book of *Against the Arians* presents a slightly different picture. To begin with, the texts under discussion are Johannine (14.10; 17.3; 10.30; 17.11). The Arians want to read these gospel texts as meaning that any human being can reach the same relationship with God as the Logos – by being obedient, they may be one with the Father. So there is a sustained argument for a distinction between the real Son of God and adopted sons of God. Then there is a switch to dealing with the incarnation as such, and gospel texts at last predominate. The difficulties highlighted by the texts quoted (and they are drawn from all over the gospels) are (1) the Son's reception of things from God, so implying he was not by nature from the Father (e.g. 'all things were delivered to me by the Father' (Matt 11.27), and similar Johannine statements); (2) his human weakness, implying he was not the true 'power' of the Father (as demonstrated by the troubling of his soul before the passion (Jn 12.27–8) and by the agony in Gethsemane, his fear, etc.); (3) his ignorance, implying he was not truly divine wisdom (examples include his asking questions at Caesarea Philippi, at the feeding of the multitude, etc.); and the problems that arise from his praying to the Father, his cry of dereliction on the cross, his not knowing the hour when the end will come, and so on. Suddenly details of the gospel narratives become the key focus of discussion.

The solution is not by proof-text or exegesis. The argument is that one has to look at the whole intent of scripture to discern what all this is about. The Johannine prologue and Phil 2.6–8 are quoted to provide an overall perspective. This is followed by stress on the soteriological imperative: he became human for our sake. The properties of the flesh are said to be his on account of his being in the flesh: hunger, thirst, suffering, being weary, and the like. The Logos bore our infirmities as his own, since the flesh was his. So, when the flesh suffered, the Logos was not external to it; and when he did divinely his Father's works, the flesh was not external; rather the body was his instrument or tool for doing them. Examples are given: when there was need to raise Peter's mother-in-law, who was sick of a fever, he stretched forth his hand humanly, but he stopped the illness divinely; in the case of the man born blind from birth, the spittle, which he produced from the flesh, was human, but he opened the eyes with the clay divinely; and in the case of Lazarus, he used a human voice as man, but divinely, as God, he raised Lazarus from the dead. Actual gospel narratives have now begun to figure large, but the exegesis is shaped contextually, by the questions raised in controversy rather than by the narratives themselves.

The rest of the book is an explanation of problem texts, and the whole either anticipates or reflects the christological struggles of the fifth century. In the Nestorian controversy the same kind of issue was sharpened up further: in the incarnation either the Logos underwent change or he seemed to. To avoid these alternatives, the so-called Antiochenes reinforced the distinction made in *Against the Arians* III between the Logos and the flesh – it was the humanity that experienced all the creaturely attributes of weakness, suffering, ignorance and so on. The so-called Alexandrians, however, insisted that, however mysterious and incomprehensible it might be, the subject of the narrative really was the Logos, who really was incarnate, accusing the others of teaching 'two Sons', the Son of David and the Son of God, and so dividing the Christ. The gospel narrative, summed up in the creeds, was in one sense at the heart of the debate. Key texts, however, were not confined to the gospels. Hebrews provided contentious material about weakness. Phil 2.7 was set against Jn 1.14: the way he 'became flesh' was by 'taking a body', not by changing. The same Philippians text furnished the notion of *kenōsis*, or self-emptying, as a way of maintaining the consistency of subject. What we see here is a process of deductive argument, based largely on a perception of what the whole story is about, a perception shaped by the Rule of Faith and summarized in the creeds, but also resting on longstanding intertextuality, the use of collages of texts to establish the underlying scriptural meaning of words. The gospels never stand alone.

So was there no biographical interest in the early church? Did the gospels not affect the development of doctrine simply by presenting the story of Jesus, so filling out a sense of his identity, his acts, his teaching, his example?

DOCTRINE, THE GOSPELS AND THE BIOGRAPHICAL IMPERATIVE

At one time it was fashionable to suggest that the gospels were not biographies. More recent scholarship has refined that judgement – they were in many respects like ancient biographies, even if they did not provide the sort of material we need to write a biography of Jesus of the kind we would expect.[22] That there was some biographical interest is further demonstrated by some of the apocryphal gospels and Acts, which again seem like ancient 'novella', and purport to give information, for example, about Jesus' boyhood. The idea that the early church had no interest in most of the narrative and teaching material in the gospels must be false. What has been challenged here is the simplistic notion that the gospels had a direct and dramatic impact on the development of doctrine.

Earlier, however, I mentioned the fact that *dogma* (Greek) and *doctrina* (Latin) simply mean 'teaching'. The teaching of the early church was broad-ranging, like that of ancient philosophy. It embraced cosmology and natural science through its interest in creation (see Basil of Caesarea's *Homilies on the Hexaemeron*, that is, the six days of creation). It included physiology as well as ethics in its anthropological thought (see Nemesius of Emesa, *On the Nature of Man*). And if we return from the cultured fourth century to the primitive second we quickly find that moral teaching about the proper 'way of life', coupled with appeal to the fact that God oversees everything, and all are accountable to God, is the predominant tone of the literature.[23] Jesus Christ is presented as teacher and example, as revealer of God's will for human beings. If we take seriously this broader meaning of doctrine, then clearly the teaching and character of Jesus have a fundamental importance.

Whether the gospels had a direct impact as early as the beginning of the second century is unclear for reasons stated earlier. The Apostolic Fathers produce collages of scriptural texts and gospel-like sayings, and may or may not have known the gospel texts. Oral tradition may have been more important in shaping the way of life taught in the church community and attributed to Jesus the teacher. However, by the middle of the second century we find Justin referring to the apostles' 'memoirs', quoting from the gospels we know, and insisting on the superiority of Jesus' teaching to that of other wise men. 'Brief and concise utterances fell from him, for he was no sophist, but his word was the power of God,' says Justin,[24] introducing a string of quotes which are largely drawn from Matthew. The selection is interesting: the first group all support chastity; then love, even of enemies, support of the needy, and not being anxious about worldly things are urged by long quotes from the Sermon on the Mount. Patience, good works, not swearing, and civil obedience are likewise grounded in gospel sayings.

Already the fact that Christians worship the maker of the universe only, and do so by spiritual, not animal, sacrifice, has been presented as coming from 'our teacher', Jesus Christ, who was born for this purpose and 'was crucified under Pontius Pilate, procurator of Judaea in the time of Tiberius Caesar'.[25] Furthermore, Justin shows interest in confirming the factuality of the story by other evidence, claiming that the birth of Jesus is evidenced in the tax declarations submitted under the procurator Quirinius and available at Rome for inspection, and that the *Acts of Pilate* confirm the miracles and details of the crucifixion.[26] Similar interest in factuality is apparent in the works of Gaius, a churchman who wrote in Rome at the turn of the second century: according to Eusebius,[27] he claimed in a *Dialogue with Proclus*, the leader of the Montanists, that he could point to the monuments of the victorious apostles, Peter and Paul, at the Vatican.

By the third century, the techniques of rhetorical criticism were being employed by Origen (for example) to assess the probability of gospel stories. In his exegesis he often develops a logic which leads to the conclusion that something was impossible and could not have happened. This then enabled him to say that the spiritual meaning was more important. There are some surprising cases: the cleansing of the Temple was 'improbable' – not only is there the problem that the accounts do not tally, but how could unclean animals be sold in the Temple? How could a carpenter's son have acted like that among myriads of people? The Son of God could hardly have taken a 'scourge of cords', surely? The point is the story is to be taken symbolically, and so the discrepancies between the gospels have a spiritual purpose and are not damaging to Christian claims.

In defending Christianity against Celsus, Origen uses the same techniques to demolish Celsus' story that 'the mother of Jesus was turned out by the carpenter who was betrothed to her, as she was convicted of adultery and had a child by a certain soldier named Panthera'.[28] Then he builds on the fact that Celsus has effectively admitted that Joseph was not Jesus' father, and mounts arguments for the appropriateness of the virginal conception in the case of Jesus. But when it comes to the baptism, which Celsus thinks is a fiction, Origen implicitly agrees – certainly the descent of the dove and the opening of the heavens were not perceptible to the senses. But of course the spiritual event happened. Debate about the factuality of the gospel narratives was clearly going on between the detractors and defenders of Christianity. Origen would not in the long run be representative of most Christians, since a more unquestioning assumption that the gospels were reliable and the difficulties were not material would prevail, but he was a skilful debater with knowledge of the kind of 'historical criticism' practised by ancient scholars of Homer and the classics.[29]

There was, then, some interest in the gospels as historical documents, especially among apologists and scholars. Furthermore, from Origen on, the gospels were a quarry for dogma in the sense of moral teaching, and moral teaching was read out of the gospel material systematically in the homiletic tradition, whether sayings, parables or actions. But this is to take dogma in its widest sense. As we have seen, in the development of doctrine in the narrower sense, it was the broad sweep of the story that really counted, the pattern of fall and redemption in the Bible as a whole, the recapitulation of Adam in Christ, and the contribution of the birth, suffering, death, resurrection and exaltation to that salvific process. The important thing was that these key events were real, had really happened, and really made us 'partakers of the divine nature' (2 Pet 1.4).

CONCLUSION

The question all this leaves us with is whether a doctrinal reading of the gospels is possible in an era when the 'original meaning' has become paramount, and the quest of the historical Jesus the chief preoccupation of scholars, Christian and non-Christian. Can doctrine really sit light to these preoccupations, as it clearly did in the early church?

Maybe the answer is that the early theologians had their eye on the ball. What really matters is not the historicity of this or that act or saying, but the overarching narrative. Doctrine provides concepts, abstractions, propositions which draw out the significance of the narrative, and doctrinal development therefore proceeded without reference to the historicity of every detail. Faith and discipleship, however, require the kind of fleshing out that presents us with a person who captures our imagination and calls us to follow. The fourfold gospel provides the rich texturing of testimony that is needed.

What I am suggesting, then, is that a doctrinal reading would be a non-reductive reading. It would take seriously the confessional framework which sees Jesus as 'the wholly human and visible icon of the wholly transcendent and invisible God',[30] recognizing that less paradoxical and more strictly historical attempts to characterize him necessarily reduce what he was. Straightforward accounts of his significance were invariably rejected as heresies.

Such a doctrinal reading would be open to illumination from liturgical reading of the gospels, and would avoid narrow definitions of Jesus Christ or his teachings. It would expect to find in the witness of the fourfold gospel a 'thick' portrait of the historical figure whose presence stimulated the extraordinary christological formulations that emerged through the controversies of the first five centuries, and it would seek to discern in the texts the appropriate way of responding to his call in the radically changed circumstances of life in the twenty-first century. By reading 'ourselves' into the text, believers may accept the prophetic challenges he offered in his day as still pertinent, as well as discerning and receiving the divine gift of new life which is mediated through him.

It was to safeguard the reality of human transformation through Christ that the fathers fought over the doctrinal definitions. But, paradoxically, they affirmed God as indefinable, in order to protect God's freedom and transcendence, the richness of God's being and grace. Routine repetition of formulas or assertions of fact, historical or otherwise, cannot be true to the intent of that doctrinal tradition. Authentic doctrinal reading demands the recognition that there can be inappropriate precision. Rich understanding requires discernment of the transcendent within the kind of narrative and drama that presents us with a character true to life, true to the circumstances of when and where he lived, true to the reality which we experience as made up of many particulars and revelatory of many facets of each person. Only through the fourfold gospel can the incarnation itself be enfleshed.

Notes

1. *Against Heresies*, III 11.8–9. ET, C. C. Richardson, ed., *Early Christian Fathers*, I (Philadelphia: Westminster, 1953).
2. Helmut Koester, *Synoptische Überlieferung bei den Apostolischen Vätern* (Texte und Untersuchungen 65, Berlin: Akademie-Verlag, 1957) argued for oral tradition and against knowledge of the texts. However, see J.-M. Sevrin, ed., *The New Testament in Early Christianity* (Leuven: Leuven University Press, 1989); and the ET of Massaux's classic thesis of 1950, *The Influence of the Gospel of Saint Matthew on Christian Literature before Saint Irenaeus* (Macon: Mercer University Press; Leuven: Peeters, 1990).
3. Quoted in Eusebius, *Church History* III 39. ET, G. A. Williamson (London: Penguin Classics, 1965).
4. III 1.1 and III 3.4.
5. *First Apology* 66–7. ET, Thomas B. Falls, *Fathers of the Church*, VI (Washington, DC: Catholic University of America Press, 1948).
6. *First Apology* 15.
7. See the references and discussion provided by Christopher Tuckett in Markus Bockmuehl, ed., *The Cambridge Companion to Jesus* (Cambridge: Cambridge University Press, 2001), 128–30.
8. Eusebius, *Church History* VI. 12.
9. See further below; also Frances Young, *The Making of the Creeds* (London: SCM Press, 1991), and J. N. D. Kelly, *Early Christian Creeds* (3rd edn, Longman, 1972).
10. Religion meant the traditional obligations to civic and familial gods, practices carried out in domestic shrines and public temples without explicit doctrines, creeds or even morals.
11. *First Apology* 32–53.
12. *Philadelphians* 8. ET, Maxwell Staniforth, rev. Andrew Louth, *Early Christian Writings* (London: Penguin Classics, 1987), 95.
13. *Trallians* 9.

14. *Catechetical Orations*, v 12. ET, Leo P. McCauley and Anthony A. Stephenson, *Fathers of the Church*, LXI (Washington, DC: Catholic University of America Press, 1968).
15. *Against Heresies*, I 8.1.
16. See further Frances Young, *Biblical Exegesis and the Formation of Christian Culture* (Cambridge: Cambridge University Press, 1997), ch. 2.
17. *The Orthodox Corruption of Scripture: The Effect of Early Christological Controversies on the Text of the New Testament* (New York and Oxford: Oxford University Press, 1993).
18. I reuse here an example given in Young, *Biblical Exegesis*, 162.
19. *Commentary on Matthew*, XI 1–4. ET, Allan Menzies, *Ante-Nicene Christian Library*, additional vol. (Edinburgh: T. & T. Clark, 1897).
20. *Homilies on Matthew* XLIX on Matt 14.19. ET, Philip Schaff (ed.), *Nicene and Post-Nicene Fathers*, 1st series, vol. x (Oxford and London: Parker and Co., 1889).
21. *Commentary on John* 9.1. ET from Norman Russell, *Cyril of Alexandria* (London and New York: Routledge, 2000), 122.
22. Richard A. Burridge, *What Are the Gospels?* (Cambridge: Cambridge University Press, 1992).
23. See the pastoral epistles, the Apostolic Fathers and the apologists; and for discussion, Frances Young, *The Pastoral Letters* (Cambridge: Cambridge University Press, 1994).
24. *First Apology* 14–17.
25. *First Apology* 13.
26. *First Apology* 34, 35 and 48.
27. Eusebius, *Church History* II. 25.
28. *Against Celsus* I 32. ET, Henry Chadwick (Cambridge: Cambridge University Press, 1965).
29. These two paragraphs are largely dependent on the work of R. M. Grant, whose book *The Earliest Lives of Jesus* (London: SPCK, 1961) explores the extent to which 'historical criticism' was practised in the first centuries, especially by Origen, and deserves to be better known.
30. This beautifully economic characterization of the 'two natures' doctrine comes from Markus Bockmuehl's introduction to *The Cambridge Companion to Jesus*, 1.

Further reading

Ackroyd, P., and Evans, C. F., eds., *The Cambridge History of the Bible*, I (Cambridge: Cambridge University Press, 1970)
Burton-Christie, Douglas, *The Word in the Desert: Scripture and the Quest for Holiness in Early Christian Monasticism* (New York: Oxford University Press, 1993)
Ehrman, Bart, *The Orthodox Corruption of Scripture: The Effect of Early Christological Controversies on the Text of the New Testament* (New York and Oxford: Oxford University Press, 1993)
Grant, R. M., *The Earliest Lives of Jesus* (London: SPCK, 1961)
Grillmeier, Aloys, *Christ in Christian Tradition* (London: Mowbrays, 1975)
Kelly, J. N. D., *Early Christian Creeds* (3rd edn, London: Longman, 1972)

Parker, David C., *The Living Text of the Gospels* (Cambridge: Cambridge University Press, 1997)

Sevrin, J.-M., ed., *The New Testament in Early Christianity* (Leuven: Leuven University Press, 1989)

Simonetti, Manlio, *Biblical Interpretation in the Early Church* (Edinburgh: T. & T. Clark, 1994)

Young, Frances, *The Making of the Creeds* (London: SCM Press, 1991)

Young, Frances, *Biblical Exegesis and the Formation of Christian Culture* (Cambridge: Cambridge University Press, 1997)

11 The gospels embodied: the lives of saints and martyrs

DAVID MATZKO McCARTHY

According to a stream of contemporary theology and biblical studies, the church's most basic interpretation of scripture is its embodiment of faith, in word and action.[1] Certainly, literary, historical and other critical tools ought to bear on how the Bible is understood, but, at its fundamental level, the truth of scripture is most fully grasped when lived out. This interpretative 'living out' is akin to 'performance'. It is analogous, for example, to an orchestra performing a symphony. The Bible, in other words, is understood genuinely and deeply when it is conveyed through human life, in the words and deeds of particular people, who venture to live out, in particular times and places, what they have heard, read and experienced of God in Christ. As a matter of consistency, according to the nature of scripture as canon, people of faith expect saints to be named where the Bible is read and the gospel proclaimed. From scripture flows a canon of saints.

In so far as interpreting the gospels through human life may be fruitful, the undertaking is necessarily extrabiblical, deeply personal and existential, and unavoidably theological. If living the gospel is a sure way to grasp it, the 'taking hold' is a venture that does not yield incontestable proof or demonstration. On the one hand, a person interprets and applies the gospels to life, and on the other, this person's life is interpreted by others in its conformity to the gospels. Each step along the way is a wager of faith. The meaning of a gospel text is mediated by people who respond to scripture as an existential call. A person's present-day is discovered in the text, as the gospel takes hold of the person; that is, his or her life is interpreted through the filter of the text.

The first section of this chapter will develop this point through a discussion of Ignatius of Loyola, whose important work *The Spiritual Exercises* has made him the saint of 'living in' the gospels. After the discussion of Ignatius and *The Spiritual Exercises*, our attention will shift to specific gospel texts that are performed by particular persons, whose embodied interpretations reflect the sense of the text for communities of Christians. I have organized the gospel texts theologically, moving through the themes of renunciation (Matt 19.21), kinship (Matt 12.50/Matt 10.37), works of mercy (Matt 25.40), and reconciliation (Lk 23.34). In doing so, I am following Ignatius' technique of setting the performance of the gospel texts within an overarching narrative of salvation. Two considerations determined the selection of specific texts. First, I began with ancient sources in order to find key texts, which are important also in the lives of modern saints. Second, I looked for texts that these modern saints not only live out, but also comment upon in their writings. By doing so, I attempt to mitigate the problem that saints are most often known for what they do, not with words or commentary on texts, but with their lives in relation to the world. In effect, Matt 19.21; Matt 12.50/Matt 10.37; Matt 25.40 and Lk 23.34 are four texts that have a history of importance in the Christian life, and have been significant in the self-understanding of exemplary practitioners in recent times.

IGNATIUS OF LOYOLA: LIVING IN THE TEXT

Ignatius of Loyola (died 1556) is known for *The Spiritual Exercises* – his guide to 'finding God's will in the ordering of our life' by reflection upon biblical themes and particular texts of the gospels.[2] *The Spiritual Exercises* offers a method for placing oneself within the life of Jesus, by prayerfully and imaginatively responding to God in Christ amid the situations of particular gospel texts. Individuals undergoing the *Exercises* place themselves within the text in order to respond to God or to examine their own motives and desires against the backdrop of Jesus' words, deeds, sufferings and temptations. Living in the text prayerfully opens the way for hearing the message of the gospel in one's own life. Ignatius is known not only for this guide for discernment, but also for living it out. *The Spiritual Exercises* reflects the process of his own conversion, after which he endeavours to walk in Jesus' footsteps, at first literally going to Jerusalem and finally taking on evangelical poverty and an itinerant life.

The Spiritual Exercises is instructive when considering the gospels embodied. Ignatius enters the rich narrative world of the Bible during a prolonged convalescence. Bedridden, he reads through Jacobus de Voragine's *Golden Legend*, the most popular collection of the lives of the saints in the medieval world. Ignatius is captivated, and his quest for honour and military fame is transformed into a desire to serve God in imitation of the saints. With the *Golden Legend* in hand, Ignatius imbibes the stories of martyrs and saints who witness and follow Christ with unrestrained passion. The saints abandon themselves to God, often suffer terribly for it, and receive the full measure of grace and God's communion in return. In the *Golden Legend*, the lives of the saints are organized according to the liturgical calendar, and instructions and commentary on liturgical practices are interspersed throughout. The stories themselves are also set within the sacramental life and devotional practices of the church. Penance and the Eucharist figure prominently in the great works and witness of the saints, along with their devotion to other saints – their own pilgrimages and prayers at a saint's or martyr's shrine.

This landscape of saints, martyrs and devotional practices is Ignatius' biblical world. While recovering from his war wounds, he also reads a popular life of Christ by Ludolph of Saxony (died 1377). Ludolph's *Vita Jesu Christi* arranges the chronology of Jesus' life according to the whole of salvation history. The events of Jesus' life are set within a narrative that spans from 'the eternal generation of the Word in the Trinity' to the last judgement and heavenly glory.[3] It also includes introductory instructions on how to reflect on key episodes in the gospels. The same approach and theological framework are used in Ignatius' *The Spiritual Exercises*. Texts of the gospels are unified by a gospel that is formed by the liturgy, the creed and a conception of God's plan of salvation. For example, Christ's post-resurrection appearances are put in a sequence of thirteen apparitions. The first is not biblical, strictly speaking, and the last four are not from the gospels. With the first, Ignatius notes that everyone knows and understands that Christ first appeared to the Virgin Mary. Then he continues by combining accounts (uncritically in modern terms) from Matthew, Mark, Luke and John. He concludes with three references to 1 Cor 15 and with what he knows from the *Golden Legend*, according to which Jesus appeared also to Joseph of Arimathea.[4]

This short review of Ignatius' use and method of 'living in' the gospel texts is offered as a guide to the treatment of specific texts that will follow. Particular texts of the gospels are embodied, but these texts are understood in terms of a unified and, in modern terms, largely extrabiblical field of interpretation. The person's own life is understood as an extension of the biblical world. This is not simply a premodern phenomenon. We will see that, like Ignatius of Loyola, Charles de Foucauld (died 1916), Franz Jägerstätter (died 1943), Mother Teresa (died 1997), and other twentieth-century figures employ a similarly unsophisticated and sacramental reading of scripture. Their desire to live out the gospels is conceived as a real possibility because historical distance has been collapsed, and the gospel narrative is already alive in the life of worship, prayer and devotion. These extrabiblical practices of the church give immediacy to embodiment and performance. To a degree, the embodiment of particular gospels texts, such as Matt 25.40, is possible because the passage is not seen or understood as a discrete text. 'Just as you did it to one the least of these my brothers' is not a text as much as a rule of faithfulness and a heuristic guide for interpreting the world.

The performance of a particular text is understood as a consequence of an encounter with God's living word. For example, Antony of Egypt (died 356) set out to found a place in the desert in response to Matt 19.21: 'If you wish to be perfect, go, sell your possessions, and give the money to the poor, and you will have treasure in heaven; then come, follow me.' In Athanasius' *Life of Antony*, the verse presses upon the saint through what he understands as providential events. While on his way to church, he ponders the lives of the apostles and the accounts in the Acts of the Apostles, where people 'had sold their possessions and brought the proceeds to lay at the apostles' feet for distribution to those in need'.[5] He enters the church precisely at the moment that Matt 19.21 is read, and he understands that, through divine inspiration, the gospel has been read aloud specifically for him. Antony responds by 'performing' the text, by selling his possessions and seeking to live by the Spirit. Likewise, Augustine and Francis of Assisi, with text in hand, allow the pages to open, by God's hand, in order to hear God's call in the serendipity of a single (although hardly discrete or freestanding) verse. The text is received as a call.

RENUNCIATION: MATTHEW 19.21

'If you wish to be perfect, go, sell your possessions, and give the money to the poor, and you will have treasure in heaven; then come, follow me' (Matt 19.21). Upon hearing this command of the gospel, Antony sets out on a course of rigorous personal discipline and constant self-scrutiny. He sells and gives away the proceeds of his family's considerable estate, retaining only a modest portion for his sister and himself. Not long after, while in church, he hears the gospel read, 'Take no thought for the morrow' (Matt 6.34). He realizes that his initial response to God's call had been measured.[6] He gives the remainder of his possessions to the poor and entrusts his sister to a community of virgins. 'Now released from all worldly ties, [Antony] eagerly entered upon a harsh and arduous way of life.'[7] He seeks to purify his heart and to live entirely for devotion to God in Christ. It is a ceaseless journey which forges a monastic path into the desert and, in the desert, Antony himself becomes a site where the power and compassion of God are revealed and conveyed.

In Athanasius' *Life of Antony*, the holy man's dispossession is as much spiritual as material; each is the medium of the other. So deeply are the two connected that, in his temptations and spiritual struggles, he is depicted as exchanging blows with demons. In the desert, Antony must face silver and gold that have been put in his path. The silver is a demonic illusion, but Athanasius notes that 'it is not clear whether the devil put [the gold] there to deceive him or whether heavenly power revealed it to prove that Antony could not be seduced even by real riches'.[8] When Antony succeeds in disciplining his body through fasting, keeping vigil night and day, and constant prayer, his spirit is strengthened. His contest with the devil is virtually won, and as his spirit is strengthened through austerities, his body is all the more beautiful in its countenance and dignified in its bearing. Even in death, 'his body looked healthier than those glistening bodies which are pampered by baths and luxurious living'.[9]

Critical to Antony's dispossession is his unwillingness to accept glory that is due to God alone. His strength of spirit is evident in his healing power, but, as the wonders increase, he is increasingly vigilant against the temptations of pride. Like Christ, he heals the daughter of a military officer without seeing or touching her. In Antony's case, however, he refuses to see the girl because of his humility. Refusing to open the door to his cell, Antony sends the soldier and his daughter away, 'I too am mortal and share your weakness. But if you believe in Christ whose servant I am, go and pray to God according to your faith and your daughter will be healed.'[10] Likewise, Antony's growing fame is always matched by his desire to be beyond notice and to give glory only to Christ. The recluse is constantly surrounded by would-be followers and by the sick and the lame. At the conclusion of his account, Athanasius instructs his monastic readers 'that our Saviour Jesus Christ glorifies those who glorify Him and grants the nobility of fame to those who serve Him and who not only long for the kingdom of heaven but also wish to lead a life of withdrawal in the remote mountain places'.[11]

Earlier in the *Life of Antony*, Athanasius includes a lengthy speech where Antony provides a rule for desert monasticism and instructions on the Christian life. He counsels monks not to be proud of their dispossession, and he suggests detachment for all. He points out that what is given up in this world is slight compared to what we will receive, for 'the whole earth, compared to the infinity of the heavens, is small and limited'. We ought to live for God, and to seek after what leads to eternal life, 'namely wisdom, chastity, justice, virtue, an ever watchful mind, care of the poor, firm faith in Christ, a mind that can control anger, hospitality'.[12] For Antony, purity of heart begins when we live without fear and no longer cling to earthly possessions, both material and spiritual. His journey begins with the concrete embodiment of Matt 19.21: 'If you wish to be perfect, go, sell your possessions, and give the money to the poor, and you will have treasure in heaven; then come, follow me.'

With Francis of Assisi (died 1226) and Clare of Assisi (died 1253), dispossession becomes the way of following Christ, not only in order to direct the mind and soul to God, but also to imitate Christ, who empties himself in obedience to the Father and for our sake (Phil 2.6–11). Christ takes on material poverty and takes a share in human suffering, so that we may be lifted up with him. According to Clare, the Lord, 'on coming into the Virgin's womb, chose to appear despised, needy, and *poor* in this world, so that people who were in utter poverty and want and in absolute need of heavenly nourishment might become *rich* in Him by possessing the kingdom of heaven'.[13] Both Francis and Clare develop a rule for their communities in which literal observance of Matt 19.21 provides entry into communal life and is the first step of the Franciscan way.

Clare connects the way of poverty with the blessings of Matt 5.13. 'O holy poverty/ to those who possess and desire you/ God promises *the kingdom of heaven/* and offers, indeed, eternal glory and blessed life!'[14] According to the rule of Clare, the requirements of poverty are strict for the cloistered community of women, who are called to take joy in it. While sharing Christ's poverty, they are called also to share his humility and love. They are called to 'be on their guard against all pride, vainglory, envy, greed, worldly care and anxiety, detraction and murmuring, dissention and division. Let them be ever zealous to preserve among themselves the unity of mutual love, which is the bond of perfection.'[15] In their poverty, humility and love, they are to be the splendid reflection of Jesus Christ.[16]

Like Antony, Charles de Foucauld seeks the solitude of the desert, but, unlike the ancient holy man, Charles receives no fame or followers of his path before he is murdered in 1916 by Algerian rebels. Foucauld dies poor, but not without joy and consolation. 'Don't be anxious at my solitude,' he writes from the Sahara to a friend in 1906. 'I have the Blessed Sacrament, the best of friends ... I have the Blessed Virgin and all the Saints.'[17] 'Does my presence do any good here?' he asks. Again he holds fast to the Eucharist. 'Jesus cannot be in any place without radiating.' Then, Charles thinks of his modest work. 'Contact with the natives [the Islamic population] familiarizes and instructs them, and gradually their prejudices and antipathies disappear.'[18] A few hours before his death, he explains that 'our effacement is the most powerful means we have of uniting ourselves to Jesus and doing good to souls ... When one can suffer and love at the same time one can do much, it is the utmost one can do in this world'.[19]

Renunciation of possessions, both inner and outer, is the leitmotif of Charles de Foucauld's life. He is born in 1858 as the heir of an aristocratic French family and pursues what comes to be a brief but promising military career. Afterward, he finds work on geographical expeditions in North Africa, and, through his contact with devout Muslims, is drawn back to his own Catholic faith. In 1886, Foucauld's road to the desert begins with his return to the Mass, with a pilgrimage to the Holy Land, then with his entrance into community as a Trappist, and later as a servant among the Poor Clares in Nazareth.[20] By 1897, he has come to the realization that Jesus Christ's words of good news were first of all shown through his actions, particularly by taking on poverty and drawing near to common labourers and the poor. He follows Jesus with Matt 10.24 in mind: the slave is not above his master. While on retreat a few years later, he writes, 'The desire to possess nothing but him cries out: detachment. His words cry out: detachment. His example cries out: detachment. His will cries out: detachment. I must resolve to see, unceasingly, Jesus in myself, dwelling within me with his Father.'[21]

Through his life, Foucauld pursues a connection between the themes of Matt 19.21 and Matt 25.40. Believing the gospel, 'that anything done for one of these little ones is done for [Christ]', Charles expects that he, like anyone who seeks Christ, should 'lose no time in becoming quite poor to alleviate all the wretchedness within his power'.[22] Sharing life with the poor and sharing their abandonment by the world are, for Charles, like crying out the gospel 'from the housetop of one's life'.[23] 'The man who receives Your words with faith: "If you wish to be perfect, go and sell what you own and give the money to the poor" . . . will lose no time in becoming quite poor . . . My God, I can't be rich, live in comfort, enjoy my wealth, while You were poor, harassed, living painfully by manual work, I just couldn't . . . I can't love like that.'[24] In the French colony of Algeria, Charles lives beside his Arab neighbours, not to convert, but to offer the presence of Christ in their midst.[25] He is finally killed by rebels because he is a symbol and representative of French rule in the land. He certainly was a French national, and his death can be understood as a dispossession of the rights of colonial rule – his final act of renunciation, material poverty and poverty of spirit.

TRUE KINSHIP: MATTHEW 12.50; 10.37

'For whoever does the will of my heavenly Father is my brother, and sister, and mother' (Matt 12.50). To leave brother, sister and mother, and to live apart from one's place in the ancient household, is among the radical demands of Jesus upon those who would follow him (cf. Mk 10.29–30). In the tradition, the renunciation of family is connected to Matt 19.12, that is, making oneself a eunuch 'for the sake of the kingdom of heaven'. Origen (died c. 250), the renowned theologian of the third century, is infamous for his literal embodiment of Matt 19.12, making himself a eunuch for the kingdom through castration. Although Origen is unusual in this regard, many Christians in the third and fourth centuries do take up Jesus' radical demands by adopting the life of virginity. For many, virginity is not merely a discipline of sexual desire; even more it is a form of renunciation that involves an alternative vision of common life. A reconfiguration of social life is possible, and indeed required, when one attempts to live apart from the typical economic and social functions of marriage and family.

At the beginning of the fifth century, Augustine looks to highlight the superiority of virginity by developing the theme of spiritual kinship in Christ, not over against, but over and above physical ties of inheritable affinity. Late in the fourth century, a monk named Jovinian had set off a controversy in Rome by arguing that marriage is a state of life equal in holiness to virginity. In his *Against Jovinian*, Jerome argues for the superiority of virginity without much subtlety and, in the process, seems to denigrate marriage. Augustine, in treatises on *The Good of Marriage* and *Holy Virginity*, navigates between what he sees as these two extremes. Against the views of Jovinian, he argues for the biblical and theological superiority of virginity. However, he also argues for the good of marriage on its own terms, for its steadfast fidelity, fellowship, procreative character and function in settling desire, over against those who were claiming that sex and marriage were evils.[26]

For Augustine, virginity is understood, not as the rejection of sex or of the body as evil, but in terms of his theological hierarchy of spirit over matter, of spiritual unity and regeneration over physical union and procreation. The spirit does not cast off the body, but includes it and orders it to what is higher, namely to God. We are born in Christ. In this sense, according to Augustine, 'the church is a virgin betrothed to the one man Christ (2 Cor 11.2),' and, if so, 'what great honour is due to those of its members who preserve even in their bodies what the whole Church preserves by faith, in imitation of the mother of its spouse and Lord'.[27] Here Augustine turns not to Matt 19.12 but to Matt 12.50. When Christ asks, '"Who is my mother? Who are my brothers?" what was he teaching us other than to value spiritual family more highly than relationship by birth, and that what makes people blessed is not being close to upright and holy persons by blood relationship, but being united with them by obeying and imitating their doctrine and way of life?'[28]

Augustine's own life represents the aspirations of this spiritual unity. As a young man with ambition, he knows that he must marry well. In Roman society, he must marry into a noble family in order to advance beyond the status of his birth. To secure such a marriage, he takes a common course for upwardly mobile members of the Empire. Until such time as he can gain some distinction and, through his reputation, can secure a proper wife, he takes on a concubine, with whom he has a son. In doing so, he is following a respectable route to a good marriage. When he is finally betrothed to a girl of 'suitable wealth and social standing', Augustine dismisses his faithful concubine, never to see her again. After his conversion to Christianity, he will remember the day as a great moral failure, when he disowned a woman who was a true wife for the sake of another of greater usefulness.[29] Augustine ultimately dissolves the betrothal and, in disavowing marriage, deliberately gives up a distinguished place in Roman social life. It is clear that the alternative to marriage is not celibacy *per se*, but a social alternative to the Roman household, that is, the circle of Augustine's particular friendships and the richness of shared life that is available to them on the periphery of Roman social institutions. Throughout his adult life, he struggles with, lives out and writes eloquently about the love and society of good friends.[30] As bishop, he dedicates himself to community with his clergy in Hippo, in a shared life of service and evangelical poverty. As a Christian, he lives for the unity of the church.[31]

The ancient and medieval household imposes restrictions primarily on the public roles of women, so that stories of the virgin saint often focus on her rejection of marriage, not only because of the intensity of her faith, but also for the sake of her calling in the world. Agnes (died 304) and Catherine of Siena (died 1380) are representatives of this tradition. Ambrose (died 397) writes of Agnes's noble birth and astounding beauty, which enchant the son of a Roman prefect. She rejects his desire for betrothal because, she claims, she is already betrothed to one far greater in all respects. It is Christ. The young man offers her riches and honour, but she continues to refuse. As a consequence, his father, a Roman prefect, pressurizes Agnes. When she resists, he confines her to a brothel and gives his son opportunity to defile her. She resists. She is protected by God and eventually suffers a martyr's death. She lays aside her noble birth and the expectations of society. Like the church, she gives birth to children through the Spirit.[32] Her virginity is of a piece with an alternative social order, with the kingship of Christ over against the powers of the world, and, after her death, this alternative is sustained at her shrine, where her status as virgin allows unrestricted intimacy with the faithful. Men and women come to her shrine calling her mother, sister and wife.[33]

Like Agnes, Catherine of Siena resists marriage and her social station in the household (and also despite her promising beauty), but, unlike Agnes, she is pressurized to marry, not by the pagan powers, but by her own family. The virgin continues to embody unqualified dedication to God and an alternative configuration of kinship, and, as a citizen of Christendom, renews and enlivens her own family's faith by resisting marriage and establishing a spiritual family. Members of her inherited family are integrated into her relations of faith. In *Holy Virginity*, Augustine points to this pattern in Mary's relation to Jesus. Here again, he cites Matt 12.50. Mary's relation to Christ, as his mother, is brought into existence through her conformity to the will of the Father. Her spiritual motherhood is anterior to her corporeal maternity. In 1967, Pope Paul VI appealed to the same theme and cited Matt 12.50 in his description of Mary as a model of faith, in her assent to God's will and as mother to us all in the spiritual family of the church.[34]

Likewise, for Catherine, virginity is the medium of her kinship with Christ. After about three years of suffering harassment at home, her patient endurance brings her father round. She is allowed to disavow marriage, to take the habit of a Dominican tertiary, and to set out on a path of solitude, prayer and self-mortification. Following a few years of seclusion in her room, she receives a vision of her betrothal to Christ. Through the vision, she is called to work for Christ in the world. Catherine's love of Christ, the same love which once led her to a private cell, is now expressed in her Christ-like love for her neighbours, whom she sees as Christ's surrogates (Matt 25.40).[35]

As a third-order Dominican, she sets out to care for the poor and to nurse the sick. She becomes a prominent public figure as well – an agent of social, civic and ecclesiological unity. She counsels political leaders in Pisa, Florence and Siena, and is the arbitrator of their disputes. She is known as a peacemaker (although she preaches a crusade). She is remembered for intervening for Urban VI among rival claimants to the papacy, and for her efforts to reform the church. Her close followers – married and single, male and female, peers and elders (including several Dominicans) – call her 'mother'. Catherine is remembered for establishing familial unity in Christ. 'That which she was to her disciples – teacher, mother, friend, counselor – Jesus was to her . . . Her followers fed upon her wisdom, warmed themselves at her love; they lived in her as in a living host offered for the love of men.'[36] This description is a hagiographical flourish, but it makes clear that the virgin saint is a site for an alternative society, outside the household and its constraints within the civic order. 'For whoever does the will of my heavenly Father is my brother, and sister, and mother' (Matt 12.50).

Mother, wife and three daughters are at the front of Franz Jägerstätter's mind as he awaits trial and then execution during the summer of 1943. Shortly before he is beheaded as an enemy of the state, Jägerstätter defends his refusal to co-operate with the Nazi war effort, not in order to petition the military court, but to justify his impending death to neighbours and countrymen in his Austrian town of St Radegund. Franz is accused by fellow Austrians of being selfish and irresponsible. Some men of his town share his animosity for the National Socialists, but they will fight for Austria. Many share his conviction that Nazi aggression throughout Europe is unjust. Franz, however, refuses to co-operate with what he sees as an evil regime. He believes that being a Nazi and being a Catholic are absolutely incompatible and that joining with the cause of the Third Reich is an offence against God. Jägerstätter is accused by his neighbours in St Radegund of being self-centred, of shaming his family and his country for the sake of 'a troubled mind'. His family will suffer for his scruples. After he is gone, they will receive harsh treatment from Nazis and scorn from fellow Austrians.

In response to accusations of irresponsibility toward family and country, Franz makes reference to Matt 10.37 and 10.28. He takes issue with the implication that his obligations to his wife and children might supersede his obligations to God. A father and husband who supports a family is not 'free to offend God by lying (not to mention all the other things he would be called upon to do).'[37] Franz, of course, feels the weight of separation from his loved ones, and he worries for their future. Nonetheless, 'did not Christ Himself say: "He who loves father, mother, or children more than Me is not deserving of My love"? Or, "Fear not those who can kill the body but not the soul; rather fear much more those who seek to destroy body and soul in hell?"'[38] Jägerstätter interprets both passages in terms of the kingship of Christ. 'Christ, too, demands a public confession of our faith, just as the Führer, Adolf Hitler, does from his followers.'[39] Franz will not swear an oath to the Führer in so far as Hitler's purposes are an offence to God. One either believes in Hitler and follows him, or plays a 'crooked game' of dishonest rationalizations and flight from our responsibilities to God, truth and justice.[40]

Franz Jägerstätter's embodiment of Matt 10.28 and 10.37 illuminates the themes of Augustine's interpretation of Matt 12.50, the martyrdom of Agnes, and Catherine's struggles and peacemaking in the family and the world. Our inheritable bonds of family are secondary to relationships founded in Christ; true kinship is founded on following God's will and way in the world. In Matt

10, Jesus sends the twelve disciples out to announce the coming of God's kingdom – without gold or silver, extra tunic, or sandals or staff – 'like sheep in the midst of wolves' (Matt 10.5–16). Jesus tells the disciples that he will set a man against his father and a daughter against her mother (Matt 10.35). In this regard, the virgin performs an act of dispossession and distinction from dominant social structures like the household. Renunciation of ancestral and inheritable ties is the beginning of God's reconstitution of family. 'For whoever does the will of my heavenly Father is my brother, and sister, and mother' (Matt 12.50).

WORKS OF MERCY: MATTHEW 25.40

'Truly I tell you, just as you did it to one of the least of these my brothers, you did it to me' (Matt 25.40). 'The judgement of the nations' in Matt 25.31–46 is the basis for a longstanding tradition of Christian practice. The parable is interpreted to mean that our true relationship to Christ is not only judged, but also revealed, in our care for and unity with the hungry, thirsty, naked, sick and imprisoned. Martin of Tours (died 397) is well known for his battlefield declaration to Caesar: 'Up till now I have fought for you; allow me now to fight for God . . . I am a soldier of Christ, I am not allowed to fight.'[41] After imprisonment by Caesar, he is released from his military obligations. He becomes a monk, and later a bishop (while also a holy man and recluse) of Tours. As bishop and monk, he is distinguished for his asceticism, miraculous works and missionary activity among pagans in the rural areas of Gaul.

Martin of Tours is also remembered for the manner of his conversion. In Sulpicius Severus' account of his life, Martin's performance of Matt 25.40 serves as a benchmark for entering into the Christian life, and as the context for Christ's summons to the saint. Pressed into military service by his father and by Rome, Martin was a reluctant soldier, and he took 'refuge in the church against his parent's wishes and demanded to be made a catechumen'. Sulpicius Severus notes that even before he became a candidate for baptism, 'he supported those in trouble, he brought help to the wretched, he fed the poor, he clothed the naked and kept nothing of his military salary for himself apart from what he needed for food each day'. [42] On a cold winter day, Martin encounters a naked beggar. He recognizes the encounter as providential, like Antony of Egypt who hears the reading of Matt 19.21 as an unambiguous message specifically to him. Martin 'who was filled with God's grace, understood that this man had been reserved for him'. Having nothing with him except his own military cloak, Martin cuts it in two and gives half to the beggar. That night, Martin entertains Christ in a dream. He discovers that 'He Himself was clothed in the person of this beggar, He was recalling his own words (for He had once said, "As often as you do this to one of the least, you have done it to me")'.[43]

Encountering Christ in the poor is a prominent theme among the saints, and two twentieth-century practitioners, Dorothy Day (died 1980) and Teresa of Calcutta (died 1997), have embodied Matt 25.40 in our time. For each, Jesus Christ is not merely represented by the poor, sick and imprisoned, but simply *is* the hungry, thirsty, ill and forgotten. Dorothy and Teresa undertake a life with the poor with deep faith, patience and hope. Eucharistic devotion plays a central role for each. For them, the centuries since Jesus' crucifixion in Jerusalem are not a barrier to our relationship to him. Christ is present now, and, with this immediacy, Matt 25.40 suggests not grand gestures but simple acts that are likely to go unnoticed, except by those whom we touch. In 1948, Mother Teresa performs a simple act by setting out into the streets of Calcutta in a simple white sari.[44] She encounters Jesus 'in the distressing disguise of the poor', and with them, she finds a life of joy – a profound happiness in the presence of Christ.[45] Many follow her along the way, and, by her death in 1997, her Missionaries of Charity care for the poor across the world.

At the age of thirty-six (in 1932), Dorothy Day is a freelance journalist, a veteran radical and a recent convert to the Christian faith. In December of that year, she meets Peter Maurin, a peripatetic (i.e., homeless) theologian and social critic, who soon becomes Day's inspiration and guide. Side by side with Maurin, Day develops a vision of social life, which puts Christian pacifism and the dignity of every person at the centre of just economic and political practices. In 1940, Day writes, 'The vision is this. We are working for "a new heaven and a new *earth*, wherein justice dwelleth." We are trying to say with action, "Thy will be done on *earth* as it is in heaven." We are working for a Christian social order.'[46]

On 1 May 1933, Dorothy and Peter take their newly printed *Catholic Worker* newspaper to the streets of New York City. The paper soon becomes Day's medium for promoting voluntary poverty, compassion for one's neighbour and love of enemy, for denouncing poverty, injustice and war, and for spelling out the details of 'practising the presence of God' through spiritual and corporal works of mercy.[47] At the same time, Day, Maurin and others put the *Catholic Worker* into practice. They share life with the poor. Dorothy and her friends offer bread and soup to the unemployed and poor of the city; she and her brother open up their own flat to homeless men, and they find funds to rent more flats for men and women. They begin to have public discussions for the 'clarification of thought', and they apply their philosophy and faith to ventures in communal farming. They depend entirely upon donations, their own unpaid labour and the work of volunteers; they live precariously from day to day. They live literally as neighbours to 'the least of these'. The *Catholic Worker* gains a wide readership, and houses of hospitality spring up in cities across the country. A movement is born.

At the centre of Dorothy's life are faith and her desire for unity with Christ. In 1953, Day would look back and remark: 'I condemn poverty and I advocate it; poverty is simple and complex at once; it is a social phenomenon and a personal matter. It is a paradox.'[48] For Day, poverty is not, first of all, a grand political strategy, but a matter of 'the little way' where we join in community with Christ and 'the least of these' through the simple matters of everyday life. Poverty is a consequence of day-to-day struggles of faithfulness. Matt 25.40 and the Sermon on the Mount (Matt 5–7) are central to this little way.

> The Spiritual Works of Mercy are: to admonish the sinner, to instruct the ignorant, to counsel the doubtful, to comfort the sorrowful, to bear wrongs patiently, to forgive all injuries, and to pray for the living and the dead. The Corporal Works are to feed the hungry, to give drink to the thirsty, to clothe the naked, to ransom the captive, to harbor the harborless, to visit the sick, and to bury the dead.[49]

Day does not romanticize 'the poor'. They have 'no halos already glowing round their heads' and 'if we hadn't got Christ's own words for it, it would seem raving lunacy to believe that if I offer a bed and food and hospitality to some man or woman or child, I am replaying the part of Lazarus or Martha or Mary, and that my guest is Christ'.[50] Matt 25.40 unveils all our apprehensions and wonder in receiving Christ. Dorothy Day embodies this gospel truth: in hospitality to the poor, we make room for Christ, and the great risk and promise of entertaining Christ is that we will become like him too.

RECONCILIATION: LUKE 23.34

'Then Jesus said, "Father, forgive them; they do not know what they are doing"' (Lk 23.34). Martyrdom is a reconciling death. While men and women stand defenceless before their accusers, the promise of Christ's crucifixion and resurrection is confirmed. The power of God in Christ is proclaimed over against the powers of the world, and, in this clash of authority, there is a repetition of Jesus' way to the cross. In typical martyrology, the saint suffers, but stands firm – sometimes impervious to blows and torments. The saint accepts suffering and death, not as a victim, but armed with faith and with God's promises of communion. In the very act of martyrdom and in the acting out of Christ's own death, there is a foretaste of union with him. As a result, the suffering of martyrdom is matched with assurance and a guarantee of sharing divine life. The martyr has a clear view of harmony and delight far greater than the misery of the moment. The authorities of the world are vanquished at the very moment when they seem most effective in their power to impose death.

In Acts 6.8—8.2, Stephen, like Jesus, is charged with making pronouncements against the Temple, and like Jesus, he forgives his accusers at the moment of his death. Stephen is no passive victim. He levels his own charge against his judges: 'Which of the prophets did your ancestors not persecute? They have killed those who foretold the coming of the Righteous One, and now you have become his betrayers and murderers' (7.52). They are enraged, but Stephen sees the heavens open and 'the Son of Man standing at the right hand of God' (7.56). They drag him out to be stoned, and he asks the Lord to receive his spirit. His last words are reserved for the forgiveness of his executioners. 'Lord, do not hold this sin against them' (7.60). Typical of the stories of martyrs, the drama does not end with Stephen's death. Saul is introduced as a consenting witness to the stoning of Stephen. It is noted that a general persecution ensues, and 'all except the apostles were scattered throughout the countryside . . .' (8.1). While 'devout men buried Stephen and made loud lamentation over him', those scattered give testimony throughout the land.

Similar themes are present in *The Martyrdom of Polycarp* (c. 155). The author of the account discerns providence in Polycarp's persecution and death, 'in order that the Lord might show us once again a martyrdom which is in accord with the gospel'.[51] Polycarp's imitation of Christ's way to death serves as a witness, so that 'we too might be imitators of him . . . For it is the mark of true and steadfast love to desire not only that oneself be saved, but all the brothers as well'.[52] Polycarp does not seek to be a martyr, but he does not resist it. The authorities set out to find him, but upon the urging of others, he flees. When found, he offers himself willingly. When his captors come to arrest him, he graciously offers them a meal and a place at his table. The soldiers who are now his guests keep watch as Polycarp prays unceasingly for two hours. His actions bear witness to his faith, and his martyrdom bears witness to Christ.

Before the magistrate, Polycarp refuses to swear an oath to Caesar and professes the kingship of Christ. 'For eighty-six years I have been his servant, and he has done me no wrong. How can I blaspheme my King who saved me?'[53] Polycarp is filled with God's gifts of courage and joy. Threatened with burning, he announces an all-consuming fire of the coming judgement. Polycarp stands confident as kindling and wood are piled around him, and he refuses to be nailed, 'for he who enables me to endure the fire will also enable me to remain on the pyre without moving, even without the sense of security which you get from the nails'.[54] Instead, he is bound with his hands behind him, 'like a splendid ram'. Polycarp prays. He gives glory to God and thanksgiving for his place among the martyrs and for the coming resurrection in Christ. As Polycarp says his final 'Amen', the fire is lit.

The fire, however, does not bring the end. The story of the martyr continues through the miraculous preservation of Polycarp's body and a burning desire of the faithful 'to have fellowship with his holy flesh'.[55] The body is the medium of holiness and unity in Christ. The fire around Polycarp takes 'the shape of an arch, like the sail of a ship filled by the wind'. The martyr's body is sheltered in the middle and does not burn like flesh, but 'like bread baking or like gold and silver being refined in a furnace'. The smell is sweet, 'as if it were the scent of incense or some other precious spice'.[56] Polycarp's accusers conspire to destroy his corpse, but after his body is submitted to cremation his bones remain. They are gathered up by the faithful, for they 'are more valuable than precious stones and finer than refined gold'. The bones become a site of gathering and 'commemoration of those who have already fought in the contest, and for the training and preparation of those who will do so in the future'.[57] The martyr is an embodiment of the church's unity *in* Christ and *with* Christ's redemption for the world.

The remembrance of twentieth-century martyrs reinforces and extends the theme of redemption. For instance, Maximilian Kolbe, a Franciscan Pole (died 1941), is remembered for taking the place of a fellow prisoner who was being sent to a starvation bunker at Auschwitz. Edith Stein (Teresa Benedicta of the Cross) is also remembered for her death in Auschwitz (died 1942). But, as a Carmelite and a Jew, her canonization as martyr has provoked controversy. Many believe that the Holocaust is being co-opted by the church. It is true that Stein understands her death as a Jew in terms of the redemptive solidarity of the cross. She accepts her arrest and imprisonment as an evil that she suffers with the Jewish people, from which her own baptism ought not to exempt her.[58] At the time of her arrest in 1942, she is in the process of completing her study of St John of the Cross, titled *The Science of the Cross*. The work reflects Stein's faith and self-understanding. 'The perfection of one's own being, union with God and work for the union of others with God and the perfection of their being are all inseparably united. The Cross gives access to all this, but the preaching of the Cross would be vain if it were not the expression of a life of union with Christ crucified.'[59]

On 4 April 1968, while standing on a hotel balcony in Memphis, Tennessee, Martin Luther King Jr is shot and killed. The first attempt on his life is made much earlier, in January of 1956, when a bomb is thrown at his parsonage in Montgomery, Alabama. In Montgomery, King is the pastor of Dexter Avenue Baptist Church and leader of the now famous bus boycott, which is the first in a series of campaigns led by King to challenge and overturn systems of racial discrimination in the United States. Outside his home, King meets with a crowd of friends and church members, who are angry at violence directed at King. Later, he would recall that he 'realized that many people were armed. Nonviolent resistance was on the verge of being transformed into violence.'[60] From his porch, he calms the crowd. 'We are not advocating violence. We want to love our enemies. I want you to love our enemies. Be good to them. Love them and let them know you love them.'[61]

During the Montgomery boycott, King gains a clear view of the purposes and goals of the movement. 'This is not a war between the white and the Negro but a conflict between justice and injustice. This is bigger than the Negro race revolting against the white. We are seeking to improve not the Negro of Montgomery but the whole of Montgomery.'[62] In 1968, the message is the same. He is in Memphis to support striking sanitation workers. In the years before, he had challenged not only legal segregation, but also discriminatory voting laws and economic injustices. He had denounced the US war in Vietnam. He had been threatened and arrested many times. On 3 April 1968, the day before his assassination, he gives his prescient 'I've been to the mountain top' speech. In the speech, he encourages those assembled. 'We've got to give ourselves to this struggle until the end . . . Be concerned about your brother. You may not be on strike, but either we go up together or we go down together. Let us develop a kind of dangerous unselfishness.'[63] Through his life, King put this message into practice.

In a sermon, 'Love in Action', Dr King attends to Jesus' words in Lk 23.34, 'Father, forgive them; for they know not what they do.'[64] He begins by noting the consistency between Jesus words and actions. On the cross, Jesus' prayer of forgiveness is an embodiment of Matt 5.38–48. Jesus 'admonished his followers to love their enemies and to pray for them that despitefully used them . . . Their lives had been conditioned to seek redress in the time-honored tradition of retaliation.'[65] According to King, Jesus' prayer offers us a contrast to the dominant social order. Jesus 'did not overcome evil with evil. He overcame evil with good. Although crucified by hate, he responded with aggressive love.'[66]

After developing forgiveness as a 'habit' and 'structure of being', King's sermon turns to the nature of intellectual and spiritual blindness (i.e., 'for they know not what they do'). He holds that moral blindness is 'a structured part of the culture' that shows its effects as respectable citizens cry 'Crucify him', or look to war as 'the answer to the problems of the world'.[67] Good and respectable citizens have perpetuated slavery and racial segregation in America. Religion, law, science and philosophy have been twisted 'to give sanction to the doctrine of white supremacy'.[68] In this regard, the cross is a higher law and greater wisdom. King points out that millions of African Americans 'have been crucified by conscientious blindness'. He proposes what is almost unthinkable, that 'with Jesus on the cross, we must look lovingly at our oppressors and say, "Father, forgive them; for they know not what they do."'[69]

For King, this embodiment of Jesus' words is *the* witness that works against intellectual and spiritual blindness. It is 'apparent that sincerity and conscientiousness in themselves are not enough'.[70] Military power and scientific discovery will not open our eyes and turn us around. We need the light that comes into the world through God in Christ and his way to the cross. Christ crucified is 'love conquering hate' and 'light overcoming darkness'. 'A voice crying through the vista of time calls men to walk in the light . . . "This is the condemnation," says John, "that light is come into the world, and men loved darkness rather than light."' King concludes. 'As I behold the uplifted cross I am reminded not only of the unlimited power of God, but also of the sordid weakness of man . . . I am reminded not only of Christ at his best, but of man at his worst.'[71] Through his life and his death, Martin Luther King Jr embodies the vision and desire to share God's way of love and righteousness. He does so until he dies a martyr's death, which sustains Jesus' prayer of reconciliation: 'Father, forgive them; for they know not what they do.'

CONCLUSION

The martyrs and saints interpret the gospels through action. Their attempts to live out the meaning of texts are wagers of faith. They endeavour to follow Jesus Christ through self-scrutiny, purity of heart and a renunciation of conventional ways of life. They seek to be transformed by a new way of living and to live in God's light. The saints attempt to show God's mercy toward their neighbours and to live out bonds of true human kinship in God. They thirst for righteousness, and desire to be peacemakers and faithful children of God. If the saints and martyrs interpret texts through a 'performance', naming and recognizing these 'holy ones' is an interpretative venture as well. This chapter, for instance, has offered a constructive proposal by naming specific saints among the canon of saints. Exemplary lives shed light upon us all. In the tradition of the church, saints are named so that we might better see and acknowledge the ways of God. The practice of naming saints suggests that our interpretations of the gospels are not finished until we put the texts into practice as well.

Notes

1. Stephen C. Barton, 'New Testament Interpretation as Performance', in *Life Together: Family, Sexuality and Community in the New Testament and Today* (Edinburgh: T. & T. Clark, 2001), 223–50.
2. George E. Ganss, SJ, ed., *Ignatius of Loyola: The Spiritual Exercises and Selected Works* (New York: Paulist Press, 1991), 121.
3. Ibid., 19.
4. Ibid., 197–200; Jacobus de Voragine, *Golden Legend*, 2 vols., trans. William Granger Ryan (Princeton: Princeton University Press, 1993), I, 276.
5. Carolinne White, trans., 'Life of Antony by Athanasius', in *Early Christian Lives* (Harmondsworth: Penguin, 1998), no. 2.
6. Ibid., no. 3/3 (White numbers by paragraph/section).
7. Ibid., no. 3/3.
8. Ibid., no. 12/11.
9. Ibid., no. 93/60.
10. Ibid., no. 48/24.
11. Ibid., no. 94/62.
12. Ibid., no. 17/17.
13. 'The First Letter to Blessed Agnes of Prague', in Regis J. Armstrong, OFM Cap., and Ignatius C. Brady, OFM, eds. and trans., *Francis and Clare: The Complete Works* (New York: Paulist Press, 1982), 192.
14. Ibid.
15. 'The Rule of Saint Clare', in ibid., 222.
16. 'The Fourth Letter to Blessed Agnes of Prague', in ibid., 204.
17. Charles de Foucauld, *Meditations of a Hermit*, trans. Charlotte Balfour (London: Burns & Oates, 1981), 176.
18. Ibid., 178.
19. Ibid., 184.
20. Robert Ellsberg, 'Charles de Foucauld', in Susan Bergman, ed., *Martyrs*, (San Francisco: HarperCollins, 1996), 285–98.
21. Foucauld, *Meditations*, 164.
22. *Silent Pilgrimage to God: The Spirituality of Charles de Foucauld*, by a Little Brother of Jesus, trans. Jeremy Moiser (London: Darton, Longman & Todd, 1974), 76.
23. Ibid., 41.

24. Ibid., 76–7.
25. Ellsberg, 'Charles de Foucauld', 292.
26. Augustine, *The Works of Saint Augustine*, I/9: *Marriage and Virginity*, trans. Ray Kearney, ed. David G. Hunter (Hyde Park, NY: New City Press, 1999), 29–32, 65–7.
27. Augustine, 'Holy Virginity,' in ibid., no. 2.
28. Ibid., no. 3.
29. Ibid., no. 5; also see his *Confessions*, VI 13–15.
30. Marie Aquinas McNamara, OP, *Friends and Friendship for Saint Augustine* (Staten Island, NY: Society of St Paul, 1964).
31. Peter Brown, *Augustine of Hippo* (Berkeley: University of California Press, 1967), 212–25, 408–10.
32. St Ambrose, *De Virginibus*, in *Patrologiae cursus completes: Series Latina*, XVI ed. J. P. Migne (Paris, 1845), no. 31.
33. *Golden Legend*, I, 101–4.
34. Paul VI, *Signum Magnum* (13 May 1967) in *The Pope Speaks*, XII, no. 3 (1967), 278–86.
35. Catherine of Siena, *The Dialogue*, trans. Susanne Noffke, OP (New York: Paulist Press, 1980), nos. 64, 148.
36. Igino Giordani, *Catherine of Siena: Fire and Blood*, trans. Thomas J. Tobin (Milwaukee: Bruce Publishing, 1959), 111.
37. 'The Jägerstätter Documents', in Gordon Zahn, *In Solitary Witness: The Life and Death of Franz Jägerstätter* (Boston: Beacon Press, 1964), 204.
38. Ibid.
39. Ibid., 191.
40. Ibid., 195–200.
41. 'Life of Marin of Tours by Sulpicius Severus', in White, trans., *Early Christian Lives*, no. IV.I.
42. Ibid., no. II.I.
43. Ibid., no. II.I.
44. Robert Ellsberg, *All Saints: Daily Reflections on Saints, Prophets, and Witnesses for Our Time* (New York: Crossroad, 1997), 393.
45. Mother Teresa of Calcutta, *My Life for the Poor*, ed. José Luis Gonzalez-Balado and Janet N. Playfoot (San Francisco: Harper & Row, 1985), 20, 28, 92.
46. Dorothy Day, *By Little and by Little: The Selected Writings of Dorothy Day*, ed. Robert Ellsberg (New York: Alfred A. Knopf, 1984), 91.
47. Ibid., p. 92.
48. Ibid., 109.
49. Ibid., 98.
50. Ibid., 95.
51. *The Martyrdom of Polycarp*, in J. B. Lightfoot and J. R. Harmer, trans., *The Apostolic Fathers*, 2nd edn, revised by Michael W. Holmes (Grand Rapids: Baker Book House, 1992), no. 1.
52. Ibid.
53. Ibid., no. 9.
54. Ibid., no. 13.
55. Ibid., no. 17.

56. Ibid., no. 15.
57. Ibid., no. 18.
58. Boniface Hanley, OFM, *No Strangers to Violence, No Strangers to Love* (Notre Dame, IN: Ave Maria Press, 1983), 55–60.
59. Edith Stein, *The Science of the Cross: A Study of St John of the Cross*, ed. Lucy Gelber and Romaeus Leuven, OCD, trans. Hilda Graef (Chicago: Henry Regnery Company, 1960), 216.
60. Martin Luther King Jr, *The Autobiography of Martin Luther King, Jr.*, ed. Clayborne Carson (New York: Warner Books, 1998), 79.
61. Ibid., 80.
62. *New York Times* (24 February 1956), quoted in King, *Autobiography*, 81.
63. King, *Autobiography*, 361–2.
64. Martin Luther King Jr, *Strength to Love* (Philadelphia: Fortress, 1981), 39.
65. Ibid., 41.
66. Ibid., 42.
67. Ibid., 43.
68. Ibid., 45.
69. Ibid., 46.
70. Ibid.
71. Ibid., 48.

Further reading

Armstrong, Regis J., OFM Cap., and Ignatius C. Brady, OFM, eds., *Francis and Clare: The Complete Works* (New York: Paulist Press, 1982)
Bergman, Susan, ed., *Martyrs* (San Francisco: HarperCollins, 1996)
Brown, Peter, *Augustine of Hippo* (Berkeley: University of California Press, 1967)
Day, Dorothy, *By Little and by Little: The Selected Writings of Dorothy Day,* ed. Robert Ellsberg (New York: Alfred A. Knopf, 1984)
Foucauld, Charles de, *Meditations of a Hermit* (London: Burns & Oates, 1981)
Ganss, George E., SJ, ed., *Ignatius of Loyola: The Spiritual Exercises and Selected Works* (New York: Paulist Press, 1991)
Greer, Rowan A., *Christian Hope and Christian Life: Raids on the Inarticulate* (New York: Crossroad, 2001)
Hanley, Boniface, OFM, *No Strangers to Violence, No Strangers to Love* (Notre Dame, IN: Ave Maria Press, 1983)
King, Martin Luther, Jr, *Strength to Love* (Philadelphia: Fortress, 1981)
White, Carolinne, ed., *Early Christian Lives* (Harmondsworth: Penguin, 1998)
Wilken, Robert L., *The Spirit of Early Christian Thought: Seeking the Face of God* (New Haven and London: Yale University Press, 2003)
Zahn, Gordon, *In Solitary Witness: The Life and Death of Franz Jägerstätter* (Boston: Beacon Press, 1964)

12 Praying the gospels: spirituality and worship
GORDON MURSELL

INTRODUCTION

Definitions of 'spirituality' are many and various. St Paul distinguishes between two different ways of living: 'according to the flesh' and 'according to the Spirit' (see especially Rom 8). In the light of such a distinction, 'spirituality' may be understood as the whole of life, seen in the perspective of humankind's relationship with God in Christ. It will have a special interest in those enduring realities that are held, in scripture and in the Christian tradition, to be of the essence of what is understood by 'spiritual' – love, peace, forgiveness, reconciliation, wholeness, salvation and so on – and in how those realities are experienced, fostered and articulated. And, since it is concerned with the whole of life, 'spirituality' will be no less interested in other realities – above all, the reality of evil – which may appropriately be described as 'spiritual', and are no less intrinsic to creaturely existence, but which may demand a very different kind of response.

On such a view of spirituality, the gospels have an exceptional importance: partly because they have much to say about all those spiritual realities that are accepted as being either constitutive of Christian life or a direct threat to it; partly because they vastly extend our understanding of what 'Christian' means – most obviously by all that they tell us about the life, teaching and significance of Jesus himself. But there is another reason for their exceptional importance: unlike almost all other New Testament texts, they seek to convey truth in the form, not of concept or of doctrine, but of story. And, like poems, stories are less easy to control than other forms of discourse available for the communication of truth, less susceptible of just one 'official' interpretation, capable of addressing in a much more direct and immediate (though also in a richly allusive and rarely predictable) manner the stories and lives of those who read them.

THE GOSPELS IN EARLY CHRISTIAN PRAYER
AND LITURGY

It is, however, important to remember that, during the whole of the first millennium of Christian history and for a considerable amount of the second as well, the gospels were far from being readily or easily accessible to those who were not members of a small minority such as the literate, or the cloistered, or the ordained. Most encountered them primarily in worship: Christianity took over from Judaism the practice of reading scriptures as an integral part of worship, and Justin, writing in the mid-second century, speaks of 'the memoirs of the apostles' being read at the Eucharist 'for as long as time allowed';[1] and by the fifth century the reading of an extract from the gospels in worship was already being accompanied by some formality and ceremony.

Even then, however, the reading of the gospels in worship was not always intended so much to offer wisdom for everyday living as to draw the worshipper out of the material realities of this world and into the life of heaven. This was especially true in the eastern (Greek) Christian tradition. The theologian Maximus the Confessor (c. 580–662) observes that listening to an extract from the gospels read during the divine liturgy is at once a costly and a transforming process for those who are present, because it demands of them nothing less than a turning away from worldly realities to the vision of the Trinity itself. They are drawn up into the eternal song of the angels to an encounter with God, so that they are 'now divinized by love and made like him by participation in an indivisible identity to the extent that this is possible'.[2]

Other difficulties in the way of making the gospels readily accessible took longer to disappear, above all that of language. In the western Christian tradition, where neither of the two biblical languages was familiar, still less vernacular, the gospels were for centuries heard only in the language of imperial Rome – Latin – whereas in the east some people at least will have understood the original Greek. In the medieval period, the earliest translations into the vernacular were intended only for the edification of those who took regular part in liturgical prayer – scholars, priests, monks and nuns; and even those vernacular translations that were aimed at lay people (such as those produced in late medieval England by the Lollards) were at first accessible only to a tiny educated elite. It is true that sermons on biblical texts, including the gospels, originated early in Christian history; but for centuries these also were not in the vernacular. And throughout the medieval west, those biblical commentaries and sermons that were intended for spiritual edification were just as likely to be on the Psalms or the Song of Songs (both of which were held to be particularly conducive to contemplative prayer) as on the gospels. In the eastern Christian tradition, the gospels did enjoy greater prominence. In the patriarchal school at Byzantium in the twelfth century, for example, the rector was also the 'professor of the gospel': his colleagues included the 'professor of the Apostle' and the 'professor of the Psalter', but the pre-eminence of the first suggests a higher priority being placed on studying and praying the gospels.

Nonetheless, and despite these difficulties, there are good grounds for arguing that even in the first Christian millennium the gospels exerted a profound and pervasive influence on Christian spirituality. In the first place it is important to remember that early Christian scholars saw no reason to separate the intellectual from the spiritual, theology from prayer: they were more likely to distinguish the literal from the allegorical, the 'surface' meaning of the text from its deeper 'spiritual' truth. But what they sought from scripture was not simply intellectual understanding but a far deeper knowledge, *gnōsis*, that derived from encountering Christ himself in the scriptures that spoke of him. In the preface to his commentary on the Gospel of Matthew, written at the end of the fourth century, St Jerome distinguishes between the *historica interpretatio* (historical interpretation) and the *intelligentia spiritualis* (spiritual understanding); but he goes on to stress the paradox that the first people to be called by Jesus to preach were unlettered fishermen, so that the conversion of the faithful could be attributed only to the action of God, not to human eloquence and teaching.[3] Similarly, early Christian writers who reflected on the gospels constantly sought to connect scripture with daily life. Thus Augustine insisted that it is the evidence of the Christian's life, not the Christian's words, that best testifies to the truth of scripture.[4]

Secondly, the gospels could be made available to people in ways that were not restricted to language and words. Countless medieval Christians will have become familiar with the contents of the gospels through wall paintings, stone carvings and stained glass, much of which was designed not just to convey the stories themselves but to connect them both with their Old Testament equivalents and with everyday contemporary life. Street theatre, popular songs, jewellery and embroidery all helped to lift the gospel stories into the heart of home and marketplace alike; and manuscripts containing biblical texts or commentaries on them could be rendered accessible to the non-literate by the addition of illustration: presentations of the Bible, such as the *Biblia pauperum* or the French *Bible moralisée*, which were produced for catechetical purposes, commonly included illustrations designed to be accessible – both directly, to those with little learning, and, as part of a complex iconographical programme, to those with much.

THE IMITATION OF CHRIST

This brings us to the question of how, and in what ways, the gospels have shaped Christian spirituality and worship through the ages. Perhaps the most influential way in which they have done this is in making it possible for Christians to see Jesus not just as the means of their salvation but as the model for their lives. Texts such as Matt 10.37–8 ('Whoever loves father or mother more than me is not worthy of me; and whoever does not take up the cross and follow me is not worthy of me') exerted an immense influence on generations of Christians thereafter; and the explicit identification of Jesus with God, which finds its fullest expression in the Gospel of John, effectively declared that a life devoted to the imitation of Christ was in itself the surest means to union with God. It is of course unclear how far the gospels, directly and (so to speak) *ex nihilo*, inspired individuals and communities to dedicate themselves to living in imitation of Christ, and how far they were used to justify particular and preconceived human initiatives; but what is indisputable is that Christian spirituality would have possessed an unimaginably different character had the gospels never been written.

In much early and medieval Christian spirituality, the imitation of Christ, while in one form or another available to (indeed mandatory for) every Christian, was in its fullest manifestation possible only for those who chose to abandon 'the world'; and here it is possible to see not only how the gospels influenced Christian spirituality but also how the Christian values and presuppositions of the time influenced people's reading of the gospels. Athanasius, the fourth-century theologian and archbishop of Alexandria, wrote a life of his near-contemporary St Antony of Egypt, in which he persuasively presented Antony as responding directly and literally to Jesus' injunction to those who wished to be perfect ('Go, sell your possessions, and give the money to the poor . . .', Matt 19.21), and thereafter as in effect dedicating his entire life to a literal imitation of one specific gospel story, the account of the temptations of Jesus by Satan in the wilderness. The world of Antony's new life in the Egyptian desert, and his lonely struggles there with the power of evil, as well as much of the imagery Athanasius adds, derive from these narratives.[5] Figures such as Antony, once canonized or written about, became themselves exemplary, just as Christ had been for them; and the long and immensely diverse tradition of desert spirituality, so persistent and powerful a feature of both eastern and western Christian piety, consequently owes its origins and character not just to the biblical narrative of the journey of the people of God from Egypt to the promised land, but also to the gospel accounts of Jesus' temptations, and to how those accounts were lived out by exemplary figures like saints and martyrs.

Other Christians sought to imitate Christ not simply by a literal re-enactment of one particular gospel story but by making their own what they took to be the whole character and dynamic of Christ's earthly life. Arguably the most famous of all such imitators was Francis of Assisi (1181–1226), for whom the gospels in their entirety were a manifesto for every aspect of the Christian life. Thus, the 1226 *Testament of St Francis* records him as declaring that God personally revealed to him that he should live according to the form of the Holy Gospel;[6] and his near-contemporary Clare of Assisi makes the same point at the start of the Rule she set down for her sisters.[7] Similarly, the eleventh-century Stephen of Muret sought to fashion the entire spirituality of the new monastic order he founded at Grandmont, in the diocese of Limoges, on the precepts of the gospels. Using words of Jesus in the Farewell Discourses of the Gospel of John ('In my Father's house there are many dwelling places', Jn 14.2) to justify the many and different (though, in his view, exclusively monastic) ways in which Christians might follow Christ and attain salvation, he went on to maintain that the only certain, and uniquely authoritative, rule of life for Christians was the text of the gospels themselves. So convinced was he of its sufficiency that he adopted none of the known monastic rules and left no written rule for his disciples.[8]

By the thirteenth century, not least as a result of the influence of charis-matic figures such as Francis, the imitation of Christ had become something accessible to lay people as well; and the presuppositions of earlier Christians like Stephen of Muret that Jesus' summons to seek perfection (in texts such as Matt 19.21) could be obeyed only within the cloister were being gradually enlarged: later devotional texts on this subject were addressed to all Chris-tians. Nor was the imitation of Christ restricted to men. In two thirteenth-century Scandinavian texts, *Grœnlendiga saga* ('The Story of Greenland') and *Eiriks saga* ('The Story of Erik [the Red]'), the central figure of the lay woman and mother Guðriðr is clearly presented in such a way as to show that the imitation of Christ is entirely possible for lay people living 'in the world'. And not only the imitation of Christ: Guðriðr's life is also based on the gospel accounts of the Virgin Mary, whom she follows not only in unselfish obedience to Christ but in pondering and meditating upon what she experiences. The two sagas thus reveal a careful and coherent concern on the part of the medieval Scandinavian church to provide role models, rooted in scriptural texts that, though reflecting current ecclesiastical priorities, could be made available and attractive to anyone. The very fact that these are sagas recalls a point made earlier: the gospels are stories, and, since the spirituality of the Icelandic and Inuit peoples (among many others) has always been centred upon stories, there were unlimited ways in which the stories of Christ the itinerant teacher and those of migrant and hunter-gatherer communities could interact with one another.[9]

Exactly what it was in the life of Christ (or of Mary or any other gospel figure) that was to be imitated was, then, something that varied according to time and place; and the church sought constantly to offer (and sometimes to impose) its own view and its own pattern. The Greek theologian Gregory of Nyssa, writing about the imitation of Christ in the fourth century in his *On Perfection*, proposed an ontological participation in the life of Christ with a particular concern to shun the passions of 'the world'. On the other hand, the fifteenth-century Thomas à Kempis advocated a quite different kind of interiority – one coupled with an individual moralism, and that demanded an even more rigorous rejection of 'the world'.[10]

Many such spiritual texts were addressed, implicitly or explicitly, to women, encouraging a conformity to particular aspects of the life and teaching of Christ as set out in the gospels (such as gentleness and obedience) and by implication the rejection of others less congenial to the church at the time.

This did not, however, prevent women from developing their own patterns of spirituality which, while no less rooted in the gospels and in orthodox Christian teaching, opened up new approaches to the imitation of Christ. Many, drawing in particular on the theology and imagery of the Gospel of John, sought union with Christ, sometimes in a direct and immediate manner which may properly be described as mystical. To give but one example: the medieval mystical writer Angela of Foligno (c. 1248–1309). Angela was a laywoman, a wife and mother, who was deeply influenced by Franciscan spirituality, but who also drew heavily in the language and imagery of union in the Gospel of John to articulate her own profound sense of union with God. At one point she describes how on one occasion she felt herself to be led into a vision in which she was told that, by seeking fully to apprehend the gospel when it is read during Mass, it is possible to be led into a profound and intimate experience of God so intense and beautiful as to render one oblivious to oneself and the outside world during it.[11] This sense of the gospel text as being intrinsically capable of leading someone to a profound mystical encounter with God is not original to Angela; but it illustrates the hidden power that the gospels in particular were believed to possess, and their potential to effect the transformation of human lives – not least those who, because of their gender or social position or both, had little likelihood of experiencing any other kind of transformation.

THE GOSPELS IN CHRISTIAN PRAYER AND MEDITATION

The influence of the gospels on Christian spirituality was not restricted to the imitation of, or search for union with, Christ: in a more general sense it affected the texture and character of Christian piety and worship across every tradition and period. But the influence was rarely one-way: the text or content of the gospels came to be understood in different ways by those who both prayed with them and sought to live by them. Late medieval Christians, for example, meditating on the passion of Christ as recorded in the synoptic gospels, understood Christ's suffering as being infinitely greater than any human suffering, because it was that of the divine Son of God as well as of the human Jesus of Nazareth. Only suffering on so cosmic a scale could begin to speak to an age afflicted by the horrors of the Black Death and the Hundred Years War. The fourteenth-century English writer Julian of Norwich ponders this theme at length in her *Showings* (or *Revelations of the Divine Love*); and it finds expression in countless late medieval depictions of the crucified Christ.

One of the most enduring ways in which the gospels influenced Christian spirituality was by various forms of meditation or reflection that were designed to enable people to imagine themselves to be actually present in particular gospel scenes, and to consider what implications that imaginative participation might have for their lives. Much Anglo-Saxon book illumination is designed to foster this kind of approach to the text of the gospels, though at this period the emphasis was placed not only, or even primarily, on considering the implications of such meditation for the present, but on seeking to enter, through prayer, into the life of heaven. The gospels were held to be a unique means, not of contemplating the past, or even of renewing the present, but of anticipating the future. Christ was believed to be present to the believer directly through the word of the gospels: hence the practice of decorating the covers or opening pages of Anglo-Saxon gospel books with ornamental crosses or symbols of the evangelists, heightening the symbolic significance of the gospels themselves. And it was Christ the eternal Word of God, and Christ the coming Judge, who was supremely revealed in this way. Thus the English monk and scholar Bede the Venerable (c. 673–735), in one of his homilies on the gospels, considers the image in the Gospel of John about the pregnant woman enduring the anguish of childbirth for the sake of bringing a new child into the world (Jn 16.21–2) as a symbol of the church, which suffers persecution even while bringing new Christians to birth, and adds an eschatological interpretation: the whole church suffers in this world as it looks and moves forward to the life of heaven, and to the Lord who will then crown those who have suffered in his name.[12]

Later in the Middle Ages, and with the focus still primarily on the life of the world to come, there developed in monastic circles in western Europe the practice of *lectio divina*, a particularly intensive form of prayerful spiritual reading in which the words of scripture were ruminated over as if the reader was like a ruminant animal: the texts and images were absorbed, then brought back into the conscious mind so as to be thoroughly digested in a period of attentive meditation that (it was believed) would eventually lead the reader into a deeper state of contemplation. The twelfth-century Carthusian monk Guigo II, prior of the Grande Chartreuse, wrote a *Ladder of Monks* (*Scala claustralium*) in which he identified four stages in the ladder of the spiritual life: reading (i.e. of scripture), meditation, prayer, and contemplation. He describes reading as 'the careful study of the Scriptures, with all the mind's attention' (*Ladder* 2), a process exactly comparable with that of eating, tasting and digesting food (*Ladder* 3); and, in ruminating upon a text from the Sermon on the Mount ('Blessed are the pure in heart, for they will see God', Matt 5.8), he speaks of the soul gradually coming to see how attractive that vision of God in eternity will be, and beginning to deploy all its efforts in seeking here and now that purity that alone can attain it (*Ladder* 4). The focus is still on the life of heaven; but the perspective is narrower, more individual, the gospel text addressed directly to the person's own life which is subjected by means of it to a searching and intimate scrutiny.

GOSPEL MEDITATION AND THE USE OF THE IMAGINATION

This kind of spiritual reading of scripture demanded the unhurried and undistracted concentration (not to mention the availability of rare and expensive texts) which was hardly possible outside the cloister. But another form of reflection on scripture, which this time focused more directly on the gospels, was much more accessible to those living 'in the world'; and, although it, too, originated in the Middle Ages, it has remained one of the commonest forms of meditation on the Bible, albeit largely within the

Catholic tradition. This was the rosary, a discipline which encouraged imaginative prayer by individuals or groups who pondered various 'mysteries' in the life of Christ and his mother Mary while reciting set prayers a prescribed number of times, and seeking to allow the stories of the gospel to address and nourish the person praying or those for whom the rosary was being recited. In 2002, Pope John Paul II added a new set of five mysteries to the existing fifteen. These, which he called the 'mysteries of light', were taken from the life of Christ in the gospels: the baptism of Christ in the Jordan, the wedding at Cana, the proclamation of the kingdom of God in the Sermon on the Mount, the transfiguration, and the institution of the Eucharist.[13]

The *Spiritual Exercises* of Ignatius of Loyola (1491–1556) are similarly designed to encourage imaginative meditation on gospel scenes, but with the specific intention of leading the person praying to open his or her heart and will to God in the active expectation of being summoned to a specific (and often costly) vocation in Christ's service. In the *Exercises*, the focus has shifted from the future (the life of heaven) to the present. Thus, in the Second Week of the *Exercises*, the person praying is invited to contemplate first the incarnation and secondly the birth of Christ, imagining himself or herself to be present at the scene of the latter, and repeating the exercise several times so as to consider what God might be asking of him or her.

Prayerful reflection on the texts of the gospels has not been restricted to the Catholic tradition. The Lutheran mystic Johann Arndt (1555–1621) insisted that merely listening to, or reading, the gospels was useless unless it was integral to the practice of a genuinely Christian life.[14] Book 2 of his *True Christianity* is a concerted attempt to make use of the whole life and example of Christ as a way of both fashioning the life and developing the prayer of the believer through a systematic programme of repentance and personal reflection. The author of the Elizabethan homily entitled *A Fruitful Exhortation to the Reading of Holy Scripture* commends medieval-style rumination on scripture, and warns of the dangers awaiting those who put human writings and fantasies before the truth of the gospel.[15] But the focus here, as in Ignatius' *Exercises*, is on the impact of the gospel on the present, and supremely on the lives of those doing the reading and praying.

It is almost impossible to calculate the impact on western Christian spirituality of the invention of printing, and with it the increasing availability of the entire Bible in the vernacular. What is unquestionable is that these things accelerated a process already begun in earlier centuries: individual and communal reflection on the gospel stories and images, in such a way as to allow those stories and images to address directly the individual's or community's own immediate life and prayer. Here (as just one example of how that reflection might find expression) is an extract from the writings of the English Protestant William Tyndale (c.1494–1536), one of the most famous of all Bible translators, reflecting on the story in the Gospel of Luke of a woman (by tradition Mary Magdalene) anointing Jesus in the house of Simon the Pharisee:

> Simon believed and had faith, yet but weakly; and, according to the proportion of his faith, loved coldly . . . But Mary had a strong faith and therefore burning love and notable deeds, done with exceeding profound and deep meekness. On the one hand she saw herself clearly in the law, both in what danger she was in, and her cruel bondage under sin . . . and . . . the fearful sentence and judgment of God upon sinners. On the other side, she heard the gospel of Christ preached; and in the promises she saw with eagles' eyes the exceeding abundant mercy of God . . . which is set forth in Christ for all meek sinners, which [ac]knowledge their sins; and she believed the word of God mightily . . . and being overcome and overwhelmed with the unspeakable, yea, and incomprehensible abundant riches of the kindness of God, did inflame and burn in love; yea, was so swollen in love, that she could not abide, nor hold, but must break out; and was so drunk in love, that she regarded nothing, but even to utter the fervent and burning love of her heart only . . . For as a man feeleth God in himself, so is he to his neighbour.[16]

Tyndale has set the gospel story in a firmly Protestant hue, especially in what he says about the primacy of true faith. But he has retained the old medieval emphasis on experiencing the presence of Christ directly through the medium of reflection on the text of scripture, as well as its concern to apply the fruits of that experience to the loving service of one's neighbour.

THE GOSPELS IN LIBERATION AND FEMINIST SPIRITUALITY

In more recent Christian spirituality, and especially in the spirituality of the developing world, this recognition, that openness to the gospels in prayer and worship demands a response not only in terms of the individual's interior life but also in active service of neighbour, has been taken much further. The work of the late twentieth-century practitioners of 'liberation theology', especially in Latin America, has encouraged Christians to see gospel texts as radical challenges to a political system which oppresses the poor. Thus Jon Sobrino interprets Jesus's preaching of the kingdom in terms of a 'spirituality of liberation', a pattern of spiritual life that underpins, and is oriented towards, a passionate commitment to social justice and a radical transformation of the unjust structures of society in favour of its poorest members.[17] Feminist readings of the gospels have not only underlined the significance of women in the life of Jesus; they have also seen in the suffering Christ not a western-style 'lord' or 'master', conveniently compatible with colonial power-structures, but 'the divine co-sufferer, who empowers [women] in situations of oppression'.[18]

In this approach to the gospels, Christian spirituality focuses less on the exalted Christ of faith and more on the historical Jesus of Nazareth. Texts like the Peruvian catechism *Vamos Caminando* ('We are always travelling along') reflect another attempt, in this case by Christians in the Catholic diocese of Cajamarca, to allow the stories of the gospel (especially those describing or addressed to the poor) to engage in dialogue with local and contemporary stories.[19] In this and similar works, such as the writings of the Nicaraguan Ernesto Cardenal, an attempt is made to recover the original context of the gospels precisely in order to let them speak directly to the social and political context of those reading them today; and Sobrino can speak of the poor 'living the paradox of the Sermon on the Mount: a life of beatitude in difficult material conditions.'[20] He does this not in order to idealize material poverty but to argue that they alone can truly pray the gospels, because they alone are in a position to perceive its fullest implications, and to take with adequate seriousness the reflections on wealth and poverty that the gospels (especially Luke) contain. Here, as in early Christian spirituality, the gospels are again read in the light of the future, with a strong emphasis on those texts that counsel an active and expectant anticipation of a new order; but in liberation spirituality that new order is envisaged in terms of the transformation of this world, not the anticipation of the next.

THE LORD'S PRAYER

Finally, it is worth recalling the significance of specific texts from the gospels which have nourished Christian spirituality throughout its history. The most prominent of these is the Lord's Prayer, which in its Matthean form has been almost universally used in Christian liturgy from earliest times, and in the daily office (albeit inconsistently) since the sixth century.

It has been in use in the vernacular in English since the beginning of the eighth century. Its interpretation, unsurprisingly, reflects the cultural and theological preoccupations of its interpreters: thus the monastic reformer Peter Damian (1007–72) exhorts the clergy and people of Milan to set their hearts on all that is heavenly as they pray it, since our Father is described as being in heaven rather than on earth, whereas the Reformation theologian John Calvin (1509–64) sees it rather as the embodiment of everything (both in this world and in the next) for which Christians ought to pray and after which they should aspire.[21] The Spanish mystical writer Teresa of Avila (1515–82) pointed out that, since the Lord's Prayer reminds us that we are all children of the same heavenly Father, it thereby warns us of our equality before God, irrespective of birth or social standing; and she maintained that the perfection of contemplation could be attained by anyone praying it.[22] And the Anglican theologian Evelyn Underhill (1874–1941) believed that it is in itself 'a complete direction for the Godward life of the soul'.[23] Most recently, the masculine imagery of the prayer has led to some gender-sensitive revisions, in the interests of a more inclusive spirituality.[24]

MUSIC AND THE SPIRITUALITY OF THE GOSPELS

In order to view in more detail how these varying approaches to the gospels in the history of Christian spirituality find expression, one particular medium suggests itself as a case study: that of music. Since the earliest Christian period, the singing of hymns and psalms has been central to worship and prayer; and throughout most of Christian history the songs in the Gospel of Luke (the *Benedictus, Magnificat* and *Nunc Dimittis*) have in particular been given an especially prominent role. The gospels themselves were described in musical terms; the second-century St Clement of Alexandria declares that 'The trumpet of Christ is his Gospel; he has blown it and we have heard.'.[25] Three different responses to the gospels in music illustrate the wide variety of possibilities music offers to inform Christian spirituality.

Johann Sebastian Bach

In the Lutheran tradition, the use of music to allow the gospel to nourish the spirituality of both the individual believer and the Christian community reached its highest point in the great passion settings of Johann Sebastian

Bach (1685–1750). These are conceived on three levels: the first is the gospel text itself, declaimed dramatically by soloists and choir; the second is a series of arias and *ariosi*, in which what is happening is reflected on theologically in such a way as to point up its implications for the spiritual life of the listener; the third is the provision of Lutheran chorales, in which the entire congregation could participate and thereby appropriate for itself the full significance of the story of Jesus' crucifixion.

A striking example of how this works may be found in the *St Matthew Passion*, where the gospel account of Jesus' arrest in Gethsemane is followed by an extraordinary aria: it begins as a melancholy and reflective duet for soprano and alto, 'So ist mein Jesus nun gefangen' ('And so my Saviour now is taken'), pondering the significance of what has just happened. Then the chorus interrupts with music and words expressive of passionate lament ('Loose him! Leave him! Bind him not!'), and after a reprise of the duet the chorus, so to speak, sweeps away the spirituality of traditional Christian mourning in favour of a fast and furious outburst:

Have lightnings and thunders their fury forgotten?
Then open, O fathomless pit, all thy terrors!
Destroy them, o'erwhelm them, devour them, consume them
With tumult of rage,
The treach'rous betrayer, the merciless throng.

This is a striking illustration of how music and words together articulate different responses to the gospel text; and the power of Bach's setting consists in the way the eloquent but rather passive reaction to Jesus' betrayal and arrest articulated by the two soloists is overwhelmed by the much more active engagement with the text sung by the chorus. The question mark in the words above is in a sense even more important than the words themselves. This is a spirituality that allows people to wonder why an innocent man should have been led to his death through the agency of his friend; and it is not unreasonable to conjecture that it was, in Bach's view, only that kind of searchingly honest spirituality that could allow the gospel story of Christ's passion to address the continuing doubt and anguish of the Christian in the face of the sorrows of his or her own day.

Black Gospel music

A very different engagement with the gospel accounts of Christ's passion can be found in the music of the Black Gospel tradition that had its immediate origins in the southern United States during the nineteenth century, but ultimately originated in the music and spiritual traditions of West Africa. Black Gospel music tends to use language of power, praise, salvation, struggle and above all hope, both for a better society in this world and for the peace and joy of the world to come. The style, rhythm and use of physical movement, as well as the way singer and audience interact, allow for a different kind of spirituality to emerge from engagement with the stories and truths of the gospel. Characteristic of it are a strongly communal sense of assurance and a vigorous expectation of a better future that can help to subvert the grim realities and injustices of the present. Some Black Gospel music is intimate and gentle in character; but here too the effect of music and words together is powerfully spiritual, drawing singer and listener alike into a deep sense of spiritual union:

In the upper room with Jesus
Sitting at his blessed feet
Daily there, my sin confesses
Begging for his mercy sweet.
Trusting his grace and power
Seeking there his love in prayer:
It is there I feel the spirit
As I sit with him in prayer.
   Oh, it's in the upper room with Jesus
   Oh, it's in the upper room with my Lord
   And your God,
   Yes, it's in the upper room
   Well, it's in the upper room
   Talking with my Lord
   Oh, my God.

The words of this song were written by Lucie Eddie Campbell (1885–1963) in 1947: it became famous when it was taken up by Mahalia Jackson (1911–72), perhaps the most famous of all Black Gospel singers. But such songs are intended not only, or even primarily, for professional soloists: countless Black churches throughout the United States and beyond have used this song as a means of entering more deeply into the last supper by encouraging worshippers to imagine themselves as being present there themselves, engaged in a personal conversation with Jesus not entirely dissimilar from those envisaged in St Ignatius' *Spiritual Exercises*.

Olivier Messiaen

A third musical response to the gospels can be found in the music of the great French Catholic composer Olivier Messiaen (1908–92), who based several of his pieces on texts or scenes from the gospels. One of the most monumental of these is the *Vingt regards sur l'enfant-Jésus*, completed between 23 March and 8 September 1944 in Paris, and dedicated to his wife, the pianist Yvonne Loriod. The French word *regard* may perhaps best be translated as 'contemplation': this is intensely reflective music, at once rigorously focused on the gospel scenes or theological truths being pondered and at the same time drawing on a highly eclectic range of sources (birdsong, astronomy, Catholic spiritual writers and much else) in seeking to fashion a spiritual response to scripture that is both intellectually complex and almost artlessly emotional. Messiaen describes its theological programme in his introduction to the piano score.[26] The child in the manger is 'regarded' from a variety of perspectives: first by the Father, later by the Virgin, the angels and so on. But Messiaen wants to contemplate the birth of Jesus in the light both of the rest of Christ's earthly life as the gospels recount it and of the eternal perspectives of the divine incarnation – as well as from the point of view of the church of his own time. Hence one of the twenty movements is entitled 'Regard de la croix' ('Contemplation [of the infant Jesus] from the cross'), and the last one (which concludes with an apotheosis of extraordinary power) 'Regard de l'Église d'amour' ('Contemplation [of the infant Jesus] from the Church of love'). The abiding character is contemplative, and many of the movements are extremely slow: it is as though every being in the entire cosmos, from the Creator to the least creature, takes its turn in 'regarding' the wonder of the Word made flesh, allowing listeners to appropriate for themselves the mystery of the incarnation through a process of great richness and beauty, but perhaps above all of almost childlike wonder.[27]

Hymns

For most Christians, however, it is in the singing of hymns that the gospels most immediately address their spiritual lives and experiences. It is not surprising to find that, from the earliest Christian period, hymns have reflected both the theological priorities and the socio-political assumptions of their age. Thus, for example, the famous hymn of Venantius Fortunatus (530–609), *Vexilla regis prodeunt* ('The royal banners forward go') not only draws on a rich variety of biblical texts in responding to the gospel account of Christ's crucifixion but implicitly articulates a political message: this

Christ (it seems to say) is royal, reigning and triumphant from the tree, and spoiling the spoiler of his prey. Amid the political upheavals of post-imperial sixth-century France, such a message has a particular relevance. And the spirituality of this hymn is unambiguously rooted in a theology of power and strength that alone could effectively sustain Christians in so uncertain an age.

A very different air is breathed in the hymns of the eighteenth-century Methodist Charles Wesley, who, like Olivier Messiaen after him, combines profound theological reflection with a deeply personal and affective piety in seeking to allow the gospels to address the lives of his fellow Christians. In one of his eucharistic hymns he reflects on the story in Luke's gospel of the road to Emmaus:

> O thou who this mysterious bread
>   Didst in *Emmaus* break,
> Return, herewith our souls to feed,
>   And to thy followers speak.
>
> Unseal the volume of thy grace,
>   Apply the gospel word,
> Open our eyes to see thy face,
>   Our hearts to know the Lord.
>
> Of thee we commune still, and mourn
>   Till thou the veil remove;
> Talk with us, and our hearts shall burn
>   With flames of fervent love.
>
> Enkindle now the heavenly zeal
>   And make thy mercy known,
> And give our pardon'd souls to feel
>   That God and love are one.[28]

This is by no means the greatest of Wesley's huge output of hymns. But it demonstrates how, through the medium of words and music, the stories and truths of the gospels could be appropriated by Christians whose lives and backgrounds were very different from that of the gospel-writers. Such appropriation was never neutral, never objective; but the astonishing diversity of ways in which it took place is in itself testimony to the seemingly inexhaustible capacity of those ancient biblical texts to address, and sometimes radically to transform, human lives and aspirations. Wesley brought the language and Protestant theology of his day to the story of the Emmaus road; but he still managed to make his own the mysterious and elusive Christ described there.

It is a long journey from the world of Venantius or Wesley to that of twentieth-century Glasgow; but the hymns of the Scottish writer John Bell (born 1949) are no less expressive than those of his predecessors in offering those who sing them a spirituality that will allow them not only to engage with, but to defy, the seeming certainties of the social order around them. In his work, the stories of the gospel reveal a God, not of power, but of compassion, justice and love, a God who subverts the arrogance of the strong. Rooted in the radical Scottish tradition of George MacLeod and the Iona Community, Bell's hymns deploy a sensitivity to language and imagery that recalls the values of liberation theology and is similarly rooted in the lives and experience of the poor:

> Before the world began
> one Word was there;
> grounded in God he was,
>   rooted in care;
> by him all things were made;
> in him was love displayed,
> through him God spoke and said
>   'I am for you.'
> The Word was in the world
> which from him came;
> unrecognised was he,
>   unknown by name;
> one with all humankind,
> with the unloved aligned,
> convincing sight and mind
>   'I am for you.'[29]

CONCLUSION

In a lecture delivered in 1994, the German theologian Johannes Baptist Metz argued that 'the language of prayer is not only more universal, but also more exciting and dramatic, much more rebellious and radical than the language of current theology'.[30] Metz was reflecting on the forms of prayer found in scripture, such as the great psalms of lament, the prayer of Job, Christ's cry of pain from the cross, and the urgent prayer ('Maranatha': 'Come, Lord Jesus!') with which the Bible closes (Rev 22.20).

To 'pray the gospels' has meant very different things to successive generations of Christians; but among the many reasons why it is important to pray them, and not simply to study them, is precisely because, as Metz points out, such prayer is capable of having a transforming effect on those praying that study alone may not equal. For it is, as we have seen, the consistent experience of such people that praying with the gospels draws them from being spectators to being participants, allowing them to bring all of themselves, including their doubts and questions, into their prayer; and it may only be in and through this kind of prayer that the purposes of the original gospel writers can be achieved.

Notes

1. Justin, *First Apology*, 67.
2. *Mystagogia* 13; ET by G. C. Berthold in *Maximus Confessor: Selected Writings* (Mahwah: Paulist Press, 1985), 200.
3. *On Matthew*, preface, in Saint Jérome, *Commentaire sur Saint Matthieu*, ed. Bonnard (Paris: Sources Chrétiennes 242, Éditions du Cerf 1977), I, 70; and ibid., I 4, commenting on Matt 4.19 (p. 102).
4. *On Christian Doctrine*, IV 27.59–60.
5. See, e.g. *The Life of Antony*, 37, where the saint explicitly quotes Jesus' words to Satan in Matt 4.10.
6. *The Testament of St Francis* 14.
7. *The Rule of St Clare* 1.1.
8. See Bede Lackner, *The Eleventh-Century Background of Cîteaux* (Washington, DC: Cistercian Publications, 1972), 196–203.
9. For Inuit spirituality and the significance of storytelling within it, see Hugh Brody, *The Other Side of Eden* (London: Faber, 2001).
10. For Gregory and Thomas, see Margaret R. Miles, *The Image and Practice of Holiness* (London: SCM Press, 1988), 21–8.
11. *The Book of Blessed Angela of Foligno*, 1.1 (the 'Seventeenth Step').
12. Bede, *Homilies on the Gospels*, 2.13.
13. John Paul II, *Rosarium Virginis Mariae: Apostolic Letter on the Most Holy Rosary* (London: Catholic Truth Society, 2002), 19–21.
14. *True Christianity* (*Vier Bücher vom wahren Christentum*), 1606, ch. 36; trans. Peter Erb (Classics of Western Spirituality; New York: Paulist Press, 1979), 155–61.
15. *Certain Sermons or Homilies Appointed to be Read in Churches in the Time of the Late Queen Elizabeth* (Oxford University Press, 1840), 1–8.
16. *The Parable of the Wicked Mammon*, 1528.
17. Jon Sobrino, *Spirituality of Liberation*, trans. R. R.Barr (Maryknoll: Orbis, 1988).
18. Jacquelyn Grant, *Black Women's Jesus*, quoted in Kathleen O'Brien Wicker, 'Teaching Feminist Biblical Studies in a Postcolonial Context', in Elisabeth Schüssler Fiorenza, *Searching the Scriptures: A Feminist Introduction* (New York: Crossroad, 1993), 376.

19. *Vamos Caminando* (Lima: Centro de Estudios y Publicaciones, 1977); ET (same title) by John Medcalf (London: SCM Press), 1985.
20. *Spirituality of Liberation* (Maryknoll: Orbis, 1988), 164. For Cardenal, see especially *The Gospel in Solentiname*, 4 vols. (Maryknoll: Orbis, 1976–82).
21. Peter Damian, Letter 84, in *Die Briefe des Petrus Damiani*, ii, ed. Kurt Reindel (Munich: Monumenta Germaniae Historica, 1988), 454; ET by Owen J. Blum OFM, *The Letters of Peter Damian 61–90* (The Fathers of the Church: Mediaeval Continuation; Washington, DC: Catholic University of America Press, 1992), 248. Calvin, *Institutes of the Christian Religion*, iii 20.34.
22. *The Way of Perfection* 25 and 27.
23. Evelyn Underhill, *Worship* (2nd edn, London: Nisbet & Co., 1937), ch. 11.3.
24. For example, that of Jim Cotter ('Beloved, our Father and Mother, in whom is heaven . . .'), in Hannah Ward and Jennifer Wild, *Human Rites* (London: Mowbray, 1995), 315.
25. *Protrepticus* 11.116.2–3, quoted in James W. McKinnon, *Music in Early Christian Literature* (Cambridge: Cambridge University Press, 1987), 31. Origen uses the same metaphor in his *In librum Jesu Nave homilia*, 7.1 in J. P. Migne, ed., *Patrologiae cursus completus, series Graeca*, 161 vols. (Paris, 1857–66), xii 857.
26. *Vingt regards sur l'enfant-Jésus* (Paris: Durand, 1944).
27. See Paul Griffiths, *Olivier Messiaen and the Music of Time* (London: Faber, 1985), esp. 119–20; and Peter Hill, 'Piano Music I', in Peter Hill, ed., *The Messiaen Companion* (London: Faber, 1995).
28. From *Hymns on the Lord's Supper*, 1745.
29. By John Bell and Graham Maule; from *Rejoice and Sing* (Oxford: Oxford University Press, 1991), 269; © The Iona Community/Wild Goose Publications.
30. Johannes Baptist Metz, *Diagnosen zur Zeit* (Düsseldorf, 1994), 79–80; ET by Linda M. Maloney in Erich Zenger, *A God of Vengeance?* (Louisville: Westminster/John Knox Press, 1996), 95.

Further reading

Barton, Stephen C., *The Spirituality of the Gospels* (London: SPCK, 1992)
Cullmann, Oscar, *Prayer in the New Testament* (London: SCM Press, 1995)
Elliott, Charles, *Praying the Kingdom* (London: Darton, Longman & Todd, 1985)
Greer, Rowan A., *Broken Lights and Mended Lives: Theology and Common Life in the Early Church* (University Park and London: Pennsylvania State University Press, 1986)
Hardy, D. W., and Ford, D. F., *Jubilate: Theology in Praise* (London: Darton, Longman & Todd, 1984)
Johnson, Luke T., *Living Jesus: Learning the Heart of the Gospel* (San Francisco: HarperCollins, 2000)
Louth, Andrew, *The Wilderness of God* (London: Darton, Longman & Todd, 1991)
Sobrino, Jon, *Spirituality of Liberation* (Maryknoll: Orbis, 1988)
Stevenson, Kenneth, *Abba, Father: Understanding and Using the Lord's Prayer* (Norwich: Canterbury Press, 2000)
Tugwell, Simon, *Ways of Imperfection* (London: Darton, Longman & Todd, 1984)
Williams, Rowan, *The Wound of Knowledge* (2nd edn, London: Darton, Longman & Todd, 1990)

13 Living the gospels: morality and politics

SCOTT BADER-SAYE

Does Jesus speak to matters that are public and political, or is his teaching directed solely to the individual believer? This question has become harder to answer in the modern world. Or, to put it better, such a question has become possible only in the modern world. The distinction between the public and the private that many today take for granted has its history in the rise of the modern secular nation and the demise of the church's political power. In the modern west, religion tends to fall on the 'private' side of the divide, while politics names the 'public' realm in which varieties of rights and interests are weighed and evaluated. Ethics continues to be invoked as both a private and a public matter, but it is generally agreed that, in order for ethics to become public ethics, all religious content must be evacuated. Only in this way, it is argued, could an ethic be binding for a religiously diverse population. While one might respect the desire to create a political body that can foster a unity of purpose across religious boundaries, the public/private split has tended to fragment our most basic human questions. 'How are we to live together?' (a political question) is separated from 'What is the good that we should pursue?' (an ethical question), which, in turn, is separated from 'Where do we come from and where are we going?' (a religious question). This tendency to fragment the human quest makes it difficult sometimes to understand the biblical world in which politics, religion and ethics are unapologetically intertwined in the pursuit of God and the good.

Jesus lived in a world where belief in God's covenant with Israel shaped the whole of life, individually and communally. This way of life had to be lived under the constraints of Roman domination, but subjugation to foreign rule did not in principle change the scope of the covenant. As E. P. Sanders notes, '*The most striking point about Jewish law is that it brings the entirety of life, including civil and domestic practices, under the authority of God. . .* "Religion" in Judaism was not only festivals and sacrifices, as it was in most of the Graeco-Roman world, but rather encompassed all of life.'[1] As Josephus, a first-century Jewish historian, put it, 'Religion governs all our actions and occupations and speech; none of these things did our lawgiver leave unexamined or indeterminate.'[2] The right worship of God, obedience to God's commands, and proper leadership in the community constituted overlapping circles which together comprised the life of the chosen people.

The history of moral and political interpretations of the gospels takes us from a time when the biblical unity of religion, politics and ethics was assumed, through a period in which this integrated worldview crumbled under the force of philosophical and political change, to a present in which the narrative world of the Bible is being reclaimed, though in a new key. Part of what is being rediscovered is the political power of Jesus' call to 'dispossess,' that is, to relinquish the power, wealth and prestige that afford some the ability to dominate others. After exploring this vision of dispossession in the gospels, we will examine St Augustine, Immanuel Kant, Reinhold Niebuhr and John Paul II as interpreters of the ethic of Jesus. In each case we will see that the intelligibility and practicality of Jesus' ethic of dispossession rests on the reader's ability and willingness to enter into the narrated world of the text, including its theological assumptions about creation, sin, redemption and resurrection.

READING THE GOSPELS: NARRATIVES OF DISPOSSESSION

A rich man came to Jesus asking for an ethic – 'What must I do to inherit eternal life?' – but instead got an invitation to pass through the eye of a needle – 'Go, sell what you own, and give the money to the poor, and you will have treasure in heaven; then come, follow me' (Mk 10.21). Jesus implies that to live the gospel is not to have an ethic but to have a life. There is a reason why the gospel writers left us stories about Jesus and not just a compendium of his teachings. The whole of Jesus' life, death and resurrection suggests more a moral pattern than a list of rules. This is not to diminish the importance of his explicit moral teaching; it is rather to say that we falsify the gospel when we distill political or moral principles from the narrative context of Jesus' whole life and witness. The story as a whole functions to make Jesus' teaching intelligible. One cannot, for instance, know either the possibility or the difficulty of Jesus' call to 'turn the other cheek' until one has read to the end of the story and witnessed his own self-giving on the cross, and one can hardly imagine following this path unless one reads further still and hears the good news of resurrection and Christ's triumph over death.

Not only does Jesus' story flesh out his moral vision, but his gathering of a community makes his moral vision liveable. In contrast to the modern tendency to individualize ethics, the gospels present discipleship as a communal endeavour. The disciples are not given a message and then sent home. They are invited to join in the community of discipleship and to follow Jesus as a body. The dispossession of power, property and privilege involved in following Jesus will prove impossible apart from a community ready to bear one another's weaknesses, burdens and vulnerabilities. Even when the disciples are sent out on mission, they are sent not alone but in pairs.

John's gospel especially challenges those who think they can follow Jesus alone and in secret to shed the cloak of darkness and cast their lot publicly with the community of disciples. Nicodemus, for instance, can under the cover of night address Jesus as 'a teacher who has come from God' (Jn 3.2), but in the light of day he refuses to confess this belief to his fellow Pharisees (Jn 7). David Rensberger comments:

> What the Gospel of John calls for on the part of the secret Christians is a public transfer of allegiance. This is what Nicodemus successfully avoids in the council of the Pharisees and rulers in John 7 . . . They are being asked, in fact, to switch sides from persecutor to persecuted. The group they are being asked to join has no status, no power, no place in the world. They are being asked to dislocate and displace themselves socially, to undertake an act of deliberate downward mobility. Quite possibly they are being asked to risk their lives.[3]

In the gospels, personal transformation and new life can be sustained and embodied only through identification with the community of disciples.

While the moral life proclaimed in the gospels takes a form that is narratively displayed and communally embodied, its content revolves around the pattern of Jesus' own dispossession and restoration. The cruciform obedience of the cross exemplifies the call to dispossession that saturates Jesus' teaching. The way of the cross constitutes a *kenōsis* (emptying) not only of power, but of wealth, influence, even life. This emptying calls for radical trust in God, since it means surrendering those possessions and powers that create a defence against misfortune. Thus, in Luke, Jesus reassures his followers of God's providential care before calling them to radical renunciation.

'Do not worry about your life, what you will eat, or about your body, what you will wear. . . For it is the nations of the world that strive after these things, and your Father knows that you need them. Instead, strive for his kingdom and these things will be given to you as well. Do not be afraid, little flock, for it is your Father's good pleasure to give you the kingdom. Sell your possessions, and give alms. Make purses for yourselves that do not wear out, an unfailing treasure in heaven, where no thief comes near and no moth destroys. For where your treasure is, there your heart will be also.'   (12.22, 31–4)

God's provision makes the radical risk of dispossession both possible and necessary. Those who are too heavily weighted with the world's power, influence and wealth will be distracted from the goods of the kingdom.

Dispossession distinctively shapes Jesus' new politics. After the last supper, a dispute arises among the disciples as to who will be the greatest in God's kingdom. Jesus rebukes them, not because his kingdom is 'non-political' but because they have misunderstood his politics. He immediately contrasts his own 'servant politics' with that of the Gentile nations: 'The kings of the Gentiles lord it over them; and those in authority over them are called benefactors. But not so with you; rather the greatest among you must become like the youngest, and the leader like one who serves' (Lk 22.25–6). Mark's gospel concludes this story with an explicit connection between servant leadership and the path of the cross: 'For the Son of Man came not to be served but to serve, and to give his life a ransom for many' (Mk 10.45). Likewise, John's gospel displays this politics of the powerless when Jesus assures Pilate that he has a kingdom but that his kingdom is not 'from this world' (Jn 18.36). What is 'unworldly' about Jesus' reign is not that it is purely spiritual but that his followers do not fight on his behalf (Jn 18.36).

It must be added that dispossession is not an end in itself; it is not an abstract endorsement of poverty or powerlessness for its own sake. In the world of the gospels, to lose one's life is to find it (Matt 10.39; Mk 8.25). The final word is not cross but resurrection. To be emptied of the things of the world is but a prelude to participation in eternal life, which is not so much the unending extension of time as a quality of time that is already present (Jn 17.3). When Peter reminds Jesus of all that he and the other disciples have left in order to follow him, Jesus responds that those who have become dispossessed will not remain so, but will receive back 'a hundredfold'. Both Mark and Luke specify that this receiving not only is an expectation of the future life, but will come to pass 'in this age' (Mk 10.30; Lk 18.30). An example of this is found toward the end of John's gospel. As Jesus dies he turns his bereft mother over to the care of John, his bereft friend (Jn 19.26–7). One family is broken through Jesus' self-giving, but a new family is born. New life grows from the soil of dispossession.

For this pattern of self-emptying and restoration to make sense, one must share Jesus' vision of a redeemed creation in which the powers of violence, greed and oppression have been overcome, despite their continued presence in the world. God's kingdom has broken in on the world's kingdoms and a new way of life has become possible, but the defeat of the powers is not always visible to the naked eye. The need and desire to see as God sees relates especially to the exercise of the imagination – the ability to view the world through some frame of reference that frees people for new and creative responses. Jesus invites his disciples not only to do what he does but to see what he sees – that the world is not only sinful and dark but also loved and redeemed. This means that discipleship in the present age, bracketed as it is between the reality of Jesus' advent and the hope of his return, requires a kind of double vision. It requires living *in* a still fallen world while living *into* a redeemed world. Such living will undoubtedly make Christians look strange. For the truth is, if Jesus has not changed the world with his coming, his ethic can only appear misguided. If death has not been defeated, then non-violence is incoherent, even reprehensible. If the reign of God has not begun, then opening one's goods to the community is a foolish risk. Without sharing Jesus' vision of a world renewed, without seeing what Jesus saw, one dare not try to live as he lived.

To sum up, the ethic of the gospels (1) focuses not on disembodied teaching but on the entire life and witness of Jesus, (2) calls for a distinctive community life of shared vulnerability, (3) urges dispossession in the pattern of Jesus' own self-giving, (4) envisions a joyous, new, resurrection life, lived in the power and guidance of the Holy Spirit, and (5) requires Christ-like vision and imagination.

INHABITING THE GOSPELS: ST AUGUSTINE

Those following after Jesus have the ongoing task of interpreting his life and words in their own time and place. According to Hans Frei, St Augustine of Hippo (354–430) engages in a certain kind of 'realistic' reading of the gospels that was widespread prior to the eighteenth century. This interpretative method was both 'literal and historical'; that is, it 'envisioned the real world as formed by the sequence told by the biblical stories'.[4] Augustine lived during great historical turmoil. Just a few decades before his birth, Constantine, the Roman emperor, had converted to Christianity, ending centuries of persecution for the church. By the end of Augustine's life he would see Rome sacked by Vandals from the north, the beginning of the end of the Empire. These transitions raised difficult questions. How was Christianity to come to grips with its newfound position of establishment, given Jesus' deep challenge to the ways of worldly power? How were theologians to engage the varied worldviews among Rome's citizens now that Christian witness could be open and public? How were Christians to interpret the political changes brought on by the demise of the Roman Empire?

Like most pre-critical interpreters, Augustine assumed the historical accuracy of the literal sense of the biblical text. He also assumed that all the disparate biblical stories fit into one cohesive narrative and that 'the interpretive means for joining them was to make earlier biblical stories figures or types of later stories and of their events and patterns of meaning'.[5] Thus, the gospel narratives became the hinge for interpreting the entirety of the Bible in so far as the unity of scripture resided in the figural pattern of Christ's life, death and resurrection. Augustine assumed that the world rendered by the biblical stories was the real and only world. The direction of biblical interpretation 'was that of incorporating extra-biblical thought, experience, and reality into the one real world detailed and made accessible by the biblical story – not the reverse'.[6] This kind of interpretation characterizes not only Augustine's readings, but most Christian interpretation of the gospels up until the period of modern biblical criticism.

One can see Augustine incorporating his own life and times into the world of the gospels in his reinterpretation of pagan virtue and his re-narration of the history and politics of Rome. Augustine uses the gospel call to dispossession as a way of contrasting Christian virtue and pagan virtue, the heavenly city and the earthly city. The moral philosophers of Augustine's day would have widely affirmed the cultivation of the four cardinal virtues: temperance, fortitude, justice and prudence. But Augustine challenges this tradition by re-situating (and thus redescribing) the virtues within the context of Jesus' command to love God and neighbour (Matt 22.34–40; Mk 12.28–31; Lk 10.25–8; cf. Jn 13.34; 15.12). Seeking the proper *telos* of the virtues, Augustine entreats, 'Let us hear, O Christ, what chief end Thou dost prescribe to us; and what is evidently the chief end after which we are told to strive with supreme affection. "Thou shalt love," He says, "the Lord thy God."'[7] So Augustine concludes, 'I hold virtue to be nothing else than perfect love of God',[8] adding also that 'our love of our neighbour is a sort of cradle of our love to God'.[9]

Classically, the virtues were understood as powers or capacities, as was reflected in the Latin root *virtus*, meaning 'strength'. But, so understood, virtue could serve the lust for glory as easily as it served the love of God.[10] If the virtues were not rightly directed towards the good of God and neighbour they were but splendid vices, for 'the virtue which is employed in the service of human glory is not true virtue'.[11] When interpreted as habits of Christian love, the cardinal virtues are rescued from the pursuit of glory and domination. So Augustine offers this alternative to the pagan tradition: 'temperance is love giving itself entirely to that which is loved; fortitude is love readily bearing all things for the sake of the loved object; justice is love serving only the loved object, and therefore ruling rightly; prudence is love distinguishing with sagacity between what hinders it and what helps it'.[12] Virtue becomes less a matter of self-possession than of self-giving. For instance, it is only as power is tempered by servanthood that true justice can be done in the home. 'In the household of the just man,' Augustine writes, 'even those who give orders are the servants of those whom they appear to command. For they do not give orders because of a lust for domination but from a dutiful concern for the interests of others, not with pride in taking precedence over others, but with compassion in taking care of others.'[13]

Alongside his reinterpretation of virtue, Augustine re-narrates the history of Rome, and indeed world history as a whole, within the narrative pattern of scripture and the symbolic world of the gospels.[14] As described in *The City of God*, all of history could be understood in terms of the rise of two cities based on the pursuit of two loves. The city of God arises from the love of God, while the city of earth arises from the love of self. Augustine figuratively incorporates the world's story into the biblical narrative, reading Roman politics, especially the founding story of Romulus killing Remus, as an extension of the lust for domination already present when Cain killed Abel.[15] He argues, not that Christians should refuse to participate in the politics of the earthly city, but rather that their participation must be radically transformed by Jesus' call to love God and neighbour. Christian rulers will renounce the love of domination and glory; indeed, they will love the reign of God more than they love their own kingdoms,[16] and they will be happier to be members of the church than to be rulers of the world.[17] In contrast, the 'Roman heroes belonged to an earthly city, and the aim set before them, in all their acts of duty for her, was the safety of their country, and a kingdom not in heaven, but on earth . . . What else was there for them to love save glory?'[18]

Augustine envisions political action that serves not the glory of particular persons or particular nations but rather the glory of the heavenly city.

Thus, he assumes that a Christian can serve as emperor, but his rule will be quite different from that of pagans. Augustine even appeals to the Sermon on the Mount as having political relevance for the Christian ruler: 'So great is the righteousness of the one who has his virtues from the Spirit of God, that he loves even his enemies.'[19] Rowan Williams sums up Augustine's politics this way:

> We arrive at the paradox that the only reliable political leader, the only ruler who can be guaranteed to safeguard authentically *political* values (order, equity, and the nurture of souls in these things) is the man who is, at the end of the day, indifferent to their survival in the relative shapes of the existing order, because he knows them to be safeguarded at the level of God's eternal and immutable providence, vindicated in the eternal *civitas dei*. Politics and the art of government take on the Socratic colouring of a discipline of dying; and only so do they avoid the corruption of the *civitas terrena*, the anti-city . . . in which value and unity rest on essentially divisive and contingent factors and yet are bitterly and unscrupulously fought for.[20]

Augustine draws on the pattern of Christian love, embodied in Jesus' own life and self-giving, imaginatively to reinterpret pagan virtue and earthly politics by fitting them into the world of Jesus and the gospels.

THE GOSPEL AS AN ETHIC: IMMANUEL KANT

Immanuel Kant (1724–1804) lived and wrote in a world far distant from that of Augustine. During the seventeenth and eighteenth centuries, in order to preserve public life from the devastating religious conflicts of the post-Reformation era, the rising nation-states in Europe began to imagine a politics in which religion was irrelevant. Believe what you want in private, they said, but do not try to bring your religious convictions into the arena of civic debate and legislation. This exclusion of religion from the public sphere not only marginalized Protestant–Catholic political manoeuvering; it also allowed the young nation–states to consolidate power over against the church, making national identity more basic and significant than religious identity.[21]

Increasingly, the political project of the nation-state eschewed not only any entanglement with religion but even the assumption that politics should be concerned with moral leadership. Unlike the classical political vision of the ancient Greek city-state or the Roman republic, the new modern nation-states were not committed to the formation of *virtuous* people. They were committed to the formation of *free* people. While certain moral standards had to be enshrined in law to protect life and liberty, the nation-state quickly retreated from the broader moral task of shaping *good* citizens, since this would require a consensus on what was 'good'. The state's withdrawal from moral formation combined with a weakening of the church's influence to create a vacuum of moral authority. So the philosophers of modernity undertook a massive renovation project: to lift the house of morality from its now shaky theological and ecclesial supports and replace it on the supposedly more solid foundation of human reason and/or experience.[22]

This task was inherited and carried forward most influentially by Immanuel Kant. Near the end of the eighteenth century, he set forth an ethic of duty guided by the universal norm (or as he called it, 'categorical imperative') that one should 'act only according to the maxim by which you can at the same time will that it should become a universal law'.[23] The insightful reader might notice the similarity of this maxim to Jesus' words, 'Do to others as you would have them do to you' (Matt 7.12; Lk 6.31), but Kant does not rely on Jesus' authority to support his principle. Quite the opposite; he argues that Jesus can be recognized as good only if he measures up to an external norm of reasonable morality. Unlike Augustine, who considered Jesus the *standard* of the good, Kant considers Jesus, at best, an *example* of the good. This displacement of Jesus comes out most clearly in Kant's comments on Jesus' interaction with the rich young man (Mk 10.17–22). Kant appeals to the passage, not to cite Jesus as an authoritative moral teacher, but to explore Jesus' response to the man's calling him 'Good Teacher' (10.17). Jesus' response is telling for Kant: 'Why do you call me good? No one is good but God alone' (10.18). Here Kant believes he has found biblical support for separating Jesus from any equation with the good. Kant argues:

> Even the Holy One of the gospel must be compared with our ideal of moral perfection before He is recognized as such; even He says of Himself, 'Why call ye Me (whom you see) good? None is good (the archetype of the good) except God only (whom you do not see).' But whence do we have the concept of God as the highest good? Solely from the idea of moral perfection which reason formulates a priori.[24]

Kant does not follow this biblical pericope to its conclusion; thus his attention never turns to the climax of the exchange when Jesus urges the man to 'sell what you own . . . then come, follow me' (10.21). Kant has little use for this command, since he gives no moral weight to the following of moral exemplars. One cannot base an ethic on following someone else's pattern of life. Kant writes, 'Nor could one give poorer counsel to morality than to attempt to derive it from examples. For each example of morality which is exhibited to me must itself have been previously judged according to principles of morality to see whether it is worthy to serve as an original example, i.e., as a model. By no means could it authoritatively furnish the concept of morality . . . Imitation has no place in moral matters, and examples serve only for encouragement.'[25] Exemplars cannot finally be helpful because duty must arise from one's own will and reside in one's own reason. The example of one person can never in itself be binding upon others as a duty. 'Man . . . is subject only to his own, yet universal, legislation, and . . . he is only bound to act in accordance with his own will, which is, however, designed by nature to be a will giving universal laws.'[26] This has significant implications for reading the gospels, where we find Jesus repeatedly urging his disciples, 'Follow me.' Such a command cannot be taken with moral force, since the pattern of Jesus' life cannot, in itself, have moral authority.

For Kant, self-possession, or autonomy, is more important to his ethic than dispossession. It is true that duty *may* require a kind of dispossession (we must be careful not to confuse Kantian duty with a utilitarian seeking of pleasure or self-interest), but the categorical imperative filters Jesus' 'do unto others' through a social-contract lens. Radical self-emptying has been replaced by a rational balancing of rights and responsibilities. And so, when Kant comes upon biblical passages that espouse radical dispossession of power, such as 'Love your enemies', he finds himself having to interpret the passage against its literal sense. He confesses that such an interpretation 'may . . . appear forced – it may often really be forced; and yet if the text can possibly support it, it must be preferred to a literal interpretation which either contains nothing at all [helpful] to morality or else actually works counter to moral incentives'.[27] So, commenting on Matt 5.44, 'I say to you, Love your enemies and pray for those who persecute you', Kant writes,

> I should try, as a first alternative, to bring the New Testament passage into conformity with my own self-subsistent moral principles (that perhaps the reference is here not to enemies in the flesh but rather to invisible enemies which are symbolized by them and are far more dangerous to us, namely, evil inclinations which we must desire to

bring wholly under foot). Or if this cannot be managed, I shall rather have it that this passage is not to be understood in a moral sense at all ... probably it merely refers to the law, valid for every state, that satisfaction for injury shall be sought in the courts of justice of the overlord, where the judge's permission to the complainant to ask for a punishment as severe as he desires is not to be taken as approval of the complainant's craving for revenge.[28]

Kant's methodology takes as a principle the need to interpret Jesus' life and teachings within a universal framework. Thus, the moral vision of the gospels must be conformed to the practical rationality of the modern mind.

To return to Hans Frei's analysis, Kant would be an example of how the direction of biblical interpretation shifted in the eighteenth and nineteenth centuries. No longer did the biblical world subsume all other reality. Rather, the Bible had to be translated into terms acceptable to the new modern worldview. The meaning of the text was seen as 'detachable from the specific story that sets it forth'.[29] Kant's search for universals led him to seek the meaning of the biblical text outside of the text itself, in an ideal moral content. Jesus, and the gospels, were not rendered meaningless by Kant, but the meaning they bore was no longer necessarily connected to the gospel narratives themselves.

THE GOSPEL ETHIC AT THE EDGE OF HISTORY: REINHOLD NIEBUHR

The apologetic attempt to situate Christian moral and political ethics within a worldview more acceptable to the modern mind continued into the twentieth century. Reinhold Niebuhr (1892–1971) was one of the most influential American Protestant ethicists of his day. Like Kant, Niebuhr saw the life and teaching of Jesus as pointing to a moral ideal, but, unlike Kant, Niebuhr concluded that it was impossible to live this ideal within the compromised and sinful world of real human history. Neither Kant nor Niebuhr thought that one could live the gospels in any direct way, but, whereas Kant believed that one could live the universal ethic that was present (though sometimes hidden) in the gospels, Niebuhr thought that one could live only *in the shadow* of this ethical ideal. In other words, at the points where Kant openly reinterpreted the text, even 'forced' a reinterpretation upon it (thus conforming the ethic to his practical moral principles), Niebuhr was more inclined to accept the text in all its idealistic difficulty and then to proclaim the ethic impractical. He writes:

It is very foolish to deny that the ethic of Jesus is an absolute and uncompromising ethic. It is, in the phrase of Ernst Troeltsch, an ethic of 'love universalism and love perfectionism.' The injunctions 'resist not evil,' 'love your enemies,' 'if ye love them that love you what thanks have you?' 'be not anxious for your life,' and 'be ye therefore perfect even as your father in heaven is perfect,' are all of one piece, and they are all uncompromising and absolute. Nothing is more futile and pathetic than the effort of some Christian theologians who find it necessary to become involved in the relativities of politics, in resistance to tyranny or in social conflict, to justify themselves by seeking to prove that Christ was also involved in some of these relativities. . . Those of us who regard the ethic of Jesus as finally and ultimately normative, but as not immediately applicable to the task of securing justice in a sinful world, are very foolish if we try to reduce the ethic so that it will cover and justify our prudential and relative standards and strategies.[30]

One cannot but admire Niebuhr's resolute determination not to confuse the high calling of Christ with the tentative and partial compromises of the world's politics. Surely it is better to hold the standard high and admit that we cannot reach it than to lower the standard and praise ourselves for our partial loves and our relative justice.

The result of Niebuhr's move, however, is to place the high standard of Jesus' ethic of dispossession beyond history. Once Niebuhr conceives of Jesus and his moral vision as 'outside of history', he must look to other moral sources to give realistic guidance in a fallen and compromised world. 'It is impossible', he writes, 'to construct a social ethic out of the ideal of love in its pure form, because the ideal presupposes the resolution of the conflict of life with life, which it is the concern of law to mitigate and restrain. For this reason Christianity really had no social ethic until it appropriated the Stoic ethic.'[31] Here Niebuhr makes two critical assumptions. First, he assumes that love is possible only once 'the conflict of life with life' is resolved. He does not seem to imagine that love could play a redemptive part in resolving the conflict. Second, he assumes that Christianity had no social ethic prior to importing Stoicism. This statement can hold true only if one has already relegated Jesus' moral vision to the unpractical realm of the 'ideal.' If, to the contrary, Jesus imagined that his followers would embody his pattern of self-giving in communities of dispossession, then one might equally say that the gospels themselves are *nothing but* a social ethic. Certainly the community of which Luke tells in the book of Acts interpreted Jesus this way: 'All who believed were together and had all things in common; they would sell their possessions and goods and distribute the proceeds to all, as any had need' (Acts 2.44–5).

What makes Jesus' teaching and pattern of life so difficult for many modern interpreters like Kant and Niebuhr is the significant disjuncture they perceive between the world as Jesus saw it and the world in which we now live. As noted above, one aspect of the ethical discourse of the gospels is the construction of a 'symbolic world that creates the perceptual categories through which we interpret reality'.[32] This includes symbolic descriptions of the character of God and the human condition. But, for Kant and Niebuhr, the 'symbolic world' of the gospels (including, most notably, the eschatological inbreaking of the kingdom of God) was not considered part and parcel of Christ's moral vision. Rather, it constituted a dispensable (because outdated) husk that could be stripped from the ethical kernel. Kant and Niebuhr imagined that Jesus' teaching could be turned into general ethical norms that could be brought into some kind of relation with the symbolic world of modernity (a worldview that assumed the inevitability of human conflict and the non-intervention of God). For Kant this meant, at times, radical reinterpretation of the plain sense of Jesus' teaching, while for Niebuhr, who refused such radical reinterpretation, this required holding up Jesus' 'love perfectionism' as an ideal that was worthy of our deepest respect but that could not be lived in the trenches of a sinful world. Both Kant and Niebuhr presupposed that the ethic of the gospels, especially as it pointed to radical dispossession, was not 'realistic' and thus was unliveable in the world as we know it.

Part of the problem with this position, however, is that it begs the question of what constitutes the 'real' in 'realistic'. Whose vision, which world-view, determines what is prudential or realistic? Apart from the symbolic world of the gospels, in which Jesus has conquered the powers and made peace possible, the attempt to love one's enemies will seem futile or foolish. But within that symbolic world, the witness of peace is the witness that triumphs and the power of the martyr is finally stronger than that of the soldier. If one attempts to situate Jesus' ethic in the context of the modern myth of a primal war of all against all, in which violent struggle becomes a *necessary* part of the created order, then one can only say with Niebuhr that Jesus' ethic is not directly relevant and stands 'outside history'. But if an 'armistice between various contending actions and forces'[33] is not all that one can hope for, and if the deepest truth is that the reign of God has come and Jesus has defeated death through the cross and resurrection, then one can risk following a path in which losing life is finding it.

LIVING THE GOSPELS: JOHN PAUL II

The gospels depict not only an ethic but the symbolic world in which that ethic can make sense. Augustine's ability to read the gospels as giving practical guidance for Christians had much to do with his perception that the symbolic world of the text was a true representation of the world in which he lived. He could set forth the pattern of Christ as normative because he imagined himself to inhabit the world of the gospels. As Frei has shown, this sense of symbolic continuity with scripture broke down in the modern period. Correlatively, the gospel ethic of dispossession, considered apart from Jesus' vision of the coming reign of God, became either unintelligible (Kant) or impossibly difficult (Niebuhr). Once Jesus' ethic was detached from his symbolic world, one was left with the choice of reinterpreting the ethic to fit the modern world (Kant) or declaring the ethic 'ideal' and thus unrelated to the modern world (Niebuhr). But as modernity has yielded to postmodernity it has become thinkable again to retrieve (analogically) and embody (figuratively) the symbolic world of scripture. This, of course, cannot be done through a simple repristination of premodern literalism. It is clear that one cannot go back and 'live in the gospels', as if there were no 'ugly, broad ditch'[34] between the biblically narrated world and today. Yet many theologians and biblical scholars are seeking new ways to bring the biblical horizon into an analogical relation with the beliefs and concerns of the present age, situating the reader *figuratively* and *analogically* within the world of the gospels even while recognizing that modern science and historical study have for ever changed certain assumptions about how the world works. Along these lines, Richard Hays describes the church's hermeneutical task as one of 'metaphor making,' and the church's life as an 'embodied metaphor'.[35] If we read the gospels as providing a *pattern* of dispossession and a *vision* of the world in which the reign of God has begun, then the living of the gospels will involve imaginative construals of God's calling in the present moment.

Once again the work of Hans Frei provides important guidance. In *The Identity of Jesus Christ*, he displays a way of reading the gospels that is neither modern nor simply premodern. Rather, he is attentive to the distance between the modern reader and the gospel world, while at the same time seeking to bridge that distance through a figurative connection between the modern world and Jesus' pattern of dispossession, death and resurrection.

For whomever [the story of Jesus] becomes the truth, it does so not by imaginative obliteration of time but by hammering out a shape of life patterned after its own shape. That does not mean that we repeat the original events literally in our lives, and certainly not completely, but it means that our lives reflect the story as in a glass darkly. The shape of the story being mirrored in the shape of our life is the condition of its being meaningful for us.[36]

For Frei the disciple is not one who follows Christ in literal imitation (since Christ's distinctive work is unrepeatable), but the one who 'follows Christ without trying to become Christ, at a distance rather than from too nearby'.[37] The disciple echoes Jesus' 'pattern of exchange', in which he empties himself so that others can be filled and dies so that others can live.[38] The church, in turn, 'is called upon to be a collective disciple, to follow at a distance the pattern of exchange, serving rather than being served'.[39]

In his encyclical *Veritatis Splendor*, John Paul II (1920–2005) carries out a hermeneutical recovery along the lines sketched by Frei. At the beginning of the encyclical John Paul brings us back again to the story of the rich young man and the challenge of dispossession. We recall that, according to the version in Matthew, the man asks Jesus, 'Teacher, what good deed must I do to have eternal life?' (Matt 19.16). John Paul notes that 'the *question* is not so much about rules to be followed but *about the full meaning of life*'.[40] In this simple observation, he situates himself over against the modern attempt to extract ethical principles from the gospels, reminding us that morality is not a *part* of one's life but rather is a way of describing the *whole* of life as it is oriented toward God. Further, the rich man's question itself is not as significant as the teacher to whom it is addressed, for 'the decisive answer to every one of man's questions, his religious and moral questions in particular, is given by Jesus Christ, or rather is Jesus Christ himself'.[41]

Jesus responds to the man, 'Why do you ask me about what is good? There is only one who is good' (Matt 19.17). John Paul's interpretation of these words differs significantly from what we saw in Kant. Jesus is not deflecting the ethical question away from himself and towards a rational principle. Rather, he is creating a determinative connection between God and the good: '*To ask about the good*, in fact, *ultimately means to turn towards God*.'[42] John Paul goes on to note that the fulfilment of the law about which the rich man asks '*can come only from a gift of God*: the offer of a share in the divine Goodness revealed and communicated in Jesus. . . What the young man now perhaps only dimly perceives will in the end be fully revealed by Jesus himself in the invitation: "come, follow me."'[43] In other words, by reading on in the story, beyond the point at which Kant stops, John Paul discovers in this final invitation the connection which links the good to following Jesus.

Unlike Kant or Niebuhr, John Paul sees Jesus' pattern of life as not only *normative* for Christian ethics but as both *relevant* and *practical*. Of course, it is true that 'if God alone is the Good, no human effort, not even the most rigorous observance of the commandments, succeeds in "fulfilling" the Law'.[44] But, as a 'gift of God', human beings are made able to share in and live in the goodness of God. John Paul has more confidence in the possibility of following Jesus than does Niebuhr, but this confidence lies not simply in his assessment of human capacities. It lies in his willingness to appropriate the symbolic world of the gospels, the narrative world in which God can and does transform lives and communities, making obedience possible.

Part of the transformation that will be required in the modern world, according to John Paul, is a transformation of the concept of freedom. As Augustine redefined virtue, so John Paul takes up freedom as a key moral concern of his age and reforms it according to the witness of Christ. 'The *question of morality*, to which Christ provides the answer, *cannot prescind from the issue of freedom. Indeed, it considers that issue central*, for there can be no morality without freedom.'[45] But modernity, following Kant's appeals to autonomy, has misunderstood freedom. 'Certain currents of modern thought have gone so far as to *exalt freedom to such an extent that it becomes an absolute, which would then be the source of values* . . . The individual conscience is accorded the status of supreme tribunal of moral judgment which hands down categorical and infallible decisions about good and evil.'[46] In contrast, John Paul argues that human freedom is 'real but limited', since this freedom is finally grounded not in the human creature but in God.

True freedom is decisively linked to the pattern of Christ's self-giving. '*The Crucified Christ reveals the authentic meaning of freedom; he lives it fully in the total gift of himself* and calls his disciples to share in his freedom.'[47] The dispossessing of the self in service turns out to be the truest act of freedom. The kind of freedom that is unmoored from any norm outside itself is but a false freedom by which people become enslaved to their own self-serving desires. Freedom is not the precondition from which one begins the moral life; it is the end goal of the journey. The church, through the sacraments that assimilate the believer to Christ, provides the place where that freedom can be developed and the journey sustained.[48] John Paul's reinterpretation of freedom in light of the cross provides a model for reclaiming an Augustinian vision without a precritical literalism.

THE PATTERN OF THE CROSS AND 9/11

An example of living the gospels in the pattern of dispossession can be seen in the response of the Episcopal Church to the tragedies of 11 September 2001. On Friday 14 September 2001, Frank Griswold, Presiding Bishop of the Episcopal Church, celebrated Eucharist near 'Ground Zero', the site of the World Trade Center attack. He noted the importance of its being Holy Cross Day on the church's liturgical calendar, and he took the opportunity to reflect on the sufferings of 9/11 in light of Christ's suffering on the cross. He wrote:

> How appropriate and right it was that our mourning and grief be rooted and grounded in the mystery of the cross. St Paul speaks of sharing the sufferings of Christ . . . . every act of violence, and all that it produces, is an instance of Christ's own suffering with and on behalf of those he came to reconcile to one another through the cross . . . The cross is Jesus' facing into all the subtle and obvious forces of evil that divide the human family, drawing us all to himself in order that we might be transformed and live in new patterns of relationship: patterns which are grounded in the awareness that – at the heart of all differences of language, race, culture and ways of believing and naming God – we are profoundly one in the mind and heart of our Creator.[49]

This capacity to see 'all differences' gathered up into the love of the Creator was made possible for Griswold by reflecting on present events through the lens of the gospel narratives. The image of the cross allowed him to see in 9/11 something more than just terror and evil (which surely were also present). Two weeks later the bishops of the Episcopal Church put out a statement responding to the events of 9/11 entitled 'On Waging Reconciliation.' Through an act of analogical imagination the bishops again brought together the suffering of the times with the cross of Christ. In so doing they were able to imagine responses other than revenge. They wrote:

> We come together . . . in the shadow of the cross: that unequivocal sign that suffering and death are never the end but the way along which we pass into a future in which all things will be healed and reconciled. Through Christ 'God was pleased to reconcile to himself all things whether on earth or in heaven, by making peace through the blood of his cross' (Col. 1:20). This radical act of peace-making is

nothing less than the right ordering of all things according to God's passionate desire for justness, for the full flourishing of humankind and all creation.[50]

Because the suffering of the cross was taken up into God's work of making peace with the world, the suffering of 9/11 can be taken up into a human project of reconciliation. Such an interpretation does not deny the horror or tragedy of the moment, any more than it denies the horror and tragedy of the crucifixion; rather, it places evil and suffering within the world of the gospels, where suffering can be redemptive and death can be defeated. Given this conviction, the bishops were able to summon the resources to speak for peace at a time when many in the United States were preparing for war. By entering the cruciform reality of the gospels, they were able to issue a call for dispossession, for relinquishing the power of vengeance in favour of a ministry of reconciliation. In so doing, they provided a powerful example of moral and political engagement with the gospels.[51]

Notes

1. E. P. Sanders, *The Historical Figure of Jesus* (New York: Penguin, 1993), 37–8, emphasis in original.
2. Josephus, *Against Apion*, 2.171, cited in Sanders, 37.
3. David Rensberger, *Johanine Faith and Liberating Community* (Philadelphia: Westminster, 1988), 114.
4. Hans Frei, *The Eclipse of Biblical Narrative* (New Haven: Yale University Press, 1974), 1.
5. Ibid., 2.
6. Ibid., 3.
7. Augustine, 'On the Morals of the Catholic Church', in *The Nicene and Post-Nicene Fathers of the Christian Church*, IV (Grand Rapids: Eerdmans, 1979), 44–5.
8. Ibid., 48.
9. Ibid., 55.
10. Augustine, *The City of God*, trans. Henry Bettenson (New York: Penguin, 1984), 213, 891.
11. Ibid., 213.
12. Augustine, 'On the Morals of the Catholic Church,' 48.
13. Augustine, *City of God*, 874.
14. In using the term 'symbolic world' I am following Richard Hays, *The Moral Vision of the New Testament* (San Francisco: HarperSanFrancisco, 1996), 209. Hays argues that the moral vision of the New Testament includes the depiction of 'a *symbolic world* that creates the perceptual categories through which we interpret reality' (209). This 'symbolic world' includes 'its representations of the human condition and its depictions of the character of God' (209). I take this to be similar to Erich Auerbach's observation that the Old Testament makes

a powerful claim on the reader: 'we are to fit our own life into its world, feel ourselves to be elements in its structure of universal history . . . Everything else that happens in the world can only be conceived as an element in this sequence'; *Mimesis* (Princeton: Princeton University Press, 1953), 15–16. The point here is that Christ's ethic cannot make sense apart from a set of theological convictions, symbolically and narratively presented in scripture (for instance, the goodness of God's creation; the covenant with Israel; Christ's defeat of evil, sin and death; the inbreaking of the reign of God; and the empowering work of the Holy Spirit). Jesus' moral vision in the gospels could be read as a description of what life would look like if this biblical account of the world turned out to be true.

15. Ibid., 600.
16. Ibid., 220.
17. Ibid., 223.
18. Ibid., 204.
19. Ibid., 212.
20. Rowan Williams, 'Politics and the Soul: A Reading of the *City of God*', *Milltown Studies* 19/20 (1987), 67.
21. For a wonderful account of the wars of religion and the rise of the state that challenges the standard narrative, see William Cavanaugh, '"A Fire Strong Enough to Consume the House": The Wars of Religion and the Rise of the State', *Modern Theology* 11/4 (1995), 397–420.
22. For a discussion and critique of the Enlightenment project to find a new basis for morality, see Alasdair MacIntyre, 'Why the Enlightenment Project of Justifying Morality Had to Fail', in his *After Virtue*, (2nd edn, Notre Dame: University of Notre Dame Press, 1984), 51–61.
23. Immanuel Kant, *Foundations of the Metaphysics of Morals*, trans. Lewis White Beck (Indianapolis: Bobbs-Merrill, 1959), 39.
24. Ibid., 25.
25. Ibid.
26. Ibid., 51.
27. Immanuel Kant, *Religion Within the Limits of Reason Alone* (New York: Harper Torchbooks, 1960), 101.
28. Ibid., 101.
29. Frei, *Eclipse*, 6.
30. Reinhold Niebuhr, 'Why the Christian Church is not Pacifist', *in The Essential Reinhold Niebuhr*, ed. Robert McAfee Brown (New Haven: Yale University Press, 1986), 106.
31. Reinhold Niebuhr, *An Interpretation of Christian Ethics* (San Francisco: Harper & Row, 1963), 91.
32. Hays, *Moral Vision*, 209.
33. Reinhold Niebuhr, *Interpretation of Christian Ethics*, 23–4.
34. G. E. Lessing, *On the Proof of the Spirit and of Power*, in *Lessing's Theological Writings*, ed. and trans. Henry Chadwick (Stanford: Stanford University Press, 1957), 55.
35. Hays, *Moral Vision*, 298–306.
36. Hans Frei, *The Identity of Jesus Christ* (Philadelphia: Fortress, 1975), 170–1.

37. Ibid., 80.
38. Ibid., 81.
39. Ibid., 160.
40. John Paul II, *Veritatis Splendor* (Vatican City: Libreria Editrice Vaticana, 1993), 7.
41. Ibid., 2.
42. Ibid., 9, emphasis in the original.
43. Ibid., 11.
44. Ibid.
45. Ibid., 34.
46. Ibid., 32.
47. Ibid., 85.
48. Ibid., 21.
49. The Most Rev. Frank Griswold, 'Overcoming Evil', 18 September 2001, <http://www.episcopalchurch.org/presiding-bishop/postings/091801es.html> (21 January 2002).
50. Bishops of the Episcopal Church, USA, 'On Waging Reconciliation', 26 September 2001, <http://www.episcopalchurch.org/presiding-bishop/postings/092601st.html> (21 January 2002).
51. Thanks to Raymond Barfield, Stephen Barton and Kelli O'Brien for very helpful comments on this chapter.

Further reading

Bonhoeffer, Dietrich, *The Cost of Discipleship* (rev. edn, New York: Macmillan, 1959)
Frei, Hans, *The Eclipse of Biblical Narrative* (New Haven and London: Yale University Press, 1974)
Fowl, Stephen, and L. Gregory Jones, *Reading in Communion: Scripture and Ethics in Christian Life* (Grand Rapids: Eerdmans, 1991)
Hauerwas, Stanley, *The Peaceable Kingdom* (Notre Dame, IN: University of Notre Dame Press, 1983)
Hays, Richard, *The Moral Vision of the New Testament* (New York: HarperCollins, 1996)
Jones, L. Gregory, *Embodying Forgiveness: A Theological Analysis* (Grand Rapids: Eerdmans, 1995)
Moltmann, Jürgen, *Jesus Christ for Today's World* (Minneapolis: Fortress, 1994)
Niebuhr, Reinhold, *An Interpretation of Christian Ethics* (New York: Harper & Brothers, 1935)
O'Donovan, Oliver, *Desire of the Nations: Rediscovering the Roots of Political Theology* (Cambridge: Cambridge University Press, 1996)
Verhey, Allen, *Remembering Jesus: Christian Community, Scripture, and the Moral Life* (Grand Rapids: Eerdmans, 2002)
Williams, Rowan, *Resurrection: Interpreting the Easter Gospel* (Cleveland: Pilgrim Press, 2002)
Yoder, John Howard, *The Politics of Jesus* (2nd edn, Grand Rapids: Eerdmans, 1994)

Index

Made in the USA
Lexington, KY
03 August 2016